Discover What's ONLINE

Other Prima Computer Books

Available Now!

Build a Web Site: The Programmer's Guide to Creating, Building, and Maintaining a Web Presence
The CD-ROM Revolution
CompuServe Complete Handbook and Membership Kit, Second Edition (with CD-ROM)
Create Wealth with Quicken, Third Edition
Cruising America Online 2.5
Cruising CompuServe
Cruising The Microsoft Network
Data Security
The Essential Book for Microsoft Office
Excel for Windows 95: The Visual Learning Guide
Interactive Internet: The Insider's Guide to MUDs, MOOs, and IRC
Internet After Hours, 2nd Edition
Internet Information Server
The Internet Warp Book: Your Complete Guide to Getting Online with OS/2
Introduction to Internet Security
Managing with Microsoft Project
Microsoft Works for Windows 95: The Visual Learning Guide
Migrating to Windows 95
Moving Worlds (with CD-ROM)
PowerPoint for Windows 95: The Visual Learning Guide
Quicken 5 for Windows: The Visual Learning Guide
Researching on the Internet: The Complete Guide to Finding, Evaluating, and Organizing Information Effectively
Sound Blaster: Making WAVes with Multimedia
Stacker Multimedia
UnInstaller 3: Uncluttering Your PC
Visio 4: Drawing Has Never Been Easier!
Web Advertising and Marketing
Web After Hours
Web Browsing with America Online
Web Browsing with Netscape Navigator 1.1
Web Browsing with NETCOM NetCruiser
Web Browsing with Prodigy
Web Browsing with The Microsoft Network
Windows 3.1: The Visual Learning Guide
Windows 95: The Visual Learning Guide
Windows 95: A to Z
Windows 95: Easy Installation Guide
The Windows 95 Book: Your Definitive Guide to Installing and Using Windows 95
WinFax PRO 7 for Windows: The Visual Learning Guide
Word for Windows 95: The Visual Learning Guide
WordPerfect 6.1 for Windows: The Visual Learning Guide

How to Order:

For information on quantity discounts contact the publisher: Prima Publishing, P.O. Box 1260BK, Rocklin, CA 95677-1260; (916) 632-4400. On your letterhead include information concerning the intended use of the books and the number of books you wish to purchase. For individual orders, turn to the back of this book for more information.

Discover What's ONLINE

WHY YOU SHOULD BE ONLINE, AND HOW TO GET THERE

Rob Tidrow

Nancy Stevenson

Dennis Hamilton

PRIMA PUBLISHING

P is a registered trademark of Prima Publishing, a division of Prima Communications, Inc.
Prima Publishing is a registered trademark of Prima Communications, Inc.
Prima Publishing, Rocklin, California 95677.

Project Editor: Kelli Crump
Acquisitions Editor: Julie Barton
Developmental Editor: Liz Reding
Technical Reviewer: Alfonso Hermida
Copy Editor: Theresa Mathias
Indexer: Katherine Stimson
Interior Design and Layout: Danielle Foster
Cover Design: Bill McCloskey

ISBN: 0-7615-0503-2
Library of Congress Catalog Card Number: 96-68071
Printed in the United States of America
96 97 98 99 CC 10 9 8 7 6 5 4 3 2 1

I would like to dedicate this book to my parents, Jack and Rebecca Tidrow,
and to my grandparents, Bill Klein, Mary and Kyle Smith, and Hobert and Mona Tidrow.

—RT

For David Hamilton, captain-in-training for the Starship Enterprise.

—DH

CONTENTS AT A GLANCE

CONTENTS

ACKNOWLEDGMENTS

No one can survive in a vacuum, particularly writers. I want to extend my deepest gratitude to the people who helped me during this project. At Prima Publishing, thanks go to Don Roche and Alan Harris for giving me an opportunity to work on this project and for continued support. Thanks to Julie Barton for providing me with the encouragement and help to get me moving, and for the pieces of chocolate. The editors and developer—Theresa Mathias, Alfonso Hermida, and Liz Reding—deserve a lot of credit for molding and shaping my text, forcing me to expand my limited point of view on some topics, and ensuring the technical accuracy of the text. Also, I want to thank Kelli Crump at Prima for taking the lead on this project and using the gentle power of persuasion and passion to make this book "happen." Finally, I want to thank my wife, Tammy, and two boys, Adam and Wesley, for letting me be grumpy and tired some days and for always keeping the coffee hot. Thanks y'all!

—RT

Many thanks to the crack team at Prima, including Julie Barton and Kelli Crump, for involving me in the project and pulling so many pieces together with such grace under fire.

—NS

Acknowledgments

I'd like to thank Julie Barton of Prima for allowing me to be a part of this terrific book, and for her patience when a bum ankle temporarily laid me up. Kelli Crump and Theresa Mathias for the terrific suggestions for the manuscript. Nancy Stevenson for making it all possible. And my family, who without complaint let me work through a long-planned vacation to get the material for this book in.

—DH

INTRODUCTION

The online world is giving many people the change to experience things they've never had the opportunity to do. It offers people a way to get beyond the four walls of their home or office and participate in a different, electronic world. These are but a few of the activities and information you can find while online.

- The Magna Carta
- Hourly hurricane reports from the National Hurricane Center
- A live interview with Tom Hanks
- Free software
- Conversations with people interested in the same subjects you are
- Animations from the movie *Toy Story*

It's been said that the online world is revolutionizing the world around us. In many ways it is. Communications between people has greatly expanded by using tools like electronic mail (e-mail for short) and online chat sessions. Having the capability to send documents and computer files around the world is making it easier and quicker for companies to publish stock reports, news and weather reports, and general information. A user in New York City, for instance, can almost instantly send a letter she is writing to a recipient in Seattle. A user in

Detroit can take a tour of the Vatican while online, without leaving the comfort of his home. None of this has ever been available before.

Who Is This Book For?

As recently as two years ago, getting connected to the online world required craftiness, computer nerd-like tendencies, and nerves of steel. For many users, getting online was as difficult as landing on the moon with a helicopter. It was nearly impossible.

Fortunately, getting connected is much easier now. This book is designed to help you understand the types of resources available online, the connections you can make, and how to get connected quickly and easily. Depending on the service you choose, getting online can be as easy as installing some software and filling out a registration form. In other cases, it may involve a few more steps, but this book takes you step-by-step through them all.

The following list describes the type of audience this book is designed for:

- Computer neophytes who are a little intimated by all the techno-speak surrounding computers and the online community. Easy to read discussions and plenty of explanations throughout the book ease you into getting online.
- Beginning users who are not sure if they have the right equipment and software to go online. If you're not sure if the computer you have at home or at work lets you get connected to the online world, this book tells you exactly what you need to get online.
- Experienced computer users who want to get online fast. You can skip around the book to learn about the various options available, and then get connected to the online service you want.
- Computer users who are not sure if the online world has anything of interest for them to explore. For many people, this is one of the main reasons why they are not connected. They don't know why or if they should be. You'll find answers here.
- Computer users who want to change from one online service to another. If you have some experience online but want to change to another service or connect to the Internet, this book discusses the three major online services (America Online, CompuServe, and Prodigy), as well as the Internet and World Wide Web.

How This Book Is Structured

You'll find this book to be set up in an easy to follow format that enables you to read it from front to back, or skip to the chapters and sections you need most. For most users, the latter way is probably the preferred method and the following Part summaries will help you find the information you are looking for.

Part I starts by introducing you to the online world, including the Internet, World Wide Web, and commercial online services. You also find out why getting connected is so popular and why it is the right time for you to get online. Part I also lets you know exactly what you need to get online.

Part II is devoted to the Internet and World Wide Web. The Internet lets you access millions of documents and files online, meet people from around the world, and send electronic mail to friends and relatives in almost every part of the planet. In Part II you are shown how to connect to the Internet using easy to follow step-by-step tutorials. The part concludes with a chapter about Internet Service Providers, which are the companies that provide you access to the Internet.

In Part III, you learn about the major commercial online services, including America Online, CompuServe, and Prodigy. You also learn how to pick the right service for you. The chapters devoted to the online services take you on "virtual" tours of the major features and highlights offered by each service.

Part IV is designed to show you how to put everything you've learned together and make the online world work for you. You will learn how to use the Internet and online services to search for information, such as how to find lost relatives. Topics covered include shopping and making travel reservations online. Finally, you will become acquainted with online security.

Enjoy reading *Discover What's Online*!!!

PART I

DISCOVER THE ONLINE WORLD

1

WHY SHOULD I GET ONLINE?

If you find yourself puzzling over the complexity of getting online or even why you should, rest assured, you're not alone. On a recent *60 Minutes* telecast, Andy Rooney was shown trying to get connected to the Internet. Although Andy admitted he's not the most computer-literate person on television, he did feel that he should be able to connect to the Internet like so many others have done. What Andy went through—configuring his modem, installing software, setting up his America Online account—was the same frustrating and confusing experience most users go through to get online. Rest assured, however. Andy's demonstration for television looked difficult, but connecting to the Internet is actually quite simple if you follow the process described in this book.

By picking up this book, you've taken the first step to discovering what's online and how to get connected to the online world. You've probably heard about the Internet, the Information Superhighway, and maybe even the World Wide Web. If you have a computer or subscribe to trendy magazines, you've undoubtedly been bombarded with advertisements from CompuServe and Prodigy. And who hasn't received a floppy disk or two from America Online? All of these companies, along with the Internet and many other services, make up the online world.

This chapter introduces you to the online world and answers the question "Why should I be online?" Further, for those who aren't sure if getting online is right for them, this chapter provides some reasons why getting online might not be the best choice for them now.

What Does "Online" Mean?

What does it mean to be *online*? For many people, getting online has been a natural extension to their workday. For others, it has been a hobby or a way to extend their recreational or educational endeavors. Still for others (perhaps this is your situation), getting online has been something they've wanted to get around to doing someday, but they're not sure of how to do it or if it's the right thing for them to do.

To be online means to be connected to a computer or series of computers (known as a *network*) by way of a *modem* or similar device across a telephone line (see Figure 1.1). A modem is a device that attaches to your computer and enables it to communicate with another computer over a telephone line. If you use a home or personal computer, your modem probably connects through a standard telephone line. If you work in a company or institution (such as a school or government agency), your computer probably connects to a dedicated high-speed telephone line through a network. The primary function of a network is to allow people and computers to communicate and share information.

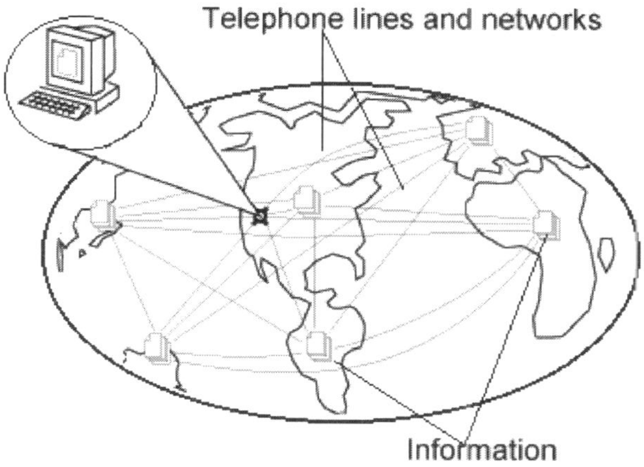

FIGURE 1.1

When you get online, you have a wealth of information and services available to you.

Defining what's available online is similar to defining what's available in the real world. You can access goods and services, documents, and technical or personal support. You can download software to use on your computer. You can communicate with friends and coworkers, find new friends, chat with people who have similar interests, and debate important topics. If you're interested in what's happening around the world, you can get the latest news, weather, and sports (see Figure 1.2).

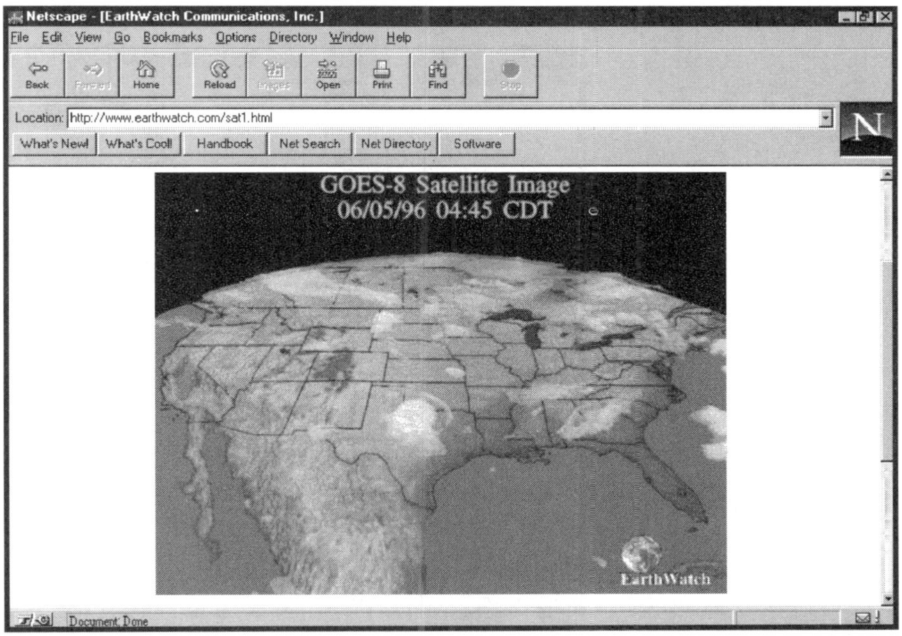

FIGURE 1.2

You can get up-to-date weather reports from the National Weather Service.

What Is the Information Superhighway?

Some terms used to define the online world are *cyberspace*, *Information Superhighway*, *InfoBahn*, and *Internet*. Of those terms, Information Superhighway comes closest to defining what the online experience is like. The connection between your computer and modem to the online world is like the highways and interstate freeways that connect you to cities and other places in the real world. Highways and freeways enable you to travel from place to place, visit other people, and find new places of interest. The Information Superhighway enables you to do the same, but instead of traveling in automobile or bus you travel using a computer and modem.

The online world enables you to go to places that can't even be reached by the highway or freeway system. Unlike the highway system, which must adhere to many physical and political limitations, people online can go wherever telephone lines or satellite links can be established. Imagine the freeway system stretching across the oceans, over the northern and southern polar caps, and even into outer space.

The Information Superhighway is a catch-all phrase that means different things depending on who you talk to. Some people define the Information Superhighway as simply the Internet. The Internet is only part of the Information Superhighway. The Internet, which you'll learn about more in Chapter 3, is a

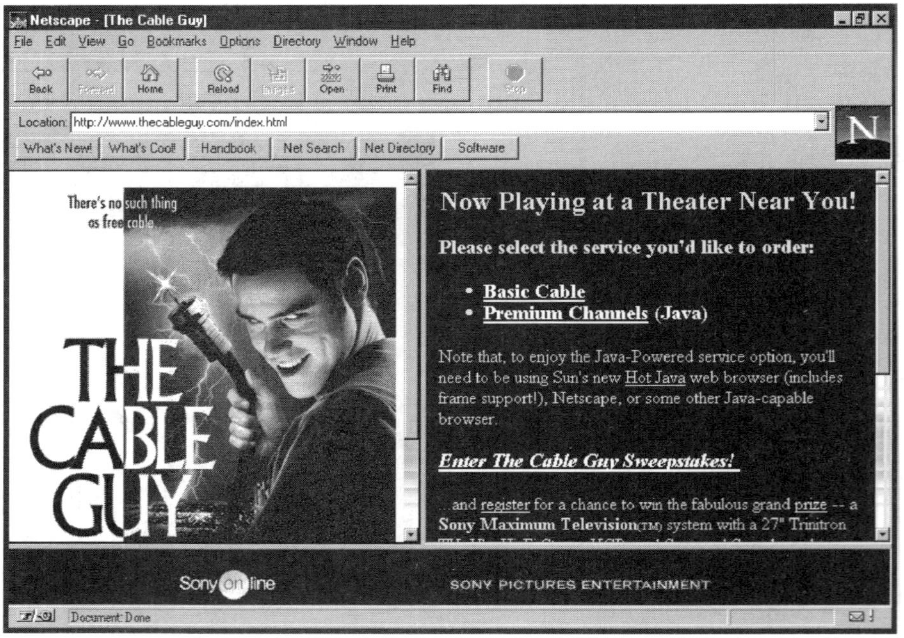

FIGURE 1.3

The Internet offers a wealth of information, communication services, and entertainment, including what's showing at the movies this weekend.

large network of computers that spans the planet and gives you access to many information sources (see Figure 1.3). There are, however, other online sources that make up the Information Superhighway. These include television networks, cable and satellite services, commercial online services (like CompuServe), and electronic transfer businesses, such as an electronic banking service.

In some ways, it's not important to know exactly what the online world is. The main point is to understand how you fit into it and how you can take advantage of it for your own needs. One way to get a better understanding of what the online world has to offer is to understand the different services and networks that make up the online world. But before you do that, you might want to spend a few moments to get familiar with some of the terms and phrases you're likely to hear and read while online.

Why Is There So Much Jargon?

As with any new area of life you discover, certain words or phrases may be new to you. Remember the first day you started your first job? At times, your co-workers and managers probably sounded like they were speaking a foreign language. They were using terms and phrases unique to the company or business, and may have taken some time for you to learn them. After you learned them, however, it became easier for you to communicate with your business associates. This is the same experience you'll have online. At first, terms and phrases might fly over your head and be confusing. After a while, however, you'll pick them up and use them in conversation as though you knew them all along.

The following list contains some general terms you'll likely encounter. You'll be able to follow along in this book easier if you read through this section first.

TIP

You might want to place a bookmark here or dog-ear this page so you can quickly return to this list as you encounter terms and jargon throughout the book.

- **Bulletin board system (BBS).** A BBS is generally a computer running software that enables people to have dial-up access to leave and retrieve messages. Some BBSes include technical support, files for download, interactive games, and limited connections to the Internet. Most BBSes are used within local areas and don't have national or international connections. So if you don't have a local phone number to dial, you end up paying for long distance charges when connecting to out-of-town BBSes.

- **Chat groups.** These are services on commercial online services and the Internet that enable two or more users to communicate in real-time with each other while online. In a chat group, each user types their remarks and posts them to the chat service—it's like talking on a telephone to several people at once but using a keyboard to talk instead of a mouthpiece. Chat groups have become one of the most popular online areas.
- **Commercial online services.** Services provided via a computer modem connection. These services include information, entertainment, and communications to their members. Major online services include America Online, CompuServe, and Prodigy. The Internet is not a commercial online service.
- **Cyberspace.** A term used in the William Gibson novel, *Neuromancer*, to describe a futuristic computer network people use to connect their brains to online information and data repositories. Many people use the term "cyberspace" to describe the online world.
- **Electronic mail (E-mail).** Text-based messages sent from one computer to another via a network, such as the Internet, or via a commercial online service. E-mail messages can contain only text (such as letters or numbers) while traveling across the Internet. You can, however, attach a binary file (such as a spreadsheet file or program) to your e-mail messages that the recipient can download and use.
- **File download.** The act of receiving a computer file from a remote computer to your local computer while connected online.
- **File upload.** The act of transmitting a computer file from your local computer to a remote computer while connected online.
- **Login.** The process of establishing a connection between your computer and a network. Usually, a unique username and password are required for users to log in to a network.
- **Logout.** The process of disconnecting a connection between your computer and a network.
- **Internet.** A collection of networks linked together to form one giant network. They all use the same protocol (TCP/IP—Transmission Control Protocol/Internet Protocol) to communicate.
- **Internet Service Provider (ISP).** Businesses that enable you to get direct connections to the Internet and the World Wide Web using a computer and modem.

- **Modem.** A device connected to your computer that enables your computer to communicate over a telephone line. Modems come in two types: internal and external. Internal modems are installed directly onto your computer's motherboard and are accessible through a port in the case. External modems are stand-alone devices that use a serial or modem cable to hook to your computer.
- **Network.** A system of computers hooked together using a common networking *protocol*. Networks can be as small as two computers connected together (such as in a small office or home), to as large as several million linked together (such as the Internet).
- **Newsgroups.** A set of discussion groups on the Internet divided into topics where users (known as members) can post and read messages about a newsgroup topic. Some commercial online services provide access to Internet newsgroups.
- **Protocol.** A set of rules or standards computers use to exchange information and communicate with one another.
- **TCP/IP (Transfer Control Protocol/Internet Protocol).** The set of protocols developed by the Defense Department's Advanced Research Projects Agency (ARPA) that is used by all computers on the Internet to communicate. To connect your computer directly to the Internet, it must be running TCP/IP software, also known as a TCP/IP stack.
- **World Wide Web (WWW or Web).** A part of the Internet that uses http (hypertext transfer protocol) to transmit text, files, graphics, sounds, videos, and other interactive content. To navigate the WWW, you use Web browser software, such as Netscape Navigator, Microsoft Internet Explorer, NCSA Mosaic, or others. The term "Web' is often used synonymously with "Internet."

As you continue through this chapter and others, you'll come across additional terms that will help you connect and journey through the online world.

What Does the Online World Offer?

Many of the things you can do online are the same functions you now do offline. For example, you can conduct research using online resources; you can send messages to friends and coworkers; you can watch videos online; and you can listen to the news. These are the same activities you can conduct offline, but when online you have more control over when these activites are delivered to you. If you want to listen to *ABC News* on the Web at 8:45 P.M. instead of at its regular time, for example, you can download and listen to the news then.

The following are some of the activities you can enjoy while online:

- Find out the latest news, weather, and sports from a number of news services, including *USA Today*, *Reuters*, *Wall Street Journal*, and others (see Figures 1.4 and 1.5). With many of these news services, such as Reuters' page on the Web, you can get the news before you hear it on the radio or see it on television (see Figure 1.6).
- Transfer a file from one computer to another. This enables you to share work you've done on your computer with other users regardless of their location.
- Get the latest information about your favorite celebrity or television show. Figure 1.7 shows a site on the Web where you can download files about the show *X-Files* on Fox Television.
- Conduct bank transactions, buy and sell stocks, and receive daily Wall Street updates.
- Chat with people from around the world who share your interests.

What you can do online depends largely on the service or type of network you're connected to. Some services, such as CompuServe and America Online, give you

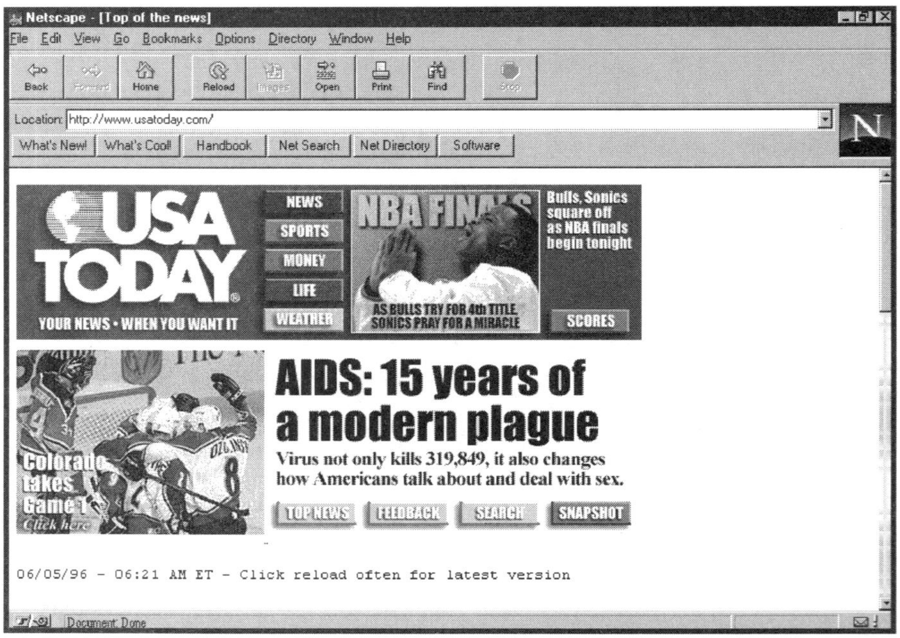

FIGURE 1.4

You can get the news online from *USA Today*.

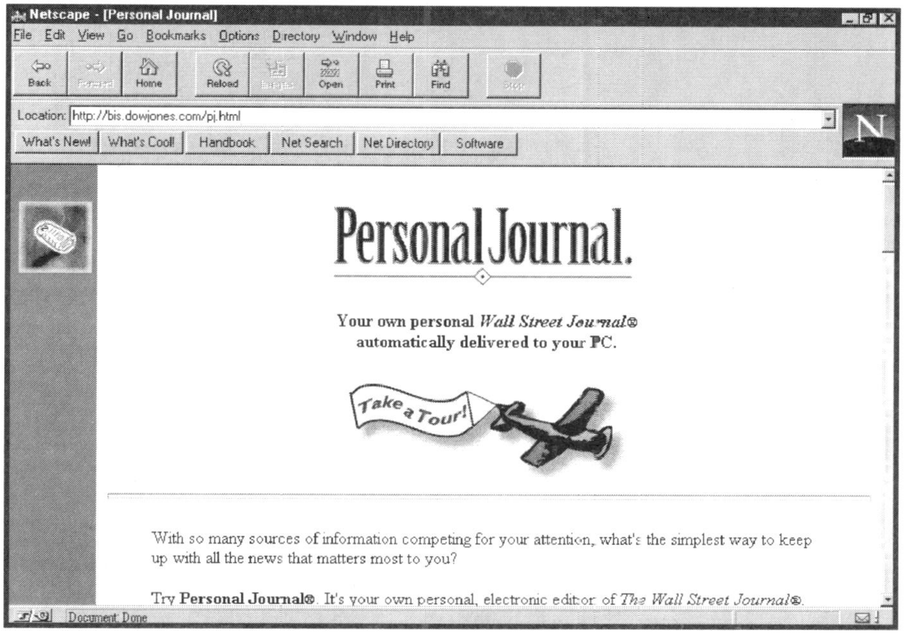

FIGURE 1.5

The *Wall Street Journal* offers a subscription service on the Web that sends you only the news you're interested in.

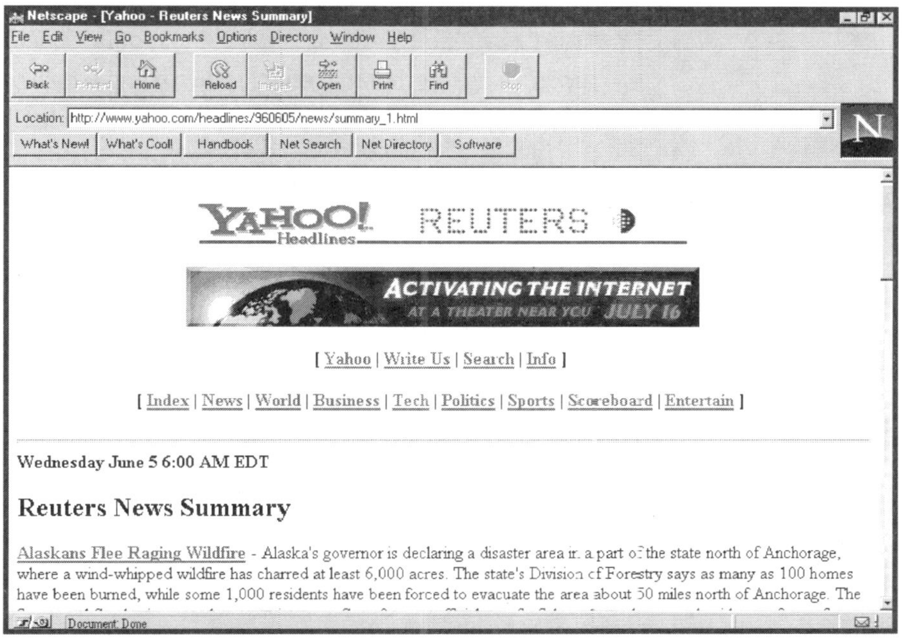

FIGURE 1.6

Reuters posts the latest news for you to read before it's even broadcast on the radio or television.

FIGURE 1.7

Fox Television posts pictures and other information about their popular television shows on the Web.

full access to the Internet and the Web, as well as offer you their own content. Other online services, such as some BBSes, offer you information and data that is only available on their service. Most online services, however, have connections to the Internet that enable you to send e-mail between other online services and BBSes, and to users who are connected to the Internet.

How Do You Get Online?

Before you can get online, you need a few basic tools. These tools let you connect to the online world, communicate with others who are also online, and download and view resources and services that you find online. Chapter 2 goes into more detail about what you need to get online, but the following list summarizes what you'll need:

NOTE

If you're connecting from work, you should first talk with your information systems manager or other technical support person to make sure your company allows employees to go online. Some company polices require all employees to use the same online service or to use special software that reduces the chances of security violations to the company's computer system.

- **Personal computer.** The first piece of equipment you need is a computer. Without a computer, you can't do anything online. The brand of computer you use doesn't make much difference. What will make a difference is the amount of memory and processor you have installed. Generally, more memory (random access memory—RAM) and a faster processor will greatly enhance the performance of your system.
- **Modem.** A modem is a computer device that enables your computer to communicate with other computers across a telephone line. Modem, which stands for Modulation-DEModulation converts the digital signals produced by your computer to analog signals, which travel across standard telephone lines. Then the modem on the other end converts the analog signal back to a digital signal so the computer on the end can interpret the data. The process works the same for the data received by your modem.
- **Phone line.** To connect to online services or to the Internet, you'll need a phone line to plug you modem into. Make sure your phone line can be connected to your modem, usually with an RJ11 (single-line) phone jack. These are the phone jacks that you probably have on your phone connectors on your wall.
- **Online service or Internet membership.** After you have your computer and modem working, you'll need a service to dial in to. The choices you can make here are numerous and include major commercial online services (such as CompuServe and America Online), smaller commercial services (like Genie), and Internet Service Providers. The latter gives you a direct connection to the Internet. You can find specific information on the different online services in Part III. Internet coverage is the topic of Part II.
- **Communications software.** Depending on the service you choose, you'll need to acquire specific software so your computer can connect to that service. Most commercial services distribute membership software free of charge; they give it away at trade shows, through the mail, and even bundle it with new computer purchases. If you connect to the Internet, you may need to get special software that lets your computer connect to the Internet. For example, dial-up software calls your Internet Service Provider and logs you into the Internet.
- **Money.** Nothing is free, and that includes going online. Unless you'll be connecting through your work or school, you'll need to pay a monthly

fee for membership to an online service or Internet Service Provider. These fees differ from service to service, but are generally in the range of $15-$20 a month for four to five hours of online time. Depending on the service, you'll need to set up some type of billing process; in most cases, this is done by credit card transaction. When you establish a membership with a commercial online service (such as CompuServe), you usually do so by connecting to the service with your modem and computer. You then are asked for your credit card number while online. Although it is recommended not to send this type of information across the Internet (because of lack of security), doing so when connnected to a commercial online service usually does not pose a great risk.

NOTE

Look for free online time with America Online, CompuServe, and Prodigy. If you're a new member, you can usually get up to 10 or 20 hours of free time to try out the service before you become a full member. The only catch to this is that you need to keep track of the time you spend online. Most services provide a free area for you to review your current charges. When you sign up to use your free hours, you'll need to provide your credit card number. After you use up your free hours, the online service automatically starts charging you for the time you spend online and submits credit card charges about every two weeks. You don't get a message telling you that the charges are being placed on your credit card. If you don't want to join the service after your free time, you need to cancel your membership with the service by calling or writing the membership department. Otherwise, you may continue to receive charges on your credit card for that service.

Understanding the Internet

The Internet is a global communications network that uses a common language, known as TCP/IP. When you think of the Internet, don't think of it in terms of one computer or one company. Instead, think of it as a collection of computers, users, and resources you can access while online. Originally, the Internet was a Department of Defense project headed by ARPA (Advanced Projects Research Department), and was called ARPAnet. ARPAnet was developed in 1969 to connect strategic military and research sites together to ensure that information could be shared with institutions and research centers, and be able to withstand a nuclear attack.

A new technology was invented called *packet switching* that sent chunks of data (called *packets*) across a network in the safest and quickest means possible. Each packet was small in comparison to the rest of the message and included information about the recipient and sender. If a recipient's computer did not receive a packet because it was interrupted or lost, the sending computer would simply resend an identical packet.

The first four ARPAnet sites that used packet switching were Stanford University, University of California, Los Angeles, University of California, Santa Barbara, and the University of Utah in Salt Lake City. This was the birth of the Internet; this ensured that if a packet of information could not get through one link, it could be rerouted through another link on the network to arrive at the intended destination.

Eventually, ARPAnet was renamed DARPAnet and began to include additional research entities, particularly universities. In 1972, over 40 sites were connected to the Internet. As more users became involved, more technologies emerged to allow more to happen online, including e-mail, file transfers (using FTP—File Transfer Protocol), and remote logins. Remote logins enabled a computer to control a remote computer over the Internet.

In 1974, Vinton Cerf and Robert Kahn released TCP/IP, which set the standard by which networks and computers link to the Internet. This enabled hundreds of sites to become part of the Internet, and lead to wider expansion of technologies to be integrated with the Internet.

From the 1970's to the early 1990's, the foundation of what is now the Internet solidified. The following technologies (see Chapter 3 for more details) emerged during this time:

- Internet chat groups
- USENET newsgroups
- Telnet
- Wide Area Information Servers (WAIS)
- Gopher sites
- World Wide Web

As recently as 1991, much of the Internet was off limits to blatant commercialization. However, many companies were starting to see the potential for using the Internet to communicate with other businesses, regional offices, and customers. Businesses wanted to exploit the global reach of the Internet to draw new customers and to promote their products and services. Through the years, the government maintained control of the Internet by way of the National Science

Foundation (NSF), which published *acceptable use policies* that forbid commercialization on the Internet.

It wasn't until after the NSF lifted restrictions on the commercial use of the Internet (there are still policies against advertising in designated USENET newsgroups) that the Internet began to explode with users. With the Web taking hold in 1993, the number of networks connected to the Internet surpassed the one million mark. The number today exceeds nine million (remember, the original ARPAnet started with four networks).

By far, the most important technology of the Internet for new users is the Web. Although you'll eventually interact with many of the other services on the Internet (such as FTP and newsgroups), you'll probably start your journey on the Internet by using the Web. As shown in Figure 1.8, the Web is a graphical network that displays text, graphics, videos, and plays sound.

You'll learn more about the Internet, the Web, and how to connect to and use the Web in Chapters 3 and 4. For now, read about the commercial online services and how they relate to the Internet.

History of Commercial Services

Commercial online services have been around as long as personal computers have been available. In fact, CompuServe was introduced in 1969, before personal

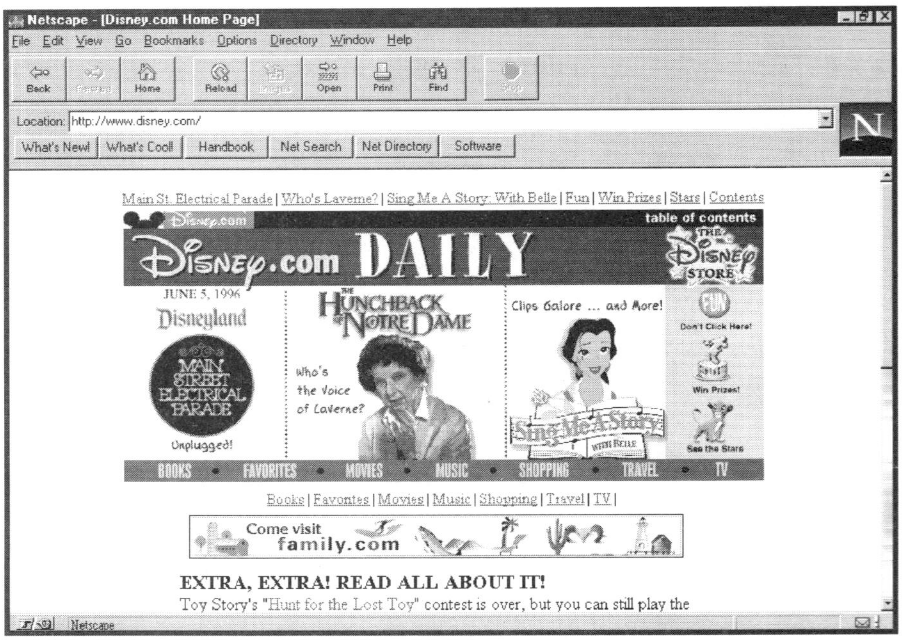

FIGURE 1.8

The World Wide Web will probably be your first encounter with the Internet.

computers existed and at the same time the Internet was developed. As personal computers became more popular in home and office settings, CompuServe started offering specialized and technical services to the mass consumer market, creating the largest commercial online service in the world. In 1995, America Online became the largest commercial online service with over six million members.

NOTE

Initally, CompuServe was an online service for financial institutions doing business with H&R Block, CompuServe's original parent company. H&R Block recently sold CompuServe, which eventually offered public stock for itself.

Some of the services offered to consumers by CompuServe included the following:

- E-mail
- Support and message forums
- Chat services, called CB Simulator
- File transfer and file download
- News, weather, and sports
- Entertainment updates, movie reviews, and exclusive photos

CompuServe was not the only commercial service to venture into the online world during the early stages of the personal computer; other services included America Online, Genie, and Prodigy. While CompuServe catered to the serious computer user looking for technical support, America Online and Prodigy tended to appeal to a more general audience. Genie, an online service owned by General Electric, became popular with a segment of the business community that needed a service to handle various e-mail formats, including sending and receiving e-mail via the Internet.

As personal computers have become more powerful and as users have matured, the needs of online services have grown. Through the years, a number of commercial services have come and gone. Many have found the competition from major online services like America Online, Prodigy, and CompuServe to be too strong. Other services have found the Web to be a more compelling business model for them.

Table 1.1 lists major commercial online services and briefly describes each one.

Online Services and the Internet

Because of the popularity and rich resources of the Internet, commercial online services began several years ago to offer Internet-related services. One of the

TABLE 1.1 COMMERCIAL ONLINE SERVICES

Service Name	Features	For More Information
America Online	Includes an attractive, easy-to-use interface; excellent news, entertainment, and Internet and Web access	1-800-827-6364
CompuServe	Includes WinCIM, a powerful interface for Windows; excellent computer product and support forums; weekly specials; allows easy access to the Web.	1-800-848-8199
Prodigy	Includes interesting travel, Internet, and sports information.	1-800-776-3449
The Microsoft Network	Includes original news and Microsoft product support; available only for Windows 95 users.	1-800-386-5550
Genie	Includes some computer technical support areas and news.	1-800-638-9636
WOW!	Designed for young users; features fun projects, stories, and Web sites for kids; owned by CompuServe.	1-800-848-8199

first implementations of this was enabling members to send e-mail to Internet users and even to members of other online services. For example, a CompuServe member can send an e-mail message to a Prodigy member. The availability of this feature made it possible for people who were not fortunate enough to be connected to the Internet at school or through a government agency to take advantage of the expansive and global infrastructure of the Internet.

Today, the relationship between the commercial online services and the Internet has grown tighter. CompuServe, for instance, offers two ways to access its services. One way is to use its connection software (such as WinCIM for Windows users) to dial directly into CompuServe's main window. From there, you can access CompuServe's original content areas, such as vendor support forums, newspaper archives, and special events pages. These are all services that require a service charge to access. Depending on the service you visit or access, the service charge may be included in your monthly membership rate. Other services, however, are pay-per-visit; these show up on your bill only when you use them.

NOTE

As you'll read in Chapter 7, when you enter a premium service area, such as the Newspaper Archives area, CompuServe displays a warning message telling you a surcharge will be placed on your bill if you decide to use this service. This way you aren't surprised by any charges that appear on your monthly billing statement.

Although this method of business and transaction has worked well for CompuServe, times have changed. Users want to access the Web as well as have access to CompuServe (or other services, like America Online). This has lead to another way that users can use their CompuServe memberships: providing online content directly on the WWW. What this means is that you no longer need to use the online service's proprietary software or direct telephone number to access the service's content. So you have access to the online service's content, and you have the wealth of information available on the Internet and Web.

An analogy for this new structure is to compare an online service to a retail store, and the Web to a shopping mall. Sometimes, you may want to run to a single store to pick up what you need. But if you're searching for a wide assortment of items or "just looking," a shopping mall is where you'll probably wind up. By letting users make one connection to access both the Internet and the commercial online service, users can select from a seemingly endless supply of online information and services, much like shoppers can from large shopping malls.

As the online world changes, so do the businesses that offer online services. Until recently, the Internet was accessible only by dedicated Internet Service Providers, universities, large businesses, and government agencies. To make sure they're bringing in the revenue needed to sustain and grow their businesses, commercial services have had to significantly change their business model. Instead of providing the one-stop shopping service, where billing was metered by the dial-up software and login processes, the commercial services are beginning to provide samples of

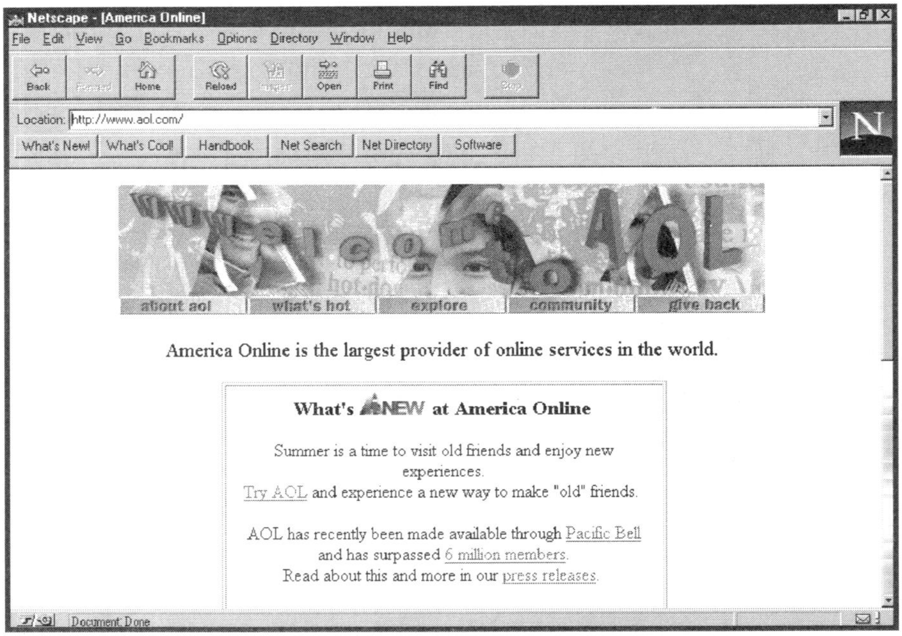

FIGURE 1.9

America Online is using the Web to draw customers to its online service.

their content on the Web to draw users to their core business area. One such company doing this is America Online (see Figure 1.9).

America Online (AOL) provides sneak previews and samples of their member areas on the Internet. You can, for example, take a tour of AOL's main business components, including the Global Network Navigator (GNN) Web service, WebCrawler search engine and directory, and AOL Community. The AOL Community is the heart of the AOL service. It includes members' and employees' home pages, and the AOL Channels. Much like television channels, or CompuServe forums, AOL Channels provide information on different subjects. Some of the AOL Channels include the following:

- **Today's News.** Features breaking news before you hear it on the radio or see it on televsion.
- **MusicSpace.** Includes a number of references to Web sites devoted to different music genres.
- **Life, Styles & Interests.** Features topics of interest for almost everyone. Unless you're dead, you'll find something here to pique your interest.
- **Kids Only.** Devoted to kids, and kids only. You can view pictures of Australian frogs, read about naked mole rats, and see the AOL Top Ten Kids Web Sites list.

- **Newsstand.** Enables you to read online newspapers, including the *San Francisco Chronicle, New York Times* Fax Edition, *San Jose Mercury News,* and *eye Weekly* (a Toronto arts weekly).

Visitors to the AOL Web site can download a copy of the AOL access software, which they then can use to dial into the AOL service and establish an account. Of course, this requires the user to first disconnect from the Internet and then connect directly with AOL.

Not only is the new customer base compelling to commercial services, the Internet offers a much more diverse platform for online members. Members are no longer restricted to the content and information provided by a single online service. Instead, they can choose from the content provided by their online service, plus the rich information sources available on the Internet and Web. The following list describes some of these sources:

- **Links to related sites.** The primary goal of any commercial service is to make money. To reach this goal, a commercial service must provide customers with services and content that will continue to draw them back. One way to do this is to make it easy for members to access sites on the Web and to keep pages updated and fresh looking.
- **New programming capabilities.** Providing to users the latest and greatest software and technological releases is paramount to retaining and adding members. During the past two years, the Web has seen some of the most compelling and interesting programming advances in computing, including multimedia software and virtual reality programs. *Virtual reality* is a term used to describe a 3-D, artificial computer world. By moving their businesses to the Internet, commercial services can take advantage of these new capabilities.
- **Business diversification.** One way to increase business is to add more clients, sell more products, or add a new service. Commercial online services are using the Web to help them launch new business ventures, including business-to-business services, Internet business networking services (called "intranets"), and electronic publishing. Prodigy, for example, recently released a new electronic magazine called *Stem* to complement their main online service (see Figure 1.10).
- **Gain international appeal.** Because the Internet is available in many countries, commercial services can appeal to international audiences they've never reached before. Although many online services offered services in other countries, they tended to focus on major cities and dense

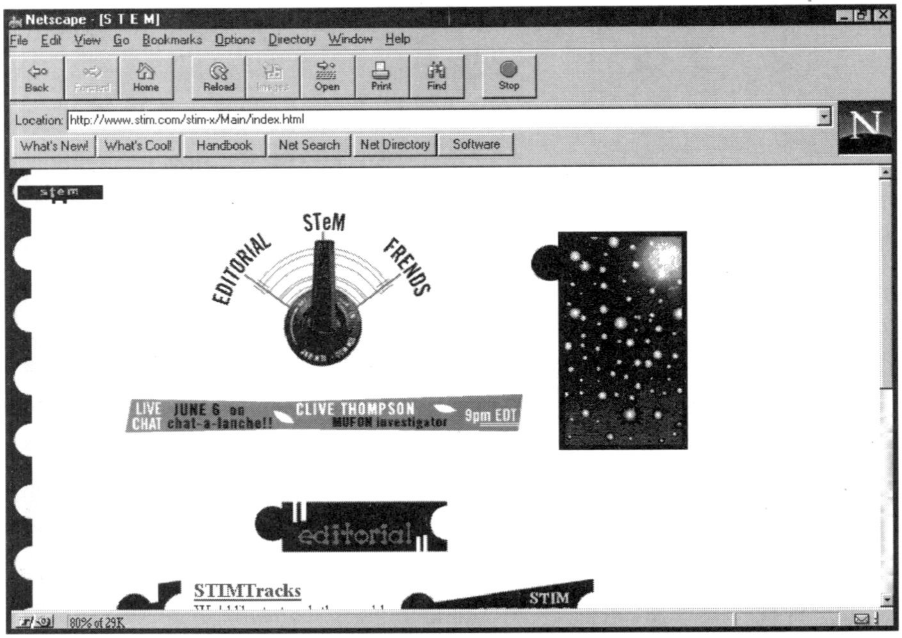

FIGURE 1.10

Prodigy's new *Stem* magazine is available only on the World Wide Web.

population areas. CompuServe, for example, offered dozens of connections in Great Britain, Japan, Germany, and Australia. Others places, such as Singapore and Norway, had relatively few connections. The Internet enables all those with Internet access to now access commercial services via the Web.

- **Conduct online conferences.** A technology that's getting a lot of attention lately is online conferencing (see Figure 1.11), which enables a group of people in different rooms, buildings, cities, or even countries to meet online and conduct meetings. Along with discussions and online chats, special software called *whiteboards* enable users to view and edit the same document while online. These types of conferences may revolutionize the way companies conduct business with internal staff, clients, and outside consultants.

As you can see, a number of reasons have driven commercial online services to take up stakes on the Internet. Even so, there are some distinctions between the Internet and commercial online services that you should know before connecting online.

How Online Services Compare to the Internet

Many people have difficulty making the distinction between commercial online services, such as CompuServe and America Online, and the Internet. As more

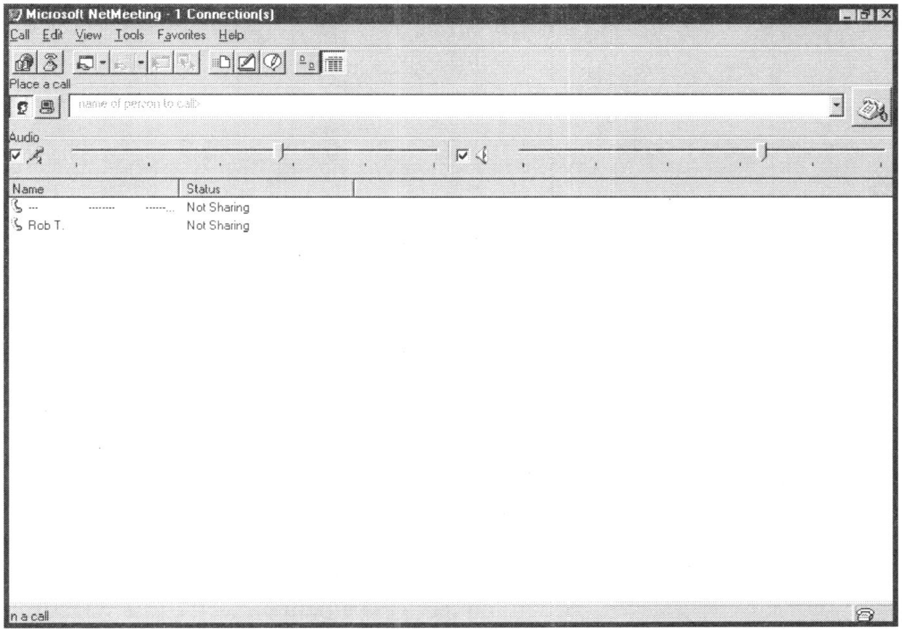

FIGURE 1.11

Conferencing software lets multiple users view and modify the same document.

and more commercial services move toward the Internet, the distinction becomes less defined. There are, however, major differences between commercial online services and the Internet.

Common Misconceptions about Online Services and the Internet

One of the problems in comparing commercial online services to the Internet has been common misconceptions about the relationship between online services and the Internet. The following are some common misconceptions about commercial services:

- **They are the Internet.** Although many online services have a presence on the Internet, specifically on the Web, they aren't the Internet. Commercial online services, along with many other networks and computers, make up the enormous world wide network known as the Internet.
- **You can't get to the Internet from commercial online services.** Most major commercial services now make it easy to connect to the Internet. CompuServe, for example, includes two kinds of software with its free connection disk. You can use the CompuServe version of Netscape or Mosaic to reach the Web directly. Or, you can use CompuServe's proprietary software called WinCIM (for Windows) or the Macintosh CIM

program to access CompuServe directly. Most online services also enable you to access different services of the Internet directly from the online service, including e-mail, file transfer protocol (FTP), and USENET newsgroups.

- **You can't get to commercial online services from the Internet.** Until recently, this was true. Now, however, most commercial services enable you to switch from one service to the next with ease. You don't have to disconnect from your Internet connection first. With CompuServe, for example, you can configure your Web browser (Netscape Navigator or Microsoft Internet Explorer) to launch CompuServe's Windows-based software to access CompuServe while still connected to the Internet (see Figure 1.12).
- **Commercial online services cost more than the Internet.** In some ways, this is true but it depends on your needs and how you want to use your online time. Commercial online services organize their information and services far better than the Internet does, so finding and using a service with a commercial online service is faster; you save time online. Recently, commercial online services have introduced new pricing structures to compete better with the way Internet services charge, including unlimited monthly charges and annual rates. In the past, commercial services usually

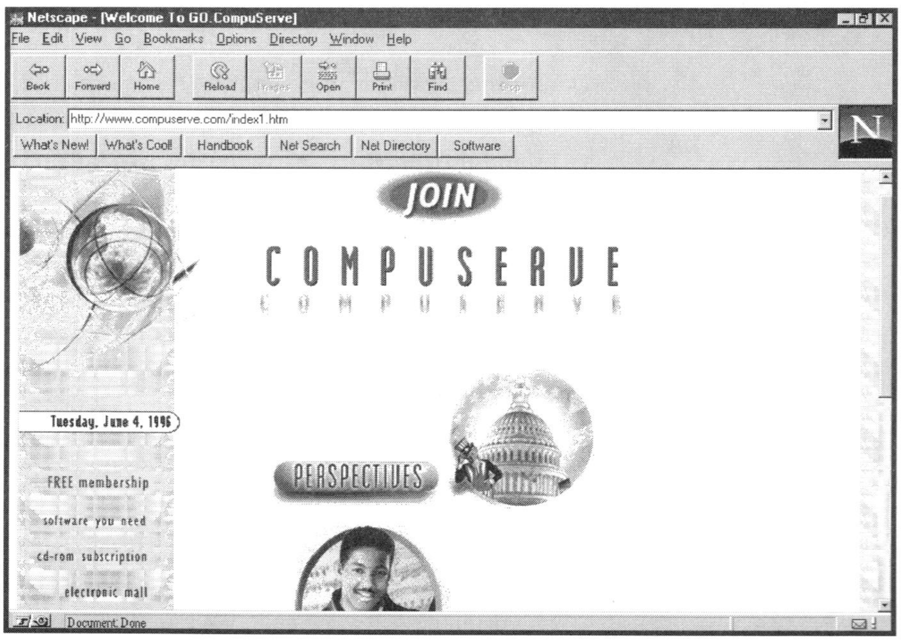

FIGURE 1.12

You can connect to CompuServe while still on the Web by setting up your Web browser to automatically launch WinCIM.

charged a monthly rate that included several free hours, then charged you an hourly rate after you used up your free hours.

Understanding how commercial online services relate to the Internet is important for several reasons. First, it helps you understand how you're charged for the time you spend online. Second, knowing what each service provides lets you know the available services and content. Finally, the way you configure and set up your computer to connect to online services and the Internet depends on the service to which you connect. Some services, for instance, require you to use proprietary software and specific modem and computer configuration parameters, while others let you choose the communications software.

Basic Differences between Commercial Online Services and the Internet

By far, the largest difference between commercial online services and the Internet is the way content is organized. When you connect to the Internet, there is no central "front door" that everyone goes through. Each user can decide where to start from. As you'll see in Chapters 3 and 4, users can start from a number of places when they connect to the Internet, including the following:

- Customized Web pages stored on the user's computer (see Figure 1.13).

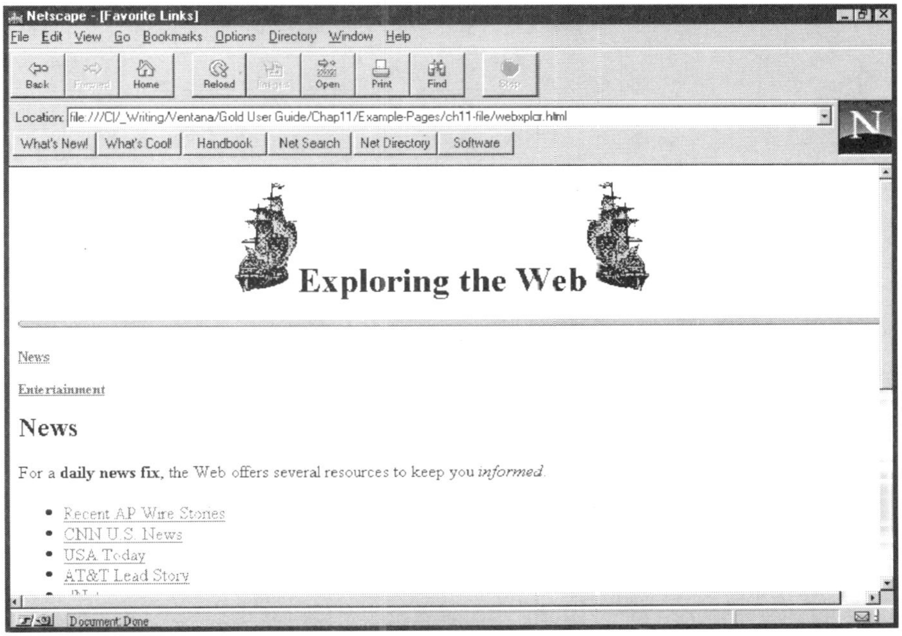

FIGURE 1.13

Many users design their own home page that displays automatically when they start their Web browser.

- Web pages established by commercial services, such as America Online, CompuServe, and Prodigy.
- Any Web page that allows you access, such as Netscape Communications, Saturn Automobiles, and *USA Today*.
- Special directory and search pages designed to let you locate information and resources using keyword or topic search criteria. Figure 1.14 shows Yahoo!, one of the most popular search directories.

Unlike the Internet, commercial online services organize information and resources in more practical and useful ways. America Online, for example, has an easy to understand main menu that you see immediately when you log in (see Figure 1.15). From this main menu, you can choose to receive e-mail sent to you; read the news, weather, or sports; join chat sessions; or visit a number of AOL services.

The way CompuServe organizes its content is by setting up *forums*. Forums are areas devoted to a specific topic of interest, company, or computer area. Forums provide the following benefits to users:

- Enables users to communicate with others who share similar topics of interest
- Provides confidential or undocumented information about software, news events, or products

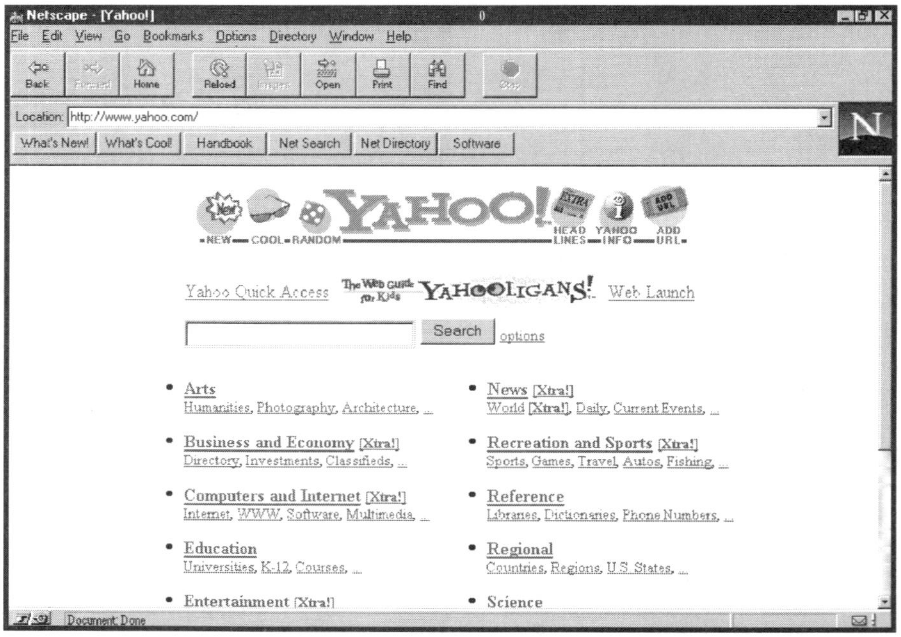

FIGURE 1.14

The Web includes several search directories (such as Yahoo!) to help you locate what you're looking for.

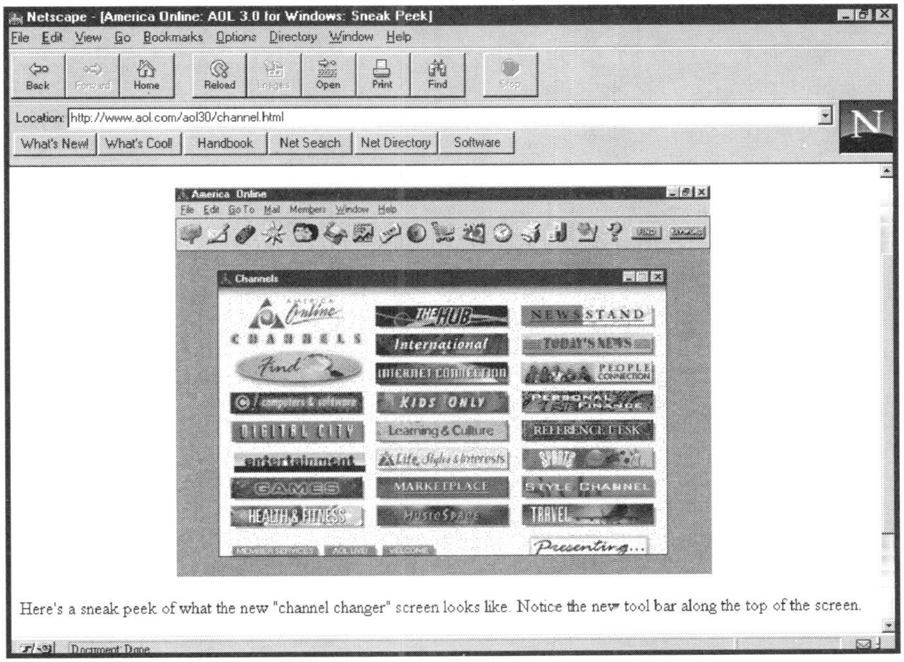

FIGURE 1.15

America Online's menu helps members find content and resources quickly.

- Includes cutting-edge technology news and updates
- Contains shareware, freeware, and other software sources for downloading
- Provides areas for debates, online discussion groups, and questions and answers about specific topics
- Includes product support areas for hundreds of computer software and hardware manufacturers.

Table 1.2 lists some of the most popular CompuServe forums and their descriptions. Notice how forum names usually let you know the type of content that will be available in it. This is different from the names and resources you may encounter on the Internet, which can be cryptic and misleading. Go phrases are the addresses you use to connect to services and forums on CompuServe.

Another distinction between commercial online services and the Internet is the control over content that is available on the online service. Because the Internet is so large and historically has had few restrictions, there has been a lack of control over the type of information available on it. No one is in charge of determining what gets posted on the Internet. If you're looking for something on the Internet and you look long enough, you can probably find it. You might even find material that is offensive, insulting, dangerous, pornographic, and rude.

Table 1.2 Popular CompuServe Forums and Services

Forum Name	Description	GO Phrase
Time News Center	Get the latest news from *Time* magazine's CompuServe service.	TEM
Education Forum	Forum dedicated to bringing together education professionals, students, and parents.	EDFORUM
WinSupport	Includes a number of topics to help users troubleshoot and use Microsoft Windows.	WIN-1
Internet New Users Forum	Devoted to helping users new to the Internet and World Wide Web.	INETNE
All-Movie Guide	Includes a movie database that can be searched by actor, title, category, AMG rating, producer, director, or genre.	ALLMOVIE
Dun & Bradstreet's Electronic Business Directory	Directory of information on over 8.5 million businesses in the United States.	DUNSEBD
easySABRE	Provides flight schedules for commerical airlines, information on millions of airfares, and access to hotel and car rental agencies. This is the travel reservation system operated by American Airlines.	SABRE

Commercial online services, on the other hand, have more control over what is posted and available to their members. Each commercial online service decides what's appropriate for their members; they decide what members can post and say on the service. Any file that gets transferred to an online service must first be approved and checked by the service before it is available for others to view or download. Interactions on message forums and chats are usually moderated to make sure the bylaws of the group are adhered at all times. This does not necessarily mean that all messages are censored. It usually means that if a discussion begins to deviate from the original intent of the group or forum, a moderator will post a message reminding members of the bylaws of the group to refocus the conversation.

Commercial online services also have strict policies against distributing illegal files, photos, and other information not owned by the person who posts the information. This is in stark contrast to the Internet, which has fewer controls over what is posted. Some sites and newsgroups on the Internet, for example, include illegally copied software that users can download for free. They may also include graphics or text that has been posted by someone who doesn't have copyright authority to do so. Commercial online services require members to read and agree to copyright infringement disclaimers that hold the members responsible for any information or file they upload to the service.

NOTE

On February 7, 1996, President Bill Clinton signed into law the Communications Decency Act (DCA) to help curb some of the problems with transmitting indecent material across the Internet and other telecommunications devices. The DCA makes it illegal to knowingly transmit and store patently offensive or indecent text, files, or images, including chat discussions, newsgroup messages, and reference materials. Although there is much debate about this law, one result has been that Web sites that contain offensive and pornographic material have begun to place warnings to viewers before any indecent images or text is displayed (see Figure 1.16). A recent district court decision deemed the DCA unconstitiutional, but the Supreme Court has yet to rule on it.

Looking at Who Should Get Online

It's not fair to say that everyone should get connected to an online service or to the Internet. What is fair to say is that everyone who wants to get online should be able to. Also, you may not be sure how to justify the expense and the time you'll spend online once you do connect. Many users find that once they have an Internet account or have signed up for their 15 free hours on a service like America Online, they can't find time to learn how the service fits into their already busy schedule.

This section shows how the online world can fit into almost everyone's life, including students, professionals, small and large business owners, homemakers, retirees, computer users, and entertainers.

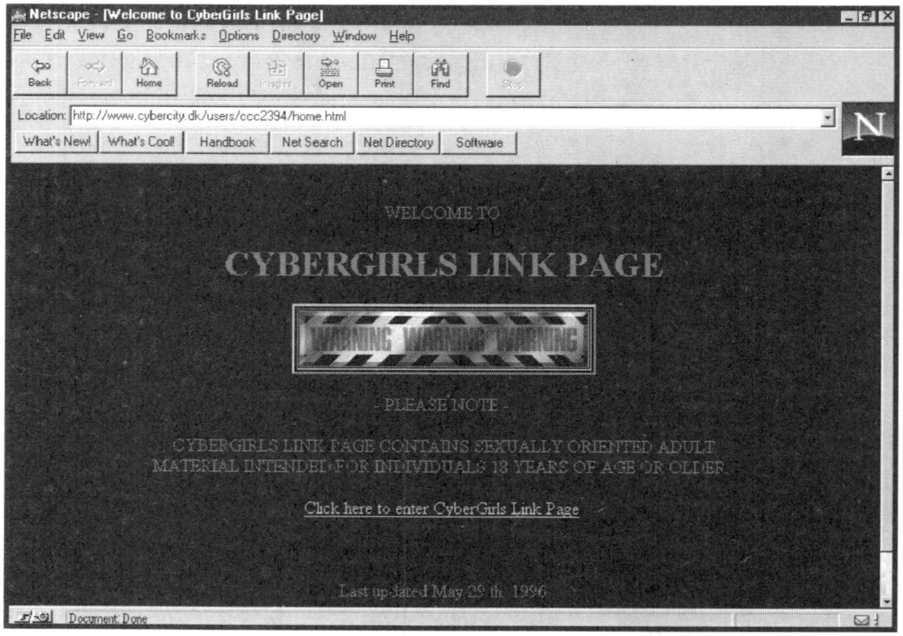

FIGURE 1.16

Since the Communications Decency Act was passed in early 1996, many controversial Web sites post warnings like this one.

Getting Connected for Work

One significant population of online users is business people. Business usage of the Internet has increased dramatically over the past two years. Some estimates show that annually, over one million users are connecting to the Internet, with the large percentage of those from the business segment.

Many reasons exist as to why business usage of online services and the Internet is booming. One reason is the rapid transaction speed online technology offers. For example, e-mail can be delivered over the Internet quicker than by any courier service (only the telephone is probably faster). Also, when exchanging files between users—whether they are in two separate buildings across town, work in different cities or states, or live halfway around the globe—nothing is faster than using the Internet or a commercial online service.

NOTE

Why not use the telephone for everything? Without a doubt, the telephone is one of the most important business tools today. An e-mail message delivered over the Internet or other online service will never replace the expediency or directness a single phone call can achieve. Technologies available online, however, are fantastic complements for phone transactions because of the diverse ways a message can be sent and delivered. An e-mail message sent at midnight from an office on the west coast to an office on the east coast, for example, can be read and replied to early the next morning in the east coast office. This exchange reduces the amount of time people have to play the infamous "phone tag" game of calling and leaving cryptic voice mail messages. A single e-mail message can sometimes reduce the need of leaving numerous voice mail messages.

Many businesses use the Internet and online services to communicate with others and receive product support and software; they also use it to promote and market their products and services. The Web is one of the most affordable ways to set up a business online by creating and publishing Web pages for the world to see. Figures 1.17 and 1.18 show business Web sites devoted to promoting products and services of the business. Regardless of the size of the company, customers can gain access to company information, upcoming products, and press releases.

Getting Connected at Home

One of the fastest growing markets of the online world is the home user market. The home user market is made up of people who go online from home for entertainment, research, education, or hobbies. Many of these users get connected by signing up for free connect time through one of the online services. America

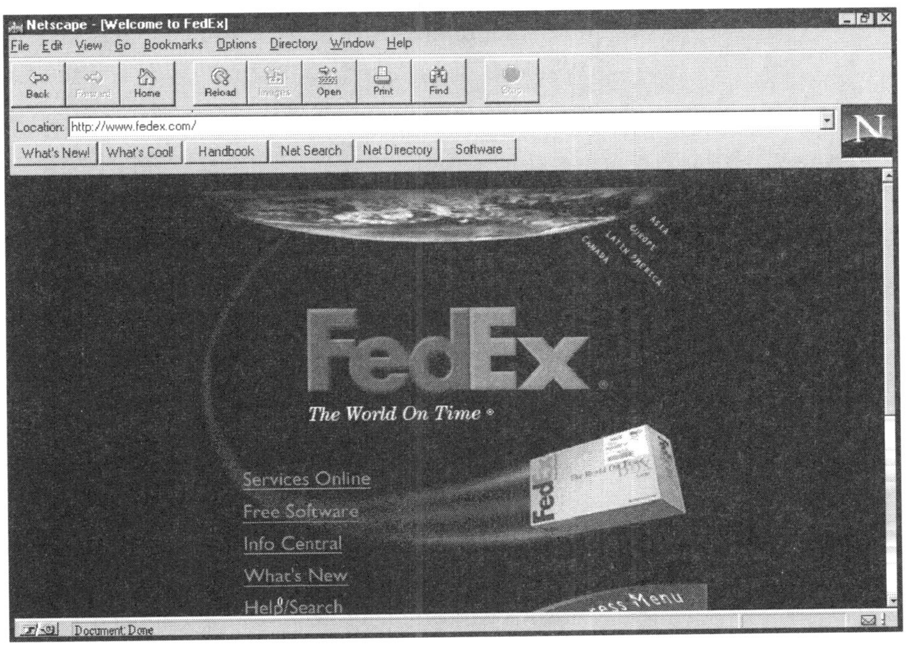

FIGURE 1.17

Thousands of large businesses like Federal Express now offer services online.

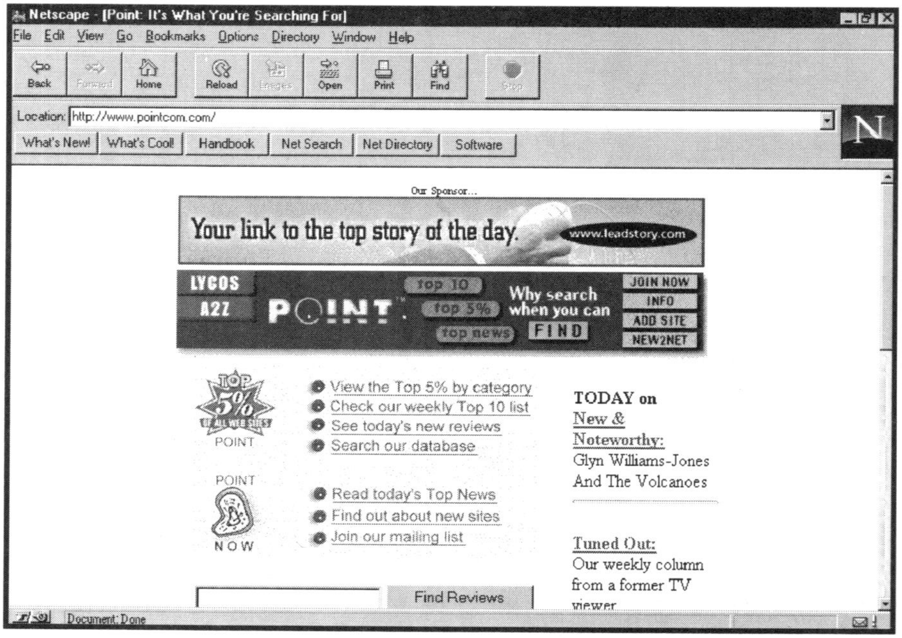

FIGURE 1.18

Small and medium-sized businesses, such as Point, are prominent on the Web.

Online, for example, provides free sign-up disks that include 10 or 15 hours of free online time to any one who uses them.

Another common way to connect to an online service is when you purchase a personal computer for home. Most computers you can buy now have modems pre-installed and have icons on the desktop that let you easily connect to one of the major online services. When you purchase a new computer that has Microsoft Windows 95 installed, for example, you will see an icon for The Microsoft Network and possibly other services as well.

NOTE

In February 1996, Microsoft and America Online agreed to install a copy of America Online's sign-up software with every copy of Windows 95. In return, AOL agreed to use the Microsoft Internet Explorer World Wide Web browser software as its default Web browser. Microsoft will start including this software sometime in mid-1996.

The reasons for home users getting connected are as diverse as the users themselves. For example, you might want to get connected to get your daily fix of news and sports. Or, you might get connected to find out more information about a topic of interest, like gardening or downhill skiing. There are lots of reasons why you might want to get connected online from home:

- To learn more about a topic, such as history, computers, sports, and more
- To communicate with others via e-mail
- To purchase products and services, including software, clothes, food, wine, coffee, books, and technical support
- To find groups of people that share your same interests or hobbies, such as genealogy and writing
- You can establish a presence online with your own Web site or forum area

What if you want to take a vacation to a place you've never been to? How about Cape Hatteras, North Carolina? How do you find the most up-to-date information on Cape Hatteras? One way is to visit the local library or bookstore and check out books and magazine articles about it. But this way, you never know if the resource is available, or if the information is current. Articles as old as twelve months may not provide the most up-to-date information about a vacation spot. You may want to know about what's changed since the last tropical storm or hurricane past by the North Carolina shore. Knowing what hotels or condominiums have vacancies during the times you want to stay is also very important.

Getting this up-to-date information, which can change daily or weekly, is almost impossible using print material. Of course, you could call tourist information centers, travel agents, or friends to find out the best places to stay and then call for reservations. At some point, you'll need to do this anyway. But spending time on the phone can be expensive and may not give you all the information you need to plan your trip.

One way to conduct all or most of your research is by using online resources. The following are some of the resources you can use to plan your trip:

- Conduct searches on the Internet and online services to locate travel information, view vacation hot spots, and download a list of hotels or restaurants in the area.
- Get updated weather conditions in the area using the National Weather Organization's weather maps.
- Make hotel or restaurant reservations on the Internet. If you don't want to make reservations directly online, you can get 1-800 numbers of many hotels and restaurants.
- Find savings and coupons online. One site on the Web, called Hot Coupons, lets you enter zip codes to receive coupons you print out for food, goods, and services.

- Locate relatives, friends, and old colleagues in the area you'll visit. By using a number of searching utilities and online telephone and address directories available on the Internet, you can do name or location searches to find people across the country and around the world.
- Find chat groups or newsgroups devoted to travel and ask others about the best places to stay and eat.

Getting Connected at School or for Research

The online world has become one of the greatest repositories of information since Benjamin Franklin introduced the concept of public libraries in the late 1700's. The Internet and online services provide you with a way to access information that you otherwise may have difficulty locating or knowing about. The Internet provides millions of pages of information relating to almost every topic, including the government, medicine, law, business, politics, and science. By running keyword searches, you can obtain abstracts of articles, white papers, literature, and other sources available online.

If your local or school library is small or lacks in quality and quantity of research information, you may want to check out the Internet for the research information you need. Because the Internet is available worldwide and because it's accessible to you via a phone connection, you aren't confined to the physical limitations of a library or research facility to retrieve information. Also, as more colleges and universities place their libraries online, you'll be able to access information from first-rate collections, such as Harvard Law School, Indiana University Education Department, MIT School of Engineering, and Northwestern School of Journalism.

NOTE

Unfortunately, one of the effects of having millions of documents available online is that people may not visit their local or school libraries. I'm not proposing that the Internet or other online services should replace the experience of visiting the library. One of the simple pleasures in life is to go to a library, rummage through shelves of books and videos, CDs, and periodicals, and then borrow any—or almost any—of those resources. One way to use online sources of information is to complement your visits to the library to help you isolate resources you may need more information about. Also, one of the limitations of being online is that graphics take a great deal of time to download, so large picture books, maps, and illustrated resources are very seldom available online in their original, or printed, versions.

Table 1.3 illustrate some examples of the type of research information you can find online.

NOTE

The Where to Find column in Table 1.3 may not make sense to you right now. In Parts II and III, you learn how to use different online and Internet connections. Then you'll be able to use these references to locate the documents listed. For now, use the table to understand the types of information and data you can find online.

Many college professors and high school teachers are integrating the Internet into their regular classroom lectures. Some instructors recommend or even require students to use the Internet to locate specific sources for information.

Here are some of the advantages of using the Internet and other online services for research:

- Availability of diverse content and resources
- Information is up to date and it's posted almost as soon as it's is available
- Electronic sources are searchable by keyword, phrase, topic, or other indexing methods
- No physical limitations on when and where you can conduct research sessions

NOTE

A current problem with information on the Internet and other online services is the lack of quality control. When you pick up a book or review a research paper, you trust that the publisher has made every attempt possible to ensure the quality and accuracy of the information. This doesn't mean some inaccuracy doesn't appear in the printed document, but publishers place an imprint of quality, or imprimatur, *on their work so readers continue reading the books that are published.*

On the Internet and many other online services, however, anyone can be a publisher of material. Individuals, big businesses, grade-school students, your next door neighbor, or you can publish documents online and claim their value to the reader. Because of this, the reader of the information must determine the value and quality of the material. This can be an almost impossible task because the reader might not be knowledgeable of the subject. For example, if a medical

Table 1.3 Types of Research Information Found Online

Documents	Description	Where to Find
Multimedia Fair Use Guidelines	Guidelines on multimedia copyrights in the digital age from the Consortium of College and University Media Center	**http://www-act.ucsd.edu/webad/fairuse.html**
The Legal Dictionary-Gilbert's Law	Full-text of Harcourt Brace Legal Publication's electronic legal dictionary with over 4,000 legal terms	GO EXCELLER on CompuServe
NBA Playoff History	Results of the National Basketball Associations championships since 1947	**http://www.usatoday.com/sports/basketball/sknhist.htm**
Hobbes' Internet Timeline	History of the Internet divided by decades, starting with the 1950s	**http://info.isoc.org/guest/zakon/Internet/History/HIT.html**
The Prevention of Prostate Cancer	Document discussing the prevention and factors that contribute to prostate cancer	**http://www.secapl.com/prostate/pienta.html**
Protection of Timber and Depredations	U.S. Code on conservation and protection of timber in the United States.	**http://orbus.pls.com:8001/cgi-bin/taos_opcode.pl**
Communications Decency Act Frequently Asked Questions	Answers the most common questions and dispels some of the myths relating to the Communications Decency Act.	**http://www.vtw.org/pubs/cdafaq.html**

student researches inaccurate pharmaceutical information on the Internet, he or she may not be prepared to prescribe suitable medicines to patients.

In Chapter 10, you'll read about conducting searches online and where to find different types of information.

Looking at Who Should Not Get Online

You've read about who *should* get connected online. How about those who should not get connected? Although this book is not intended to discourage anyone from using the wealth of information and services available online or to censure anyone, there are some caveats you might consider before connecting.

First, if you want to use the Internet or an online service to cause harm or to ridicule someone, consider another forum for it. There's already an overabundance of users who have polluted the Internet with false claims, questionable and pornographic material, annoying messages, and other wasteful content. If your sole purpose is to fool or con other users, you should reconsider your motives. This is not to say that opinions, satire, and debates should not be online. But they are generally not used as a way to purposely hurt or offend anyone.

On the other hand, if you're easily offended by graphics that would embarrass your uncle Jimmy, messages that are racially motivated, and information that may be false, you may not want to go online. Because of the behavior of some users and the different cultures that have access to online services and the Internet, you need to adopt an open-minded spirit.

Finally, you shouldn't go online if it will consume your entire life. Like anything else, you should moderate the amount of time you or family members spend online. Not only is this a matter of economics, but the electronic world cannot replace the real world. If you find yourself spending every waking hour online, get away for awhile and re-evaluate why you went online in the first place. The Internet and Web can be highly addictive. They have even been known to destroy strong relationships and marriages.

Examining Online Risks to Children

Growing up, you were taught not to talk to strangers. As parents and adults, you want to protect children from dangers and from people who want to hurt them. Most of the dangers you encountered growing up still exist, but a new one has emerged with the technology revolution. Now people can prey on children while online, and you should learn how to protect yourself and your family while connected.

One of the toughest responsibilities parents have with regard to children going online is how to balance the good with the bad. You want your children to have access to the multitude of online information, but you don't want them exposed to something that may hurt them. You want your children to experience and discover on their own—that's how we all grow—but you don't want them uncovering inappropriate text or graphics they're not ready for.

You wouldn't drop off your kids at a city block full of drug addicts, porno shops, or prostitutes, so you shouldn't let your kids wander through cyberspace without a guiding hand. Ironically, the reason that the online world has grown so rapidly and has worldwide appeal—its capability to allow users to access it regardless of geographic and political boundaries—is one of its shortcomings when it comes to controlling where and what your children access. You can't move to the suburbs of cyberspace to keep your kids away from the problem sections of the inner city. You need to rely on other measures to keep the good stuff accessible and the bad stuff out of reach. You can read about these measures in the following sections, and in Chapter 12.

Ways Children Are Targeted

Children are subject to the following online safety risks:

- Communications with older users who prey on kids. This can be in the form of e-mail, chat sessions, or newsgroup messages (where users place messages to the public). You don't let children talk to strangers on the street or approach "dirty old men" in cars. Warn them against this while they're online as well.
- Exposure to inappropriate text or graphics. As you'll learn in Chapter 3, the Internet includes areas where users can download pornographic pictures or read subversive and inappropriate documents.
- On the Internet, there are over 200 sexually-explicit newsgroups on topics like bestiality, bondage, erotica, prostitution, and fetishes. Regardless of your viewpoint on these topics, you need to keep your children away from them as they develop into adults. With the major online services, you can access these newsgroups just as you can on the Internet.
- Availability of racially oriented information generated by hate groups, anti-Semitics, and other groups that disseminate information you may not want to have your child exposed to.

Simple Ways to Protect Children

One of the ways to ensure that your children are not exposed to some of the risks online is to become involved and to learn about the online world. Don't expect your child to teach you or to share with you problems they encounter. They may be hesitant to let you know about questionable areas they visit; they may fear that you'll take away their online privileges.

Children should never use their full names, give out phone numbers or addresses, nor disclose their age to anyone while online. They should also never agree to meet anyone in person who they have met online. Some users will use an alias and a bogus age to lure lonely children to meet them at a park or area around the child's school.

WARNING

As a parent, one of the worst fears you can have is that of your child disappearing or being abducted. Several cases about men seducing children via the Internet to meet them in person have been in the news the past year. One case involved a teenage girl who was sent an airplane ticket from the abductor so she could fly to Florida to meet him. Fortunately, the girl was located by law enforcement officers and returned home without incident. Unfortunately, this may not always be the case, so warn children against the dangers of sending personal information and about trusting anyone they meet online.

Another way to keep children away from potentially harmful sites and information is to use software designed to block access to these places. One of these products is called SurfWatch (1-800-458-6600), which lets you block sexually explicit material on the Internet. When you use SurfWatch, you can set it up so children in your household are not allowed to access specific newsgroups and World Wide Web sites. Other members of the household, however, can have full access rights to the Web and newsgroups.

In short, don't let the computer be a babysitter without first checking out its references. Become involved with your children's experiences online and let them know that you're available to help them if they have questions. Even more important, by getting involved, you let children know that you understand the computer well enough that you can check up on their online activities.

What's Next

Ready to get online? If so, continue to Chapter 2 to see what you need and how to connect your computer to the online world. That chapter shows you how to prepare your computer to go online, how to configure modem settings, and how to establish connections to the Internet, CompuServe, and America Online.

2

WHAT DO I NEED TO GET CONNECTED?

Chapter 1 focused on some of the issues of why you would want to get online, as well as what commercial online services and the Internet have to offer. Once you decide to go online, you need to put together the necessary tools and equipment so you can make a connection.

If you're lucky, everything you need is already installed and configured on your computer. When you purchase a new computer, you usually can get an internal modem and membership software for one or more major online services. If you purchase a computer with Windows 95 pre-installed, you have the Internet Jumpstart Kit that helps you connect to the Internet.

On the other hand, you may need to obtain one or several of the required tools to get connected online. This chapter shows you what you need and leads you through the process of putting it all together to get you online.

Understanding the Components Needed to Connect Online

Before you start dreaming about flying through cyberspace, you need to wake up, roll up your sleeves, and get your computer setup to get connected. For some users, this process can seem daunting at first; it can even intimidate the most expert of computer users. But don't worry! This chapter walks you through—step-by-step—and attempts to cater to as many situations as possible.

NOTE

A special message to Apple Macintosh users: Before you get too involved with this chapter, you should note that this chapter is written exclusively for computers that run the Microsoft Windows operating system. If you need help configuring hardware or software on your Macintosh, consider consulting the documentation that came with your computer or picking up another book that focuses on the Macintosh system.

The tools you need are divided into four primary areas: hardware, operating system, communications software, and a telecommunications device. The telecommunications device is simply the telephone line, or in some cases a cable link. The following sections discuss each of these areas in more detail.

Hardware Needed to Go Online

The first piece of equipment you'll need to go online is a computer. This book focuses on IBM-compatible computers that run the Microsoft Windows operating system. As you'll see in the next section, you can be running Windows 3.1, Windows for Workgroups 3.11, or Windows 95. If you don't have a computer yet, read through the recommendations listed here first. Although almost any computer can connect online, some computer systems perform better for online activities than others.

The following list suggests minimum system requirements for an online computer:

- 80486- or Pentium-based computer (80486 is usually shortened to simply 486)
- 14" VGA color monitor
- 14,400 bps internal or external modem
- Mouse or joystick
- 4MB of memory; 8MB if running Windows 95
- 20MB to 50MB of free disk space
- Floppy disk drive

If you purchased a computer in the past two years, your system probably meets these standards. Even if your system processor is slower than the recommended 80486 (such as an 80286 or 80386), you still can have a fulfilling and rich online experience. The faster 80486 and Pentium processors are recommended because those are the most frequently sold now. Plus, the faster the processor you get, the better.

Another way to speed up your system performance is to install as much random access memory (RAM) as you can. Most computers you purchase have at least 8MB of RAM. But that's barely enough to run Windows and your online software. When you start browsing the Internet and downloading information to your system, you'll want to have as much memory as possible to keep the performance of your computer at an adequate speed. If you use an application like Netscape Navigator 2.0 to navigate the Web, you'll find that it performs best with more than 12MB of RAM on your system.

For this reason, the following list shows the recommended system if you have the purchasing power to obtain it:

- Pentium 133MHz processor
- 17" SVGA (Super VGA) monitor
- 28,800 bps internal or external modem
- Mouse

- 16MB of memory
- 50MB of free disk space
- Floppy disk drive and 6X CD-ROM drive
- Sound card and speakers (to hear audio files available online)

Because some of the preceding equipment is not known by all readers, the following sections discuss processors, monitor settings, and modems in more detail.

A Brief Look at Processor Speeds

If you aren't sure of the speed of your processor, you can find this information in a number of places. First, look at the front of the computer case. Sometimes the model number or feature list includes the processor speed. Look in the documentation or invoice that came with your computer system. If you're using Windows 95, you can look up the processor size in the System Properties page. To do this, use the following steps:

1. On the Windows 95 desktop, right-click the My Computer icon.
2. Choose Properties from the context menu. The System Properties sheet appears. Make sure the General tab is selected (see Figure 2.1).
3. Near the bottom of the page, look for the Computer setting. Under that setting you can see the type of processor, such as the Pentium. You can also determine the amount of memory installed.

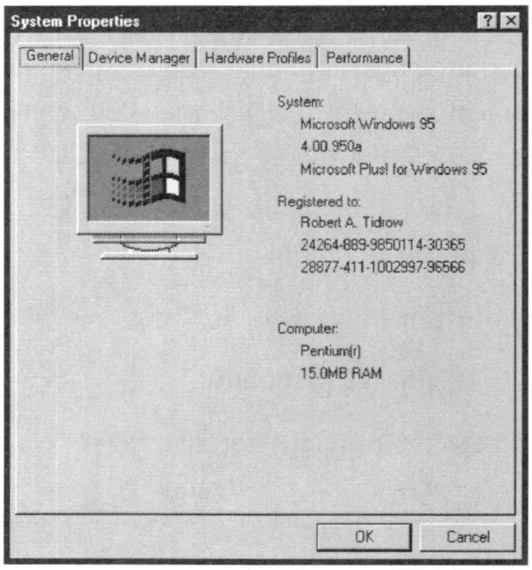

FIGURE 2.1

You can determine your computer's processor speed by looking at the General page of the System Properties sheet.

Monitor and Video Settings

The type of monitor you have isn't as important as the resolution settings the *video adapter* supports. The video adapter, or *video card*, is the interface card (or device) that plugs into your computer inside its case. You usually don't have to worry about the video adapter except when you plug in the monitor to the back of the computer case. Normally, monitors support resolutions of 640×480. This means that the picture you see on your screen paints 640 *pixels*, or small dots, across the width of the screen; and it paints 480 pixels across the height of the screen.

Because the Web and commercial online services include a large amount of graphics and multimedia files (such as full-motion videos and games), you'll want to make sure your monitor can support resolutions of up to 1024×768. If your monitor cannot support this, you should at least attempt to get support for up to 800×600.

Figures 2.2 and 2.3 illustrate the size differences between 640×480 and 800×600. The larger the setting (such as 1024×768), the more information that can display on the screen at once. The drawback to a large setting is that everything displayed is small. Depending on the image or content, it can be indecipherable.

If you don't know the resolution your monitor and video adapter supports, you can usually find out by looking at the documentation that came with your monitor.

FIGURE 2.2

This Web page is displayed at the standard resolution, 640×480.

FIGURE 2.3

Here's a Web page displayed at 800×600 resolution.

If that's not handy, you may have to try resetting your monitor resolution using Windows. Before you do this, you should have your video and Windows system disks handy. You may need them as you work through the following steps. The following steps show you how to change your video resolutions with Windows 95. A nice feature of Windows 95 is that it doesn't require you to reboot your computer for the new video resolution to work. You can, as Microsoft terms it, change resolutions "on the fly."

NOTE

Changing resolutions "on the fly" doesn't work with all monitors or video adapters—particularly those manufactured prior to the release of Windows 95. If your monitor doesn't support this feature, you'll need to shut down and reboot your system to make the changes take effect.

1. Right-click the Windows 95 desktop. A context menu appears.
2. Click Properties to open the Display Properties sheet (see Figure 2.4).
3. Click the Settings tab (see Figure 2.5).
4. Under Desktop Area, move the slider to the new setting. For example, if the setting is currently at 640 by 480 pixels, move the slider to the right

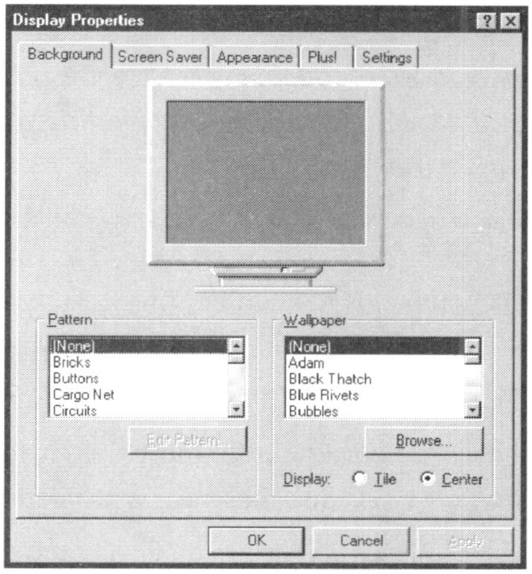

FIGURE 2.4

The Display Properties sheet includes several options to change the way Windows 95 works.

until it is at 800 by 600 pixels. You might also want to set the number of colors to either 256 colors or high color, depending on your video adapter. Notice how the sample display at the top shows you an example of how your display looks.

5. Click Apply to change the resolution setting.

6. Windows 95 displays a message letting you know that your monitor will flicker and may go black for a few seconds.

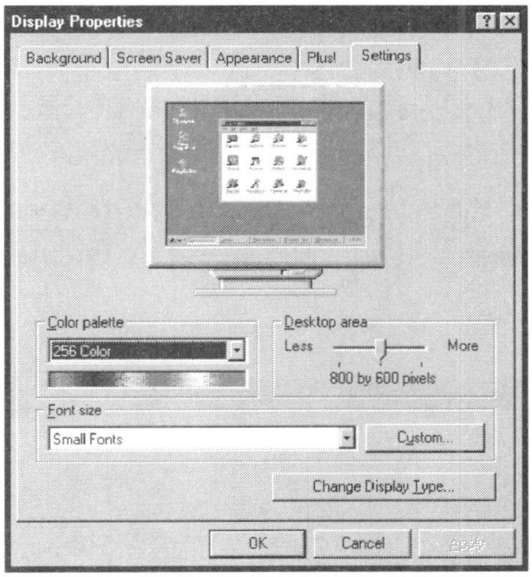

FIGURE 2.5

Use the Settings page to change monitor resolutions in Windows 95.

NOTE

If your monitor or video adapter doesn't allow the resolution setting you changed, Windows 95 will display an error message letting you know that the old resolution setting will be used.

7. Click OK. After this momentary black out, your monitor returns to normal with the new resolution setting. You may need to supply the video adapter's system disk or the Windows 95 system disk at this point.

   If your monitor blacks out for more than 15 to 20 seconds, you may need to reboot your system—there was a problem.

8. After the new setting takes affect, the Monitor Settings dialog box appears (see Figure 2.6). If you want to keep the new settings, click Yes. Otherwise, click No to return to your previous setting.

9. Click OK on the Display Properties page to save the settings.

Modems

In addition to the computer, the most important piece of equipment you need is a *modem*. Modems let your computer communicate on telephone lines. You need a modem because computers "speak" one language, while normal telephone lines understand another language. Your computer speaks in binary data, which you can think of as a series of ones and zeros, to determine how data is sent. The telephone line, on the other hand, understands analog data, which is like our normal speech patterns. This is why you and your friends can talk on the phone without a device like a modem to interpret your speech waves.

Modems come in two flavors, internal and external, and in various speeds. For practical purposes, the main difference between an internal modem and an external modem is that one sits inside the computer and one is on the outside. (Hint: The internal modem is the one inside the computer. You figure out the rest.)

I won't go into the details of installing a new modem, but there are some things to look for when you do. You may get an internal modem included with the

FIGURE 2.6

The Monitor Settings message box lets you return to your original monitor settings or accept the new resolution.

purchase of a new computer. To know if you have one, look at the back of the computer for a place to plug in a standard telephone jack. If you see this, you have an internal modem. This is great, because you won't need to install it yourself. Because it goes inside the computer, you must remove the computer's cover to install one, which requires you to pick up a screwdriver and physically install it (or paying someone else to do it for you).

TIP

If you use Windows 95, look for a Plug and Play compliant modem. Plug and Play modems are automatically recognized by Windows 95 and greatly reduce the amount of time needed to install and configure them.

An alternative to installing an internal modem is to purchase an external one. External modems are self-contained devices that sit next to your computer and are hooked to your computer using a serial cable.

As listed in the suggested requirements, you should get a modem that is rated at 14,400 (also called 14.4) or 28,800 (also called 28.8) *bps (bits per second)* or *baud rate*. What does this mean? The baud rate or bps settings is the speed at which the

Don't Forget to Buy...

A common problem with purchasing an external modem is remembering to purchase a serial cable that connects your modem to the computer. In almost every case, modem manufacturers don't include these cables with their modems. Before you rush out to buy a cable, however, look at the connections on the back of your computer. You'll need to find a COM port (communications port) or serial port to which to connect the cable. Some computers include decals labeling these ports. Write down the type of connection the port has. It will be one of a few different configurations. It can be a 25-pin male connector, for which you'll need to purchase a 25-pin female connector cable. It may be a 25-pin female connector, so you need to purchase a 25-pin male connector cable. You might also have a 9-pin male connector, or 9-pin female connector, which requires a 9-pin female connector cable and 9-pin male connector, respectively.

To tell what type of connector you have, count the number of metal pins or holes in the port. The 25-pin ports have 25 holes or pins, whereas the 9-pin ports have nine holes or pins. When you purchase the cable, make sure the cable has the correct connections for the cable and for your computer. When working with a sales associate, pull out the paper on which you wrote down your port type and let him know what your computer has. Double-check before you leave the store. You don't want to come back later just to pick up a new cable.

data moves from your computer across the telephone line, and from the telephone line to your computer. When you connect to an online service or to the Internet, you must determine the speed of the connection. Sometimes this is determined by the service you're connecting to. Some areas of the country, for example, only have 14.4 connections to CompuServe or America Online. You can use a faster modem to access a 14.4 connection, but the fastest rate of transfer is limited to 14.4.

To get the most out of your connection to the Internet and the Web, you should get a 28.8 modem. In fact, this is still very slow compared to the speed the Internet can transfer data. You'll read more about the transfer speeds of the Internet in Chapter 3, but 28.8 is the bare minimum you'll want for viewing graphics and downloading files on the Web. (14.4 modems are just too slow for graphics.) Otherwise, you'll spend more time waiting for Web documents to display than actually reading the documents once displayed.

The price difference between 14.4 and 28.8 modems is usually not a barrier to purchasing the faster one. In fact, in some places you can buy a 28.8 at about the same price as a 14.4 because modem manufacturers are pushing their 28.8 stock. You can find specials where 28.8 modems are priced at under $100, while 14.4 modems are routinely priced in the $50 to $90 range. Normally, 28.8 modems range between $120 and $200.

NOTE

One area where you'll find a major difference between prices of 14.4 and 28.8 modems are PC card modems (which used to be called PCMCIA). During the spring of 1995, you could purchase a 14.4 PC card modem for less than $70; a 28.8 PC card modem was priced at more than $250. If you plan to use your laptop to connect to the Internet (where PC cards are generally used), the extra cost may be well worth it. However, if you plan to use your laptop mainly to receive e-mail, and not for downloading large graphics or browsing the Web, a 14.4 modem should satisfy your needs (especially at the low cost).

To tell the speed of your modem, you can use two quick methods. First, if it's an external modem, look on the outside of the case. Sometimes it will appear on the back or bottom of the modem. For internal (and external) modems running under Windows 95, you can use the Device Manager, as shown in the following steps:

1. Right-click the My Computer icon on the Windows 95 desktop.
2. Click Properties to display the System Properties sheet.

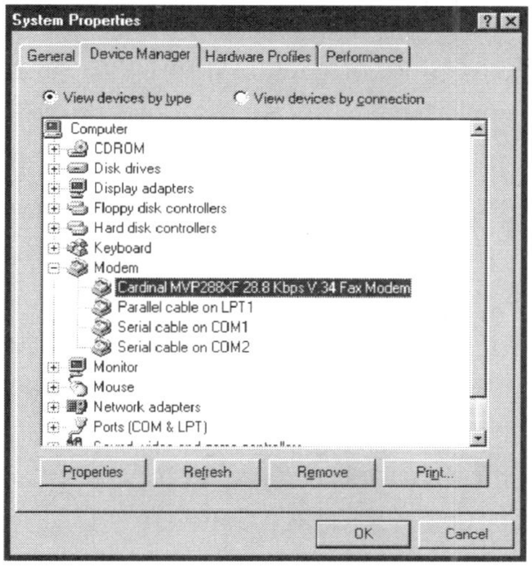

FIGURE 2.7

You can find the modem speed by using the Device Manager in Windows 95.

3. Click the Device Manager tab (see Figure 2.7).
4. Click Modem in the list box. The listing of modem devices and ports on your system expands.
5. Read the setting of the modem, such as Cardinal MVP 288XF 28.8 Kbps V.34 Fax Modem. For this example, a 28.8 modem is installed.
6. Click OK to close the System Properties sheet.

Operating Systems Needed to Go Online

An *operating system* is the underlying software that tells your computer how to work. The type of operating system installed on your system is of little consequence to the online world. In fact, much of the Internet is built on an operating system that most users don't use—UNIX. The majority of users, particularly business and home users, rely on a version of Microsoft Windows to power their computers.

Operating systems make the most difference when you're choosing the software needed to navigate online services and the Internet. For many users, having access to the latest software, including new WWW browsers, multimedia programs, and supporting files, is very important. Since the release of Windows 95, most new software being released is first released for Windows 95, then migrated to other operating systems, such as Apple Macintosh, UNIX, and Windows 3.1. Because Windows 95 was built using an advanced technology (called a 32-bit architecture—as opposed to a 16-bit architecture), more powerful programs can be developed for it. For this reason, some programs are no longer being developed for older versions of Windows. This means if you want to stay current with technology, you'll have to opt for Windows 95 or later products.

Don't worry if you're using Windows 3.1 or Windows for Workgroups 3.11, and don't want to migrate to Windows 95. There are hundreds of powerful programs that run very well under older versions of Windows. However, you'll find that it can be tougher to configure Windows 3.*x* to connect to the Internet than Windows 95. This is because Windows 95 includes several built-in programs designed to work with the Internet; Windows 3.*x* doesn't have these applications. With that said, however, Windows 3.*x* is still not difficult to set up for the Internet if you have all the right tools and proper procedures to follow, as explained in the section called "Communications Software."

TIP

When referring to Windows 3.1 and Windows for Workgroups 3.11, the term *Windows 3.x* is usually used.

The following are some of the features included in Windows 95 that make it an excellent operating system for online connections:

- **Built-in TCP/IP support.** In Windows 3.*x*, separate software is required to add TCP/IP support. TCP/IP, as you learned in Chapter 1, is the protocol used to connect computer networks together on the Internet.
- **Built-in e-mail application, called Microsoft Exchange.** Exchange is a universal e-mail "inbox" that lets you send and receive e-mail from the following services: the Internet, internal networks, CompuServe, and The Microsoft Network.
- **Microsoft Internet Jumpstart Kit.** The Microsoft Internet Jumpstart Kit is included with pre-installed versions of Windows 95 to help you easily configure Windows 95 to connect to the Internet (see Figure 2.8). With this application, you can connect to the Internet using The Microsoft Network as your provider, or you can use a separate Internet Service Provider (ISP). The kit is also available with the Microsoft Plus! software, which is a separate product distributed by Microsoft.
- **Microsoft Internet Explorer.** After you connect to the Web, you can use Microsoft's Internet Explorer Web browser to navigate from site to

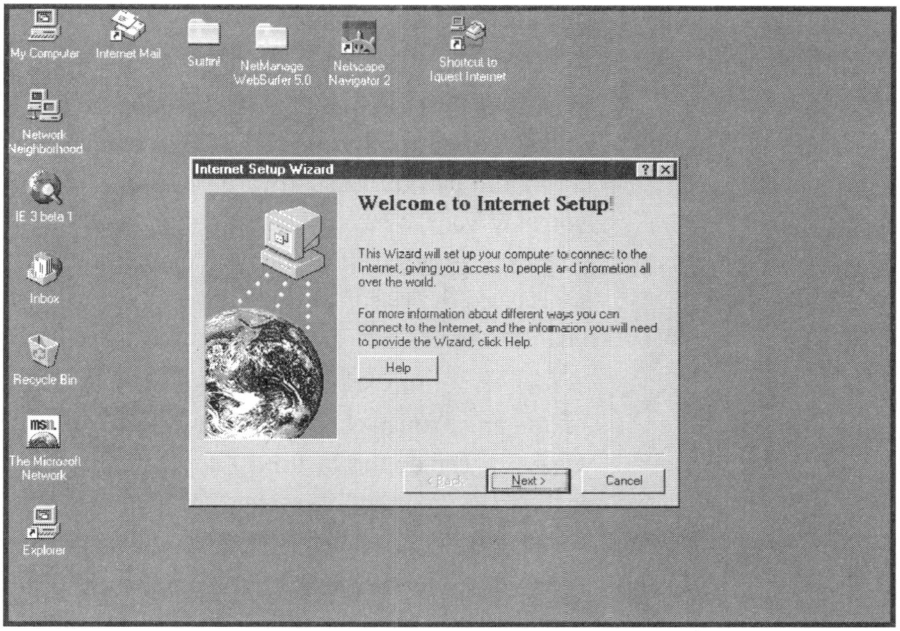

FIGURE 2.8

The Internet Jumpstart Kit includes Wizards that walk you through installing and configuring your Internet connection.

site. The Microsoft Internet Explorer is a competitive product to Netscape Navigator, which is discussed later.

- **Built-in dial-up software.** As you'll see in the section "Communications Software," you need a separate program to dial your Internet access provider. This program is called a *dial-up program*. An Internet access provider is usually called an Internet Service Provider (ISP).
- **Native FTP and Telnet applications.** Two common Internet services are FTP and Telnet (you'll learn about these in Chapters 3 and 4), and Windows 95 includes character-based applications for these services.
- **PPP and SLIP software.** PPP (Point to Point Protocol) and SLIP (Serial Line Internet Protocol) are the two protocols used to allow computers to access the Internet. Windows 95 includes this software.

Communications Software

After you have your hardware in order, you need to decide what type of online connections you'll want to make. Do you want to connect solely to the Internet and the Web? Is a commercial online service all you need? Does the free trial time offered by America Online or CompuServe seem tantalizing enough to try out?

Whatever the case, you'll need to acquire certain types of software to take advantage of all the resources you find online. Online software can be broken down into two groups: Software necessary to make a connection and software you may want to have. The first group, necessary software, includes communications programs, TCP/IP software, dial-up software, Web browsers, and Internet tools (such as FTP software). If you connect to most commercial online services you need to use their proprietary software to connect to their services.

The second group, software you may want to have, is used to complement your online time. You might, for instance, find a library of graphics files you want to view. You can do this by using a separate graphics program, such as Paint Shop Pro (see Figure 2.9). This second group of software is usually called *utilities* because they help you take advantage of the resources you find online.

In the next few sections you'll read about the software you need to get connected online, as well as the utilities you might want to have to take advantage of the numerous resources you find when you're finally online.

Connection Software You Need

The type of connection software you need varies depending on the service you use and the operating system you have. Each of the major commercial online services provides its own connection software, while you generally have to piece together the software needed to connect to the Internet. Some Internet Service Providers send you a collection of Internet software after you sign up with them;

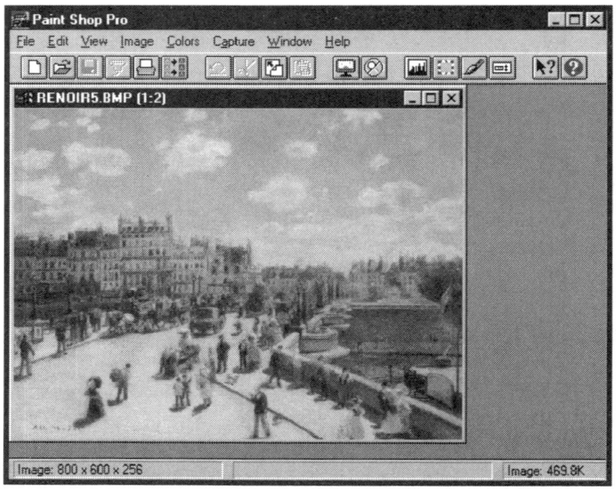

FIGURE 2.9

Paint Shop Pro is a must-have program for any online user who wants to view and edit graphics found online.

however, others assume you have the software or can find it on your own. You can also purchase software suites that provide you with most of the software you need, but you should check the suites to make sure they have everything *you* need.

The following list describes the software you need for each of the major commercial online services. All of the connection software for these services is free, although regular connection fees (when applicable) apply when you connect to the service.

- **America Online (AOL).** You need the America Online for Windows 3.0 software. For this latest version, call 1-800-827-6364, download it from their Web site at **http://www.aol.com**, or look for a copy of it bundled with magazines at your local bookstore.
- **CompuServe (CIS).** To use all of CompuServe's features, you need the CompuServe Information Manager for Windows (WinCIM) version 2.01. This software lets you connect to CompuServe or use CompuServe's Web browser to connect and navigate the Internet. To obtain WinCIM 2.01, call 1-800-848-8199, download it from their Web site at **http://www.compuserve.com**, or look for a copy of it bundled with magazines. Unlike the other online services, you don't need CompuServe's proprietary software to access it. You can use other communications software, such as HyperTerminal (which comes with Windows 95). This method is not recommended or discussed here because it limits the number of services and types of content you can use on CompuServe.
- **Prodigy.** You need the Prodigy 1.2 installation software for Windows to connect to Prodigy. To obtain it, call 1-800-PRODIGY, download it from their Web site at **http://www.prodigy.net**, or look for it bundled in magazines.
- **The Microsoft Network (MSN).** Only available if you have Windows 95 installed on your system. Use The Microsoft Network icon on the Windows desktop to register with MSN and to connect to the service. At the time of this writing, MSN was in the process of moving all their content and services to the Web. When this happens, you will no longer need to make a separate connection to MSN. You can simply connect to the Internet and navigate over to the MSN area on the Web.

NOTE

Although I'm assuming that you're new to the online world, you may have access to the Internet or online service from another source, such as work or school. You'll see references throughout this section that lists Web addresses (such as ***http://www.aol.com****) to obtain most of this software. If you don't understand this addressing scheme, read Chapter 3. If you do understand it but you don't have access to the Web at this time, you can obtain the listed software by one of the other ways mentioned.*

A trend in the computer industry is to install one or more setup programs for these online services on new computers. When you purchase a computer, the software is pre-loaded, many times with icons on the desktop informing you to "Double-click to start" or some similar instruction. This makes it easy for you to register with a service, but it may be confusing if you don't realize that these services aren't free. In addition, even if software for an online service is installed, it doesn't necessarily mean there's a modem installed on your computer. You still need a modem to connect to them.

To obtain Internet software requires a little more effort and sometimes a little more money. Depending on the software you use, you may pay as much as $100 or as little as nothing. The following list describes some of the more popular Internet connection software for Windows:

- **Netscape Navigator 2.0 Personal Edition.** Includes the number one Web browser—Navigator 2.0—plus software that helps you configure your computer easily to connect to the Internet. Navigator 2.0 is available for either Windows 95 or Windows 3.*x*, so make sure the copy you purchase is correct for your operating system. The Registration Wizard provides you with a list of national ISPs you can choose to use as your ISP. If you would rather use a local provider, you can configure Navigator to use that provider. Navigator 2.0 includes built-in e-mail and newsgroup applications, and support for FTP and Gopher. Netscape Navigator 2.0 Personal Edition is available at many retail stores, computer stores, and bookstores and sells for about $39.99. You can order a copy by calling Netscape at 415-937-3777. You can download a copy from their Web site at **http://www.netscape.com**.
- **Microsoft Internet Explorer 2.0 (MSIE 2.0).** This is included with Windows 95 on computers that come with Windows 95 pre-installed. You also can get MSIE with the CD-ROM version of Windows 95 and with the Microsoft Plus! pack. Or if you're connected to the Web, you can download it from the Microsoft Web site. MSIE is a free Web browser with support for accessing FTP and Gopher sites, but you need separate soft-

ware for e-mail and newsgroups. Yet it is available for Windows 3.*x*, with e-mail, TCP/IP, and dialer software. The address of the Microsoft Web site is **http://www.microsoft.com**. You can contact Microsoft at 1-800-426-9400.

- **Internet in a Box.** This software is from Spry CompuServe/Internet Division and includes a Web browser (Spry Mosaic), access to the Internet through the CompuServe service, and Internet connection software. Although Spry Mosaic is a good Web browser, it does lack some of the advanced features you can find in Netscape Navigator. Internet in a Box is found at retail stores, computer stores, and bookstores and sells for about $90. It's available for Windows 3.1 and higher, including Windows 95. A version for children, Internet in a Box for Kids, is also available.
- **InternetSuite 2.** Available from Quarterdeck. It contains several Internet applications, including Quarterdeck Mosaic for Web browsing, connection helper, QuickTime for Windows, Global Chat, and Adobe Acrobat Reader. InternetSuite 2 is available in most computer stores or by direct mail and sells for about $39.95. As a bonus, InternetSuite 2 includes CYBERsitter, which lets you control the types of sites your children can access on the Web.

NOTE

At the time of this writing, new versions of Netscape Navigator 3.0 and Microsoft Internet Explorer 3.0 were being tested. By the time you read this book, those new versions may be available instead of the versions previously mentioned. The new version of Navigator 3.0 will include several new features, including enhanced security, software enabling you to make telephone calls across the Internet, and support for 3-D files and videos. Microsoft Internet Explorer 3.0 also has new features, including enhanced security, a customizable toolbar, and support for advanced Web page elements, such as frames (see Figure 2.10). (You use frames *to divide the main browsing window into separate windows.)*

After you pick out the connection software, you can start building an online software collection to enhance the time you're online.

Supporting Software You Need

Regardless of where you work or what you do, there are universal tools or equipment that are used. In an office building, for example, everyone has a stapler,

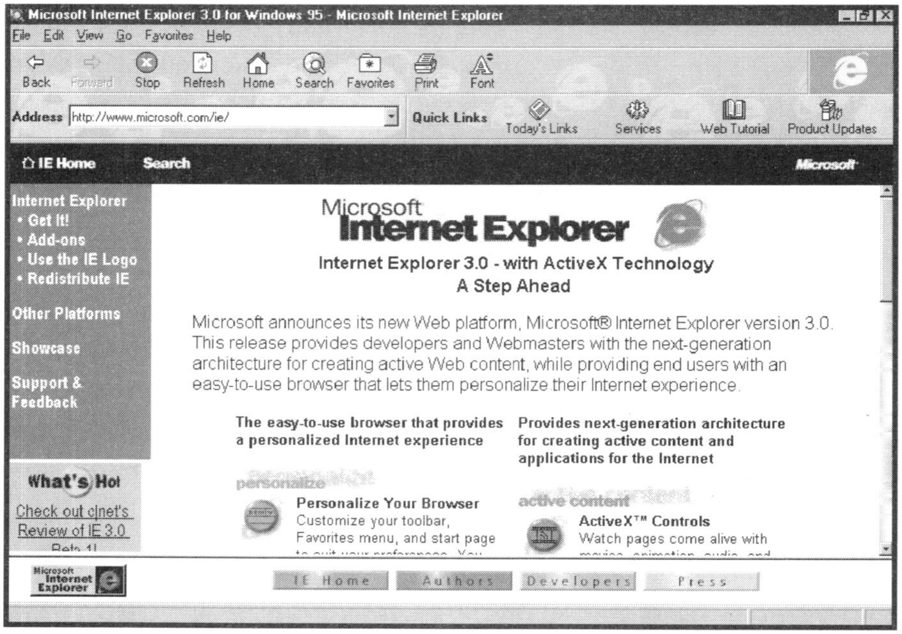

FIGURE 2.10

Microsoft Internet Explorer 3.0 includes a new customizable toolbar and support for advanced Web page features, like frames.

roll of tape, drawers of pens and paper, a telephone, and a coffee mug. These are things you can't do without. Similarly, there are certain programs you'll want to have as you become more involved online.

There are literally thousands of programs available that you can use to complement your online activities. Table 2.1 lists and describes several of the most popular ones.

In addition to these programs, there are applications that users on the Internet and the Web just to have in their cache. First, you'll need a Web browser, which was discussed in the previous section. Next, you need applications that let you view files you find on the Internet, communicate with other people connected to the Internet, and experience multimedia files on the Web. One way to get many of the applications for Web navigating is to purchase Netscape Communication's Power Pack. In it, you get the following applications:

- **Chat.** Enables you to conduct online chats with users from around the world about topics as diverse as the people on the chat.
- **File viewers.** Includes products that let you view many of the multimedia files you find on the Web. It includes Adobe Acrobat document viewer, Xing Technologies' StreamWorks real-time video and audio player, Apple's QuickTime video player, and RealAudio Player from Progressive

TABLE 2.1 ONLINE UTILITIES		
Program Name	**Type**	**Description**
Paint Shop Pro	Graphics	Full-featured graphics program that lets you edit, view, and create graphics. You can view GIF, JPG/JPEG, TIF, and many other file formats.
LViewPro	Graphics	Although it's similar to Paint Shop Pro in its function, LView Pro tends to display GIF and JPEG files in higher resolution than Paint Shop Pro.
GhostView	Graphics	Displays and prints PostScript files, which is a page-description language used by many professional desktop publishers, printers, and publishers. Some files you encounter online will be saved as PostScript files (they have the extension PS).
VuePrint	Graphics	Opens, saves, prints, and views graphics in GIF and JPEG format.
MPEGPLAY	Video	Plays back MPEG movie clips, which are compressed videos that play on Windows.
Video for W		ays back Video for Windows video files. Windows 95 ludes built-in support for Video for Windows files, but 'll need this separate application for Windows 3.*x*.
Wplany		s most of the sound files located online.
WinZip		presses and uncompresses files saved in ZIP format. are compressed to reduce their size for faster ding and downloading.
Enigma for Wind		cryption program that enables you to encrypt files for ssion so only the recipient can read them.
Wincode		you to decode and encode binary files transmitted Internet and other services in message format.

Program Name	Type	Description
Table 2.2 Internet and Web Applications		
Eudora	E-mail	One of the best e-mail applications. It enables you to receive, read, compose, and delivery e-mail over the Internet.
Pegasus Mail	E-mail	An alternate e-mail program to Eudora. Pegasus has advanced filtering settings that enable you search your messages.
NewsXpress	Newsreader	Enables you to read and post messages to the more than 14,000 USENET newsgroups available on the Internet.
WinVN Newsreader	Newsreader	One of the easiest newsreaders to use and configure.
Gopher for Windows	Gopher	Before the Web, Gopher let you access text and graphics easily. Although most Web browsers let you access Gopher resources, you might also want to have a stand-alone Gopher application.
WS_FTP	FTP	Enables you to easily connect to and access FTP (file transfer protocol) sites.

Networks. The RealAudio player lets you listen to audio files transmitted over the Web.

- **SmartMarks.** Scans Web pages and lets you know which ones have changed since you last visited them.

Table 2.2 describes some other applications you may not want to be without.

Now you have the tools to get online. If you want to connect to one of the major commercial online services, see the following chapters:

For America Online, refer to Chapter 6, "America Online."

For CompuServe, refer to Chapter 7, "CompuServe."

For Prodigy and other services, refer to Chapter 8, "Prodigy and Other Online Services."

Use the next sections to find out how to install the software and how to get connected to the Internet using Windows 95 and Windows 3.*x*.

Configuring an Internet Connection

The next few sections discuss in detail the basic requirements for configuring an Internet account, how to use Windows 95 built-in Dial-Up Networking software, and how to use the Microsoft Internet Jumpstart Kit. The section "Installing Internet Access for Windows 3.*x*" discusses how to set up Windows 3.*x* to connect to the Internet. To set up Windows 95, however, continue with the next section.

Installing Internet Access for Windows 95

When compared to Windows 3.11, Windows 95 is a breeze to configure for accessing the Internet. Microsoft even offers an add-on product, the Internet Jumpstart Kit, that helps you configure your Internet connection. The Internet Jumpstart Kit is part of the Microsoft Plus! Companion software. It's also available on new computers that come with Windows 95 pre-installed. Because every Windows 95 user may not have access to the Internet Jumpstart Kit, this chapter shows you how to configure Windows 95 with or without the kit. If possible, you should use the kit because it's usually faster and less complicated than the manual way detailed in this chapter.

If you decide to use Windows 95 to connect to the Internet—whether you use the Internet Jumpstart Kit or not—you must make sure you have all the necessary components in place to make everything work. First, you need to install Windows 95 and have it working before you can get started. You also need the following components:

- **Internet Service Provider (ISP).** This is the service that enables you to access the Internet and the Web. This can be a commercial provider, an institute, or an educational facility. Some of the newest entries into the ISP market include long-distance phone carries, such as AT&T and MCI.
- **Modem or LAN connection.** Depending on the method you use to connect to your ISP—via a dial-up connection or a network—you must have a modem or network adapter installed and working. If you're connecting to the Internet from home, you'll have a modem connection. If your company is "getting on the Internet," you'll probably connect to the Internet through a local area network (LAN).
- **TCP/IP support.** TCP/IP is the language (called a *network protocol*) of the Internet. If you didn't install TCP/IP when you installed Windows 95, you'll need to install it before your Web browser will work. (The steps for doing this are explained in the section called "Installing TCP/IP Support.")

- **IP address information.** An *IP address* is a unique number for you while you're on the Internet. Sometimes you are assigned permanent numbers (such as when you have a LAN connection), or you're assigned a different one when you connect to your ISP. The ISP assigns you an IP address based on a set of IP addresses the ISP receives from an Internet governing party. A typical IP looks like this: 198.36.70.36.
- **Connection software.** You need software that will enable you to communicate with the Internet. For many Windows 95 users, the built-in Dial-Up Networking application is the best choice. For others, software such as Trumpet Winsock can be used. Finally, if you connect to the Internet via a LAN, your network administrator will need to set up and configure the connection software on your local machine. (This topic is beyond the scope of this book, however, so check with your network administrator.)

The following sections discuss each of the preceding items in greater detail. If you have the Internet Jumpstart Kit and want to use it instead (it's faster), skip ahead to the section "Using the Microsoft Internet Jumpstart Kit" after you read the next section on getting an Internet account.

Acquiring an Internet Account

For most users, the first step to Internet access is setting up an account with an *Internet Service Provider (ISP).* ISPs are businesses or institutions that allow you to access the Internet for a fee. Some ISPs are national, such as AT&T, MCI, PSINet, and UUNET, and some ISPs are local entities that offer services to regional users. Most major cities in the U.S. have providers that sell accounts at reasonable rates. Even some colleges and universities are offering connections for a certain fee to offset some of the cost of running and maintaining Internet services.

If you connect to the Internet through your company's LAN, your LAN will need to be connected to the Internet through an ISP. For the most part—unless you're the person responsible for setting up a LAN connection to the Internet—you won't need to bother setting up an account with an ISP. Your network administrator should handle all the details and give you all the necessary information to configure your Internet access software.

When you establish an account with an ISP, you're required to pay a fee. Fees generally are structured in two ways:

- Some ISPs offer a flat monthly fee that gives you a set number of online hours per month. When you exceed this number, you pay an additional

TABLE 2.3 INTERNET SERVICE PROVIDER FEE STRUCTURES		
ISP Name	**Web Site Address**	**Fees**
AT&T	**http://www.att.com/worldnet/**	$19.95 for unlimited access
CERFNet	**http://www.cerf.net**	$20.00/month for 15 hours
Iquest	**http://www.iquest.net**	$15.00/month for 120 hours
MCI	**http://www.internetmci.com**	$19.95 unlimited access
Netcom	**http://www.netcom.com**	$19.95 unlimited access
*PRICES EFFECTIVE JUNE 21, 1996.		

amount per hour. Reasonable rates, depending on the speed at which you connect, can be between $15 to $40 per month. This type of service may give you in excess of 100 hours per month for this rate.

- Another type of fee structure you may encounter is a monthly fee plus an hourly fee. In this case the monthly fee is generally low, perhaps $4.95, with two or four hours of "free" service. For every hour thereafter, you're charged an hourly rate, usually $1 to $3 per hour. Of course, all these rates vary depending on the service provider and local competition.

Table 2.3 includes a sampling of the fee structures for some of the most common ISPs in the U.S. and their rate schedules for the first quarter of 1996. (Most ISPs offer additional fee structures as well.) As you can see, each plan requires that you think about the number or hours you may use the Internet in a given month. Most ISPs also offer quarterly, semiannual, and annual rates that enable you to stay online as long as you want and not worry about hourly charges. Chapter 9 goes into more detail about picking a service provider, if you don't already have one.

A possible hidden cost of going online is telephone tolls. If you use an ISP that isn't local—or if you live in a rural area that doesn't have a local exchange—you'll need to dial long distance to the ISP. This means you'll have charges for the ISP, as well as for normal long-distance fees. Keep this in mind as your online time may get expensive after several hours on the Internet. Providers such as AT&T and MCI are beginning to provide toll-free numbers to rural customers to reduce the cost of long distance charges.

You can find ISPs by looking in your local phone book under topic headings such as Internet, Computers, and so on. You also can find them by contacting local computer stores and asking them for references to reputable ISPs.

NOTE

As you read in Chapter 1, some commercial online services are providing Internet access. One drawback to using these services is that their fees may be a little higher than a regular ISP that provides only Internet access. At the time of this writing, a basic account with either CompuServe or Prodigy cost $9.95 per month. That plan gives you complete access to basic services, including Internet access, for five hours of usage per month. Additional hours cost $2.95 each. Note, too, that some services carry an additional charge.

Understanding PPP and SLIP Connections

When you talk with an ISP to establish a connection, you may be asked if you want a Point-to-Point Protocol (PPP) or Serial Line Internet Protocol (SLIP) account. You must have one or the other to have full Internet access, including Web access. PPP and SLIP give your computer direct access to the Internet system through an ISP. PPP and SLIP (sometimes referred to as *PPP/SLIP*) trick the Internet system into thinking your computer has a dedicated line to the Internet (although PPP and SLIP are really dial-up communication protocols that need modems or networks as intermediaries between Internet hardware and your computer).

Because PPP is a newer protocol than SLIP and because it doesn't rely on the UNIX operating system, Windows 95 has better support for PPP. Windows 95 does offer SLIP support, but you must have the CD-ROM version of Windows 95. However, most ISPs offer PPP connections, so you shouldn't have a problem finding one that supports it. Generally, the only time you'll need to worry about using SLIP software is when you already have a SLIP account established and want to migrate to the Windows 95 operating system. You learn in the section "Installing TCP/IP Support" how to install the PPP and the SLIP software for Windows 95.

Data for and from the ISP

When you set up your account with an ISP, be prepared to ask questions, answer questions, and take detailed notes. (You can find a comprehensive list of some of the questions you might ask in Chapter 5, under the section called "Sample ISP Questionnaire.") You'll need to provide information to the ISP representative so he or she can set up your account properly. Depending on the ISP, you may be given access to the Internet as soon as you call them and arrange payment plans, or it may be several hours or even a week before your account is established. Some ISPs are very busy and need some time after you call to get your account activated.

You should have the following information before calling the ISP:

- **Operating system.** Are you using Windows 95 or Windows 3.*x* or some other operating system to access the Internet?
- **Modem speed.** You'll need to know the bits per second (bps) of your modem. Is it 9,600 bps, 14,400 bps, 28,800 bps, or higher? You can find out in Windows 95 by double-clicking on the Modems icon in the Control Panel. When the Modems Properties sheet appears, look at the listing for your modem on the Generals page. This listing usually tells you the name and speed of your modem. If this doesn't show the bps rating, you can highlight the modem and then click the Properties button. This will show you the maximum speed of your modem and give the ISP an idea of your modem's speed. You also can simply refer to the modem documentation for its speed.

NOTE

The Modem Properties sheet also includes a Connect Only At This Speed check box. Because you can't regulate the speed at which you'll connect to your ISP each time you log in with them, you should keep this check box unchecked.

- **PPP or SLIP connection.** In the preceding section, "Understanding PPP and SLIP Connections," you read that you should go with the PPP account. If the ISP doesn't ask you which type of connection you want, be sure to tell them PPP. If your ISP offers only SLIP connections, that's OK—you'll just need to take a few extra steps when setting up your machine. Refer to the section "Adding SLIP Connectivity to Windows 95" later in this chapter.

- **Type of dial-up software.** You'll need to let the ISP know if you plan to use the Windows 95 built-in Dial-Up Networking software (which is recommended) or use another dial-up utility, such as Trumpet Winsock. For most beginners, the best bet is to use the Dial-Up Networking software. (If you plan to set up a network server account with the ISP, you'll need to use a different type of software for connecting to your ISP, so dial-up software is not an issue.)

Some of the information that the ISP will give you includes a password, a username, and some critical technical information—all of which you must write down. This information may be sent to you in the mail or given to you at a later date after your account has been established, depending on your ISP. Table 2.4 is set up as a fill-in-the-blank table for you to write in the information you need from the ISP to set up Windows 95 to access the Internet (you fill in the right side of the table). Be sure to keep this record for the future. It's necessary to get every number, period, and word just right when setting up your connection. Some of these terms may be foreign to you now; they're explained when you use them during setup.

If the ISP representative doesn't give you all of the information shown in Table 2.4, ask him or her if you'll need this information. In almost every situation, you'll need all this information to configure your Internet connection properly. The only place where you may have a blank is your IP address. Your ISP may assign you an IP address that you'll need to use each time you log into the Internet. The other alternative would be for the ISP to assign you a *dynamic* IP address, which means that your IP address would change each time you log in. In the section "Configuring the TCP/IP Host," you learn how to configure each type of IP address.

NOTE

Some ISPs will send you software utilities that they have customized to help you set up your Internet connection. These utilities include all the information shown in Table 2.4, and they'll have simple setup instructions for you to follow. The upside to these utilities is that you don't have to worry about reading the rest of these installation instructions. The downside is that good documentation usually doesn't accompany these utilities, so you're on your own when you encounter problems. More than likely, you'll need to call the ISP's technical support line to fix any problems or to reconfigure a setting.

TABLE 2.4 INFORMATION YOU NEED FROM THE ISP

Type of Information	Information
Access phone number	
Logon name (or username)	
Password	
Domain name	
Your IP address	
DNS server	
Your host name	
Gateway IP address	
IP Subnet Mask	
IP address of the DNS server	
ISP's modem speed	
Internet e-mail address	
Name of Internet mail server	
Name of Internet news protocol	

Setting up a Modem or a LAN Connection

While the scope of this book doesn't cover how to install a modem on your computer or how to set up a network connection, you can run the Add New Hardware option in Control Panel and follow its prompts to help you set up your modem. You also can access the online Help application (by clicking the Start button and clicking Help) and read the information in the Setting Up Modems topic. This will lead you through setting up a new modem.

To set up a network adapter on your system to work with Windows 95, see the Help topic called Setting Up Your Computer for Networks. That topic will show you the steps necessary to set up the hardware and software necessary for network support.

Installing TCP/IP Support

Now that you have an Internet account set up, you're ready to begin setting up Windows 95. You begin this process by installing TCP/IP support. In short, TCP/IP is the language that the Internet network understands. All computers must "speak" TCP/IP before you can send or receive anything from the Internet. TCP/IP is an acronym for the following:

- **Transmission Control Protocol (TCP).** This protocol breaks your outgoing messages or files into packets called *datagrams*.
- **Internet Protocol (IP).** This protocol routes the datagram packets through the Internet system in search of a target router (a computer that directs Internet traffic to other computers on the Internet). When the datagrams find the router, they navigate to the destination computer, where TCP on the other computer reassembles the packets into their original form.

TIP

Isn't TCP/IP more complex than that? Yes, by a factor of about one million. Luckily, when setting up your computer for Internet access, all you really need to know is how to set up your TCP/IP support and software. The rest of this section will explain that.

You may hear the TCP/IP program called the TCP/IP *stack*, because the various functions of TCP/IP occur in vertical layers from the application programs to the network hardware level. The application programs are at the top of the stack, and the network hardware is at the bottom of the stack. If someone asks if you have a "protocol stack," you will now know what they're talking about.

To start adding TCP/IP support to Windows 95, you need to create network support for Windows 95. The following steps lead you through this procedure:

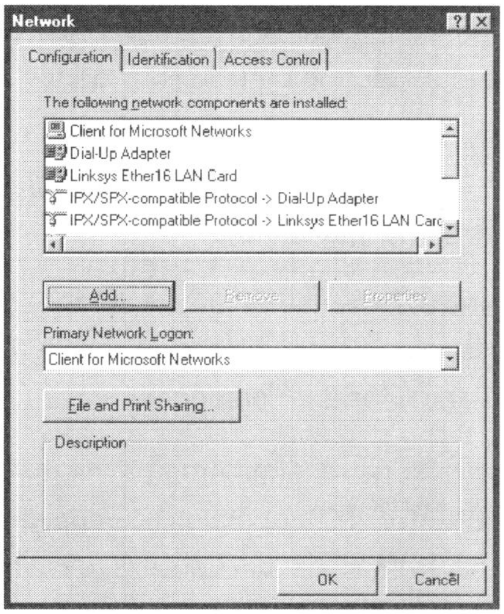

FIGURE 2.11

You can use the Add button to install TCP/IP support on your computer.

1. Double-click the Network icon in the Windows 95 Control Panel.
2. The Network dialog box appears (see Figure 2.11). This dialog box may include only one tab—Configurations—or three, depending on whether you have network configuration or not. If you have not configured a network connection, the Configuration tab has no items listed. Otherwise, you may have a few items already installed.
3. Click the Add button. The Select Network Component Type dialog box appears showing four items (see Figure 2.12). These items are the network components you can install on Windows 95:
   - Client. This is the type of network you want to install. For this example, you need to install the Microsoft Client. Other predefined clients include Novell, Banyan, SunSoft, and others.
   - Adapter. This is the network interface you set up. In many cases, this is a hardware device that you insert into your computer, some-

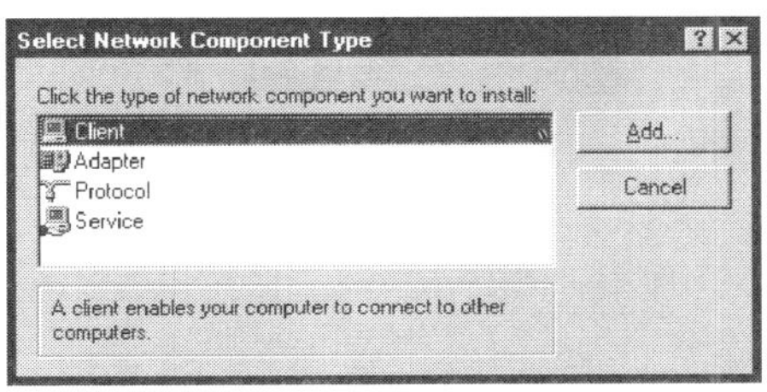

FIGURE 2.12

Double-click the Client option to tell Windows 95 that you want to establish Microsoft Network client support.

times called a *network interface card* (NIC). In this situation, you need to add the Dial-Up Networking adapter to dial your ISP.

- Protocol. This is the language that the computer uses to communicate with other computers. As mentioned, you need to install TCP/IP for this section.
- Service. This enables the network to share files, printers, and other resources. For your Internet connection, you won't have to set up anything for this component.

4. In the Select Network Component Type dialog box, double-click Client. The Select Network Client dialog box appears, with several types of network clients from which to choose (see Figure 2.13).
5. In the Manufacturers list, click Microsoft.
6. In the Network Clients list, click Client for Microsoft Networks.
7. Click OK.

You now have set up the initial network support on your system, including four network items. This gives you basic network support if you want to configure your machine to communicate with another computer running Windows 95 (that is, if both machines have network cards installed and cables attaching them to one another). The problem is, you want to communicate on the Internet. To do so, you now need to add the TCP/IP protocol to the system. Follow these steps:

1. Click Add from the Configuration tab of the Network dialog box. The Select Network Component Type dialog box appears (refer to Figure 2.12).
2. Double-click Protocol. The Select Network Protocol dialog box appears (see Figure 2.14). This dialog box includes several networking manufacturers and the Windows 95–supported network protocols.

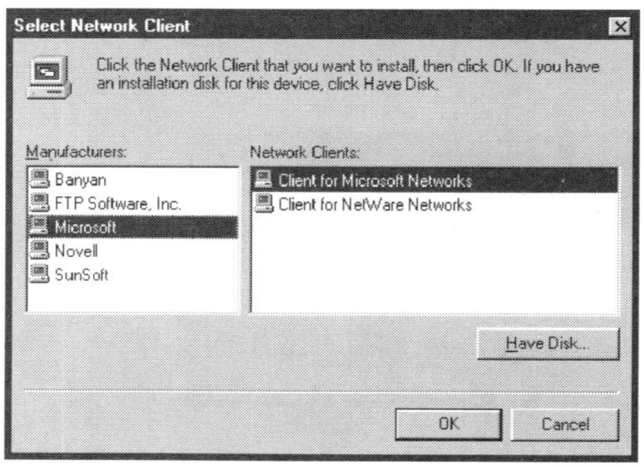

FIGURE 2.13

Select a network client from the Manufacturers list.

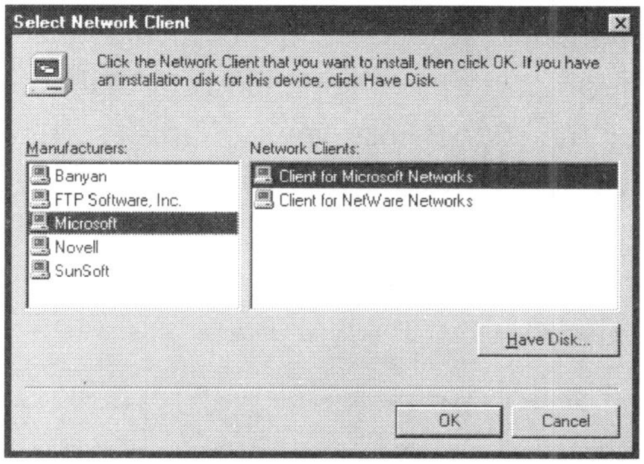

FIGURE 2.14

Use the Select Network Protocol dialog box to install TCP/IP on your system.

3. In the Manufactures list, click Microsoft.
4. In the Network Protocol list, double-click TCP/IP.

You return to the Configuration tab of the Network properties sheet. The TCP/IP selection now appears in the Network Components list, as shown in Figure 2.15.

Windows 95 will need some files from your Windows 95 installation disks or CD, but it won't ask for them until you close the Network dialog box. Because you will use this dialog box again to configure your dial-up software, save some time and just move on to that step now without closing the Network dialog box.

Configuring Your Dial-up Software

You've already seen that it takes several pieces fitting together just to get an Internet connection started. Continue your installation by adding the

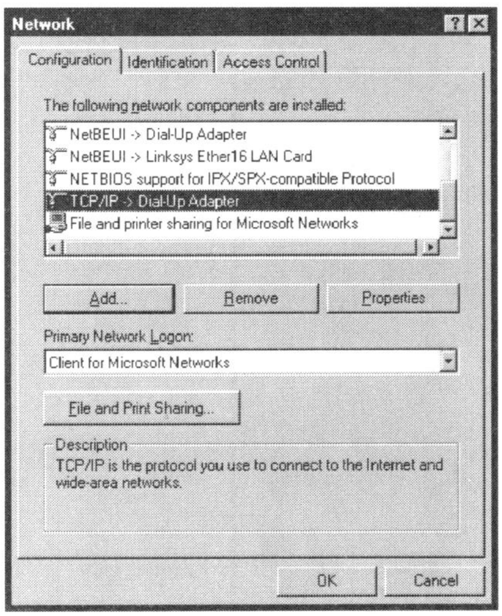

FIGURE 2.15

The TCP/IP protocol component is added to your growing list of network components.

first component that lets you dial out from your computer to the ISP. First, you set the properties for the Windows 95 Dial-Up adapter. Later, after you've configured the TCP/IP host, you can finish setting up your dial-up software by specifying the communication information, including phone numbers and passwords.

TIP

If you closed the Network dialog box, you can open it by double-clicking the Network icon in the Control Panel settings.

Use the following steps to configure your dial-up software:

1. In the Configuration page, double-click the TCP/IP → Dial-Up Adapter item in the Network Components list. The Dial-Up Adapter Properties sheet appears (see Figure 2.16).
2. Click the Bindings tab.
3. Check the TCP/IP check box to activate it. If it is already checked, leave it alone.
4. Click the Advanced tab.
5. In the Property list, make sure the Use IP Header Compression entry has a Yes associated with it in the Value list. If you need to change it, click the Use IP Header Compression item and click the Value down arrow. Click Yes and click OK. (The other entries in the Property list should be set to No.)

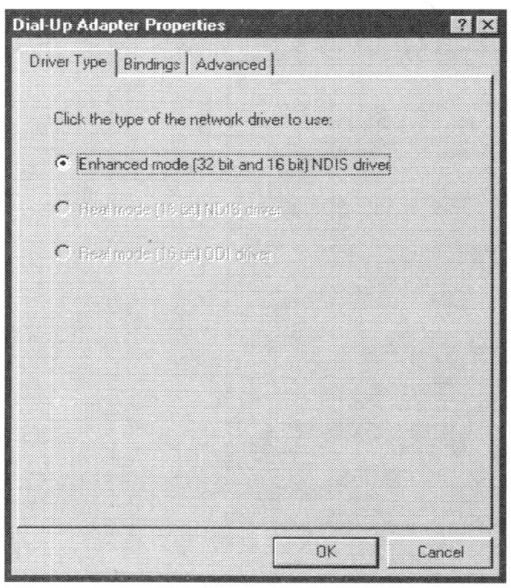

FIGURE 2.16

You need to configure some of the settings for the Dial-Up Adapter before configuring your TCP/IP host.

You return to the Network dialog box, with the Configuration tab displaying. Without closing the Network dialog box, continue to the next section. You finally get to use some of the information your ISP gave you, including those long strings of numbers called IP numbers.

Configuring the TCP/IP Host

This section shows you how to configure the Windows 95 TCP/IP host to your specific Internet protocol information. The numbers you enter are critical to your success or failure in gaining Internet access. Be sure you follow each instruction carefully.

Follow these steps:

1. In the Configuration page, double-click the TCP/IP entry in the Network Components list.
2. The TCP/IP Properties sheet opens displaying six tabs (see Figure 2.17). You will be working with four of the six tabs.
3. Click the IP Address tab. The IP Address page includes two options:
   - Obtain An IP Address Automatically. Select this option if you have a dynamic IP address when you dial into your ISP. This means that each time you dial into the Internet, your ISP assigns you an IP address.

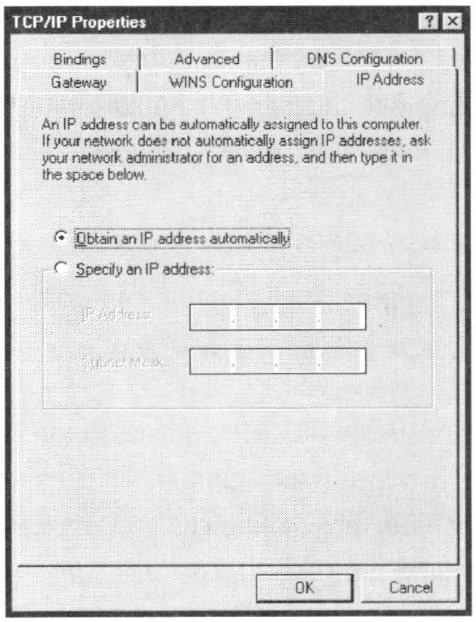

FIGURE 2.17

The TCP/IP Properties sheet is one of the most important sheets to fill in when getting connected to the Internet.

- Specify An IP Address. For static IP addresses, fill in the four-segment numbers here after you select this radio button. A static IP address is one that you will use every time you log into the Internet.

WARNING

One mistake that's easy to make here is confusing the four-part Domain Name Serve (DNS) address with your IP address. The DNS address is the information you placed in Table 2.4 next to the IP Address for DNS Server entry. If you confuse these numbers, you won't have any luck connecting to the Internet.

4. Enter the IP address information. Double-check the four-part number if you have a static IP address. Make sure the periods fall in the same place on-screen as they do in the actual number.
5. In Subnet Mask, fill in the IP Subnet Mask number that your ISP gave you. In most cases, this number is 255.255.255.0.

You have configured your IP address. Next, you must configure your provider's DNS information. Follow these steps:

1. Click the DNS Configuration tab and select the Enable DNS radio button.
2. In the Host text box, enter the user ID your ISP assigned to you. Some networks require additional information in the Host field, such as a "1" or some other character. Your ISP or network administrator should provide this information to you.
3. Enter your provider's domain name in the Domain text box. This could be something like iquest.net (domain name components are separated by periods). Be sure to include the periods as part of the domain name.

NOTE

You can learn more about domain name components in Chapter 3.

4. Enter your provider's DNS IP address in the DNS Server Search Order text box. After you enter the number, click the Add button. Enter as many numbers as your provider gives you, including a primary DNS address, secondary DNS address, and so on. Some ISPs will have only one DNS address, so don't worry if you have only one to enter here.

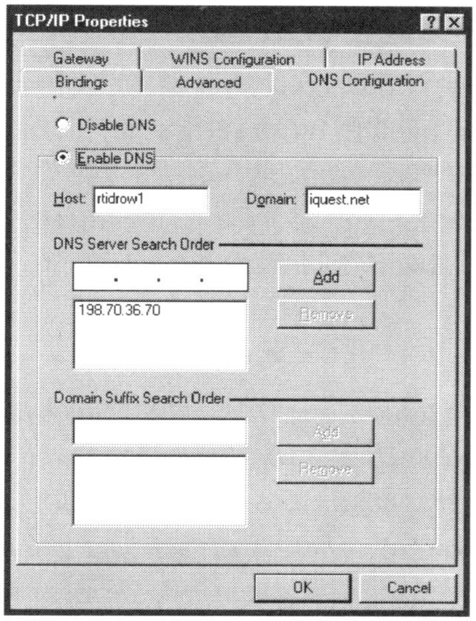

FIGURE 2.18

You need to fill in the information that pertains to your ISP on the DNS Configuration page.

5. Enter your provider's domain name in the Domain Suffix Search Order text box . Click the Add button. This helps identify your computer on the Internet. You may be able to leave this area blank and still connect to the Internet. If you are not given this item specifically from your ISP, you can use the tail end of your Internet address. For example, for the Internet address rtidrow@iquest.net, the domain suffix is iquest.net. Figure 2.18 shows how the DNS Configuration page should look now.

6. Click the Advanced tab and check the Set This Protocol To The Default Protocol check box.

7. Click the Bindings tab. This is where you tell Windows 95 which components will use TCP/IP. You want the Client for Microsoft Networks to use TCP/IP to connect to the Internet.

8. Check the Client for Microsoft Networks check box. Next, click the OK button to finish the TCP/IP Properties configurations.

9. Windows 95 may prompt you to insert your Windows 95 Setup CD or, if you have the Windows 95 Setup floppy disks, a specific floppy disk into your system. Windows 95 will copy any necessary files from the disks onto your system to enable you to use TCP/IP on your machine.

When the System Settings Change dialog box displays, click Yes to reboot your computer. The changes you just made will then take effect.

Adding a Dial-up Network Folder

After your system reboots, your system will be ready to communicate on the Internet. You now need to finish setting up the Dial-Up Networking feature to add the communications capability to the TCP/IP configuration so your computer can dial your ISP and connect to the Internet. Use the following steps to add the Dial-Up Network folder to your system.

NOTE

You may not need to do these steps. First, check in the My Computer folder to see if you have a Dial-Up Networking folder. If you do, you can skip these steps and go to the next section, "Creating a Dial-Up Icon." Otherwise, you need to complete the following steps. Also, make sure you have your Windows 95 disks or CD-ROM handy. Windows 95 may ask for them during these steps.

1. In Control Panel, double-click the Add/Remove Programs icon.
2. The Add/Remove Programs Properties sheet appears. Click the Windows Setup tab. This page contains a list of component programs you can install.
3. Double-click the Communications program. The Communications dialog box appears.
4. Click Dial-Up Networking and click OK.
5. You are prompted to insert the Windows 95 setup CD-ROM or floppy disks.

After the software is installed, the Dial-Up Networking folder appears in the My Computer folder.

Creating a Dial-up Connection Icon

Windows 95 enables you to create a dial-up connection icon that launches an Internet session connecting your computer to a specific source or provider. If you use more than one ISP, such as one for work and one for home, Windows 95 enables you to set up additional dial-up connection icons for those ISPs. Each icon locates information about your Internet account and provider that you stored earlier in Windows 95. This is handy, particularly if you have more than one on-ramp to the Internet.

If you use a third-party TCP/IP stack, such as the Netmanage Internet Chameleon, to access the Internet under Windows 95, you still must install the TCP/IP stack using the Control Panel. However, you don't need to create a dial-up connection icon. Many third-party TCP/IP programs include their own software for establishing the connection.

Now you can create a dial-up connection icon configured for your Internet service provider's host by following these steps:

1. Open the Dial-Up Networking folder you just created. Double-click the Make New Connection icon.

2. The Make New Connection Wizard opens, in which you enter the information about your service provider. In the Type A Name For The Computer You Are Dialing field, enter an identifying name for your provider, such as **Iquest Connection**. Your modem should be identified in the Select a Modem field. If not, select it from the drop-down list box. Click the Configure button located under the modem name.

3. The Modem Properties sheet appears. Click the Options tab.

4. Under Connection control, uncheck both of the check boxes, including the Bring Up Terminal Window After Dialing check box. In the same page, click the Display Modem Status check box under Status control. Click OK. The Make New Connection dialog box returns. Click the Next button.

5. In the Make New Connection dialog box, enter your provider's area code and dial-up (not voice) telephone number. Choose United States of America (1) or another country in the Country Code drop-down list box. Click the Next button.

TIP

If you have call waiting on your phone line, you can disable it by preceding the telephone number in step 5 with a disable call waiting number. This number varies depending on the phone service you have. For example, if you use Ameritech, you can usually use *70 to disable call waiting. Check with your local phone carrier on how to do this. If you don't disable call waiting and you receive a phone call while you're connected to your ISP, you will probably be disconnected.

6. Windows 95 will display a message that you have successfully created a new connection for your provider. Click Finish. An icon for your provider appears in the Dial-Up Networking folder (see Figure 2.19).

FIGURE 2.19

Your new icon for your Internet dial-up appears in the Dial-Up Networking folder.

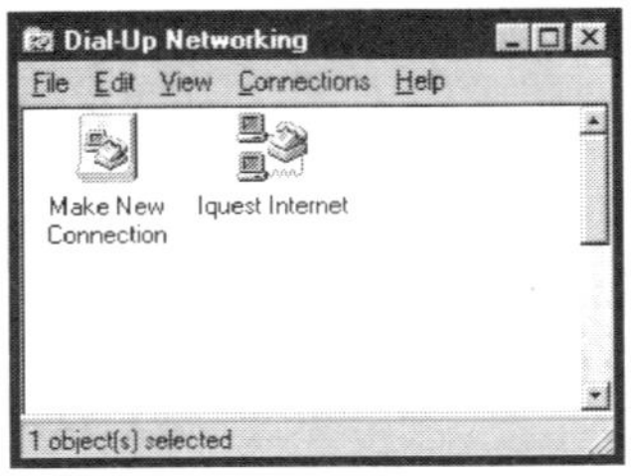

You're almost ready to dial into your Internet provider and start a PPP or SLIP session! However, there are a few more dial-up configuration steps left to go:

1. Open the Dial-Up Networking folder and click on the icon representing your provider to highlight it. Right-click the provider's icon. From the context menu, click Properties.
2. The provider's general configuration property sheet appears (see Figure 2.20). Enter the area code and telephone number of your provider's system in the appropriate text boxes. If the call to your provider is a local call, you can leave the Area Code text box blank.
3. If you're calling from an internal telephone system, you need to add 8 or 9 in front of the provider's telephone number, such as 9,765-4321, to reach an outside line. Add the comma (,) after the 8 or 9 exit code to allow a short pause while Windows 95 gets an outside dial tone.
4. Select the country you're calling from, such as United States of America (1), from the Country Code drop-down list.
5. Check the Use Country Code And Area Code check box.

FIGURE 2.20

Ensure that your modem is properly identified in the Connect Using list box of the General page.

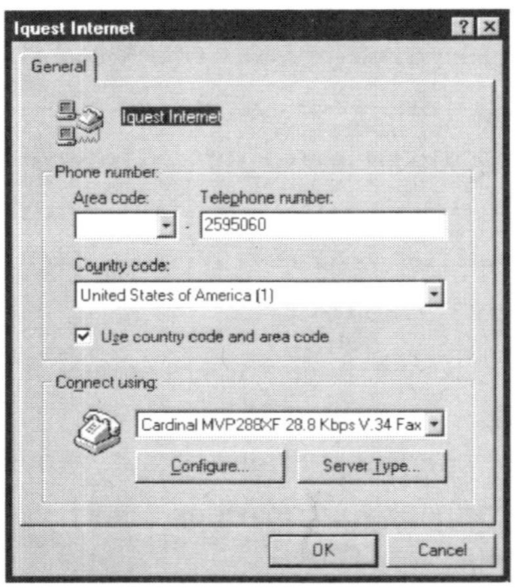

6. Select your modem from the Connect Using list box.

7. Click the Configure button. The Modem Properties sheet appears, with the General page showing. Select your modem's COM port (from the Port drop-down list) and Maximum Speed from the General page.

   Don't check the Only Connect At This Speed check box. Although you want the connect rate to be as fast as possible, your dial-up may not always achieve that maximum rate. If you check the Only Connect At This Speed check box, the dialer will only work at the connect rate selected and will not perform at a lower, and probably viable, speed. If your connect rate doesn't reach the setting you entered, Windows 95 will hang up the connection even though you could have used the lower line speed you encountered.

8. While still in the Modem Properties sheet, click the Connection tab (see Figure 2.21). Ensure that Data Bits is 8, Parity is None, and Stop Bits is 1; this is sometimes referred to as "8N1."

9. In the Modem Properties sheet, click the Options page (see Figure 2.22). Check the Bring Up Terminal Window After Dialing check box. Check the Display Modem Status check box. Click OK. The provider's General page reappears. Click the Server Type button.

10. The Server Types dialog box appears. If you have a PPP connection, select PPP: Windows 95, Windows NT 3.5, Internet from the Type Of Dial-Up Server drop-down list. If you have a SLIP connection, select SLIP: Unix Connection.

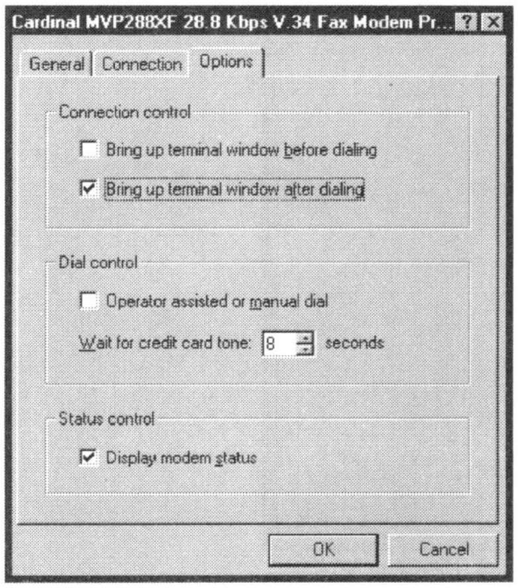

FIGURE 2.21

Set the connection preferences to 8N1 (8, None, 1).

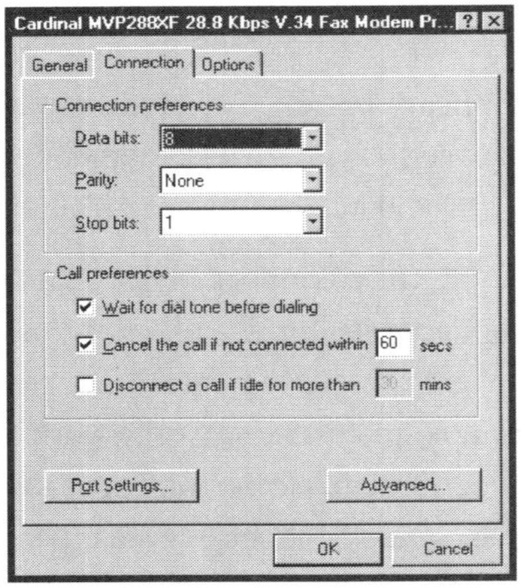

FIGURE 2.22

The Display Modem Status check box option tells Windows 95 to display a small message box with connection information when you are connected to your ISP.

WARNING

You may not see the SLIP selection. Windows 95 doesn't automatically install SLIP connection software on your system. You must install it using the Add/Remove Programs icon in Control Panel. See the next section, "Adding SLIP Connectivity to Windows 95," for more information.

11. In the Advanced Options area, check the Log On To Network and the Enable Software Compression check boxes.
12. In the Allowed Network Protocols area, check the TCP/IP check box. Uncheck the NetBEUI and IPX/SPX Compatible check boxes unless you have another network attached to your computer (see Figure 2.23).

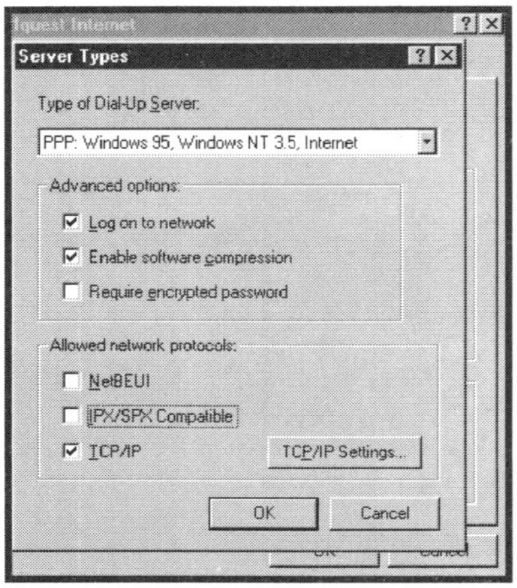

FIGURE 2.23

Make sure TCP/IP is selected so Windows 95 can connect to your ISP using TCP/IP.

13. Click the TCP/IP Settings button. The TCP/IP Settings dialog box displays.

14. If you use a dynamic PPP account, select the Server Assigned IP Address radio button. If you use a static PPP account, select the Specify An IP Address radio button and enter your specific IP address. Select the Specify Name Server Addresses radio button and enter your provider's Primary DNS Number and Secondary DNS Number—if there is a secondary number—in the text boxes under the radio buttons. Check the Use IP Header Compression and Use Default Gateway On Remote Network check boxes. Click OK.

    If you already have an existing TCP/IP program (such as Trumpet Winsock or Internet Chameleon) on your hard drive, you can continue to use it if you don't want to use the Windows 95 TCP/IP stack. If you're going to delete your current TCP/IP program, you should install and configure the Windows 95 stack and ensure that it works first.

15. Click OK in the Server Types dialog box. Click OK in the General tab.

Adding SLIP Connectivity to Windows 95

Windows 95 Dial-Up Networking supports SLIP and can connect to any ISP using the SLIP standard. SLIP is available only on the Windows 95 CD-ROM and you must manually install it after you install Windows 95.

To install SLIP, follow these steps:

1. Double-click the Add/Remove Programs Properties icon in Control Panel. Next, click the Windows Setup tab on the Add/Remove Programs Properties Sheet. Click the Have Disk button.

2. In the Install From Disk dialog box, enter the path name **D:ADMINAPP TOOLSDSCRIPTRNAPLUS.INF** and click OK.

3. In the Have Disk dialog box, select the SLIP And Scripting For Dial-Up Networking option (see Figure 2.24). Click the Install button.

4. Click OK when the Add/Remove Programs Properties sheet appears.

The SLIP software is now available on your system and you can select it in Step 10 in the previous section "Creating a Dial-Up Icon."

NOTE

Because SLIP servers cannot negotiate TCP/IP addresses, you must configure the Dial-Up Network connection to display a terminal window after you connect to your ISP. To do this, check the Bring Up Terminal Window After Dialing check box

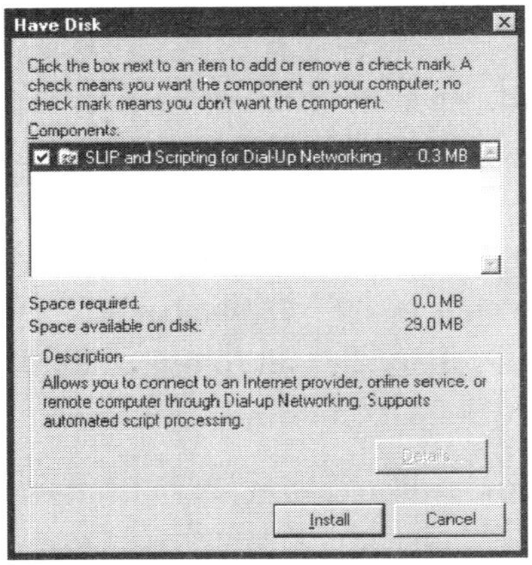

FIGURE 2.24

You must have your Windows 95 installation CD to have access to the SLIP connection software.

on the Options tab of the Modem Properties sheet in step 9 of the previous section, "Creating a Dial-Up Icon." In most cases, your ISP will display the IP host address and your IP address. Write down these addresses and place their values in the SLIP Connection IP Address dialog box that displays. Click OK.

Testing Your Internet Connection

You're now ready to dial into the Internet to test your connection. You can use a Windows 95 built-in Internet application to test the connection. To dial into your ISP provider, follow these steps:

1. Double-click the provider dial-up icon. The Connect To dialog box appears (see Figure 2.25).
2. In the User Name and Password text boxes, enter the user name and password that your provider's system expects to see from you.

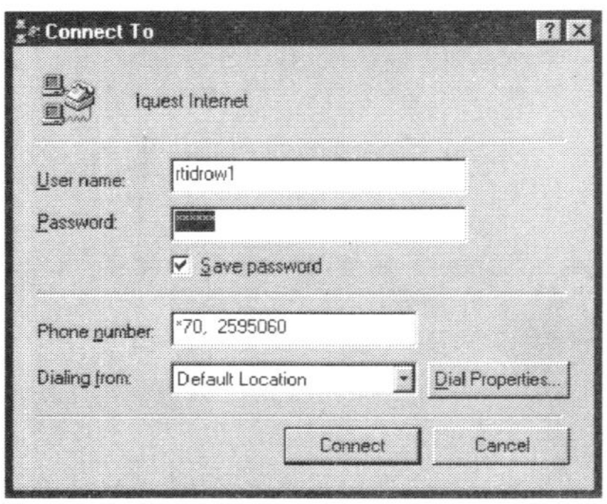

FIGURE 2.25

A Connect To dialog box.

3. Check the Save Password check box for Windows 95 to save your password from session to session. If you leave this check box empty, you'll need to fill in your password each time you dial your ISP. Your provider's data line telephone number should appear. If it doesn't, enter it in the Phone Number text box. Default Location is normally selected in the Dialing From drop-down list. If you are dialing from another location, such as from a hotel, you might have other locations configured here. Select the one for your situation. (For more information on setting up dialing locations in Windows 95, see the online help provided by Windows 95.)

TIP

If you work in an office or area that is not secure, leave the Save Password check box empty. This way other users cannot access the Internet from your account, which may also give them access to your Internet e-mail messages.

4. Click the Connect button. Windows 95 begins the dial-up process.
5. Once connected, the system will alert you that you're connected. You can minimize the Connected dialog box by clicking the Minimize icon in the upper-right corner of the dialog box.

Using WINIPCFG and Ping to Test Your Internet Connection

Windows 95 includes an IP configuration utility called WINIPCFG, which you can use to display all the current TCP/IP network configuration values of your computer (see Figure 2.26). Your computer must be running Microsoft TCP/IP to use WINIPCFG. To run WINIPCFG, click the Start button, click Run, and type **WINIPCFG** in the Open text box. Click OK.

When you run WINIPCFG, you can see the current IP address allocated to your computer and other useful data about the TCP/IP allocation. The IP configuration utility does not, however, dynamically update information. If you make any changes, such as disconnecting from your ISP. You must close the IP configuration utility and restart it.

If you're a little intimidated by the WINIPCFG utility, you can try another Windows 95 Internet utility to test your Internet connection. You can use the Ping command to quickly get your answer. The Ping command is an Internet command that sends a message out to a specific IP (such as the Microsoft FTP server),

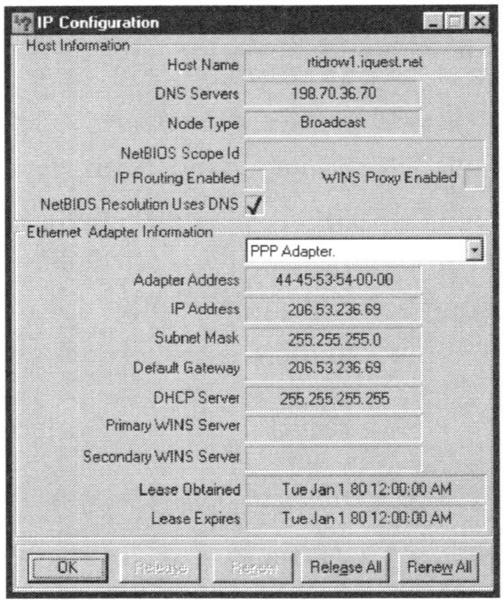

FIGURE 2.26

To see current IP settings, use the WINIPCFG utility that's available with Windows 95.

which returns a message indicating whether your connection is working or not. To use the Ping command, open a DOS window in Windows 95 and type the following address for the Microsoft FTP server:

```
ping 198.105.232.1
```

If this works, then TCP/IP is set up correctly. You'll see a response similar to the following:

```
Pinging 198.105.232.1 with 32 bytes of data:


Reply from 198.105.232.1: bytes=32 time=248ms TTL=48
Reply from 198.105.232.1: bytes=32 time=236ms TTL=48
Reply from 198.105.232.1: bytes=32 time=222ms TTL=48
Reply from 198.105.232.1: bytes=32 time=226ms TTL=48
```

If you aren't successful, you'll receive a Request timed out response. This means you need to try connecting to the Internet again.

The hard part about getting on the Internet is over. Once you have your connection set up, it's best not to change it unless you're sure that any new settings you make will be correct.

You now are ready to begin navigating the Internet. For more information on this, turn to Chapter 3, which explains what the Internet and World Wide Web are.

Using the Microsoft Internet Jumpstart Kit

If you have the Microsoft Internet Jumpstart Kit on your computer, you may want to use it to set up your Internet connection instead of using the previous sections. Using the Internet Jumpstart Kit (which starts the Internet Setup Wizard), is probably the easiest way to connect to the Internet. The wizard format follows the same paradigm of other installation wizards in Windows 95. It leads you through each step with easy-to-follow instructions. It also automatically installs most of the software and networking components—so you don't have to concern yourself with manual installation.

To use the Internet Setup Wizard, follow these steps:

1. Click the Start button, click Programs, Accessories, Internet Tools, and Internet Setup Wizard to start the Internet Setup Wizard. You also may see an icon named The Internet on your desktop that you can double-click to start the setup procedure.

2. In the Internet Setup Wizard Welcome screen, click the Next button to proceed with the setup. The How to Connect screen appears. You can select to connect via a phone line (using a modem) or through a local area network (LAN).

   If you are connected to a LAN, the Internet Setup Wizard displays a dialog box asking you if you want to connect to the Internet through a LAN or using a modem. Choose the LAN option only if your LAN is using TCP/IP and is connected to the Internet. Click Next to continue.

3. You now need to specify whether you want to connect via The Microsoft Network or a PPP account that you have with an ISP (see Figure 2.27). For this example, select the I Already Have An Account With A Different Service Provider radio button. Click Next to continue.

4. The Internet Mail screen appears. Determine whether you want your e-mail handled by Microsoft Exchange, the built-in e-mail tool within Windows 95. Unless you already have Exchange set up, select No here if

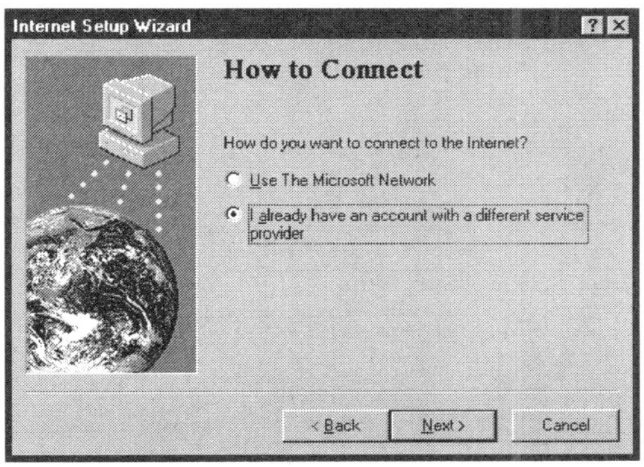

FIGURE 2.27

The Internet Setup Wizard asks you to specify how you will connect to the Internet—via The Microsoft Network or via an ISP account.

your Web browser has its own e-mail reader and creator (such as Netscape Navigator 2.0).

5. The Internet Setup Wizard now asks you for the name of your ISP. This is the name that will become the name of your connection in the Dial-Up Networking folder, so make it descriptive. Click Next.

NOTE

At the bottom of the Service Provider Information screen, you are warned that your ISP must have PPP support. If you have an ISP that has only SLIP support, close the Internet Setup Wizard and see the section "Installing TCP/IP Support." You will need to set up your account manually. When you get to step 10 in the section "Creating a Dial-Up Icon" you can select SLIP as the type of dial-up server for your account.

6. The Phone Number screen appears (see Figure 2.28). Enter the telephone number you'll use to access your ISP network. Remember, this number will be different from the phone number you use to call your ISP to set up your account.
7. Select the Country Code setting for your country, such as United States of America (1).
8. Check the Bring Up Terminal Window After Dialing check box. This enables you to enter any appropriate information in a terminal window after you've dialed and connected to your ISP. If, after you use the dial-up connection, you don't need the terminal window displayed after connection, uncheck this check box. Click Next.

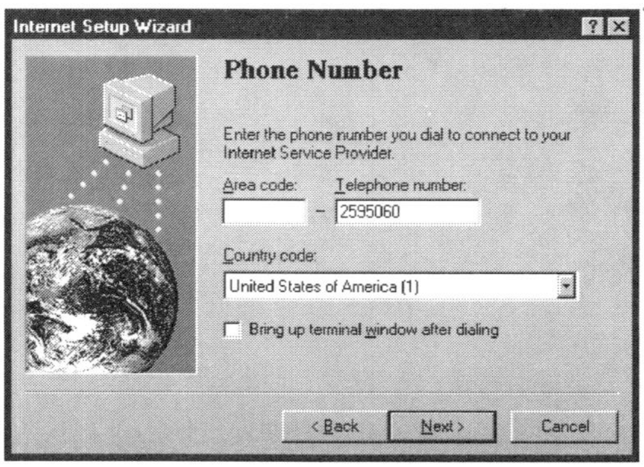

FIGURE 2.28

Fill in the Phone Number screen with your ISP's phone number.

9. The Internet Setup Wizard prompts you to fill in your username and password. You obtain this information from your ISP (and you probably filled it in Table 2.4). Be sure to type in the password correctly. Click Next.

10. The IP Address screen appears, asking you for your IP address (see Figure 2.29). You have two options here:

    If you have a dynamic IP address, select the My Internet Service Provider Automatically Assigns Me One radio button.

    If you use a static IP address, select the Always Use The Following radio button. Then, enter that number in the IP Address text box. This is a four-part number. Enter a Subnet Mask number, which in most cases is 255.255.255.0. This denotes a Class C connection (a type of Internet connection), which most home users have. If you are connecting from work, ask your system administrator or ISP what the subnet mask number is for your site.

11. Click Next. The DNS Server Address screen appears (see Figure 2.30). This asks for information about your ISP's machine. This is also a four-part number or set of numbers (for backup numbers) that your ISP gave you when you signed up.

12. Click Next. The Finished Setup screen appears, letting you know you've completed the setup process. If you selected Microsoft Exchange as your e-mail application in step 3, the Internet Mail screen appears instead of the Finished Setup screen (see Figure 2.31). Enter your Internet e-mail address and mail server. You can obtain both of these from your ISP. Your e-mail address is the combination of your username (such as rtidrow) and the DNS host name (such as iquest.net). Putting these together gives

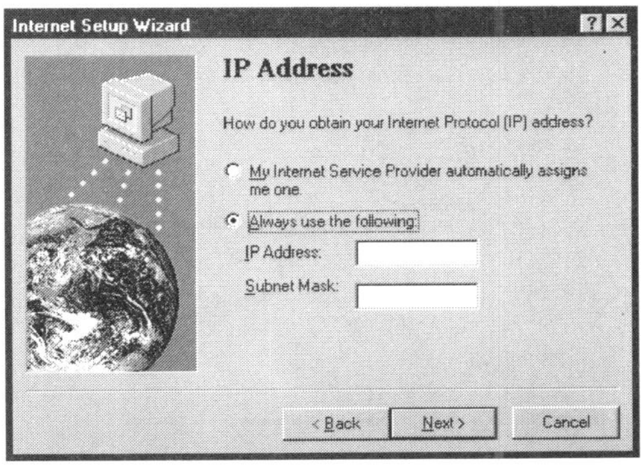

FIGURE 2.29

You must fill in the IP Address screen correctly or your Internet connection will not work.

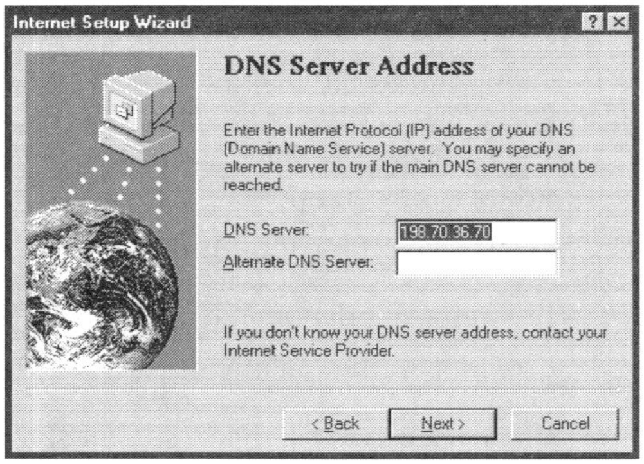

FIGURE 2.30

You need to fill in the DNS information in this screen.

you an e-mail address that will look similar to rtidrow@iquest.net. The Internet mail server will be something like pop.iquest.net. Click Next when you have this filled in.

13. You may see a dialog box that tells you to restart Windows 95 to complete the setup. If you already have all the networking components installed, you may not need to restart Windows 95. After your machine reboots and Windows 95 starts, you can install your browser software, which is discussed in Chapter 4.

Installing Internet Access for Windows 3.*x*

The previous sections showed you how to configure systems running Windows 95 to connect to the Internet. This section shows you how to connect to the Internet and the Web if you use Windows 3.11 or Windows for Workgroups 3.11 (referred to as Windows 3.*x* in this book). Unlike Windows 95, Windows

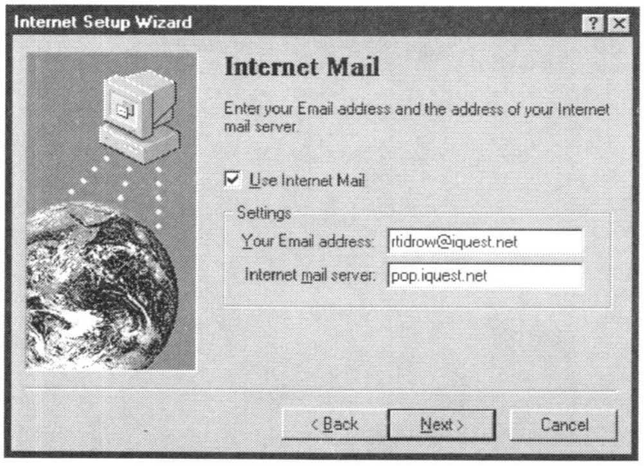

FIGURE 2.31

The Internet Mail screen is used only if you opted to use Microsoft Exchange for your e-mail application.

3.*x* doesn't include built-in software to connect to the Internet or the Web. Because of this, you need to take a few more steps to make Windows 3.*x* connect properly to the Internet.

The first thing you'll do in this chapter is find out what you need to connect to the Web. Next, you'll install the necessary software and then make a connection.

NOTE

During the past three years, Microsoft has upgraded Windows 3.1 several times, including versions called Windows 3.11 and Windows for Workgroups 3.11. For this reason, this chapter refers to those two operating systems specifically. If you are using Windows 3.1, however, you should have no problem using the software described in this chapter, as well as the specific instructions listed.

Setting up a Modem or LAN

This book is not designed to show you how to install a modem on your computer or how to set up a network connection. If you don't have a modem installed yet, consult the documentation you received with the modem. With your modem, you should have a floppy disk that contains a setup routine or drivers that let you configure the modem for Windows 3.11. Be sure to install these so your modem operates efficiently with Windows 3.11.

Unlike Windows 95, which includes an application that guides you through setting up hardware such as modems, Windows 3.11 requires you to do most of the installation manually. Make sure you have the following configured properly:

IRQ and DMA channels. These refer to the interrupt request lines (IRQs) and the direct memory address (DMA) channels of your computer. Each device you have on your computer (such as a mouse, keyboard, modem, and so on) must have these parameters assigned to them. You can find which device is using which parameter by running the Microsoft Diagnostic tool at the MS-DOS command line. Make sure you exit from Windows 3.11 first (you cannot run this tool from a DOS prompt within Windows) and then type **MSD**. Record the IRQ and DMA channels that are currently free. Use these settings when you're installing your modem. If your modem cannot use these open settings, which often occurs, you may need to switch other devices to those open settings. You can do this by consulting the hardware guides that came with your computer and individual hardware components.

Port setting. Your modem uses a communications port to send and receive data. Communications ports are referred to as *COM ports* or *serial ports.* COM ports are denoted as COM1, COM2, and so on. Your mouse may also use a COM port, so you need to make sure your modem is set up to use a different one from your mouse. Otherwise, you'll lose the functionality of your mouse after you've set up your modem. You can find port settings using the MSD tool and by opening the Ports application in the Windows Control Panel.

Setting up a network connection to Windows 3.11 is a process that's best left to the system administrator at your company. If you're the one responsible for setting up network connections, you should reference the *Microsoft Windows for Workgroups 3.11 Resource Kit* or another source that details configuring Windows 3.11 for network support.

Disabling WIN32s 1.15 and Previous Versions

There was a time when the latest Web browsers were written using 32-bit programming code, which required Windows 3.11 users to add 32-bit libraries to their systems. The Win32s extension libraries from Microsoft became a hot item on the Internet and other online services. Many users installed Win32s on their machines to run programs like Netscape 1, Mosaic, and various other versions of Mosaic. (Mosaic was the first graphical Web browser that triggered the explosion of the World Wide Web.) Other, non-Web programs (such as a game called Freecell) also used the Win32s files but they were not as popular as the browsers at that time.

Now, however, most Web browsers (such as Netscape Navigator for Windows 3.11) are written in 16-bit code and don't require Win32s to be installed on your machine. In fact, if it's on your system, Netscape will not install. For that reason, you should do one of two things. First, you can remove it from your system. Second, you can upgrade to a newer version.

If you're running Win32s version 1.15 or below, you will be unable to install Netscape unless you upgrade to version 1.20 of Win32s or remove Win32s. To find out which version (if any) of Win32s is on your system, open File Manager and select the WIN32S.INI file stored in the WINDOWSSYSTEM directory on systems running Windows for Workgroups 3.11. If you are using another Windows version (such as 3.1 or 3.11), select the WIN32S16.DLL file in the WINDOWSSYSTEM directory. Choose File, Properties. You'll be able to see the version number in the Version line.

If you can't find one of the preceding Win32s files on your system, then you don't have to worry about Netscape or other browser not installing.

If you want to remove Win32s from your system, follow these steps:

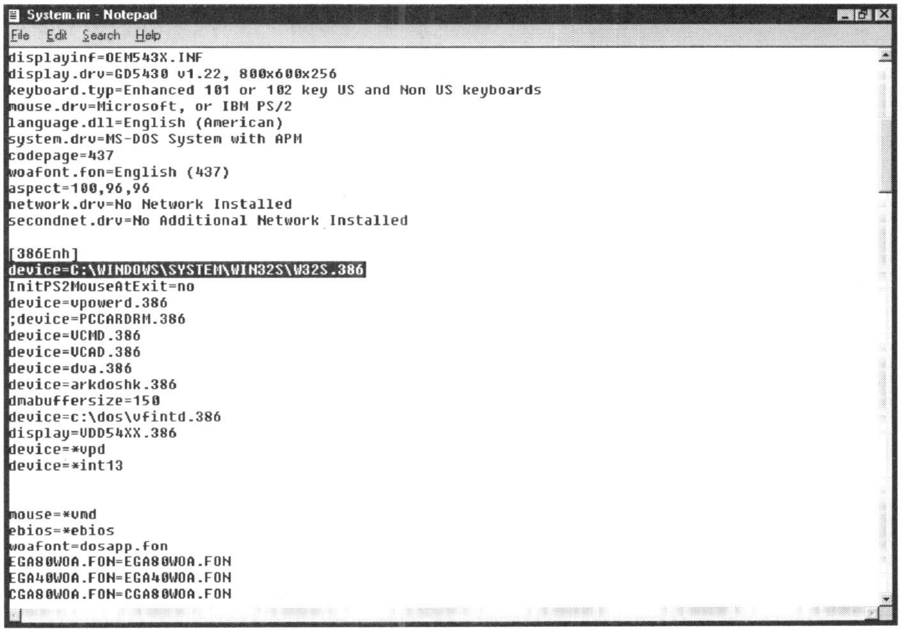

System.ini - Notepad

File Edit Search Help

```
displayinf=OEM543X.INF
display.drv=GD5430 v1.22, 800x600x256
keyboard.typ=Enhanced 101 or 102 key US and Non US keyboards
mouse.drv=Microsoft, or IBM PS/2
language.dll=English (American)
system.drv=MS-DOS System with APM
codepage=437
woafont.fon=English (437)
aspect=100,96,96
network.drv=No Network Installed
secondnet.drv=No Additional Network Installed

[386Enh]
device=C:\WINDOWS\SYSTEM\WIN32S\W32S.386
InitPS2MouseAtExit=no
device=vpowerd.386
;device=PCCARDRM.386
device=VCMD.386
device=VCAD.386
device=dva.386
device=arkdoshk.386
dmabuffersize=150
device=c:\dos\vfintd.386
display=VDD54XX.386
device=*vpd
device=*int13


mouse=*vmd
ebios=*ebios
woafont=dosapp.fon
EGA80WOA.FON=EGA80WOA.FON
EGA40WOA.FON=EGA40WOA.FON
CGA80WOA.FON=CGA80WOA.FON
```

FIGURE 2.32

The [386Enh] section of your SYSTEM.INI file contains a reference to the WIN32s application.

1. Open your SYSTEM.INI file in Notepad or in the Sysedit utility. You may want to make a backup copy of SYSTEM.INI before you start editing it.
2. Locate the section named [386Enh] and delete the following line (see Figure 2.32):

   ```
   device=C:\WINDOWS\SYSTEM\WIN32S\W32S.386
   ```

NOTE

Your WINDOWSSYSTEM directories may be different if your Windows is installed in a different directory.

3. Locate the [BOOT] section in the SYSTEM.INI file. Delete winmm16.dll from the following line:

   ```
   drivers=mmsystem.dll winmm16.dll
   ```

4. Save the SYSTEM.INI file and close it. Open File Manager.
5. Locate the WINDOWSSYSTEM directory, and remove the following files:

   ```
   WIN32S16.DLL
   W32SYS.DLL
   WIN32S.INI
   ```

6. Delete all the files in the WINDOWSSYSTEMWIN32S directory. Delete the WIN32S directory. Don't delete the SYSTEM directory.

7. Exit and restart Windows.

You may need to retain a copy of Win32s on your system for other programs to use. Netscape and some other browsers can work with versions of Win32s newer that 1.15, namely 1.20. To obtain a copy of it, you can download one from the Microsoft Download Service (MSDL) using your modem. Dial 206-936-6735 and download the file named PW1118.EXE. You can also find it on Microsoft's FTP site (**ftp.microsoft.comsoftlibmslfilespw1118.exe**). If you have an account with CompuServe, look for it in the Microsoft file library (GO MSL) and search for PW1118.EXE.

PW1118.EXE is a self-extracting compressed file, meaning you just need to place it in a directory on your system (an empty directory works the best) and then run the file or double-click it while in File Manager. This extracts all the files, including a file named SETUP.EXE. Run this file to set up Win32s on your system. You may need to exit and restart Windows after you install the software.

Installing TCP/IP Support

Now that you have an Internet account set up, you're ready to begin setting up Windows 3.11. You'll begin this process by installing TCP/IP support. To add TCP/IP support to Windows 3.11, you'll need a separate program, such as Trumpet Winsock. The following steps show how to install Trumpet Winsock to establish TCP/IP support in Windows 3.11.

1. After you install Trumpet Winsock on your computer, open your computer's AUTOEXEC.BAT file. You can use Notepad or the Sysedit utility to do this.

2. Find the PATH line and add the directory name for the Trumpet program. For example, if you placed Trumpet Winsock files in the TRUMPET directory, your PATH statement would look something like the following:

   ```
   PATH c:\windows;c:\dos;c:\trumpet;
   ```

   Be sure not to remove any other PATH entries you may already have there.

3. Save the AUTOEXEC.BAT file, exit Windows, and reboot your computer. After it reboots, start Windows.

You're now ready to configure the Trumpet Winsock application. Before you do this, make sure you have all the information filled out in Table 2.4. Next, continue with the following steps:

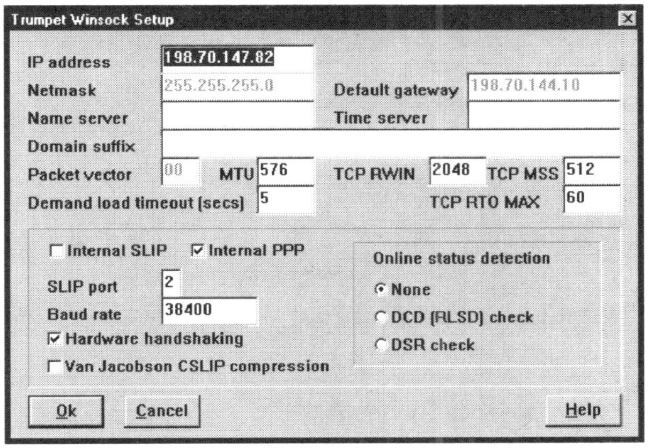

FIGURE 2.33

The Trumpet Winsock dialog box contains settings you must first obtain from your ISP.

1. In Program Manager, choose File, Run. The Run dialog box displays.
2. Enter the path to the Trumpet Winsock file named TCPMAN.EXE in the Command Line text box in the Run dialog box. Click OK.
3. The Trumpet Winsock Setup dialog box appears (see Figure 2.33). Fill out the following information:
   - **IP Address text box.** Specifies your Internet IP address that your ISP gives you. Make sure you enter this number exactly as it was given to you. IP addresses are always four-part numbers separated by periods. An example is 198.80.152.182.
   - **Name Server text box.** Use the DNS (Domain Name Server) number your ISP gave you. This is a four-part number, separated by periods.
   - **Internal SLIP check box or Internal PPP check box.** Check the check box of the type of network connection you have established with your ISP. Most services now use PPP, but you need to ask your ISP about this.
   - **SLIP Port text box.** Even if you use PPP to connect to the Internet, you need to specify the COM port your modem uses. This number is 1, 2, 3, or 4.
   - **Baud Rate text box.** Set this number to the maximum baud rate for your modem. If you use a 14,400 bps modem, set this to 38400. If you use a 28,800 bps modem, set this to 57600.

You don't need to configure any of the other options on the Trumpet Winsock Setup dialog box.

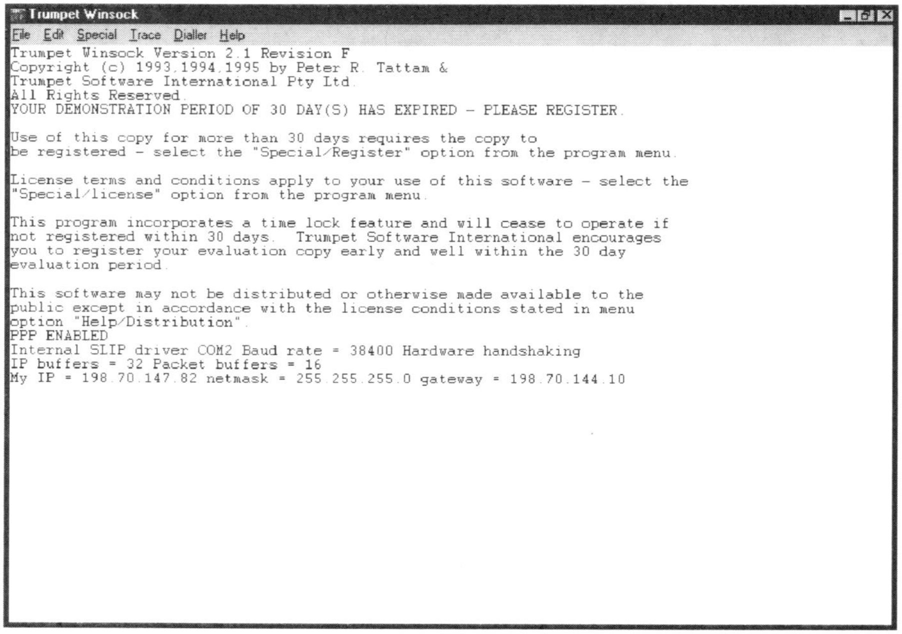

FIGURE 2.34

The Trumpet Winsock window is used any time you want to establish a connection to the Internet.

4. Click Ok. The Net Setup dialog box displays, which informs you that you need to restart Trumpet Winsock for your configuration changes to take place. Click OK.

5. The Trumpet Winsock window appears (see Figure 2.34). Close it and re-open it so the changes you just made will be used.

You're now ready to try out your new connection with Trumpet Winsock. The following steps show you how to manually connect with your ISP:

1. In the Trumpet Winsock window, choose Dialler, Manual Login. Trumpet Winsock displays the message SLIP DISABLED (or PPP DISABLED if you're connecting via a PPP connection) below the text. You'll also see the cursor blinking on the last line.

2. Type **ATDT** and the phone number to your ISP. Press Enter. This line will look something like this:

   ATDT 555-1234

   The ATDT command is an AT command that tells your computer modem to access the dial tone on a regular phone connection. AT commands are standardized command sets for modems.

If your modem is configured to have its speaker turned on, you'll hear a series of tones as your modem and the remote system's modem communicates with each other. Once connected, the Trumpet Winsock window will display the opening login message from your ISP. Typically, you'll see the name of the ISP company and then a login line.

3. Enter your login name as provided by the ISP (refer to Table 2.4) and press Enter.
4. The next line is usually the password line. Enter the password as provided by the ISP. Passwords are generally case-sensitive, so be sure to use upper- and lowercase spelling where necessary. Press Enter. You may see a message on-screen telling you that your login name and password are being validated by the server. If you've entered everything correctly, you'll see a message about SLIP or PPP access and some directions. Read the directions and respond as necessary. Each ISP is different, so there's no rule here. Some ISPs, for example, display an Acceptable Use or Policy Statement dialog box that requires you to respond Yes if you want to continue with the logging in process.
5. Respond to any questions and press Enter.
6. Press Esc to enable the SLIP or PPP protocol. You'll see a message that says SLIP ENABLED (or PPP ENABLED) to show that your connection is established.

Now you're ready to start using Internet applications, such as Netscape Navigator. The only problem at this point is that you haven't installed any of your programs yet. You do that in the Chapter 4. For now, read the following steps to learn how to log out of your ISP and close Trumpet Winsock.

1. When you finish using Trumpet Winsock, choose Dialler, Bye. This runs a script file named BYE.CMD that disconnects you from your ISP.
2. A screen appears that says Closing Trumpet Winsock may cause instability with network applications. Click OK.
3. Close Trumpet Winsock by double-clicking the Control menu at the upper-left corner of the window.

What's Next

If you got through this chapter in one piece, you've done well. The majority of the pain associated with the Internet is configuring your system to connect to it.

After you configure Windows 95 and Windows 3.*x* to work with the Internet, either through an ISP or LAN connection, you shouldn't have any problems unless you change modems or decide to use another dial-up application.

The next chapter goes into more detail about the Internet and the Web. You'll learn what the Internet is, what is on it, how to find things, and what services it supports. For example, you'll learn that there's more to the Internet than the World Wide Web.

PART II

THE INTERNET AND WORLD WIDE WEB

3

BROWSING THE INTERNET AND WEB

You learned in Chapter 2 how to configure your system to access the Internet and World Wide Web. This chapter shows you the basics of the Internet and Web, and introduces you to the other services you can use on the Internet. Although the Web is the most popular part of the Internet, you learn in this chapter that the Internet has more to offer than just the Web. These other services include FTP, Telnet, e-mail, Internet Relay Chat (IRC), USENET newsgroups, and mailing lists.

What Is the Internet?

Chapter 1 introduces the Internet and gives a brief history of it. At its simplest, the Internet is a collection of computers linked together from around the world. They're linked by telephone lines, networking cables, satellites, wireless devices, and coaxial cable.

If you wanted to take a look at the Internet, maybe take your family there on a vacation, that would be impossible. There is no Internet place or headquarters. It's not a building or even a computer. Surprisingly, there's no master computer controlled by one person, business, or government agency. Rather, the term "Internet" describes the overall collection of computers linked together.

These computers are all over the world. The Internet connects over 25 million people, many of whom are from countries outside the U.S. This makes it easy to learn about other cultures, to meet people from foreign countries, to communicate with family or friends in other place, and to learn other languages. On the Internet, you can transfer e-mail, send computer files from one computer to another, transmit information, conduct real-time chats, and advertise and market products and services. For this reason, the Internet is often termed the Information Superhighway.

You can think of the Internet in terms of a highway road system that stretches across the world. The Internet has a main *backbone* of high-speed networks that are similar to the interstate highways in the U.S. Backbones are primary networks that enable high-speed communications and transmissions of files. The backbones also can support millions of users, much like interstate highways have a capacity for millions of automobiles.

Connected to the Internet backbones are smaller *networks* that are similar to state highways. These networks provide a way for companies, organizations, and schools to access the Internet. Types of networks that fall into this category are Internet Service Providers (ISPs) and commercial online services. These networks provide "on-ramps" to the Internet, often by way of personal computers and modems. Many large businesses, such as Microsoft, Coca-Cola, and

McDonalds, use an ISP to lease high-speed, large-capacity connections to the Internet. Individuals, on the other hand, use slow modem connections to connect to the Internet.

Just like your company isn't just one department, but several linked together to achieve the same goals, the Internet is not just one service. Several services make up the Internet to provide users with different ways to transmit and receive information. The primary services in the following list are discussed in this chapter.

- World Wide Web
- Gopher
- File Transfer Protocol (FTP)
- Chat
- Newsgroups
- E-mail
- Telnet

Who Controls the Internet?

Nobody controls the Internet. Probably the closest you could come to saying who runs the Internet is to look at the National Science Foundation (NSF) and its role in the development and management of the Internet. The NSF, an independent government agency, funded one of the primary network backbones of the Internet. The backbone the NSF created in 1986 was called the NSFnet and included the following five computer centers:

- Princeton University
- University of California, San Diego
- National Center for Supercomputing Applications (NCSA), University of Illinois
- Theory Center, Cornell University
- University of Pittsburgh

The NSF played an important role in establishing policies for what the Internet was used for. Although the NSF had jurisdiction over only the NSFnet area, their standards and policies were used over most of the Internet. One of the most crucial steps to setting the way the Internet worked—and still works in principle—was the publication of the NSFnet Backbone service's Acceptable Use

Policy, which is available on the Internet at **ftp://nic.merit.edu/nsfnet/acceptable.use.policy**. The Acceptable Use Policy outlines acceptable and unacceptable uses of the Internet. These are a few of the acceptable uses:

- The NSFnet can be used only for transferring education and research information.
- The NSFnet should be used efficiently to maximize its resources and to minimize interference and traffic congestion.
- Users cannot advertise commercial products. You can, however, advertise education and research products and services.
- Commercial vendors are allowed to answer questions about their products. They cannot, however, advertise products within the responses.

In 1991, the NSF lifted the restrictions on commercial use of the Internet to allow businesses and commercial entities to use the Internet. If businesses were not allowed on the Internet, you probably would have to connect to the Internet from a research facility, government agency, or school. Without a doubt, you wouldn't be able to connect using a commercial online service, and you would be hard pressed to find a local ISP that didn't have stiff restrictions on how you used the Internet.

The NSFnet is not the only network to comprise the Internet backbone. Several others do, including commercial networks from Sprint, MCI, and the *Commercial Internet Exchange*. The Commercial Internet Exchange (CIX) is a group founded by several commercial entities in 1991 to establish a commercial presence on the Internet. NSFnet created a corporation called *Advanced Network and Services, Inc. (ANS)* to be responsible for the NSFnet backbone. ANS included *Merit* (Michigan Education and Research Infrastructure Triad), MCI, and IBM. Until 1995, when the NSFnet backbone rerouted its networks through separate networks, the ANS influenced much of the way the Internet was used.

In 1993, NSF created *InterNIC* (see Figure 3.1). InterNIC was formed to provide Internet services, including the following:

- **Registration services.** This part of InterNIC makes sure no two people, companies, or organizations have the same address on the Internet. When a site is established on the Web, the owner must first register for a domain name from InterNIC (see the section, "Getting Started on the World Wide Web," later in this chapter for more information on domain names). Each domain name costs $50 for a two-year period.

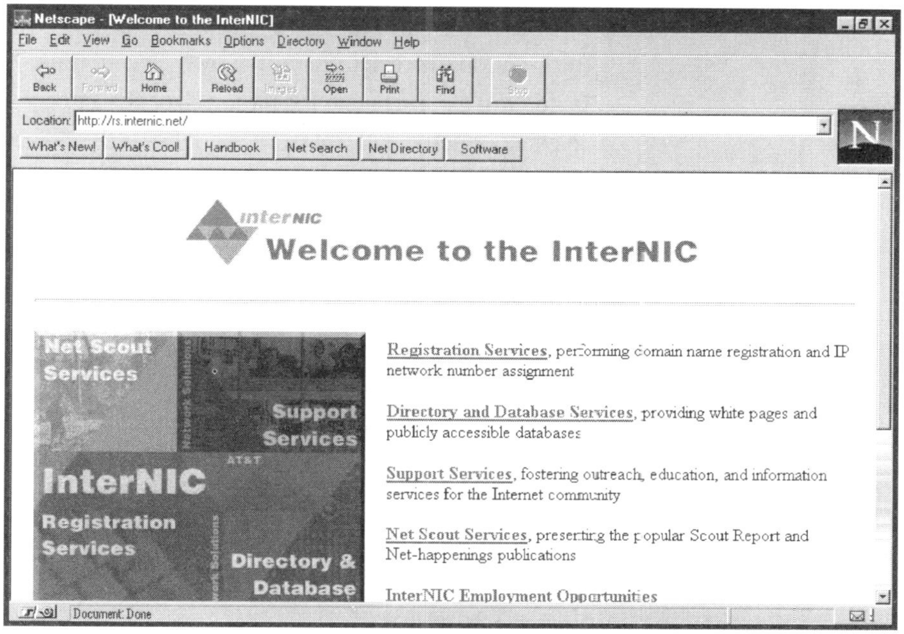

FIGURE 3.1

The InterNIC home page on the Web offers many online services.

- **Internet directory and database services.** This service has a list of all e-mail addresses on the Internet. It's maintained by AT&T.
- **Information services.** Includes the NSFnet policies and procedures, some Internet standards, and the NSFnet resource guide.

The number of people who connect to the Internet—particularly the Web—has grown significantly. This means the number of companies required to provide Internet access has needed to grow. Companies like UUNET, Cerfnet, AT&T's Worldnet, Netcom, and many others now make up a large part of the Internet infrastructure, but they still adhere to many of the policies and standards the NSF established years ago.

In 1995, NSFnet "pulled the plug" on its part of the Internet to allow commercial and private networks to take over the main backbone of the Internet. Also, in April 1995, NSFnet and MCI established a very-high-speed network backbone called *vBNS* (very high speed Backbone Network Service). vBNS links supercomputer centers to provide a network infrastructure for research on fast networks and application development.

How Fast Is the Internet?

The Internet uses high-speed data communications lines to connect thousands of computer networks and millions of computers together to form an interconnected network. The speeds along the Internet are measured in the amount of computer information that are transmitted over a given time. The faster the connection, the faster you can receive information over the Internet. Initially, you may just want to get connected and not worry about speeds. However, this becomes a real issue when the time you spend online is dictated by the speed of your modem. Moreover, the time you spend online usually costs you money, so you want the fastest connection to get the most out of your time online.

One way to think of this system is to consider your city water system. The water pressure in your kitchen and bathroom sinks and showers is adequate for what you need them for. You're charged a fee each month for the amount of water you use. Assume, however, that you're charged not by the amount of water you use, but by the amount of time it takes to fill your tub and sink, how much time you spend in the shower, how long it takes to water the grass, and so on. Now the water pressure issue is a completely different problem for you. You would want to run out and tap into the fire hydrants, which have enormous water pressure settings.

Instead of gallons of water, data is measured in *bits per second*. *Bits* are the primary units for computers. Computers work by using a binary numbering system, which uses ones and zeros to represent the bits. A *byte* of date is created when you have eight bits put together. A byte is equal to one letter or character on your computer screen. The rate that data streams through the Internet is usually not in bits; instead, data is sent by thousands and millions of bits of information per second. The common measurements you read about are kilobits per second (Kbps) and megabits (Mbps).

The backbone of the Internet is fast. You might question this when the data you access is downloading as slow as molasses on a cold day. The original NSFnet backbone carried only 56Kbps of data (most modems carry 28Kbps), but has since switched to a line that carries 45Mbps, which is commonly known as a *T-3 line*. The amount of data that can flow across a T-3 line is roughly equivalent to the amount of information that's in several standard novels in about one second.

NOTE

Don't try to get a T-3 connection, however. Most connections to a T-3 line have been taken up, but many companies use a T-1 line, which is rated at 1.5 mbps. Your local ISP may have T-1 lines available, but expect to pay a premium price for them. A T-1 is a dedicated, high-speed telephone line that the local phone company installs and leases to its clients. T-1 lines can cost up to $10,000 to install, $1,000 a month to rent, plus a service charge from the ISP.

Now, how badly do you want that T-1 line? If you still have the "need for speed," an apartment complex in New York City recently announced apartments for lease that include T-1 connections, much like a home or apartment wired for cable television. Reportedly, the apartments will rent for about $1,500 month, plus the price of the Internet service, which wasn't announced.

The speeds at which individuals usually connect to the Internet are 14.4 and 28.8Kbps. These are determined by the modems connected to their computers. As the Internet grows and more people connect to it, access speed becomes important. At work, you may have the luxury of connecting to the Internet by a high-speed connection. At home, however, you probably have a relatively slow connection through a modem. Even a 28.8 baud modem is very slow when you are downloading large graphics and files. Some areas of the country have begun offering two technologies that give homeowners and businesses high-speed access to the Internet: ISDN and cable.

ISDN (Integrated Services Digital Network) telephone lines are voice and digital network services combined in a single line. This means your regular voice conversations and modem transmissions can take place over the same phone line simultaneously. With a regular telephone line, you can do only one type of action at a time. In addition, ISDN lines are substantially faster than regular phone lines, allowing up to five times the speed of 28.8Kbps modems and eight times the speed of 14.4Kbps modems. ISDN enables users to access the Internet at speeds of 64Kbps (for two simultaneous calls) or a combined speed of 128Kbps for a single call.

Currently, ISDN is not available in all areas of the country, but many telephone companies are beginning to offer ISDN to their customers. ISDN lines are priced higher than regular phone lines with monthly fees of $30 to $130, plus one-time installation fees ranging from $100 to $600 depending on the company. Additionally, you must purchase ISDN modems (costs usually start at $180) and have ISDN software for your computer. You must also use an Internet Service Provider (ISP) who offers ISDN access to the Internet, usually at a premium rate. If you want ISDN connections, consider these extra costs, plus the limited availability area.

The following list includes a few companies offering ISDN services:

Company: Ameritech
Phone: 800-832-6328
Areas available: IL, IN, MI, OH, WI

Company: BellSouth
Phone: 800-428-4736
Areas available: AL, FL, GA, KY, LA, MS, NC, SC, TN

Company: GTE
Phone: 800-438-4926
Areas available: CA, FL, HI, ID, IL, IN, KY, NC, OH, OR, PA, TX, VA, WA

Cable is a more familiar technology to most people because of its prevalence in homes for television viewing. Some cable companies are experimenting with providing Internet access via the same cable connection used to bring cable television into your home. With cable access to the Internet, there are two primary advantages over dial-up connections. First, many homes are already wired for cable, with new home contractors offering cable as a regular feature. Also if you live in most urban areas and in some rural ares, you probably have cable. Second, cable is almost 1,000 times faster than regular modem connections, making it possible to have real-time video (such as movies and television programming), teleconferencing, and high-speed networking resources only available now to the desktop computer. In simple terms, files that take 20 minutes to download with a 28.8Kbps modem take less than one minute with cable.

Currently, companies offering cable access to the Internet are relatively few and far between. Some companies, such as TCI (TeleCommunications Inc.) and Viacom, are conducting trial connections in limited areas. In the next year, however, look for many cable operators to offer it. Also, unlike modems that you purchase, cable modems may at first be leased to you by the cable companies, much like cable boxes are leased for television viewing. Prices for cable access to the Internet are speculative now, but will undoubtedly be reasonable and competitive to other Internet access services within two or three years. For now, your best bet is to start with a regular dial-up connection using a 14.4 or 28.8 modem.

Services on the Internet

You've heard the saying, "There's no right way to eat an Oreo cookie." Well, you also can say, "There's no right way to use the Internet." It comes down to what you like (do you eat the middle first for a burst of sweetness), what you need to do, or for the nourishment. Most people connecting to the Internet do so for the Web resources. The Web is the multimedia and graphic service of the Internet; it gives users experiences that glossy magazines and television shows do. On the other end of the Internet spectrum are services like FTP and Telnet, which can give the inexperienced user cold sweats (like eating the cookie part of the Oreo without a glass of milk handy).

The following sections examine each of the services available on the Internet.

Understanding E-mail

As much as the personal computer and the Internet have allowed us to stay in the comfort of our homes and offices to explore the world they also have brought many of us closer and expanded our ties to one another. E-mail enables someone in middle America to converse with someone in downtown Melbourne, Australia in a matter of minutes for a relatively low price. E-mail enables companies with multiple branches—that may be separated by state or country—to stay in touch quickly and efficiently. E-mail also has led to many interesting relationships on a personal level, with couples coming together because of "virtual" meetings they've had online.

The first activity performed on the Internet was to send messages back and forth between researchers. Today, that's still the number one use of the Internet. E-mail is a technology used to send a simple text message between users. If you work in a company that has a local area network (LAN) installed, you may be familiar with e-mail already. The primary difference between LAN-based e-mail and Internet e-mail is the number of potential recipients; there are many more on the Internet than on your LAN. In some companies, LANs are hooked to the Internet so you can send messages to Internet users. Figure 3.2 shows an example of an e-mail message.

To use Internet e-mail, you need a few items. First, you need access to the Internet. Second, you need to install an e-mail application that lets you send and receive Internet e-mail. Several e-mail applications are available, some of which are discussed in detail in Chapter 4. A popular way to use Internet e-mail is to have it integrated as part of a Web browser, so only one application—the browser—needs to be installed and executed on your system. One such program is Netscape Navigator 2.0 (refer to Figure 3.2).

Finally, you need to know an address to which to send a message. When you want to send a letter through the Postal Service (sometimes called *snail mail*), you include a mailing address to indicate the recipient. You can't just say "To Jack" or "To Mom" and expect it to arrive at the other end. Certain protocols of addressing letters are used. Likewise, Internet e-mail requires a proper addressing protocol. E-mail addresses are usually a lot shorter than snail mail addresses and can be attached to messages with the click of a button using electronic address books (see Figure 3.3). Another advantage is that you don't need a stamp,

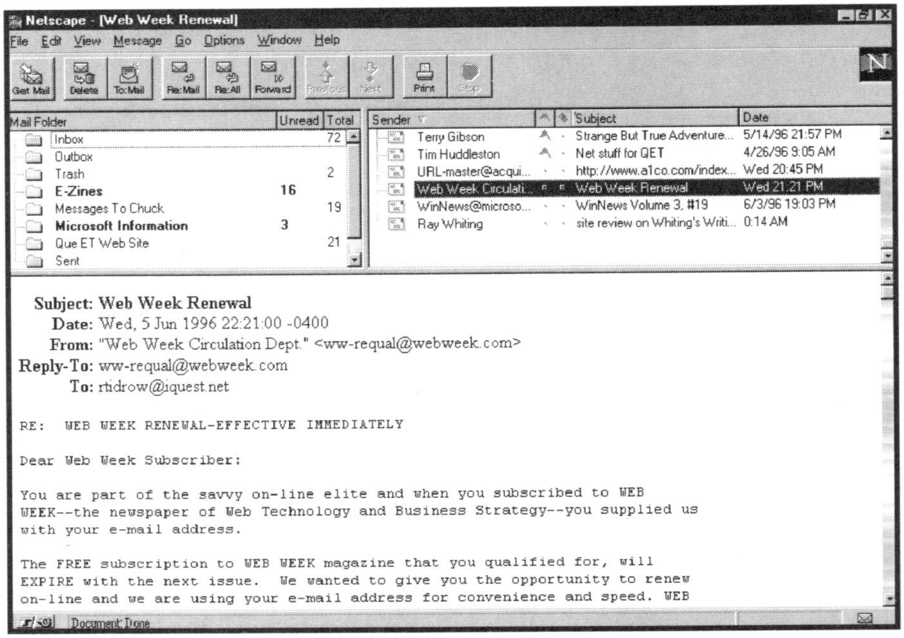

FIGURE 3.2

Electronic mail is revolutionizing the way people communicate.

so no excuses for not writing e-mail messages to your mother or Aunt Sally if they're online.

E-mail addresses are assigned to you by your ISP or network administrator. You also get an e-mail address when you sign up with a commercial online service, such as America Online. At first, they may look a little strange, but you'll soon be spouting yours off at trade shows, auctions, family reunions, and funerals. Internet e-mail addresses look like this:

dtrump@towers.com

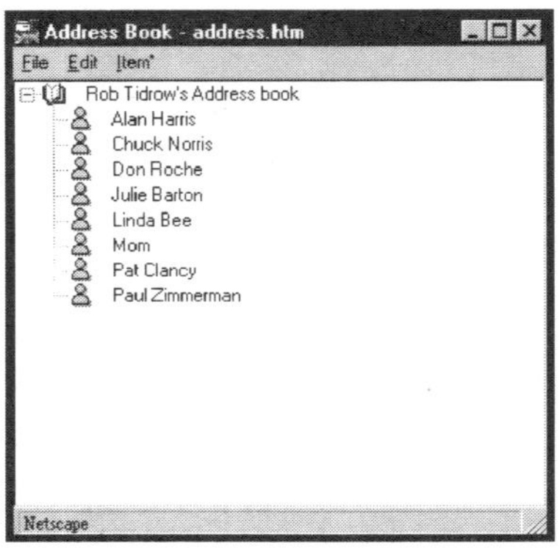

FIGURE 3.3

Electronic address books make it easy to address your e-mail messages.

Do I Have to Use E-mail?

A common question many new Internet users ask is "Do I have to use e-mail?" You don't have to use e-mail to use the Internet or the Web, but you'll miss one of its great features. You'll miss the opportunity to communicate with people who have similar interests. You'll miss the interaction you get by subscribing to mailing lists that provide you information on a wealth of topics, ranging from abortion to zoology. (Mailing lists are discussed later in this chapter.) You'll also miss the chance to send e-mail to your family, friends, congressman, or coworkers. Although there may be times when you find yourself inundated with messages, there are also times when you can't wait to receive the next message from someone you care about or are anxious to hear from.

Notice how the address is divided in three parts (separated by an "at" (@) symbol), and that it is all lowercase characters. The lowercase characters are used as a standard because of the proliferation of UNIX computers on the Internet. You should get in the habit of addressing your e-mail messages with lowercase letters to ensure you don't encounter delivery problems.

NOTE

UNIX *is an operating system developed by Bell Laboratories and found on many different types of computers. Because of its capability to run several programs at once (called* multitasking*) and use more than one processor in a computer, UNIX traditionally has been the favored operating system for businesses, institutions, and colleges setting up Internet and World Wide Web servers.*

On the left side of the @ symbol is the recipient's username, in this case "dtrump." This usually is created by using the first letter of the first name and the last name up to eight characters (some companies use the first name up to seven letters and the first letter of last name). On the right side of the @ symbol is the domain name, "towers.com," which is a unique identifier registered to the company or organization (called the *host*) in which the user has his or her Internet account. This can be the company the user works for, an ISP, or another organization. The "towers" part tells you where the host is located (such as a university, business, government agency, or similar type of host). The last part, ".com," is called the first level domain and indicates the type of host it is. There are six first level domains used in the U.S.:

- **.com** denotes commercial hosts, such as microsoft.com.
- **.gov** denotes government hosts, such as whitehouse.gov.

- **.net** denotes network hosts. (Some ISPs use this first level domain.)
- **.edu** denotes education hosts, such as purdue.com.
- **.org** denotes organization hosts, such as Public Broadcasting System (PBS).
- **.country_code** This is a variable domain that denotes foreign countries, such as .ja for Japan.

NOTE

It's important to remember that the e-mail address must be typed exactly as given to you. Unlike the U.S. Postal system, which has human beings deciphering our illegible handwriting and incorrectly spelled names and addresses, the Internet e-mail system cannot "guess" to whom you may be sending a message. If the e-mail address is entered incorrectly on your end or if the e-mail address doesn't exist, your message will be returned to you stating that it was undeliverable.

Mailing Lists

A *mailing list* is a service that redistributes mail messages to anyone who has subscribed to that list. Mailing lists are organized groups of people who communicate with each other via e-mail; they can reach many people who are interested in a topic. There are thousands of mailing lists to which you can subscribe, on such topics as auto racing, Windows 95, genealogy, sex, and cooking. Mailing lists come in two flavors: *moderated* and *unmoderated*. The moderated lists are controlled by a moderator who's responsible for ensuring that each message that gets posted on the mailing list is relevant to the list topic. Unmoderated lists don't have these control points, but users usually police themselves when messages stray too far from the list's original intent.

When you subscribe to a mailing list, you receive all the messages posted to that mailing list. Depending on the topic, you may receive 5-10 messages in a day, or as many as several hundred. These are received in your e-mail application, just like any other mail message. You can use any e-mail application to read, post, and reply to messages you get from a mailing list.

When you send a message to a mailing list to which you belong, that message is then sent to all the other users who belong to that mailing list. You may find this confusing at first, because you send your message to only one e-mail address—the address for that particular mailing list. After you send the message, it might be first read by a moderator, who approves of the message for that list and then forwards it to the other members of the list. Moderated lists are usually the best lists to subscribe to if you're interested in a focused, well-behaved list that sticks to the subject. When subscribing to a mailing list, you'll usually get a reply back to you letting you know how to get more information about the mailing list and whether the list is moderated or not.

When you create a message to be posted to a mailing list, just make sure that the e-mail address is the address to the mailing list, not to an individual on the mailing list. This might be something like the following:

> hwg-guide@netcom.com

The "hwg-guide" part of the address is a computer address that automatically routes your message to a moderator or, if the list is unmoderated, sends the message to everyone on the mailing list.

NOTE

You can send e-mail messages to other individuals on a mailing list, but these are private messages between you and that other person. Some users don't mind getting these individual e-mails if they have difficulty receiving mailing lists postings. Others don't want another set of e-mail messages cluttering their inbox. Also, if you have a comment, suggestion, or answer that is directed toward one person, it may be of benefit to others. So, post it to the entire mailing list to benefit everyone.

To subscribe to a mailing list, you send an e-mail message to the mailing list server (the computer that controls the mailing list) requesting to be on list. If the list is open to the public (some have restricted access), you'll usually receive notification from the mailing list that you're now a part of the list. You also should receive detailed instructions on how to *unsubscribe* from a mailing list. Mailing lists have different ways to unsubscribe. Here is an example of how to unsubscribe from the Microsoft WinNews mailing list:

> Send mail to enews@microsoft.nwnet.com with a blank subject line and the body of the message should only say in the text: **UNSUBSCRIBE WINNEWS**.

NOTE

It's easy to find yourself subscribing to a dozen or so mailing lists that pique your interest. This is fine, if you want to give up working or having a life. Some mailing lists are very busy—posting hundreds of messages per day. Some are slower, but still trickle in 20-30 messages a week. What this means is that you get every one of these messages, whether you read them or not. For this reason, make sure you read and keep any instructions on how to unsubscribe from a mailing list. Tuck these instructions away in your safety deposit box if necessary. You'll be thankful that you've kept them.

Another way to control the number of messages you receive from a mailing list is to look for digest formats of the mailing list. Digests compile messages posted to mailing lists into one large message that gets sent out every day or several times a day to members of particular lists. With digests, you can read the same information you can get from a regular mailing list, but in larger collections. Not all mailing lists have digests.

Understanding Newsgroups

Internet *newsgroups* are like bulletin boards hanging on the walls of your home, church, and office where you can announce important events, leave messages, or disseminate important information. With Internet newsgroups, however, many people post messages to be read by a worldwide audience. Newsgroups enable you to communicate with people around the world about topics of mutual interest. These topics can be educational, political, personal, or just fun. Individuals, educational institutions, government agencies, and businesses can be part of any newsgroup. Each newsgroup focuses on a topic in which its members share an interest.

Each newsgroup contains messages (also called *postings*—articles that people *post*, or send) pertaining to the newsgroup topic. To give you an idea of what kind of newsgroups you can find and their content, Figure 3.4 shows an example of some message names and the text from one of those messages.

Messages are transmitted by systems of networks (such as the Internet) to servers, then to the computers to those who access, use, and interact with the newsgroup. There are thousands of individual newsgroups accessible on the Internet; they fall under the umbrella of *USENET*. USENET is simply one component of the Internet; that is, it's a collection of servers that provide space for individual newsgroups.

NOTE

You'll frequently hear people say "USENET newsgroup" instead of just saying "newsgroup," even though that's redundant. You may also hear inexperienced Internet users refer to newsgroups as "forums." That's because Internet

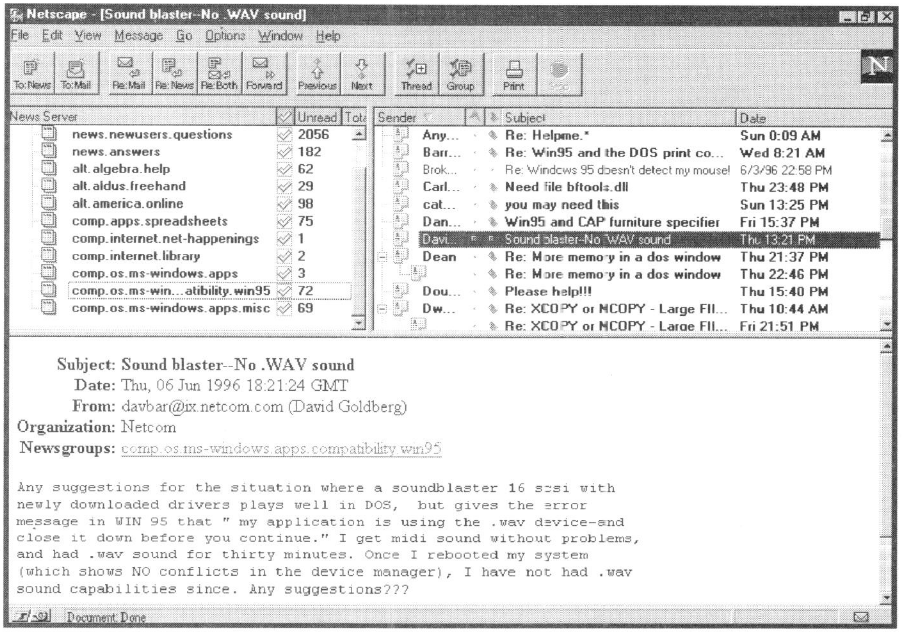

FIGURE 3.4

An example of a newsgroup message in the Netscape Navigator News window.

newsgroups are similar in nature to the message forums found on services such as CompuServe and America Online.

Understanding the Newsgroup Naming System

You need to understand how newsgroup names are formatted, just as you have become familiar with the formatting of Web site names. The name of the newsgroup reflects the topic of interest to that particular newsgroup. Newsgroup names are unique because of the words they contain, along with the periods that separate the categories and newsgroup topics.

Here are some examples of newsgroup names:

news.announce.newusers

comp.sys.mac.graphics

alt.online.service

rec.games.board

As you can see, even though the newsgroup naming system allows each newsgroup to have a unique and distinctive name, it still allows for consistency in the naming schemes. This makes the names easy to understand when you know the system. After you know the system, you can easily guess what all the names mean.

You can think of a newsgroup's name as forming a hierarchy: the most general part of the name appears at the left end of the name and the name gets more specific as you move to the right. Take the name "rec.games.board" as an example. The newsgroup falls under the major interest area of recreation ("rec"), which can cover a pretty broad range of topics. Then the name gets a little more specific; the next part of the name tells you that this particular group likes to discuss games. The next part of the name is even more specific, it tells you that this group focuses on board games (as opposed to computer games or video games).

Newsgroup names are always divided by periods—called *separators* in computerese. These simply help you string together the various pieces of a newsgroup's name, and make it easier to interpret.

Remember that newsgroups are categorized by major areas of interest, such as computers, academics, and so on. The first part of a newsgroup's name—its *prefix*—identifies the *category* to which the newsgroup belongs. The following list describes some of the major newsgroup categories you may encounter:

- **alt.** The newsgroups in this category offer a range of topics that are *alternative*. They range from the inane to the very serious. The alt group includes newsgroups such as alt.support.cancer, alt.gopher, alt.sex, and many more. Some news servers don't include all the alt newsgroups because of their controversial nature.
- **bit.** Pertains to *Bitnet* messages. Bitnet is a message and file-retrieval network with a long history in the education community. Bitnet originally consisted of its own phone lines and networks, some of which are still in use today. Most of the Bitnet features have been absorbed by the Internet, or have become obsolete.
- **biz.** Groups with this category designation are devoted to the discussion of *business*. Many of these groups have an advertising and marketing focus, and many of the postings appear to be advertising pieces, or "get-rich-quick" schemes.
- **comp.** These newsgroups are devoted to computer science, computer hardware and software, operating systems, applications, and general interest topics for computer users. Many of these newsgroups are devoted to UNIX-based systems, so if you're interested in Windows 95 or Windows 3.1, make sure you're in the right newsgroup for you. You'll want to

find newsgroups that are labeled "ms-windows," for example. Otherwise you may be in an X-windows discussion (which is UNIX).

- **news.** This category includes discussions about the USENET network, newsreader software, general USENET news questions (usually for beginners), and important information and announcements for new users. The first few times you explore newsgroups, be sure to check the newsgroups **news.announce.newusers** and **news.newusers.questions**. These closely moderated newsgroups contain only articles that are essential to first-time USENET users.
- **rec.** The designation for *recreation*, which includes newsgroups devoted to hobbies, music, arts, sports, and entertainment. If you can't find a newsgroup devoted to your kind of music or favorite sport here, try the alt listings.
- **sci.** Includes discussions on scientific research and applications not related to computer science. Many research institutes and educational facilities belong to these newsgroups.
- **soc.** Discussions about social issues, politics, and much more.
- **misc.** Includes discussions and topics that can't fit conveniently in other groups, such as **misc.jobs**, **misc.forsale**, and so on.

Who Runs Newsgroups?

No one person or group controls USENET as a whole. Some individual newsgroups do have a moderator, but that moderator works only within that newsgroup, and has no power over any other areas. This means that when you interact with a newsgroup, you're on your own for the most part. A newsgroup's moderator tries to keep the discussions focused on the newsgroup's primary topic of interest, and may filter out any messages that don't pertain to the topic. In some newsgroups, the moderator is charged with removing postings that may be considered offensive by some members.

You can read postings and reply to either the e-mail address of the individual who originated the posting, or to the newsgroup directly. If you reply to the newsgroup, your posting becomes visible to all the members of the newsgroup soon after you send it. However, if a newsgroup has a moderator, you usually will need to submit your posting to the moderator for approval before the posting can appear in the newsgroup.

Before you become actively involved in any newsgroup, you need to arm yourself with a basic understanding of the USENET's culture. When you become part of the USENET, you immerse yourself in a truly diverse, multi-cultural experience. When you exchange messages via a newsgroup, remember that you may be dealing with other people from many different parts of the world, who speak many languages, and who use vastly different hardware and software than you do. It's true that some newsgroups concern local topics and are run locally for a small group, but the overwhelming number of newsgroups are accessed around the world. Keep this in mind, and your presence will be welcomed on the USENET. Be aware of potential language barriers or cultural differences, and be precise in making your point when you post to a newsgroup so others won't be confused about your meaning.

But like most good things, USENET also has an unattractive side. You're likely to see *flames*—angry, admonishing messages—flying across USENET from time to time. In fact, some newsgroups are notorious gathering spots for hard-core flamers, who love to harass, insult, and be nasty toward other members, and especially to naive first-time visitors. Because no one moderates the USENET network (remember that a newsgroup may or may not have a moderator), users who encounter a posting they don't like or don't approve of often send flames. Flaming occurs for many reasons: perhaps because people feel a posting strays from the true focus of the newsgroup, or because someone blatantly advertises over many newsgroups. For example, if an individual posts an advertisement to sell their goods or services in a newsgroup whose intent is to provide free assistance to new users, the group's members may post flames to encourage the individual to cease this sales-related activity.

NOTE

Spamming *is a term you may hear a lot when reading newsgroup messages. Spamming is when someone sends the same message to many different newsgroups. Sometimes this is done by people advertizing a product or service, or by someone who enjoys wasting other people's time. Advertising in not encouraged in newsgroups, unless you're in a biz newsgroup that specifically allows advertising. The term "spam" originated from a Monty Python skit about Hormel's Spam product.*

Getting Familiar with a Newsgroup

Experienced USENET users universally offer one piece of advice to first-time newsgroup visitors: Don't jump into a newsgroup without first acclimating yourself to that newsgroup—just as you wouldn't walk up to a group of people you don't know and force your way into their discussion. Visit the newsgroup before posting to it. Read the current entries in a newsgroup to ensure that you won't post a message that duplicates another posting. Reading but not contributing is called *lurking* and is perfectly acceptable behavior. Get the feel for the community that comprises a particular newsgroup. When you do post, be sure you're posting an item that's pertinent to that newsgroup's interests.

You may disagree with statements (whether they're fact or opinion) that others post in a newsgroup. You also may choose to ignore postings from certain members whose opinions differ from your own. Resist the temptation to flame them. Remember, this is a global community—your boss, sister, spouse, or mother may be reading your postings. How people perceive you is a reflection of the quality and courtesy present in your postings.

Understanding File Transfer Protocol (FTP)

The concept of *FTP* is probably the easiest of all Internet services for new users to understand, but it can be difficult and frustrating to implement. You use FTP to transfer files between computers. These files can be graphics, software, documents, and multimedia files. When you use FTP, you request a file or set of files from a *remote* computer (the computer at the other end of the line) to be downloaded, or transferred, to your computer. There are thousands of sites available on the Internet that allow FTP transfers.

You also can use FTP to upload files from your computer to a remote computer. You would do this if you want to share documents or files with other users who may connect to that same remote computer. Also, if you design your own Web pages (called HTML documents), you usually use FTP to transfer the finished Web pages from your computer to post them on the Web *server* (the computer that stores HTML pages) for others to view.

Historically, FTP has been difficult to use for most Windows users not comfortable with the UNIX operating system. Because most of the computers that allow FTP on the Internet are UNIX-based, users accessing these files via FTP have had to pick up a few UNIX commands. Until a few years ago, the common FTP applications available were character-based and looked like the one in Figure 3.5. In fact, this FTP program is included as part of Windows 95, which is quite a shock to those users just learning to use graphical programs. In Chapter 4, you learn how to use this utility; you also learn a few UNIX commands that you may need when connecting to a FTP server. Many of the commands shown are similar to ones used in MS-DOS, which millions of users already know.

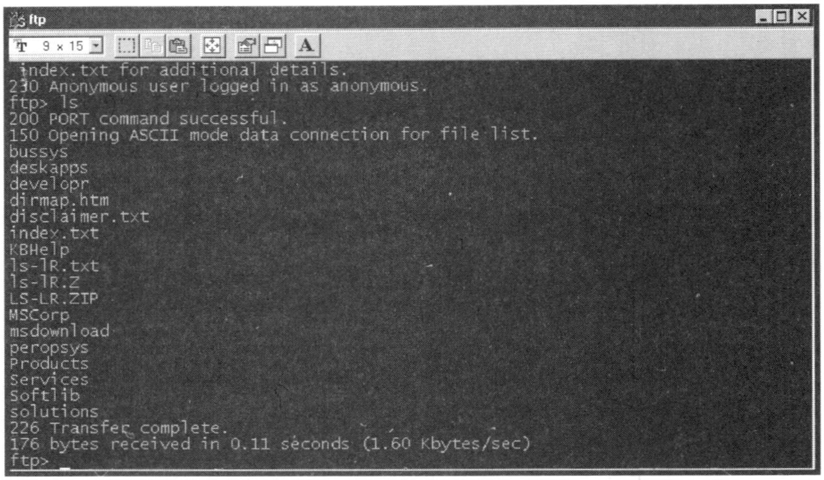

FIGURE 3.5

The Windows 95 FTP application is character-based and requires you to understand FTP and UNIX commands.

Fortunately, several Windows-based FTP applications are available that hide most of the drudgery of UNIX commands, such as WS_FTP for Windows. Also many Web sites include links to FTP sites from within the Web page. This makes it easy and intuitive for users to access and download files from an FTP server. Figure 3.6 shows the WS_FTP program logged into the same FTP server shown in Figure 3.5. Which application would you rather use?

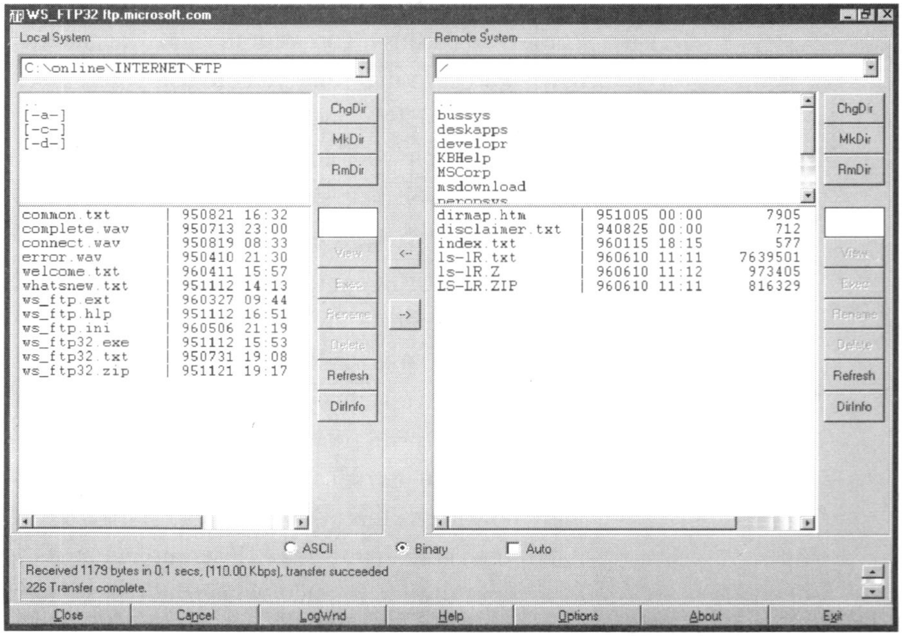

FIGURE 3.6

WS_FTP makes the FTP experience more enjoyable.

When you connect to a computer that allows FTP transfers (called an FTP server) on the Internet, you're required to log in. This enables the owners of the FTP server to keep track of who's accessing files from their computer. You need a username and password to log into each FTP server. When you finish accessing files on an FTP server, you log off the server.

Many FTP servers restrict who can log in to control who can access the documents and files. Companies and organizations often use FTP servers to allow their employees to access files from a remote computer, such as from a branch office across town or in another country. These files may be sensitive documents that relate only to that company, so it's vital for the company to let in only those authorized to view them and keep out everyone else. These types of FTP servers are called *full-rights* servers.

To access a full-rights server, you must be assigned a username and password from the FTP administrator. Your username may be your regular e-mail username, but usually is something unique so others can't use your FTP username to break into the FTP server. The password you're assigned usually is something cryptic so others can't easily guess it, such as my73tpu.

A small percentage of Internet FTP sites are set up as *anonymous* FTP servers. These FTP sites enable anyone to log into their server and access files from it, usually from a public directory (usually called /pub). When you log into an anonymous server, you use the username **anonymous** and your e-mail address for

ARCHIE TO THE RESCUE

Even with a small percentage of FTP sites allowing anonymous log ins, there are several thousand servers and millions of files available to you. Finding these files is like finding a gift for your father at Christmas. You know there's something out there, you just don't have a clue what it is or where it's located. With FTP, fortunately, you can use an Internet tool called Archie.

Archie servers have two parts to them. First, they maintain a database of files you can search on the Internet. You can use this database to search for a file or type of file you want. For example, you may know the name of the file but don't know where to get it. Or, you may want to search for files that match a specific criteria, such as "telecommunications" or "games."

Second, Archie servers store a collection of all the Internet computers that have files you can download. Periodically, the Archie servers update this collection by combing the Internet for FTP servers, and then update the Archie databases to list files found on the FTP servers. Chapter 4 shows you how to use Archie servers to find what you're looking for.

the password. The reason you must use your e-mail address is so the owner of the FTP server can keep tabs on who accesses files on the server.

As you'll see in the section called "Getting Started on the World Wide Web," some of the resources you encounter on the Web are FTP. Some Web browsers, such as Netscape Navigator 2, have built-in support for FTP so you can access those files without leaving the Web browsers. Other browsers, however, require you to execute a separate FTP program (such as WS_FTP) when you encounter an FTP file.

Understanding Telnet

Telnet is an Internet application that lets you log into a remote computer and run applications from the remote computer. A research scientist, for example, can access a high-speed supercomputer in another state or country from her relatively slow computer by using Telnet to connect to the remote computer. Closer to home, you can even register for a conference by using the Internet. Some conferences let you use Telnet to log into the server to sign up for the show.

TIP

You may encounter many forms and sign-up pages on the Web. Although many Web sites have these features, there are still some sites that require you to use Telnet to register for a show or conference. Fortunately, these sites are rapidly moving to the Web to make the experience much more enjoyable.

Telnet has the same problem FTP used to have in that it's intimidating and difficult to use for new users. Windows 95 includes a built-in Telnet application, which looks a lot like its FTP application (see Figure 3.7). Fortunately, most Internet and Web users will never have to use a Telnet resource. If you do, you're stuck using character-based applications and learning obscure commands and procedures. Chapter shows you an example of using a Telnet application.

Understanding Gopher

Before the World Wide Web, there was *Gopher*. Gopher was introduced in 1991 by researchers at the University of Minnesota (their school mascot is the golden gopher). Users (educators, researchers, government personnel, and so on) who had been using FTP and Telnet to navigate the Internet, flocked to Gopher because it presented information and files in a logical way. For example, instead

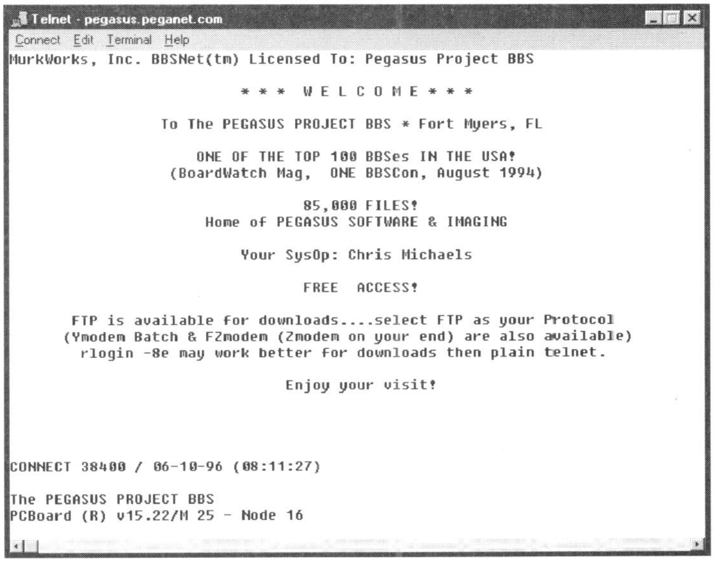

FIGURE 3.7

Windows 95's Telnet program can be as intimidating as its FTP program.

of seeing the short file descriptions shown in FTP directories, Gopher menus include longer descriptions and let you know what the file type is (see Figure 3.8). Gopher organizes and presents Internet files in menus, which remind many users of table of contents found in books or magazines. Instead of looking at a blank screen that requires you to initiate the transaction (which character-based

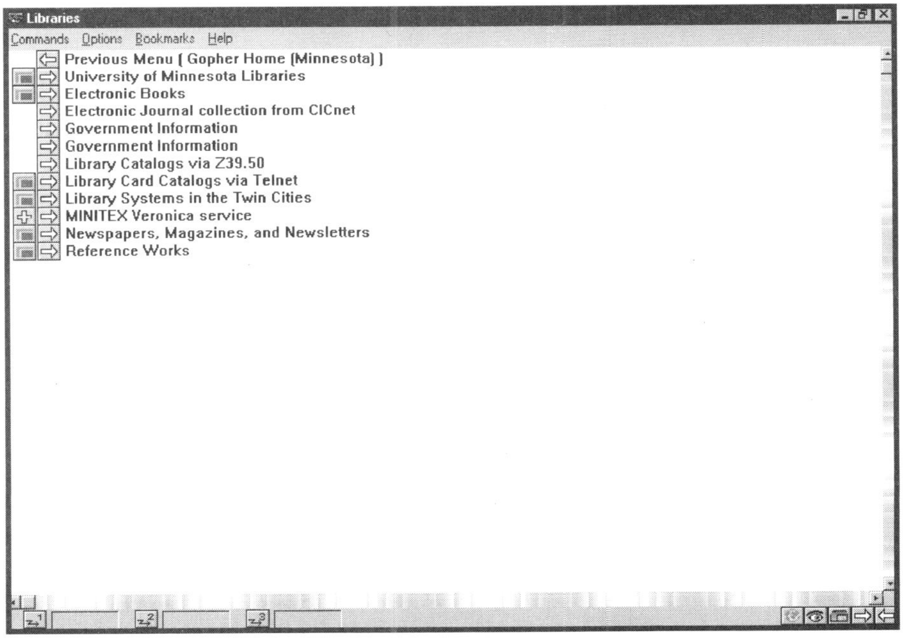

FIGURE 3.8

Hgopher for Windows provides an easy way to navigate Gopherspace.

FTP applications require), Gopher sites present you with information in organized ways, to let you view documents online or download files to your computer.

To connect to a Gopher site, you enter its address and a login ID. Sometimes login IDs are not required. After you connect to a Gopher site, you navigate Gopher menus by selecting a menu choice on-screen or going to another screen at the Gopher site. Unlike FTP and Telnet, Gopher enables you to switch to another Gopher site without logging out of the first site. Many Gopher menus include other Gopher sites, which lets you jump from one Gopher site to another in Gopherspace. If another site is not available, you simply enter the Gopher address of another site. (*Gopherspace* is the global interconnection of Gophers servers on the Internet.) Table 3.1 lists some popular Gopher sites.

WARNING

As you begin using Gopher and accessing information, you'll notice a disturbing trend. Many of the available documents and files are outdated. In fact, many are dated 1994 or earlier. This is because the Web started becoming more popular about that time, and development of Gopher servers was outpaced by Web servers.

Understanding Internet Relay Chat (IRC)

You've already learned two important ways to communicate on the Internet: e-mail and USENET newsgroups. Although these forms of communication are the most popular ways to interact with others on the Internet, you may want to interact with others in real time, as if you were in a room conversing with one another. You can do this with a feature called *chat*. Chats are used to conduct quick online meetings, answer a quick question, or set up a meeting. Chats also are viewed by many other users as a novelty item that can grow old after the first ten minutes of using it. (Especially if you end up in a chat session dominated by teenagers talking about some TV show.)

Chats enable you to carry on electronic conversations with one person or dozens of people in real time by entering comments on your keyboard. This capability is possible through an Internet service called *Internet Relay Chat (IRC)* that chat programs use to connect to IRC servers. One such application, Netscape Chat, is available from Netscape Communications. A recently announced chat product is called Comic Chat from Microsoft (see Figure 3.9).

Address	Login ID	Location
gopher.nato.int		North Atlantic Treaty Organization (NATO)
gopher.info.umd.edu		CNN Headline News
gopher.unr.edu		University of Nevada
gopher.maine.maine.edu		Amateur Radio Information
gopher.ohiolink.edu	gopher	Ohio University
gopher.uiuc.edu		Illinois University
wsuaix.csc.wsu.edu	wsuinfo	Washington State University
gopher.msu.edu	gopher	Michigan State University

TABLE 3.1 GOPHER SITES ON THE INTERNET

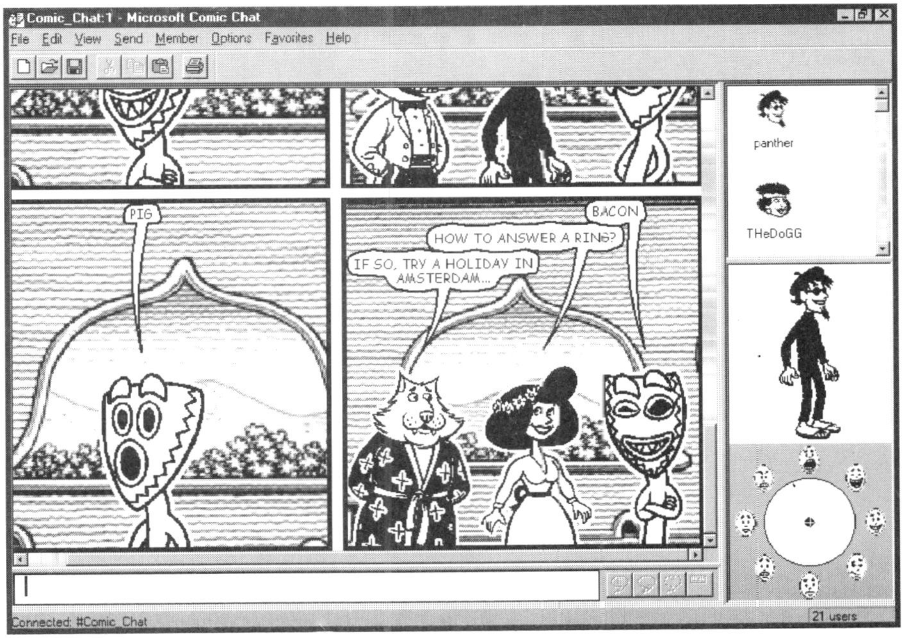

FIGURE 3.9

Microsoft's Comic Chat uses a comic strip metaphor to make chat sessions entertaining.

NOTE

The term real time, *in this sense, means that the two-way communication is happening right now; you don't send out a message and then wait an indefinite period of time for a reply. When you type a contribution to a chat conversation, your words appear on the screens of other "chatters" as you type them.*

If you're on a LAN at work, you already may have a chat program that enables you dial up someone else on your LAN and talk with them in real-time. The way this works is that chat programs typically have two windows. In one window, you type in your comments to the other user; in the other window, you see the comments or responses from the other user.

Internet Relay Chat operates under the same concept. Instead of communicating across a LAN, however, you communicate across the Internet. Also, most LAN-based chat programs only allow you to talk to one person at a time, while IRC is designed to handle many users simultaneously.

NOTE

IRC is based on the TCP/IP network protocol and uses servers and clients to enable you to talk to others. The client *is the application (such as Netscape Chat) that resides on your machine and on the machines of the other users involved in the chat session. The* server *is the computer to which you connect that provides the support for IRC.*

You must first connect to an IRC server then select an IRC channel to make contact with other users; in that sense, IRC chat is sort of like using a television. *Channels* consist of topics that you can choose to chat about, such as computers, sex, fantasy, food, and much more. If it's a busy day or night on a particular channel, you may find 30 to 50 people chatting at the same time. On slow channels, you may be the only person. (Not much give and take, but you won't have to worry about someone contradicting you!) The servers maintain information on the available channels at any given time. As new channels are added, information about the new channels is sent to every other IRC channel on the Internet.

At the time of this writing, more than 100 IRC servers were available on the Internet. You direct your IRC application to the server you want to connect to by entering an address for it. These addresses look like other Internet addresses (such as irc.indiana.edu). Technically, it doesn't matter which server you connect to, but you should look for an IRC server in your geographic area in order to shorten the distance that your messages must travel between your client and the server. In turn, this means that your message will appear to and be read by others quicker.

If you've ever walked into a room with a lot of people carrying on several conversations, you probably had difficulty following one conversation without hearing bits and pieces from other conversations. Chatting on IRC is similar, except you talk by typing and reading responses instead of listening to them. In IRC conversations, you can't block out other conversations; rather, other messages and responses intermingle with your messages and messages from the person or persons to whom you're talking.

Although you can find channels that have one large conversation (in which all participants are talking about the same topic at the same time), for the most part, what you'll find are many smaller conversations going on simultaneously, (as well as two people asking the same person different questions at the same time). What you get is a kind of schizophrenic conversation that resembles a television press conference spiralling out of control. Figure 3.9 shows an example of an online conversation in Netscape Chat. In Chapter 4, you learn how to use Internet Relay Chat.

Getting Started on the World Wide Web

When you get a connection to the Internet, you'll more than likely spend the majority of your time on the Web. The Web is a massive collection of documents and files, many of which are linked together via the Internet. The Web is a part of the Internet that allows you to view, or otherwise interact with, information in very graphical and intuitive ways. This makes the Web a popular way to receive and transmit information for a variety of media, including academic,

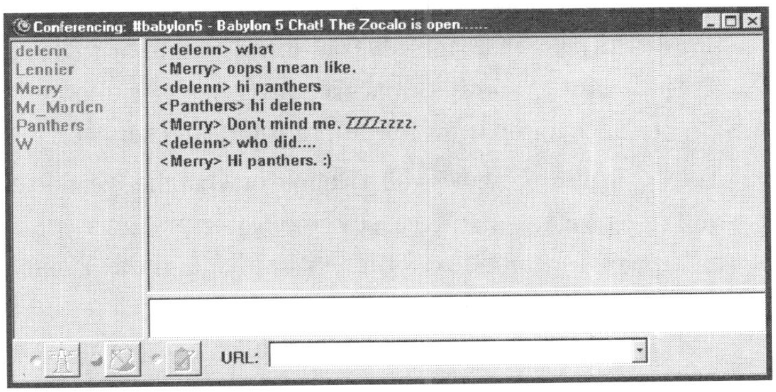

FIGURE 3.10

Internet Relay Chat (IRC) is used to discuss a number of various topics, including the television show *Babylon 5*.

commercial, institutional, and governmental. Some of the types of information you can find on the Web includes the following:

- Commercial advertisements
- News, weather, and sports
- Research papers
- Various pictures, including famous people, travel sites, animals, and more
- Government documents, including Congressional news, IRS forms, and election information
- Interactive games
- Multimedia files, including video clips, sound files, and teleconferencing software
- Computer software, including applications that work with Navigator Gold

NOTE

The World Wide Web has been responsible for much of the growth of the Internet the past two to three years. More people are using the Internet because of the way the Web presents information in graphical and organized ways. If you are getting connected to the Internet, you're probably doing so because of the popularity of the Web. Also, because of the graphics that display on Web pages, you'll want to make sure you have the fastest connection to the Internet as possible (usually a 28.8Kbps modem from home).

These are just *some* of the types of information you can find on the Web. In the next chapter, you'll visit many of these types of sites to help you get an idea of what the Web has to offer. Before the Web was introduced in 1991, many of these same items on the list were available on the Internet. However, they were in formats that weren't as intuitive to find or to use as they now are on the Web. Many of these formats required the user to enter arcane commands and learn specialized tools for different Internet services.

Figure 3.11 shows you a sample of what the Web looks like if you're using Netscape Navigator 2.0. Basically, Navigator presents you with *Web pages*, documents that include text, graphics, sound, and other objects. Web documents also include links to other documents and resources on the Web and Internet. These links are called *hypertext links*. Furthermore, Web documents are called

FIGURE 3.11

World Wide Web has much to offer, including updated headlines like the ones you can find on the *USA Today* site.

hypertext documents and are created using a document language called *HyperText Markup Language (HTML).*

Understanding Hypertext

Hypertext is a way in which information can be presented so that certain words, pictures, or other items can be linked to more information. A Web page, for example, may present information on the solar system, with each planet linked to additional information. As you read the document about the solar system, you have the option of clicking on one of the planet names, such as Jupiter, to read about it. You then can return to the original article about the solar system, or if a link is included on the Jupiter page, you can click on it. Figure 3.12 shows how this looks graphically.

In Figure 3.12, if you click the word "Jupiter" in the main document, you're shown a page that describes Jupiter in more detail. This is sometimes referred to as *jumping, hyperlinking,* or *following a link.* On that page, you can read the information about Jupiter, return to the previous page, jump to another page that contains information on Jupiter's moons, or maybe jump to an animation about the Galileo space probe.

Text isn't the only item that can be linked to other items. Sometimes you can click pictures or icons to display other documents or larger versions of the picture

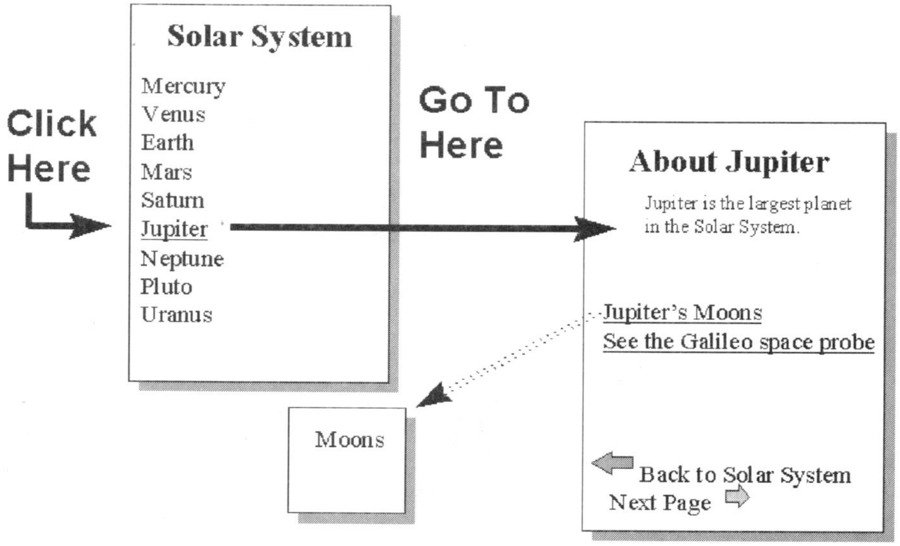

FIGURE 3.12

Hypertext documents let you "jump" from one document to another.

itself. You also may encounter links that enable you to download software or files to your computer.

In a Web document, when text or a graphic is connected to another document, file, or image, it is said to be *linked*. A linked object is denoted on-screen by special highlighting (it's usually underlined in a different color than the surrounding text). By default, most Web browsers highlight the text using a blue font and underline the linked word or phrase. For pictures or other shapes that are linked, browsers sometimes enclose the linked object with a blue rectangle, depending on the way the document was designed. Links are further differentiated by your mouse pointer. When you move the pointer over a link, the standard arrow pointer changes to a hand pointer.

Examining Uniform Resource Locators (URLs)

Each document on the Web has a unique address. These addresses are called *Uniform Resource Locators*, or URL for short. (You may hear them referred to as "Earls" for short.) An URL is an address that specifies where on the Web a specific document is stored. It also specifies the type of Internet service that your Web browser uses to retrieve the document.

An URL consists of a prefix, followed by the name of the computer on which the document is located, then the path and file name of the document. The prefix represents the type of Internet services involved. Table 3.2 lists the URL prefixes for the types of Internet services some browsers can access.

TABLE 3.2 INTERNET SERVICES SUPPORTED BY WEB BROWSERS

URL Prefix	Service	Description
http	World Wide Web	Transfers documents using the Hypertext Transfer Protocol
ftp	File Transfer Protocol	Transfers files using File Transfer Protocol
news	Network News Transfer Protocol	Access newsgroups via NNTP
file	Local hard disk or ftp	Access a local file stored on your hard disk or from an FTP site
telnet	Telnet session	Opens a telnet session to enable you to log into a remote computer.
Mailto	E-mail	Sends e-mail to another user.

TIP

Not all Web browsers support all Internet services, so check the documentation for the browser you use to see what it supports. If your browser does not support a service you want to use, then you need to obtain a separate application that does.

The computers on which Web documents are located are known as *servers*. Each server on the Internet and Web is assigned a unique server name, such as **www.microsoft.com** (the Web server name for the Microsoft Corporation site). The server name becomes part of the URL, along with path names and the name of the document or file.

URLs are like regular postal addresses. Your home, for example, has a unique address that no other home, office, or other entity shares. This enables others to send mail to your address and (for the majority of the time) have the mail end up at your home. Your address is made up of various names and codes that may be shared by other people, but not in the same order or combination as you.

This is true for Internet and Web addresses as well. Your home address, for example, may be the following:

Tom Smith
123 Walnut Street
Dayton, Ohio 12345
USA

Notice how each of the address entities are not unique. 123 Walnut Street may be an address for someone living in Columbus, Ohio for example. But when all the entities are combined in a single address, the entire address *is* unique. Likewise, an URL is made of several items that, when combined in a specific order, direct your browser to locate a specific document or file on the Web. The following is an example of the Web address for the White House:

http://www.whitehouse.gov

In this example, "http" instructs the browser to connect to a Web site. The two slashes (//) indicate that you want to attach to a server. If you want to access a Web document stored on your local hard drive, you would use three slashes (///).

The next section, "www.whitehouse.gov," is the server name—or *domain name*. Because computers communicate in binary language, not English or German or other natural languages, they must use integers as address schemes on the Internet. These are known as *IP addresses* (IP stands for Internet Protocol), and they look something like this:

`164.109.213.7.`

The problem with this is that it makes it difficult for people to remember these numbers (especially if you want to remember several of them for different sites). To get around this, the IP addresses are translated to domain names to make them easier to read, such as **www.whitehouse.com**.

You usually don't need to worry about IP addresses because an automatic service called the *Domain Name System* (DNS for short) on the Internet handles translating domain names to IP addresses and vice versa.

Within the domain name, there's an identifier that lets you know what type of organization owns the server. These are the three-letter abbreviations (such as gov, com, and edu) described in the section, "Understanding E-Mail," earlier in this chapter.

As you can see, the White House address has a gov designation to indicate that it's a government site. Most businesses, such as Ventana or McDonalds, have com designators to indicate they are commercial sites. PBS, which is a not-for-profit business, uses the org designator.

After the server name, URLs sometimes contain more information. Additional information could be the name of a specific path and document or file, and could look like the following:

http://www2.whitehouse.gov/WH/Welcome.html

In this example, the path name includes /WH/Welcome.html. The "/WH/Welcome.html" part denotes the directories or folders in which the document is stored, much like you have directories or folders on your local computer. The document displayed at this address is called Welcome.html, and is shown in Figure 3.13. The extension HTML is the standard extension for Web documents. Depending on the system your using to view the document, this extension may also be HTM.

If you put it altogether, an URL address can be diagrammed much like the one shown in Figure 3.14.

In Chapter 4, you learn how to "surf" the World Wide Web and use Internet tools.

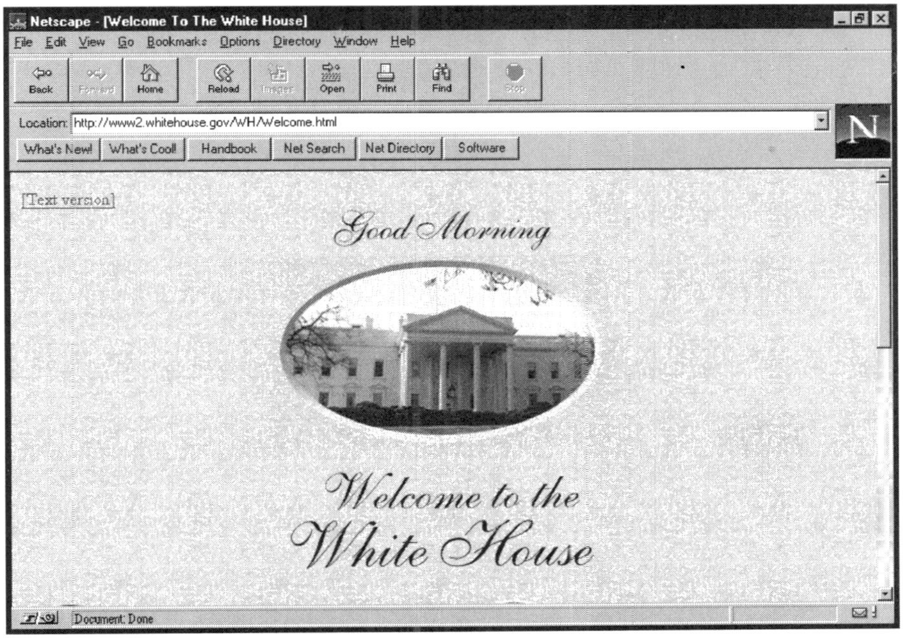

FIGURE 3.13

The White House "Welcome" page on the World Wide Web.

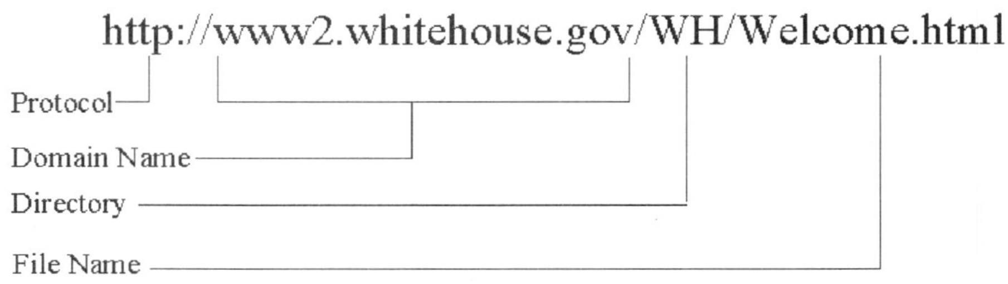

FIGURE 3.14

An URL with its components diagrammed.

What's Next

If you've been following along through the last three chapters, you're probably ready to get your hands dirty and start using the Internet and the Web. The next chapter should satisfy your need to get online and start navigating the rich resources of the Internet. The bulk of Chapter 4 is devoted to installing and using Web browsers (Netscape Navigator and Microsoft Internet Explorer). But you also learn how to use other Internet tools and supporting applications.

4

USING ONLINE TOOLS

In Chapter 3, you got an overview of the Internet and the services available on it. The best way to learn about the Internet, however, is to use it. If you're a little confused by some of the terminology and tools discussed in that chapter, don't worry. Most users are confused by the Internet before they've had a chance to experience it first-hand. Once you get online and tap into everything the Internet offers, many of the services you read about in Chapter 3 will start making sense.

The primary focus of this chapter is to introduce you to the World Wide Web, the fastest growing part of the Internet. You learn how to install and use Netscape Navigator 2.0 as a Web browser to access Web sites and other Internet services, such as e-mail, newsgroups, FTP, and Gopher. You also learn how to use leading Internet tools to access other Internet services while also using Netscape Navigator, such as WS_FTP and Netscape Chat.

Your Maiden Voyage on the Internet

Regardless of how you connect to the Internet—through an ISP, your work, or a commercial online service—you'll quickly learn one thing: You're basically on your own. Unlike the major commercial online services that offer support and guideposts along the way, the Internet (and the Web) is a wide open system that requires you to look for what you want. Until you understand how to navigate, you may feel lost and unable to take the first steps in cyberspace, let alone use it to its fullest.

There are fundamental skills you must learn to feel comfortable using the Internet. These include understanding basic addressing schemes, knowing computer file types and formats, learning searching techniques, and recognizing the type of Internet tool you need. You can use the information in Chapter 3 to help you understand the different Internet services. Use the information in this chapter to help you learn how to use the tools necessary to access those services.

Knowing Where to Start

For most new users to the Internet, using the Web is the best starting point. This is because of the Web's graphical environment and easy to use browsers. As you read in Chapter 3, the primary task of a Web browser is to display documents written in a series of codes called Hypertext Markup Language (HTML). This means HTML is read on Windows machines, as well as Apple Macintosh, IBM OS/2 UNIX, DOS, mainframes (those big computers you see in war games movies), and other systems.

Another reason the Web is great for new users is because of its hypertext features. *Hypertext*, as described in Chapter 3, is a technology that provides links from one document to another document or file. Web documents written in HTML usually contain links for readers to follow to related information, files, or to other places on the Internet. For example, you might find a document containing information on the 1996 Summer Olympic Games in Atlanta (see Figure 4.1). By clicking links found on that page, you can link to related Olympic information (see Figure 4.2).

You travel from one page to another on the Web by linking from other documents, or you can access a site directly by entering the URL of the site. Several resources are available to help users locate addresses of sites on the Web and Internet, including online search tools, print magazines and books, and lists of favorite sites. Many pages on the Web include the author's lists of favorite sites that he or she found interesting or relevant to a discussion. This is how many users find new or exciting information on a topic. For example, you might start at a page discussing art history (see **http://oksw01.okanagan.bc.ca/fiar/home.html**), and wind up reading that in 1969 Canada introduced the breathalizer to test for drunken driving.

Knowing How to Start

If you configured your computer to access the Internet (see Chapter 2), the first place you need to do is install the software to let you navigate the Web. Although

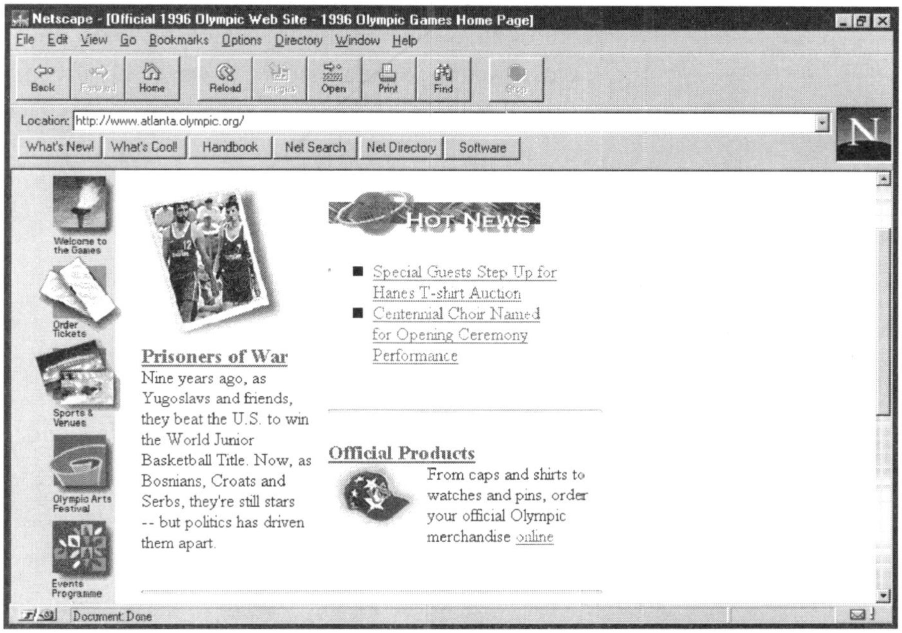

FIGURE 4.1

Web pages contain links that enable you to jump from one source to another.

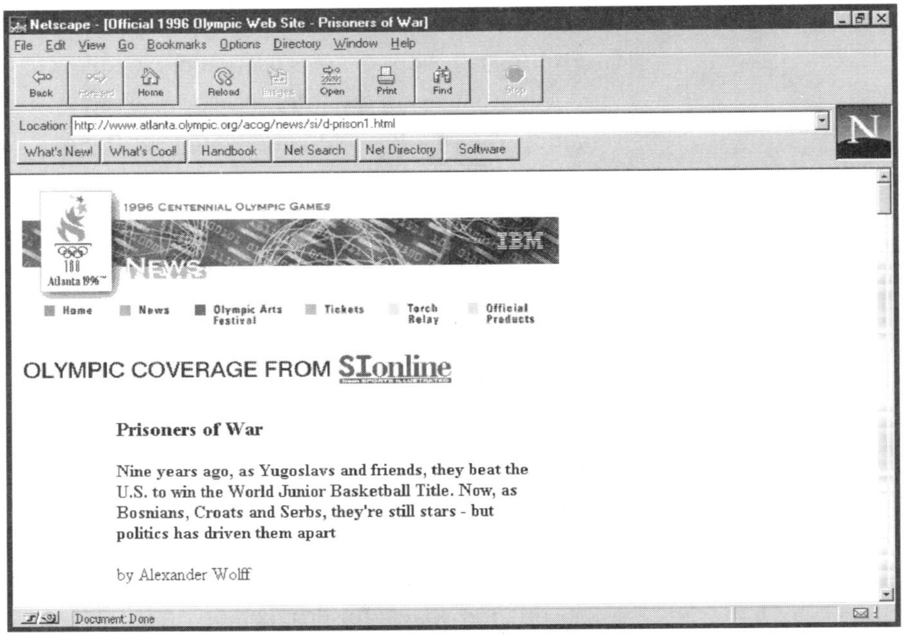

FIGURE 4.2

This page was found by links in the Web page shown in Figure 4.1.

this chapter focuses on Netscape Navigator for Windows 95, you can use the general steps here to install another Web browser, such as Internet Explorer. In fact, according to recent statistics published by Dataquest, approximately 70 to 80 percent of all Web users use Navigator, but most have a second Web browser too. When installing other browsers, however, be sure to read any accompanying documents or help files for specific setup instructions. Overall, most Web browsers are easy to install under Windows 95 or Windows 3.*x*.

Installing Netscape Navigator

The time has come for you to install Navigator and begin your adventure on the Web. Fortunately, installing Navigator is a piece of cake compared to installing and configuring your system for basic Internet access (see Chapter 2). Navigator comes with a standard Windows 95 Setup program that walks you through the installation process and helps you place Navigator on your system.

There are two primary phases to installing Navigator. First, you need to run the Navigator Setup program. Second, you need to configure Navigator to work with your system. For some systems, the second phase isn't necessary or doesn't require a large time investment. The following sections walk you through the Navigator Setup program.

Running Netscape Navigator Setup

To start the Navigator Setup program, make sure you have Windows 95 running and that all other applications are closed, including your Internet connection. Many applications share system files with other applications, so when you have one program running while installing another, you run the risk of these shared files not being updated properly.

Next, you'll need to activate the Setup program by locating it on the Navigator installation disks or by running the program from your hard drive (if you downloaded Navigator from the Netscape Web site). The following steps assume that you're using a floppy disk in drive A: to install Navigator. If your system uses a different drive letter for your floppy disk, substitute that drive when you encounter instructions for drive A:. Follow these steps to install Navigator:

1. Insert the Navigator installation disk 1 in your floppy drive.
2. Click the Start menu and choose Run.
3. In the Run dialog box, type **A:SETUP.EXE** and press Enter.
4. The Netscape Navigator Setup program starts, displaying the Welcome dialog box (see Figure 4.3).
5. Click Next. The Choose Destination Location dialog box displays telling you the folder in which Navigator will be setup (see Figure 4.4).

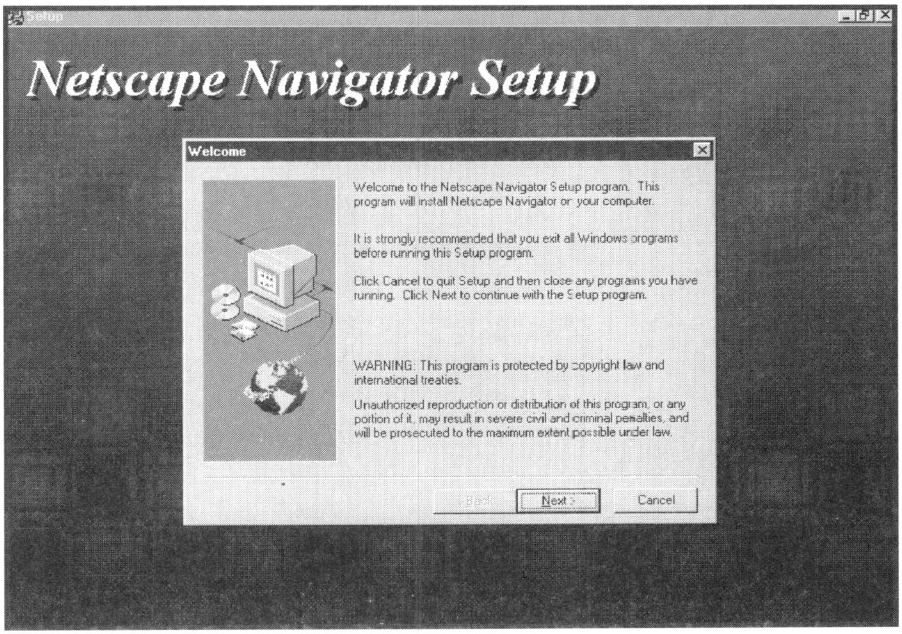

FIGURE 4.3

The opening Netscape Navigator Setup screen.

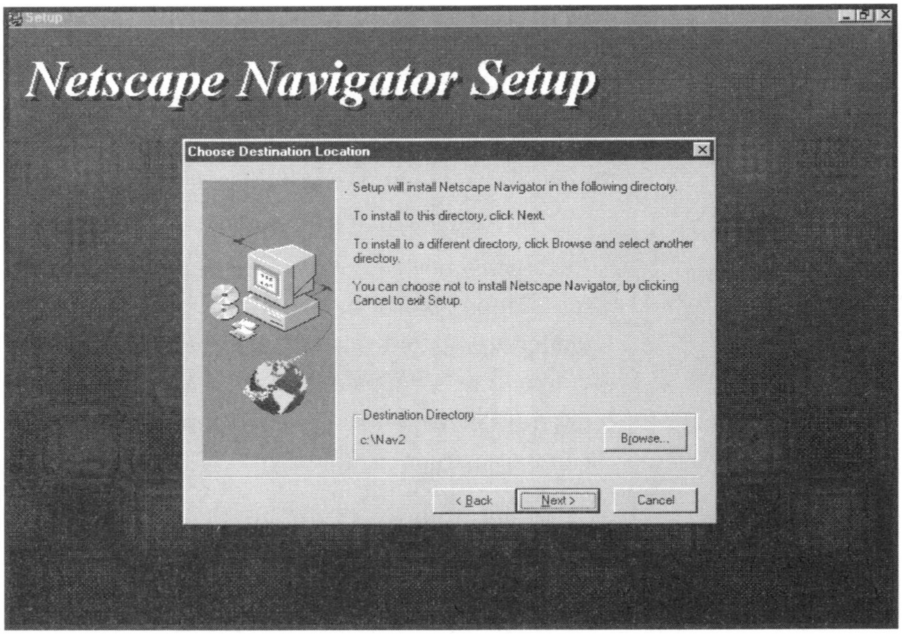

FIGURE 4.4

The Web browser offers a default folder in which to setup Netscape Navigator.

If you want to place Navigator in a different folder, click Browse and enter a new path in the Path text box of the Choose Directory dialog box (see Figure 4.5). Or, you can click the folders in the Directories list to select a directory with your mouse. If you want to install Navigator on a drive other than the C: drive, click the Drives drop-down arrow and select a different drive. Click OK to return to the Choose Destination Location dialog box.

NOTE

You also can choose a mapped network drive (if you're on a network) by clicking the Network button and selecting or entering the appropriate mapped drive.

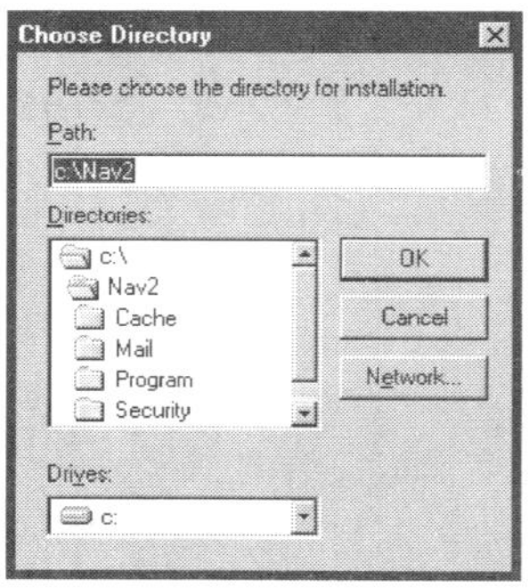

FIGURE 4.5

The Choose Directory dialog box enables you to select a different folder in which to install Navigator.

6. Click Next. The Setup screen appears, showing you the progress of files being set up on your system (see Figure 4.6).
7. When Setup finishes, a screen displays informing you that Navigator is installed and that you can start it by double-clicking its icon in the Netscape folder.
8. Click OK.
9. A screen appears asking if you want to view the Navigator Readme file. For now, click No to continue.

NOTE

The Readme file is a text file that contains important information from the Netscape developers at Netscape Communications. Sometimes you can find critical information for your system in these files. You don't have to read the file now, but remember that it's available in case you experience problems running Navigator later. The Readme file may offer a quick solution to your problem.

You're now back to the Windows 95 desktop. You can start Navigator and begin your online voyage.

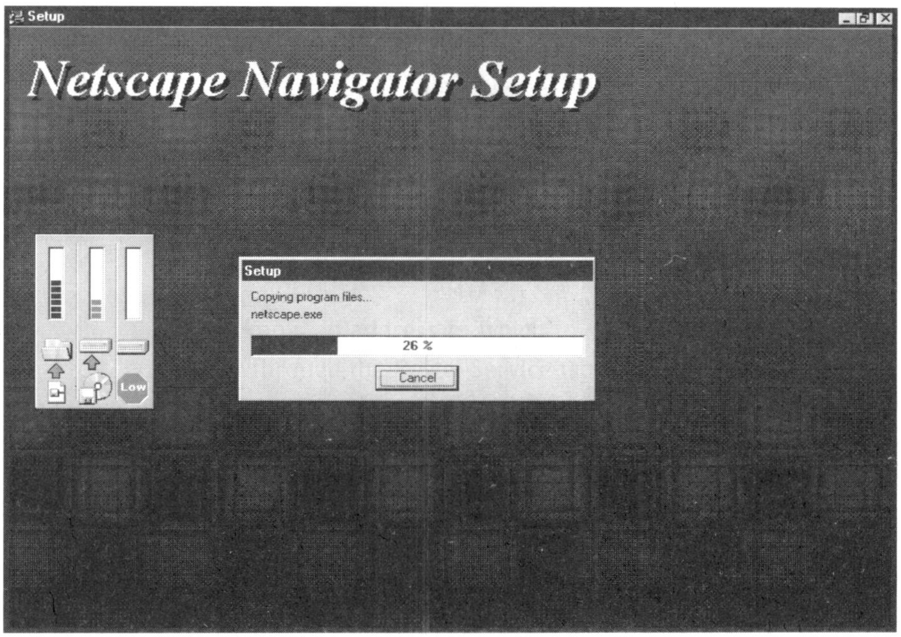

FIGURE 4.6

Netscape Navigator Setup screen showing you the progress of the files being copied to your hard disk.

Testing Your Navigator Connection to the Web

Even if you followed all of the installation steps, you may still encounter some problems when you use Navigator for the first time. Follow these steps to test your Navigator installation and connection to the Web.

1. Double-click the Netscape Navigator icon in the Navigator folder on the Windows 95 desktop (see Figure 4.7). Navigator starts for the first time on your system.

   At launch time, Navigator is designed to connect to the Netscape Communications World Wide Web site. When you start Navigator now, the Netscape Home Page displays. Navigator cannot connect to the Netscape WWW site until you first connect to the Internet with your modem (or other connection, such as a LAN). By default, Navigator knows to display your dial-up program to let you connect to your ISP. This example shows the Dial-Up Networking utility included with Windows 95 (see Figure 4.8). Depending on the dialer software you installed in Chapter 2, your screen may look different.

TIP

You can disable the Internet AutoDial feature by clicking the check box next to Don't Use Internet AutoDial On The

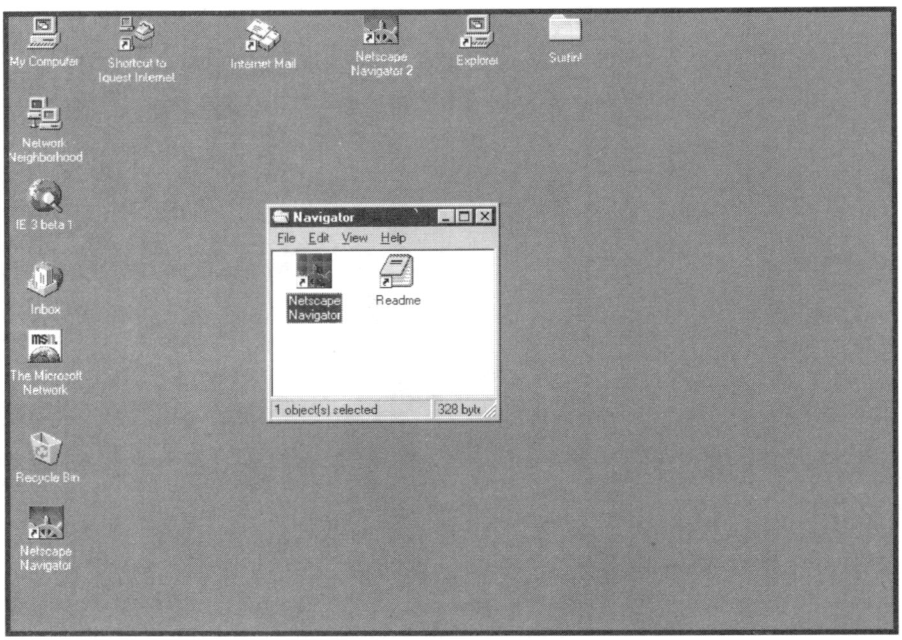

FIGURE 4.7

The Netscape Navigator folder contains an application shortcut you double-click on to launch Navigator.

FIGURE 4.8

By default, Navigator tries to connect to the Netscape Communications Home Page at start up. It will display your dial-up software automatically if you are not currently online.

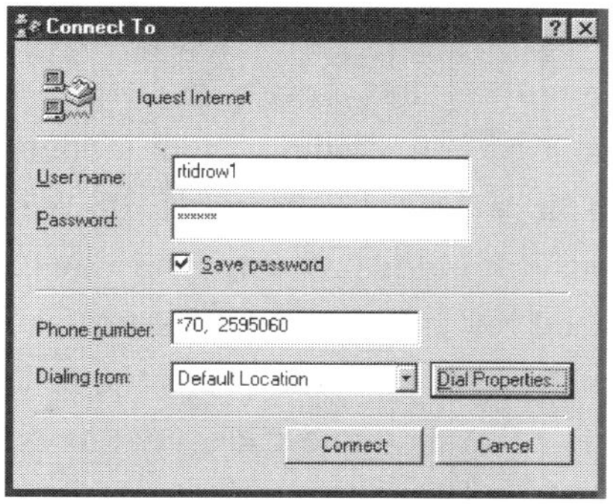

Internet AutoDial Dialog Box. You then can start Navigator without displaying this dialog box.

◆ ◆

2. Click OK and then click the Connect button on the Connect To dialog box to establish a connection to the Internet. Once connected, Navigator takes over and continues connecting to the Netscape Web site. (You'll learn about Web sites, Web documents, basic navigational skills, and more later in this chapter. For now, just make sure you can connect to the Netscape site.)

Troubleshooting Installation and Configuration Problems

Regardless of how well you followed the steps in the previous section, you may encounter some problems when you use your Internet connection. The problem may be a typographical error, a missing piece of information, or a problem with your particular setup working with your ISP or online service. Unfortunately, there's never just one answer that corrects all possible problems. For example, you may receive an error because the DNS number is wrong. You may receive the exact same error if your modem isn't turned on and you attempt to connect to an online Web site.

The following section should help you pinpoint some problems you may encounter using Windows 95 and an ISP connection.

Getting Network Protocol Errors

You may launch the Windows 95 Dial-Up Networking icon to dial your ISP and get an error message telling you that it cannot resolve an appropriate network protocol.

There are a few ways to correct this error. Clear the error message and try connecting again using the same process as before. Sometimes Windows 95 has difficulty establishing a connection to your modem. If this doesn't work, check to make sure you modem is set up to work with Windows 95 and that it's turned on. If your modem is working properly, you may have to check the IP information you've entered on the TCP/IP Properties sheet (see Chapter 2 for more information). To check those settings use the following steps. Open the Windows 95 Control Panel and double-click the Network icon. On the Configuration tab, click the TCP/IP Dial-Up Adapter setting and click the Properties button. On the DNS Configuration tab of the TCP/IP Properties page, make sure you selected the Enable DNS radio button and that you filled out the Host, Domain, and DNS Server Search Order areas according to the information you obtained from your ISP or network administrator.

Receiving DNS Errors

Another error you may receive is a DNS error. After connecting with your ISP and starting Navigator, you may receive the following error when you attempt to connect to a Web page:

```
Netscape is unable to locate the server:

www.examplepage.com

The server does not have a DNS entry...
```

This means that a few things may be wrong:

1. Double-check the address for the WWW site (the URL) you typed. Make sure it's exactly right or you'll encounter this error.
2. The site may be busy or may require specific authorization (such as a password or ID number). Start deleting segments from the end of the URL and try accessing the site again For example, if you are trying to access http://www.microsoft.com/windows/, remove the "windows/" part and try again. Sometimes specific documents on a site are not available, but the main home page is.
3. The site may have moved locations or shut down.
4. You've lost connection to your ISP and you didn't know. Check the open Dial-Up Network connection to see if your connection is still live. If not, reconnect.

   You may not have your IP addresses set up properly in the network connection areas. In the TCP/IP Settings dialog box, make sure the IP addresses are entered correctly. You may need to call your ISP technical support line to reconfirm your IP address.

You also may receive a DNS error if the Netscape Communications home page is too busy or if it's down for repairs or updates. Web sites often need to go offline because the Web site administrator (the person who maintains the Web site) needs to add new content, reorganize existing content, update the Home Page, or perform system-level duties (such as updating hardware or software). Another reason Web sites are offline is that they've been discontinued by that company or organization.

If you see a screen similar to the one shown in Figure 4.9, you have successfully installed your Internet software and set up Navigator on Windows 95. If you don't see that page, or if you encounter an error like the one shown in Figure 4.10, you may have a problem with your Internet configuration. See the next section on how to troubleshoot common installation problems. If everything seems fine, skip ahead to the "Using Your Web Browser" section.

Using Your Web Browser

You are now more than ready to launch Navigator and begin your online Web journey. This section shows you how to start Navigator (in case you haven't yet), how to enter URLs to locate specific sites, and how to use some of the Navigator utilities.

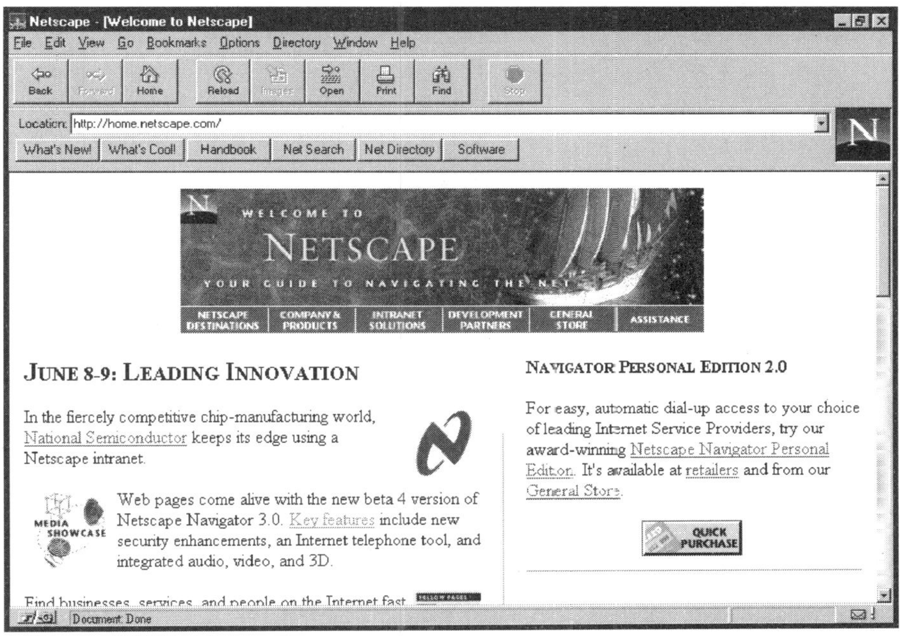

FIGURE 4.9

Connecting to the Netscape Communications Home Page is a welcome sign after configuring Windows 95 to access the Internet.

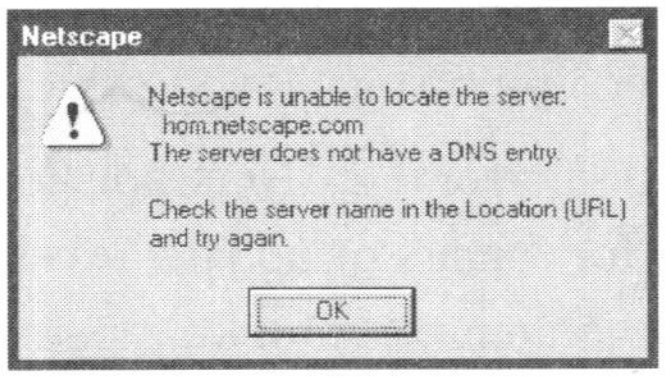

FIGURE 4.10

This error message is a common one when the IP address wasn't entered correctly.

If you don't have a live connection to the Internet right now, establish one by using the steps shown in the previous section, "Testing Your Navigator Connection to the Web". If you've already logged onto the Internet, start your Web browser.

The first time you start Navigator, you'll see the Netscape Navigator License Agreement dialog box. Choose Accept to agree to the terms specified in this document. If you choose the Do Not Accept button, Navigator won't start.

After you click the Accept button, Navigator starts and automatically displays the home page for Netscape Communications (refer to Figure 4.9). If you're new to the Web, this may be the first Web page you've seen—other than the ones shown in this book.

If you don't see the same page as the one shown in Figure 4.9, this can mean a couple of things:

- You may have configured Navigator to load a different starting page upon execution. (You learn how to do this later in this chapter in the section, "Going Home.")
- If you have another Web browser, you'll start at a different Web page. Usually, this first Web page is designed to help you find more information about the browser's company, additional sites to link to, our help on navigating the Web. Figures 4.11 through 4.13 show examples of different browsers and the pages displayed by them.

Moving from Document to Document

The Netscape Communications Home Page (like many other Web pages) includes information, pictures, and links to other sources. As you read earlier, you can click these links to move to another Web page or to download a picture or listen to a sound clip. Links are usually shown underlined and in blue text (the color of the link can vary). After you click a link, the link color changes to indicate you already visited that specific site. This way, you know which link you followed in case a page contains multiple links and you forget which link(s) you clicked.

For now, click a link on the Netscape Home Page to get a feel for how Navigator works. In the Netscape Home Page , you can click the Personal Workspace link,

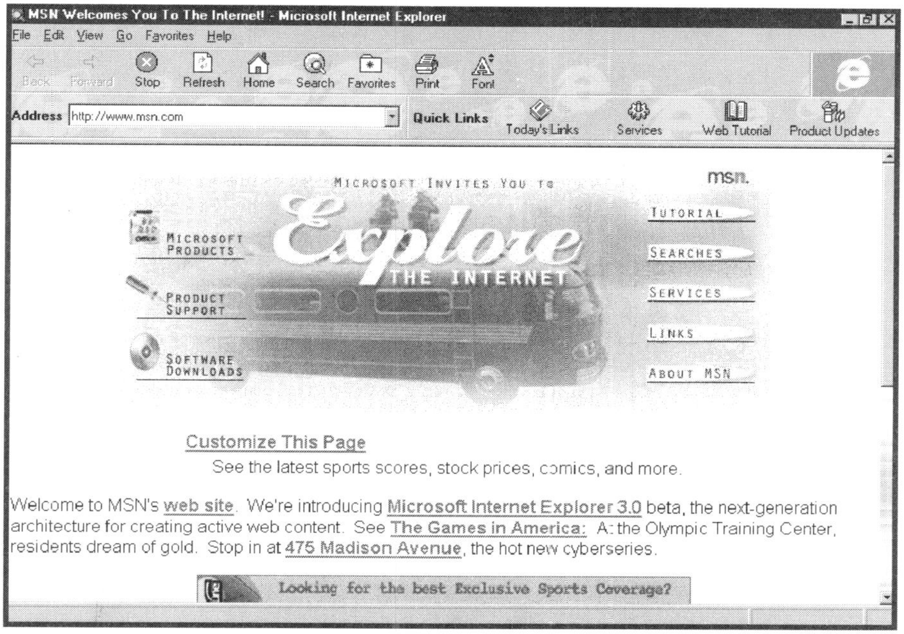

FIGURE 4.11

This is the starting page you'll see if you use Microsoft Internet Explorer 3.0.

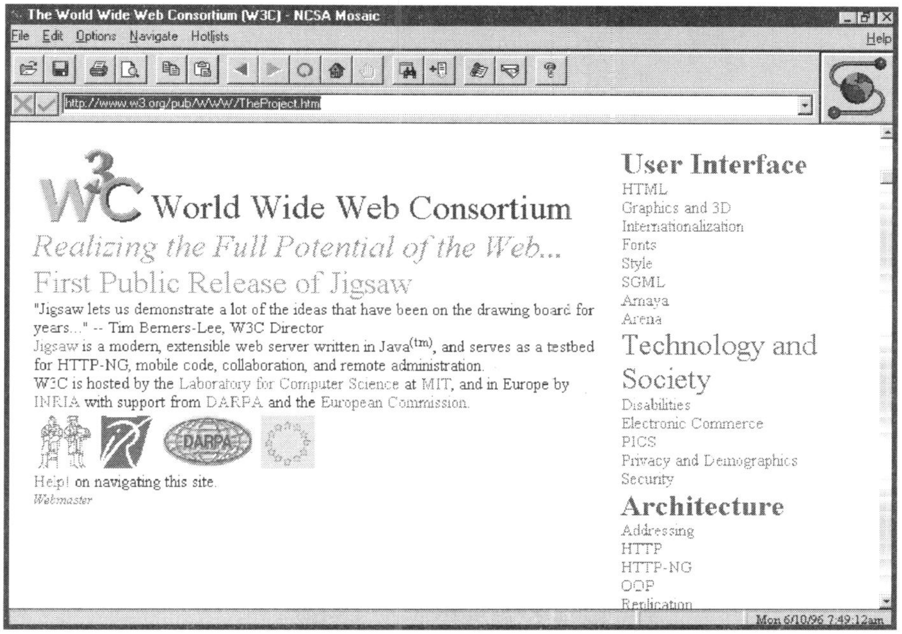

FIGURE 4.12

This is NCSA Mosaic 2.0's Home Page.

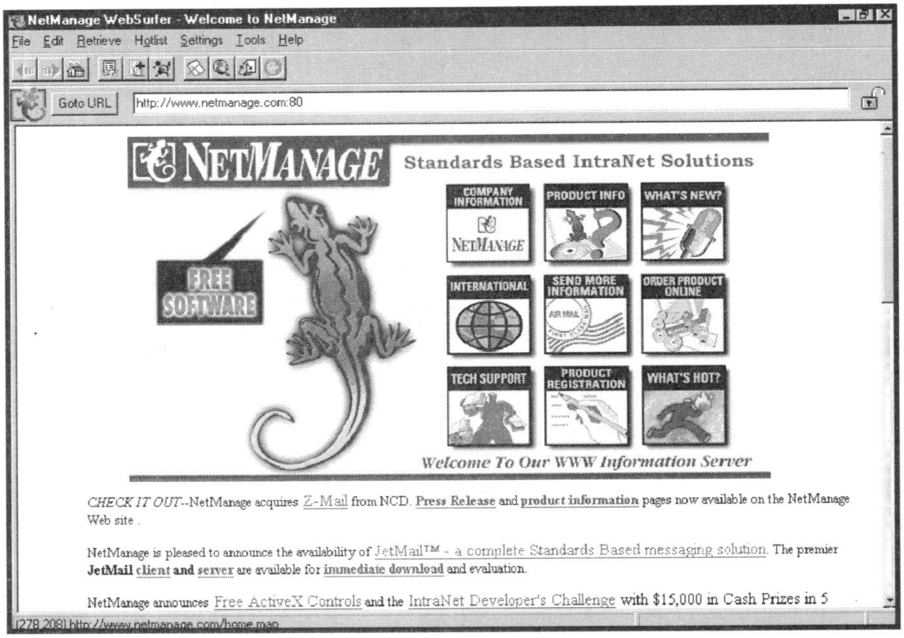

FIGURE 4.13

This is the starting page if you are using NetManage's WebSurfer browser.

which appears toward the bottom of the page. You may not see the same link on your display. This is because Netscape Communications has modified their Web page with updated or new information. If this is the case, simply find another link on the page and click it.

When you click a link, another Web page displays that shows you new information or offers you links to other sites, graphics, or similar links. If you click the Exploring the Net link found at the bottom of the page, for example, you see a new page called What's New? (see Figure 4.14). You're still at the Netscape Communications Web site—just on a different page. This is similar to turning a page in a book. With Navigator you flip through Web pages set up at the Netscape Communications site.

NOTE

The term home page is thrown around as loosely as the term Information Superhighway. Many people call any Web page a home page. This isn't technically correct. Home page *generally has three meanings.*

- *A home page can be the first page of a site, analogous to the front door to a store or business.*

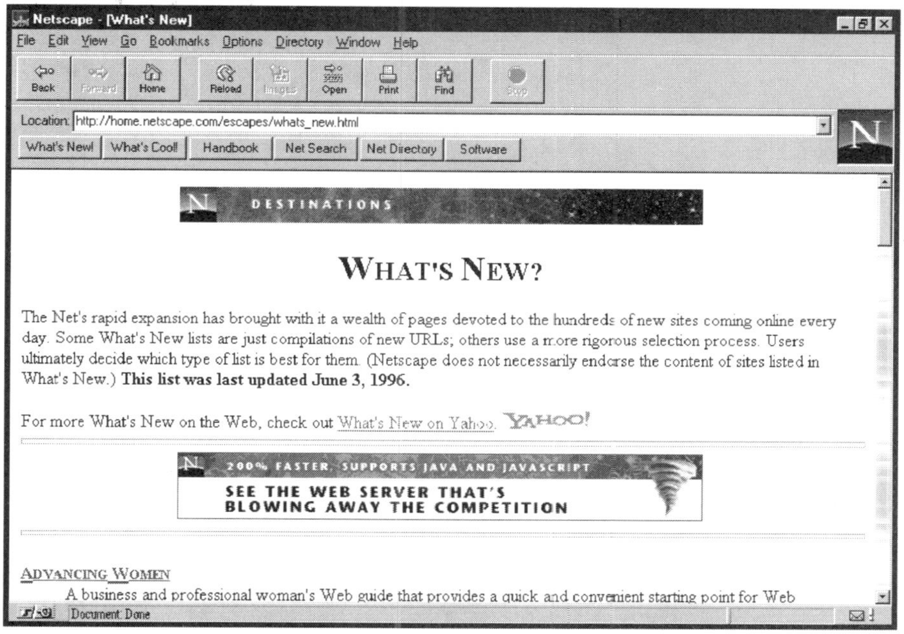

FIGURE 4.14

The What's New? page on the Netscape Communications Web site.

- *It can be the page you specify as the default page to load when you start your browser.*
- *A home page can be a personal Web page that you create. Typically, these pages can contain your favorite links, perhaps a few pithy statements about life or some other topic, and a copy of your resume.*

Now click the Back button on the Navigator toolbar (or choose Go, Back) to return to the preceding page. This is a useful tool when you want to return to a previous page you just visited. You can click the Back button to display all the pages you visited in the current session. For example, if you've viewed two pages, you can back up only once. When the Back button is dimmed or the Back command isn't available on the Go menu, you're out of pages to back up to.

You can also use the Forward button (or choose Go, Forward) to navigate between documents. The Forward button returns you to the page you just backed from. If you decide to return to the page you just left, click the Forward button.

There are also Back and Forward options on the context menu in Windows 95. You can see the context menu by right-clicking a Web document (see Figure 4.15). You can then choose either Back or Forward.

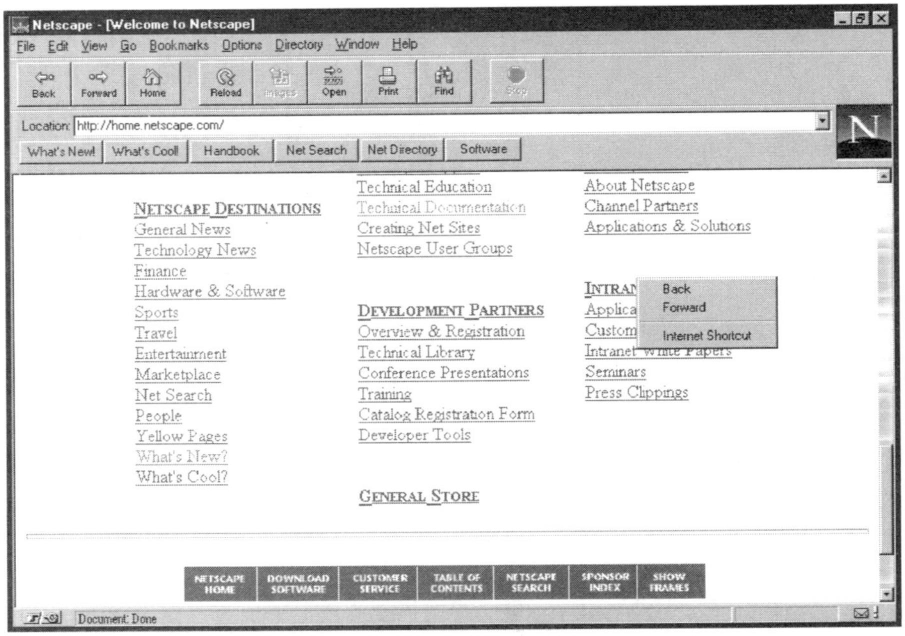

FIGURE 4.15

The context menu in Windows 95 offers the Back and Forward commands to help you quickly navigate to Web pages you visited recently.

Another type of link you'll encounter is graphical in nature. These are pictures on a page that link to other documents, sites, or files. If a picture has a link, you can click it and a new page or picture displays. Not all pictures are linked, however. Many linked pictures show a blue box around them to indicate that they're linked, but some pictures don't. The choice to have graphical links is up to the author of the Web page. To tell if a graphic is linked, move your mouse pointer over the image. If the pointer changes to a pointing hand, then the image is linked; otherwise, the image is simply used as decoration for the page.

You've already seen how hypertext links work to take you to another part of a Web site, or to another Web site altogether. Regardless of where you end up, the links contain vital information that your Web browser uses to determine where to go. This information is in the form of an URL reference. (You learned what an URL is in Chapter 2.)

The URL is one part of a link. The other part is called an *anchor*. Anchors are what you see on screen and give you clues to other links. The anchor can be a word, phrase, or a picture. You've already seen how a text anchor works. Text anchors are colored (usually in blue), so users can easily discern that it's a hyperlink. Sometimes the text anchor says something like "Click here for more information." Other times the text anchor is part of a sentence that has terms, ideas, or other words that are linked to another page or resource.

TIP

A quick way to see an URL that is associated with a link is to run your mouse pointer over the link. When you do this, the URL appears in the status bar of the browser.

When text anchors are part of the text and are not set apart from the main body of text, they're referred to as *embedded anchors*. Text anchors also can be set apart from text into bulleted lists or tables. This allows the user to quickly see all the possible links for an associated topic. On many Web pages, you'll see both embedded anchors and anchors that are not embedded. They function the same way.

Using URLs to Move from Page to Page

If a Web page doesn't include links to other sites, you aren't stuck at that site. Navigator enables you to go directly to another site by entering the address (URL) of that site.

As you learned in Chapter 2, an URL (Uniform Resource Locator—pronounced "earl") is a standard addressing scheme used by all documents and files on the Web. The URL for the Netscape Communications Home Page, for example, is **http://home.netscape.com**. You can see the URL of the site you're visiting in the Location list box of the Navigator window (see Figure 4.16). You can also use the Location list box as a way to move directly to other sites.

TIP

If the Location list box isn't visible on your screen, you can show it by choosing Options, Show Location from the Navigator menu bar.

To use the Location list box to move from one document to another, follow these steps:

1. Click the Location list box. This highlights the entire URL that is currently displayed there.
2. Type the entire URL of the site you want to visit, and press Enter. You may notice that the word "Location" changes to "Go to:" when you enter an URL in the list box. This label changes back to "Location" when you press Enter to download the new page.

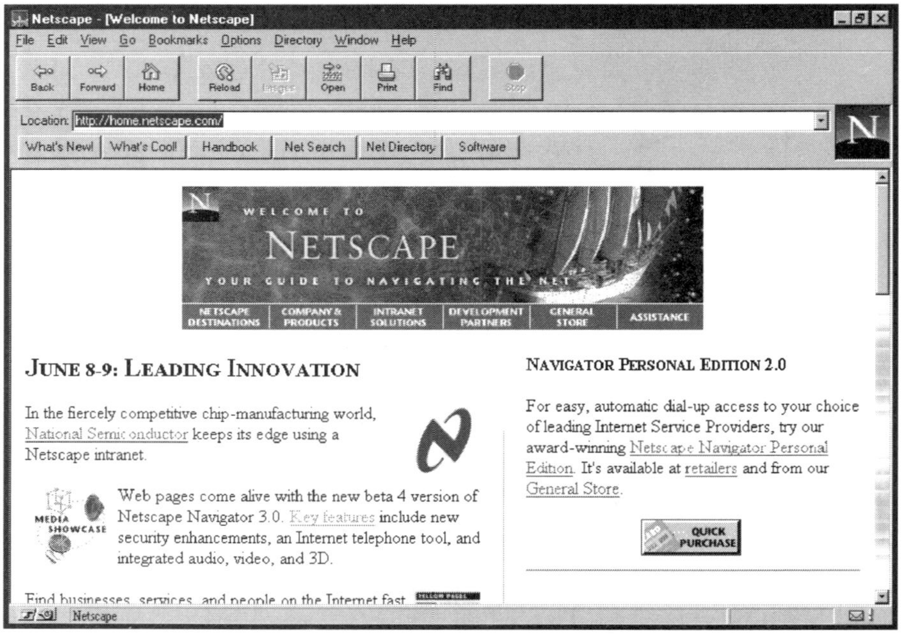

FIGURE 4.16

The Location list box shows the URL of the current Web page and lets you type in an URL to move to a different page.

Try entering the following URLS in the Location list box to get some practice using URLs. More than one site is provided in case a particular site isn't responding when you perform this exercise.

http://www.senate.gov (U.S. Senate Home Page)

http://www.crayola.com (Crayola Crayon Home Page)

http://www.microsoft.com (Microsoft's Home Page)

http://www.dilbert.com (Dilbert cartoon Home Page)

http://www.process.com/win95/win95tip.htm (Windows 95 tip site)

http://www.usps.gov/nscs/aq-zip.html (U.S. Postal Service Zip Code lookup page)

http://www.internet.net (Internet Shopping Network)

http://www.monopoly.com (Home page for the game Monopoly)

http://www.disney.com (Walt Disney home page)

http://www.webcom.com/~law/ufo (Beyond the UFO Conspiracy Home Page)

NOTE

All of the URLs in the previous list are Web documents. You can tell this by looking at the first part of the URL, in this case http. HTTP stands for the Hypertext Transport Protocol, which is the main "roadway" for the Web. In many browsers, you aren't limited to accessing just Web documents. You can access Gopher, FTP, Telnet, and other Internet sites by using that service's protocol in place of http. To access an FTP site, such as the Microsoft FTP site, enter **ftp://ftp.microsoft.com**.

You can watch the page's download progression by looking at the Progress bar at the far-right bottom of the Navigator screen. The Progress bar is a light gray bar that grows as more of the Web document is downloaded. When the full page is displayed, the Progress bar disappears from your screen. (If you're using NCSA Mosaic 2.0, the words "NSCA MOSAIC" are filled in inside the status bar.)

If you don't want to display the Location list box, but still want to enter an URL for a site, choose File, Open Location. The Open Location dialog box appears. Enter the complete URL you want to visit and press Enter or click OK.

The Location list box includes another feature you can use. By clicking the drop-down arrow of the Location list box, you can see the ten most recent locations you entered in the Location list box. These are *not* the last twenty sites you have visited; they're the URLs you actually typed in.

To use this drop-down list, follow these steps:

1. Click the drop-down arrow of the Location list box to display the list of recently visited sites (see Figure 4.17). Your list may be blank if you haven't entered an URL yet.
2. Click the URL of the site you want to access. As soon as you click the URL, Navigator automatically starts connecting to that site.

The URLs that appear in the Location drop-down list carry over to your next Navigator session—even if you exit Navigator and shut down Windows.

Using the History List

As you've just seen with the Location drop-down list, Navigator saves a limited number of previously entered sites. The only problem with this list is that it's limited to those URLs you type in. What about those sites you link to from another page? They're saved in the History list, found at the bottom of the Go menu (see Figure 4.18). You can also access this list from the History window by choosing Window, History.

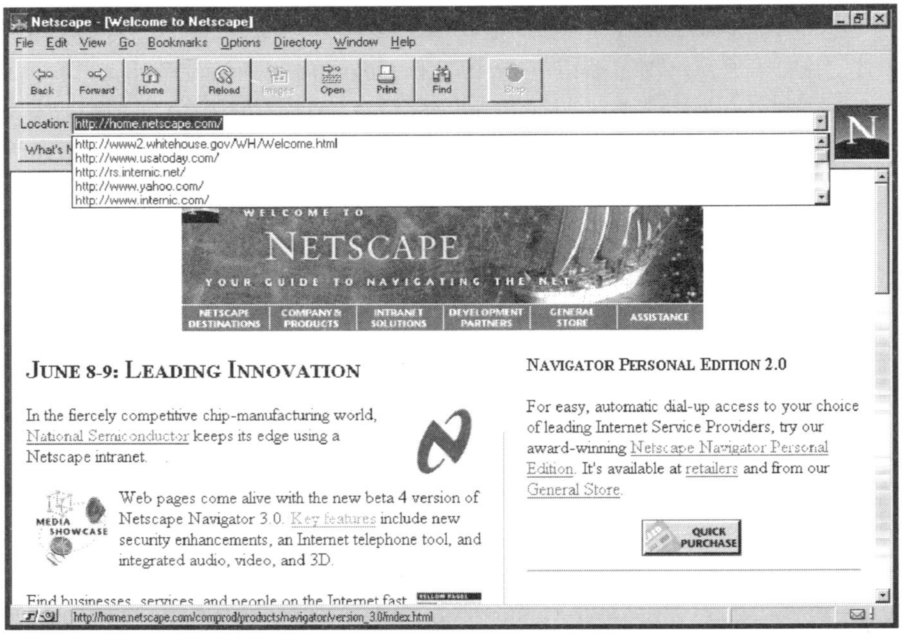

FIGURE 4.17

The Location drop-down list shows the recent URLs you have visited.

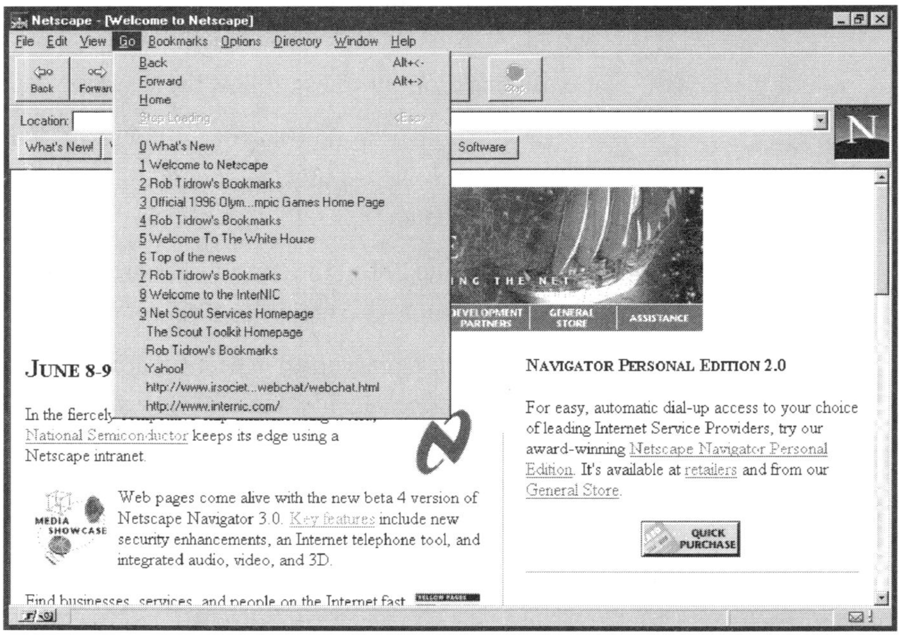

FIGURE 4.18

Use the History list to return to a page you visited earlier in your session.

The History list shows you the pages you have accessed during your current session. These are references to the pages you have downloaded, and they reflect those pages that are in a *lineage*. For example, if you link to three pages—Solar System, Jupiter, and Mars—all three of these pages appear in the History list. If you then select a link to the Solar System page (which contains the links to Jupiter and Mars), the History list changes to show only the Solar System link. This is because the Jupiter and Mars links were linked to from an earlier lineage (Solar System).

Unlike the Location drop-down list that shows only URLs in its list, the History list displays the actual names of the pages. This makes it easier to know which site is which when you want to return to a page. Another difference between the History list and the Location drop-down list is that when you exit from Navigator, the History list is erased.

TIP

Use the History list to quickly jump back to a site you've recently visited. This is less time consuming than repeatedly using the Back button to find that site.

To return to a site from the History list on the Go menu, simply click the item. Navigator automatically returns to the page. A check mark next to a Web page name indicates the page currently displayed in Navigator.

To use the History list from the History window, choose Window, History (see Figure 4.19). From this window, you can see the name of the page and the URL. You can double-click one of the sites in the list to return to that page, or highlight the site and click the Go To button. After you finish with the History window, click the Close button to close it.

NOTE

When you have the History window displayed, you can click the Create Bookmark button to save a selected page to Navigator's Bookmark list. This enables you to return to that Web document during a later session, as well as organize the page reference in the Bookmark list.

Stopping Pages during Downloading

In the middle of downloading a Web page, you might decide you don't want to view it after all. Maybe you entered the wrong URL, or you clicked the wrong

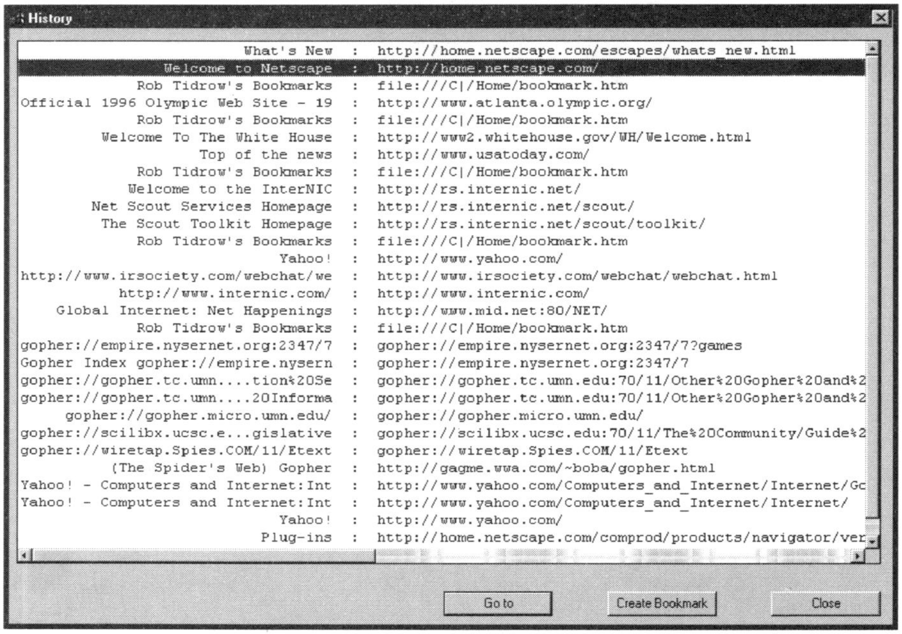

FIGURE 4.19

You can use the History list in the History window to return to recently visited sites.

hyperlink on a page, or maybe you just grow impatient while waiting for a large document or graphic to download.

In Navigator, you can stop a download in progress by clicking the Stop button on the toolbar. You can also choose Go, Stop Loading, or press the Esc key. The download is immediately halted, and you see only the part of the page that has been received to that point. The way the display looks at this point varies depending on how much information has been sent to your computer. You might even see a blank screen if nothing has been received so far.

What you do next is up to you. You can interact with the information displayed, such as clicking a hyperlink if one is displayed. You can return to a previous page by using the Back button or History list. You can change your mind again and continue downloading the current page.

If want to continue downloading, click the Reload button or choose View, Reload. This restarts the download. However, because some of the data already was received by your system, Navigator doesn't need to download the parts already displayed. Your screen will refresh the material already displayed and proceed to display the remainder of the Web page.

Reloading and Refreshing a Web Page

As you've just seen, the Reload command comes in handy when you've interrupted a download and want to finish retrieving the page. You can also use the

Reload button when you want to grab a fresh version of the page you're viewing from the Web site. Items like graphics, forms, and other features may require that you continually receive updated information from it while you visit the site.

You can also choose View, Refresh to refresh your copy of a Web page. The Refresh command, however, reloads the current document from your local hard disk—not from the Web server. When a Web document downloads, Navigator (and most other Web browsers) places a copy of it in your computer's memory and on your hard disk. This is known as *caching* (pronounced "cash-ing"). When you choose the Refresh command, Navigator looks in the cache and pulls out that version of the Web page. This means that every HTML document and image file (usually in GIF or JPEG format) you see on a Web page is being stored on your hard drive.

The main reason Navigator caches documents and files is speed. Caching uses the speed of your computer and its RAM to increase the speed with which a document can reload into Navigator. The speed with which Navigator can access a Web page from your hard disk is much faster than downloading the same page from the Web using a modem or other connection. You pay a price for this caching in terms of memory and disk space, but when connecting to the Web with low-speed modems it's well worth the price.

Each time you return to a Web site, the page is reloaded into Navigator using the cached images and text from your system, which speeds up the time it takes for the Web page to display on screen. Because the Web is dynamic and changes often, you can set Navigator to check a Web page for any changes since the last time you visited it, making sure you are always viewing the most recent document.

Configuring Cache Sizes

Navigator includes an option that enables you to control the amount of memory and hard disk you want to dedicate to a cache. When you visit a Web site, information from that site is stored in both the memory cache and the hard disk cache. When an item is in the memory cache, Navigator can access it more quickly than an item stored on the hard disk. Items stored in the memory cache are temporary and are emptied automatically during a Navigator session when the memory cache limit is full or when you exit Navigator. The hard disk cache, on the other hand, stores the information after you quit a Navigator session. The next time you start Navigator, the information in the disk cache is available.

NOTE

Even before you set the values of your hard disk and memory cache settings, you should think about how each setting affects your system. There are some advantages and disadvantages of large cache values. Even though memory caches are much quicker than disk caches, devoting more RAM to this type of cache can slow your computer's overall speed. If you plan to run Navigator with other programs, you need to make sure you have ample RAM to run all your applications. Usually, having 16MB of RAM with a Pentium processor is enough memory to run Windows, Navigator, a word processor, and a few other small applications without experiencing too much of a performance hit. As you go below 12MB, however, you may consider running Netscape and only one other application to achieve adequate speeds on your machine.

Also, large hard disk cache settings eat up your hard disk space very quickly. It's not uncommon to fill 5MB of disk space very quickly each time you surf the Web. Simple math tells you that after five or six Navigator sessions, your hard drive is getting full of cached Web pages and images.

Navigator enables you to specify the amount of memory and hard disk space it uses for caching. Use the following steps to specify these cache sizes and set other options related to cache:

1. Choose Options, Network Preferences. The Preferences property sheet appears. Click the Cache tab (see Figure 4.20).
2. Enter the size of the memory cache in the Memory Cache text box. The default setting is 600KB of RAM (about .5MB of memory). Unless you have a large amount of memory on your system (16MB or more), you may want to keep this setting where it is. Otherwise, you can try setting it at 1,024KB to see if your browsing speeds increase.

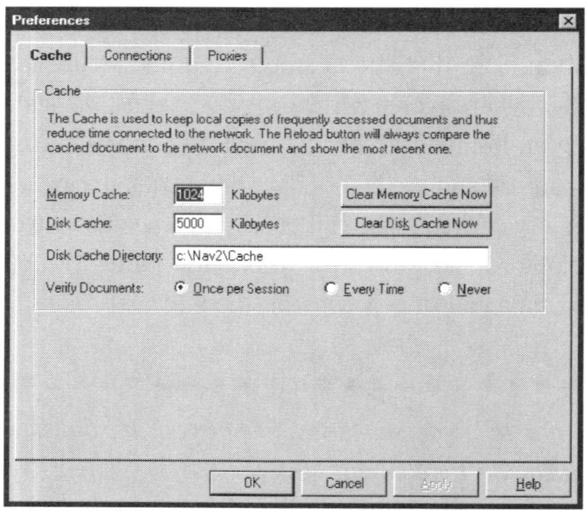

FIGURE 4.20

The Cache tab is used to manage the amount of hard drive space and memory you allocate for caching.

3. Enter the amount of hard disk space you want to reserve for a disk cache in the Disk Cache text box. The default setting is 5,000KB (5MB) of hard disk space. On most newer computers that come with hard disks of 450MB or more, you shouldn't have a problem reserving 5MB or even 10MB for this cache.

TIP

Experiment with the sizes of both the memory cache and the hard disk cache to determine the best settings for your system. If you tend to use Navigator without other applications running at the same time, you can set the memory cache much higher to make Navigator run quicker. If you tend to run Navigator with other applications that need large amounts of memory, keep the memory cache low, around 600KB. This ensures that each application will have ample RAM to run properly.

4. Enter the directory or folder in which Navigator stores the cached items in the Disk Cache Directory text box. By default, Navigator creates the CACHE folder in the Netscape Navigator folder during installation. For example, if you store Navigator in a folder called NAV, this setting will appear as C:NAVCACHE. You can change this to another directory if you want, but you should have no problems if you leave it alone.

5. To clear the current content from your disk or memory caches, click Clear Memory Cache Now or Clear Disk Cache Now. When you click either of these buttons, Netscape asks if you're sure you want to clear the selected cache (see Figure 4.21). Click OK to confirm that you do; click Cancel if you change your mind.

   Depending on how much navigating you do or how often you visit a site, you may want to periodically clear a cache setting. Having a memory cache decreases the time it takes to access sites that you've recently visited, but it does increase the strain on your local computer. When your memory

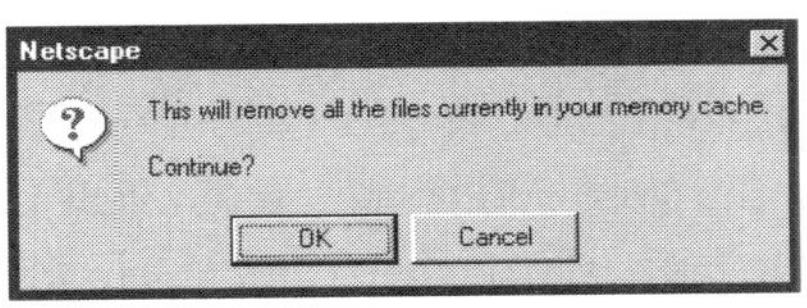

FIGURE 4.21

This message asks if you are sure if you want to clear your memory cache now.

cache is set to a high value, the amount of memory devoted to Navigator cannot be used by other resources when Navigator is running. This slows down your machine when you run these other applications. Also, you may want to clear the memory cache if you've been online for several hours and you feel your machine responding sluggishly. After you clear the cache, you should notice an improvement in your computer's performance.

6. Click one of the radio buttons in the Verify Documents section. If a document is revised that has been stored in cache, you'll want to see the revised document rather than the old document previously stored in cache. These buttons specify how Navigator checks the Web for document revisions:

   - **Once Per Session.** Checks for page revisions only once during the time you start and quit Navigator. This is the default setting.
   - **Every Time.** Repeatedly checks for changes when you request a Web page. Because Navigator is constantly checking the cached item against the Web page, you encounter a little performance degradation when you use this option.
   - **Never.** Performs no verifications; a page available in cache is always brought from cache. Not a good selection if you want to see the latest offerings on a Web site.

7. Click OK to return to Navigator.

TIP

You can also clear the disk cache by manually deleting the files in the Cache folder. To do this in Windows 95, use the Explorer; to do this in Windows 3.x, use File Manager. Don't delete the file named FAT.DB or you may experience problems using Navigator the next time you run it. You can delete any other files that appear in that folder, including those with HTM, GIF, and JPG extensions.

Going Home

Most of us feel the safest in the comfort of our own home. This is true even when you're navigating the Web. When you feel overwhelmed or a little lost while navigating, you can go back to where you started by clicking the Home button (or choosing Go, Home). This takes you to your home page. Unless you change the default, this page is the Netscape Communications Home Page that you saw when you first launched Navigator.

For this short discussion (but not for this entire chapter), *home page* means the page you specify as the default page to load when you start your browser. You may decide that you want a home page that's suited to your interests or job. You can use an URL of an existing Web page; or you can create a simple page to keep on your local hard drive and add links to it as you find more interesting sites during your navigation sessions.

To create a document that can serve as your home page, you need to learn how to create HTML documents. Although it is a fairly simple language to learn, HTML is not discussed in this book.

For now, learn how to use another Web page as your home page. The following steps show you how to change your home page in Navigator:

1. Choose Options, General Preferences. The Preferences property sheet appears.
2. Click the Appearance tab (see Figure 4.22).
3. Click the Home Page Location radio button and enter the URL of the home page of your choice in the Start With text box. The following Web sites can serve as nice home pages for new users to the Web:

   http://home.netscape.com/home/internet-search.html
   (Netscape's Net Search page)

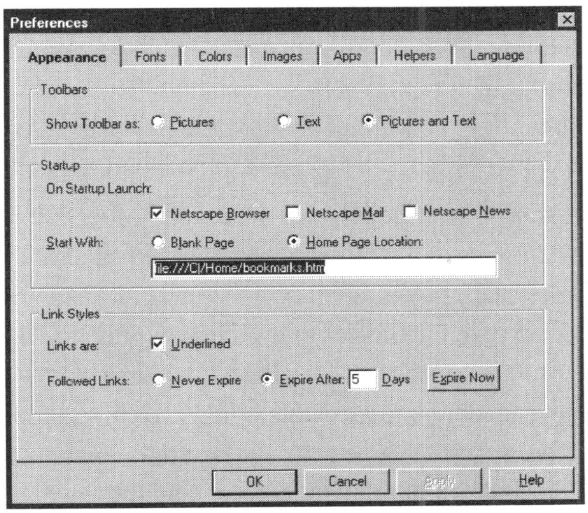

FIGURE 4.22

You can change the home page in Navigator using this property sheet.

http://home.netscape.com/home/internet-directory.html (Netscape's Net Directory page)

http://www.yahoo.com (*Yahoo* is a comprehensive directory of Internet and Web sites)

http://www.altavista.digital.com/ (Digital Equipment's search page)

TIP

If you don't want an opening page when you start Navigator, click the Blank Page radio button. A blank window will appears when you launch Navigator.

4. Click OK to save your changes.

Now when you start Navigator or click the Home button, the home page that you entered appears.

Using Bookmarks in Netscape Navigator

Not surprisingly, you'll find yourself moving back and forth among many documents on the Web. You'll often find a Web page that contains a wealth of links associated with topics that interest you, and you'll want to return to that page many times during a session. You can add a permanent reference to that page so you can quickly find it the next time you start a session. These references are called *bookmarks.*

Bookmarks in Navigator are the electronic equivalent of the 'dog-ear' or bookmark you use to mark your place in a textbook or novel. They enable you to jump straight to that Web site. Without bookmarks, you would need to enter an URL to sites you weren't able to locate from link. As you've seen, some URLs can get very long and cumbersome to type and remember.

Bookmarks are really URLs (and some other information about the site) that Navigator saves in a list on your computer's hard drive in an HTML file (usually named BOOKMARK.HTM). When you find a Web document or site of interest, you can save the URL for that site to your Bookmark list, which grows as you add items to it (see Figure 4.23). Even if you exit and return to Navigator later, your bookmarks are still available. Plus, you can customize the way your bookmark list looks. You can give bookmarks different names, organize them specific ways, and include additional information about them that will help you remember the

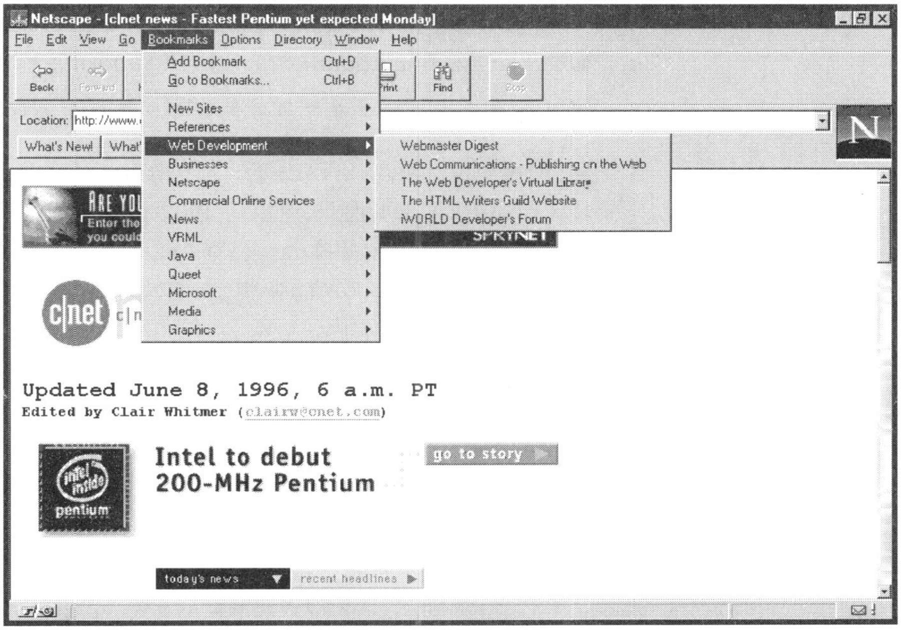

FIGURE 4.23

Bookmarks keep track of your favorite Web sites.

site's content at a later date. You also can delete bookmarks that are outdated or are simply no longer use to you.

NOTE

Bookmarks are called Favorite Sites in Internet Explorer, and are located on the Favorites menu.

The following sections describe how to create, use, and delete bookmarks, as well as how to effectively manage them on your system.

Adding a Bookmark to Your List

One of the easiest and most powerful features of Navigator is adding a bookmark. When you're at a Web page that you want to save as a bookmark, choose Bookmarks, Add Bookmark. That's it. Your bookmark is added to the bottom of the Bookmarks menu immediately. To take a look at it, open the Bookmarks menu and look at the bottom of the menu.

NOTE

You read earlier how you can use the History list to save items to the Bookmark list. As a reminder, you do this by choosing Window, History. Click the site you want to create as a bookmark, and click the Create Bookmark button. Click Close when you've finish adding items to the bookmark list.

Another way to add a bookmark is to make one from a link you find on a page. To do this, right-click the link. From the context menu, choose Add Bookmark For This Link. The only difference is that the URL of the site is saved as the bookmark, not the name of the site. You are shown how to rename a bookmark in an upcoming section.

You can create a bookmark by typing it in as well. Follow these steps:

1. Choose Bookmarks, Go to Bookmarks. The Bookmarks window appears (see Figure 4.24).
2. Choose Item, Insert Bookmark. The Bookmark Properties sheet appears (see Figure 4.25).
3. In the Name text box, enter the name of the new bookmark. This can be the same name of the site, or a name that you want to identify with the site. In the Location (URL) text box, enter the complete URL for the site—make sure you enter it exactly.

TIP

An accurate way to enter an URL of a site you are visiting is to double-click the Link icon next to the Location list

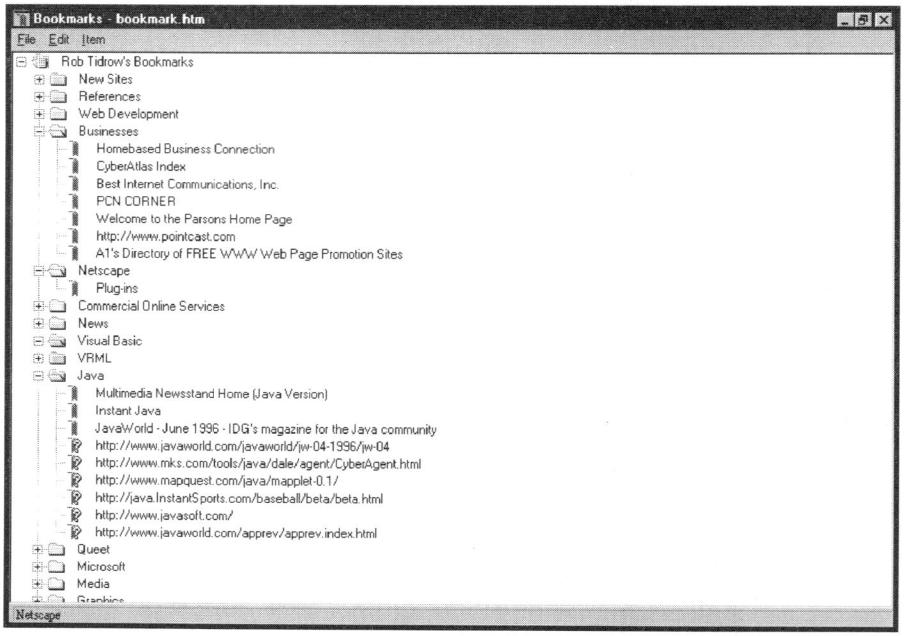

FIGURE 4.24

Your bookmarks will become as important to you as your office Rolodex. You won't want to lose them.

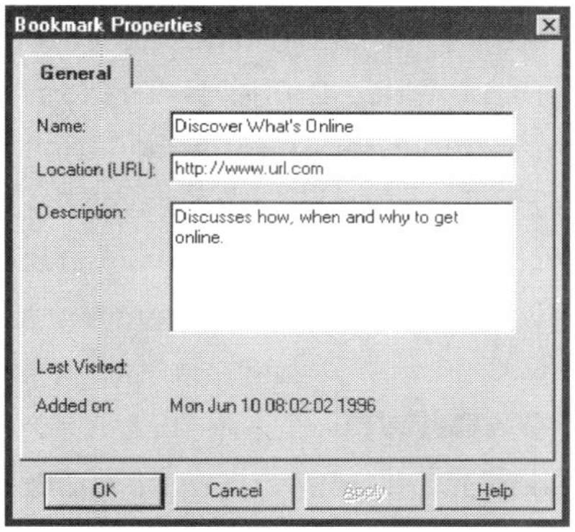

FIGURE 4.25

The Bookmark Properties sheet enables you to name and enter the location for a new bookmark.

box in the Navigator browser window. This places the current URL in the Windows Clipboard. Next, switch to the Bookmark Properties sheet, click in the Location (URL) text box, and press Ctrl+V. This pastes the URL of the site into the Location (URL) text box.

4. *Optional:* You can enter a description of the site in the Description text box. It can be as lengthy as you want.
5. Click OK to save your new bookmark.

The process for changing a bookmark name, URL, or description is similar to the preceding steps. In the Bookmark window, select the bookmark you want to modify and choose Item, Properties. The Bookmark Properties sheet appears, and you can change the name, URL, or description (refer to Figure 4.25).

In Windows 95, you can also right-click a bookmark in the Bookmarks window and choose Properties from the context menu. The Bookmark Properties sheet appears, and you can make your changes.

TIP

When using Windows 95, a quick way to save an URL of a site you're currently visiting is to right-click the Web page and choose Internet Shortcut from the context menu. The Create Internet Shortcut dialog box that appears contains the name of the site and the URL. Click OK to place the Internet shortcut on your desktop. You can then double-click the shortcut to jump to that site.

Two features of the Bookmark Properties sheet that you may be interested in are the Last Visited and Added On fields. The Last Visited field shows you the date of the last time you visited that particular site. If it was only a matter of hours, you'll see hours listed rather than days. The Added On field displays the date when you added this bookmark to the Bookmark list. You may want to add this information if you revisit sites that may have changed since your last visit.

Using a Bookmark

After you create a bookmark, you can create another bookmark using the same process or try out the new bookmark. To use the bookmark, simply double-click the bookmark in the Bookmarks window. Navigator connects to the site and downloads the Web pages from that site. If you want to see the Navigator screen better, you can minimize the Bookmarks window or close it.

Another way to use a bookmark—the most popular and easiest way—is to access the list of bookmarks from the Bookmarks menu. When you open this menu, all of your saved bookmarks appear at the bottom (refer to Figure 4.23). Simply click the bookmark of your choice to connect to that site.

Deleting Bookmarks

You may need to do some housekeeping at times on your ever-expanding list of bookmarks. To delete a bookmark, follow these steps:

1. Open the Bookmarks window by choosing Bookmarks, Go to Bookmarks.
2. Select the bookmark you want to delete and press Delete. Alternately, you can choose Edit, Delete.
3. Close the Bookmarks window by choosing File, Close, or by clicking the X button in the upper-right corner of the window.

In step 2, you can select more than one bookmark to delete by using the Ctrl and Shift keys as you click the bookmarks. The Ctrl key enables you to select non-contiguous items; the Shift key enables you to select contiguous bookmarks.

Organizing Bookmarks

Your Bookmark list may begin to look cluttered if you continually add lots of sites. Just like that junk drawer in your kitchen, your Bookmark list will end up with everything thrown into it after a while. Then, when you really need to find a site you want, you won't be able to find it quickly.

With Navigator, you can use a hierarchical structure for your bookmarks. This hierarchy is the same that directories and subdirectories or folders and subfolders use on your hard disk. Your Bookmark list has folders in which bookmarks, or other folders, can be stored. You also can place separators between items to further organize similar Web sites.

Figure 4.26 shows the Bookmarks window with the different items pointed out. Notice how the structure of this list looks similar to how your directories and files that are displayed in the Windows 95 Explorer.

Main heading

Bookmark listing

Folders

Separator

You can see in Figure 4.27 how this same list of bookmarks looks from the Bookmarks menu. Notice how the separators add a nice touch to the organization of the bookmarks.

The main reason to use this hierarchical approach is to regulate the number of bookmarks that display at a given time. If you don't do this periodically, you'll end up with a list of bookmarks that seems to go on forever. When this happens, Navigator truncates your Bookmark list when you view it from the Bookmarks menu. Any bookmarks that cannot fit on the screen, cannot be seen until you select the More option at the bottom of the list. Navigator then displays the

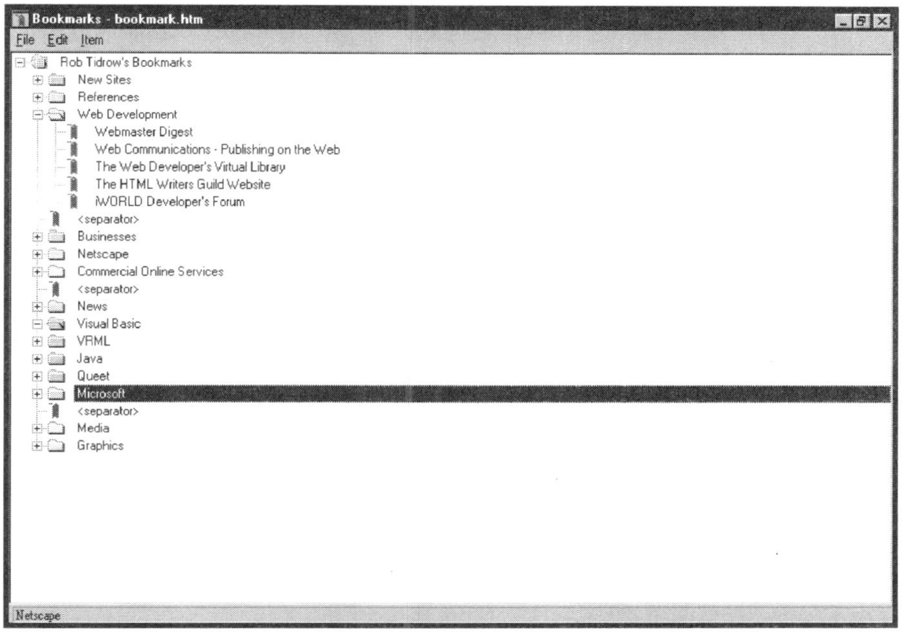

FIGURE 4.26

Netscape uses a hierarchical structure to organize your bookmarks.

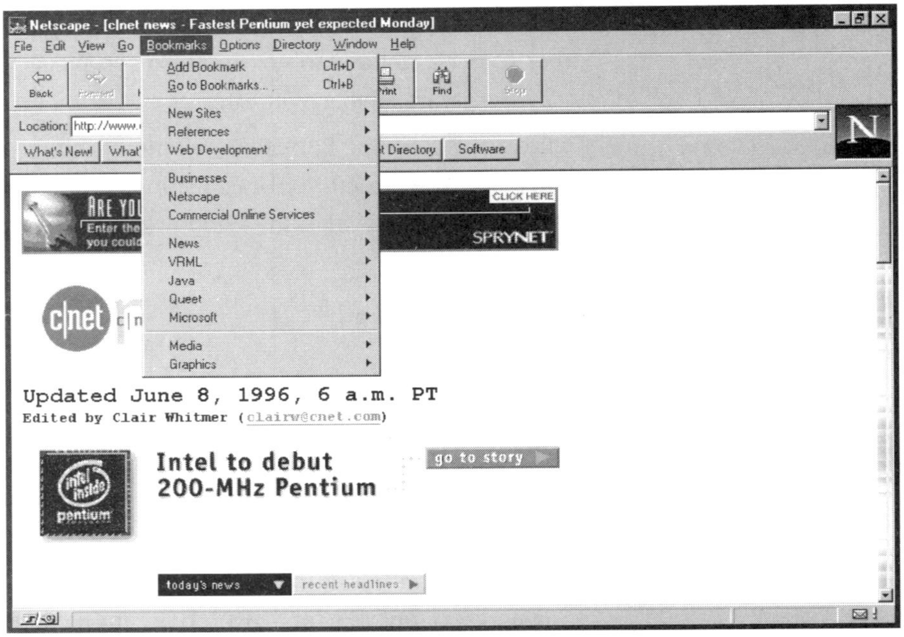

FIGURE 4.27

The Bookmarks menu shows how the bookmarks shown in Figure 4.26 display in Navigator's main window.

Bookmark window, from which you can view your bookmarks. To avoid this problem, periodically perform some maintenance tasks on your Bookmark list.

Adding Folders to the Bookmark List

Folders are used in Navigator as category headers in which you place bookmarks. One way to use these folders is to set up individual folders for different *categories* similar to the way you have folders and directories in Explorer or File Manager. Categories can be anything you want. If you frequent sites that are art-related, for example, you may want to set up an Art folder. As you add art sites to this folder, you may be able to add subfolders for Paintings, Art History, Biographies, and so on. The idea is to create an organization in which you can quickly find the right site when you want it.

To organize your Bookmark list by adding folders, use the following steps:

1. Choose Bookmarks, Go to Bookmarks. The Bookmarks window displays.
2. To specify where in the list you want the new folder to appear, click on the bookmark or item that you want the new folder to appear under.
3. Choose Item, Insert Folder. The Bookmark Properties sheet appears, with the General tab showing.
4. In the Name text box, enter the name of the new folder (see Figure 4.28).

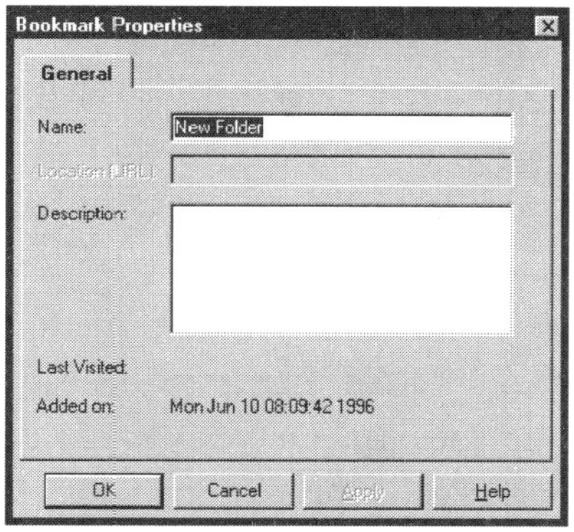

FIGURE 4.28

The General tab on the Bookmark Properties dialog box can be used to name a new folder.

5. *Optional:* You can fill in a description in the Description text box.
6. Click OK.

The new folder appears directly under the item you selected earlier. If you decide to change the name of the folder, click the folder and choose Item, Properties to open the Bookmark Properties sheet. In Windows 95, you can choose Properties from the context menu when you right-click a folder.

You may want to have a bookmark appear in more than one folder. For example, you might want to set up two folders that contain information relating to herbs—a folder containing links to general information about herbs and another folder containing links to specific herbs grown in North America. In some cases, you'll want to add the same Web site to both folders. To do this, you can make an alias of the original one and place the alias in another folder. In the Bookmark window, choose Item, Make Alias after you click a bookmark name. After you create the alias, move the duplicate to another folder.

When you change, update, or delete the original bookmark, the change is reflected in the duplicate bookmark. You can open or close folders. A plus sign to the left of the folder icon in the Bookmarks window designates a closed foler—you can't see the contents of the folder. This helps when you're performing maintenance tasks on your Bookmark list by reducing the number of bookmarks showing at one time. When you open the Bookmarks window, you'll see only the first two layers of folders open. If you have more then two layers, these folders will be closed.

You can click the plus sign to open the folder and show its contents. When a folder is open, you can see bookmarks, separators, and the other folders that are nested within.

You can move a folder and everything within that folder by dragging and dropping the folder to a new location. You may find it easier to collapse any open folders to its closed state before dragging the folder. You also can drag individual folders and bookmarks or a group of folders and bookmarks to a folder by selecting the bookmarks and dragging and dropping them onto a folder.

Another feature of Navigator 's Bookmark window is the Set to New Bookmarks Folder option. This feature enables you to select a folder in your Bookmarks list and make it the default bookmark folder. The folder selected for new bookmarks has a purple tag on it (see Figure 4.29). Instead of new bookmarks appearing at the bottom of the Bookmarks menu, you can designate a specific folder to which these bookmarks go.

To designate a folder as the default, select the folder in the Bookmark window and choose Iterm, Set to New Bookmarks Folder. The next time you add a bookmark in the Navigator Browser window, the bookmark appears in the folder you just specified as the default.

You can limit the bookmarks on your main Bookmarks menu. Say you have a long list of bookmarks that you want to keep, but you don't want them to show up every time you click the Bookmarks menu. You can limit the bookmarks that appear by choosing Item, Set to Bookmark Menu Folder. In the Bookmarks window, place all of the bookmarks you want to appear on the Bookmarks menu in one folder. Select the folder and choose Item, Set to Bookmark Menu Folder. An icon that looks like a sheet of paper with a list on it appears on the folder icon

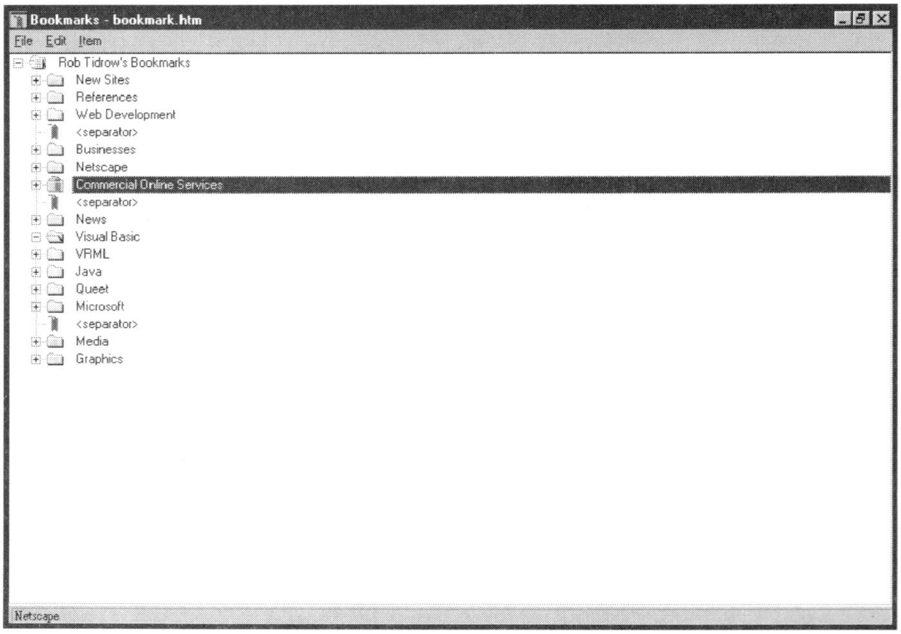

FIGURE 4.29

Use the Set to New Bookmarks Folder feature to designate where new bookmarks will be saved when using the Add Bookmark command.

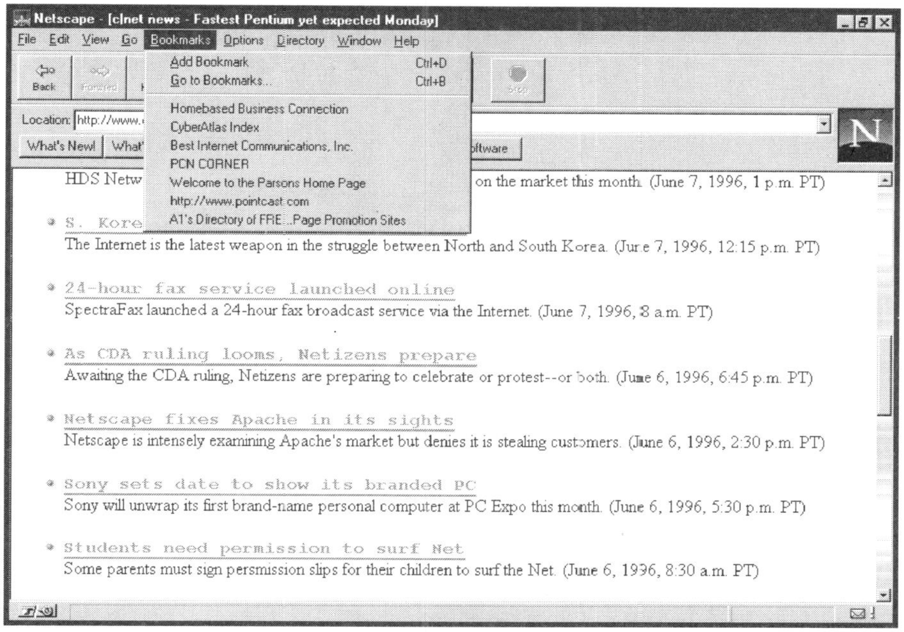

FIGURE 4.30

Limiting your bookmark folders helps you use only those in the selected folder.

you've selected. Now, when you open the Bookmarks menu, all you see are the bookmarks contained in the selected folder (see Figure 4.30).

Adding Separators to Folders

In Figure 4.26, you saw how Navigator uses separators to further segregate items in a bookmark list. Separators are used in Windows-based applications on menus to group together commands and options that are similar.

For example, if you have a folder that includes links to biographies of different baseball pitchers, you may want to separate the list into starting pitchers, middle-inning relief pitchers, and finishing relief pitchers using two separators. This way you can open the folder called Pitchers and then have starting pitchers listed at the top of the list, then have the middle-inning pitchers listed in the middle of the list, followed by the final-inning relief pitchers.

Figure 4.31 shows an example of using several separators on the Bookmarks menu.

To add a separator to the Bookmark list, open the Bookmark window and click the item above where you want the separator to be inserted. Choose Item, Insert Separator. This places a separator directly below the item you selected.

Separators don't have properties associated with them as many other objects do in Navigator. You cannot, therefore, name them or add any characteristics to them. They're simply lines that appear in the Bookmark list. You also can't move

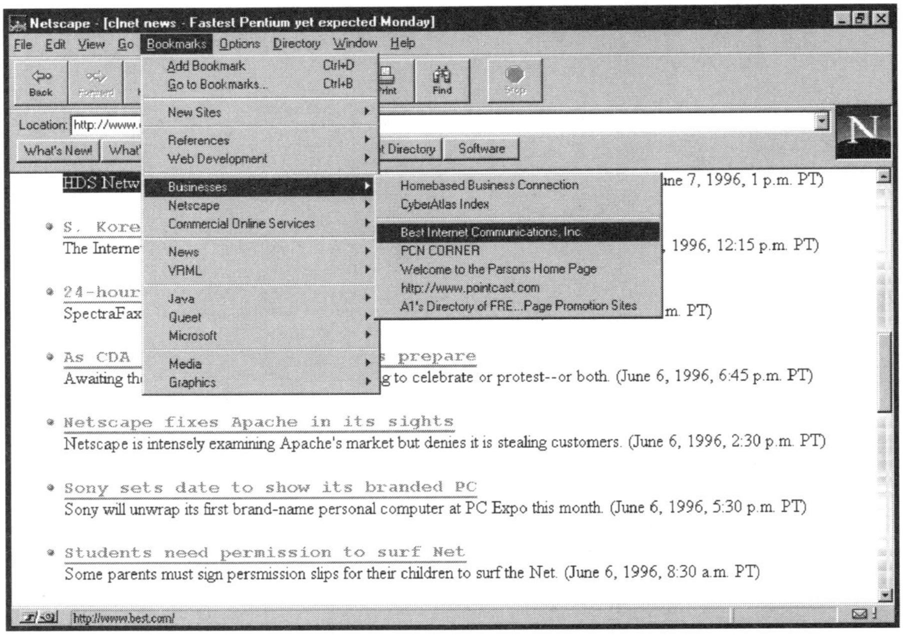

FIGURE 4.31

Use separators to further organize your Bookmark list.

them from one place to another. If you want to have a separator in another spot on the list, delete the old one by selecting it and pressing Delete (or choosing Edit, Delete), and inserting a new one in the new location.

TIP

You can quickly sort your bookmarks in the Bookmarks window by clicking a folder, and then choosing Item, Sort Bookmarks. Your bookmarks will rearrange alphabetically.

One quirk you should note about this feature is that all your separators appear at the top of the Bookmark list. You'll need to move the separators into a new placement to make them useful again. Or, simply delete them by clicking them and pressing the Delete key.

Understanding the What's New? Bookmark Feature

With Navigator, you have a feature that lets you automatically find out if a site has been updated since the last time you visited it. You can, of course, manually go to each site. But to reduce that hassle, you can use the What's New? feature. The What's New? feature works by connecting to each site you've selected (all of your bookmarks or just a group of them) and then checks to see if that site has changed since your previous visit. The following steps lead you through this task:

1. Choose Bookmarks, Go to Bookmarks to open the Bookmark window.
2. Select the bookmarks you want to have Navigator check for you. If you want to check all of your bookmarks, you don't need to select any bookmarks at this point.
3. Choose File, What's New?. The What's New? dialog box appears.
4. Click the All Bookmarks radio button to instruct Navigator to check all your bookmarks (see Figure 4.32). Click the Selected Bookmarks radio button to check only those bookmarks you selected in the Bookmarks list.
5. Click Start Checking. Navigator displays a window that shows you the progress of the checking process and then displays the status of the Web sites and whether they've changed since you last visited them.
6. Click OK after reading the window.

If Navigator locates any sites that have changed, it marks them with a "flash" icon next to the bookmark. This icon resembles a tiny fire cracker exploding. Items that have not changed are not marked. The time it takes you to check on your list of sites varies depending on the number of sites you've selected and the amount of traffic on the Internet at the time. If you select only a couple of items, it takes only 5 to 10 seconds to complete the checking process.

NOTE

The busiest time on the Internet is between the hours of 11:00 AM and 1:00 PM EST. This is due in large part to the number of people using the Internet during their lunch breaks. If you notice a degradation in accessing sites during that time, you might want to try surfing at an earlier or later time in the day.

FIGURE 4.32

Navigator can check for changes in any Web sites listed in your Bookmarks list.

Sharing Bookmark Lists

The Bookmark list is an HTML document. This means that you can copy the HTML file to other systems you're using, or share the document with other users. So if you find a number of sites that a friend or coworker would be interested in, you can simply make a copy.

Because the Bookmark list is a file, you can also make a backup copy of it. You should do this periodically. Open the Windows 95 Explorer or File Manager in Windows 3.11 and copying the BOOKMARK.HTM file to another directory or backup disk. You can find this file in the main folder of the Netscape Navigator folder. For example, if you installed Navigator in the NAV folder, the path for your bookmark file would be C:NAVBOOKMARK.HTM.

To import a bookmark list into your current list, you need access to the list that you want to import. For example, you may acquire a bookmark list from an e-mail message or from a central server on a local area network. Whatever the means, make sure you can access it and that you know where it is. Then follow these steps:

1. Choose Bookmarks, Go to Bookmarks.
2. Click the item in the bookmark list under which you want to insert the imported bookmarks.

TIP

First, you may want to add a new folder (such as Imported Links) to which the new bookmarks would initially import. After you import the bookmarks, you can decide if you want to reorganize your entire Bookmark list. However, if you want to quickly delete them, you can delete the whole folder in which you placed them. This approach may be easier then importing the bookmarks in the middle of previously created bookmarks.

3. Choose File, Import. The Import Bookmarks File dialog box opens.
4. Locate the bookmark file you want to import. The file can be named anything that has an HTML or HTM extension to it.
5. Click the Open button. The imported bookmark list appears in your Bookmark list, underneath the item you selected in step 2.

NOTE

Instead of using the Import feature to merge another list with your Bookmarks list, you can open an HTML file in the Bookmarks window. To do this, choose File, Open and select the HTML file from your system. This is handy when you want to replace your existing Bookmark list with another one.

The bookmarks are now part of your list—as if you created them yourself. You can move them, rename them, organize them, or delete them like regular bookmarks.

As an example, let's say you're responsible for finding Web sites on a particular subject, such as weather. Say you're also a member of a news team that's compiling a research area on the Web that includes news, weather, sports, and human interest. After you find all the Web sites that you can, you want to share the list with the director of the team. You could give the director a long list of hand-printed sites and URLs that she would then need to input manually into the master Bookmark list. Instead, you can save your Bookmarks list and hand it over to the director as a file. The director then can import the bookmarks as previously shown.

To export a Bookmarks list, use the following steps:

1. Choose Bookmarks, Go to Bookmarks to open the Bookmarks window.
2. Choose File, Save As. The Save Bookmarks File dialog box appears (see Figure 4.33).

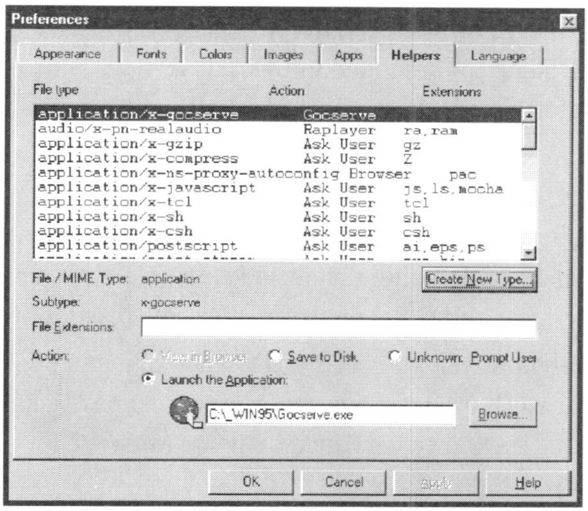

FIGURE 4.33

You can export a copy of your Bookmarks list to share with other users.

3. In the File Name text box, enter a file name. Select a file type from the Save As Type list box (save the file as HTML or HTM). You also can select a folder in which to store the file if it's other than the current one.
4. Click the Save button to save the file.

You now can send or copy the file to another user or system.

Encountering Different Web Page Elements

As you navigate the Web, you'll encounter a number of types of elements. You've already see how to handle basic text, links, and some graphics. Although text is the predominant element on the Web, there are lots of other items you'll see:

- **Graphics.** Some graphics can be viewed and downloaded, while others can be viewed, downloaded, *and* clicked on.
- **Forms.** Many sites include *forms* for registration, to get more information, or for other purposes. Although navigating forms is easy, there are a few tricks to help you use them, as you'll see in the section called "Using Web Forms."
- **Tables.** Web documents use *tables* to organize and display text, graphics, links, and other elements.
- **Frames.** *Frames* divide the screen into different windows. Although Netscape created frames, some other Web browsers support them, including the new Microsoft Internet Explorer 3.0.
- **Audio.** A number of sites include sound files for you to download.

Each Web browser is different. The one you use may or may not support all of the elements described in this list. To find out if your browser supports these features, consult its documentation.

Many sites are created using features that the most cutting-edge browsers support. Because Netscape and Microsoft are leading the pack for new and innovative features, you'll see references to these browsers on many of the Web sites you visit. Most Web sites that include features not supported by every browser (such as frames and tables) will offer alternate pages for those browsers to download.

First, however, you need to learn about helper applications and Netscape plug-ins, which will help view many of these types of elements. Plug-ins are covered in the section called "Understanding Netscape Plug-ins."

Understanding Helper Applications

As you've learned, Web browsers can display only certain file formats, such as HTML documents and some graphics. There are hundreds of other file formats used in the computer industry that you can download from the Internet, such as word processor files, spreadsheet files, and database files (such as DOC, XLS, and DB2).

If you find a file not supported by your Web browser, you have three choices. You can ignore it and move to another file or page. You can download it and open it in an application that supports the file. Or, you can assign a *helper application* in your Web browser to activate when you encounter a certain file format (also known as file type). Helper applications are so named because they execute when your Web browser needs "help" to display a file.

You can set up helper applications for most Web browsers, including Navigator and Internet Explorer, using configuration options. To set up helper applications, use the Helpers tab of the Preferences property sheet (see Figure 4.34). This tab can initially causes undo anxiety for some users. If you feel this way, don't worry. When you feel comfortable with its components, the Helpers tab is rather simple to understand and use.

You can use almost any program as a helper application. The secret is to use the best application for each file type and to have it installed on your computer. Most helper applications you use can be executed separately from Navigator. For example, you can use the Windows Paint program (called Paintbrush in Windows 3.1) to create pictures in a bitmap format (BMP). You then can use Paint to view BMP and PCX files that you may encounter on the Web.

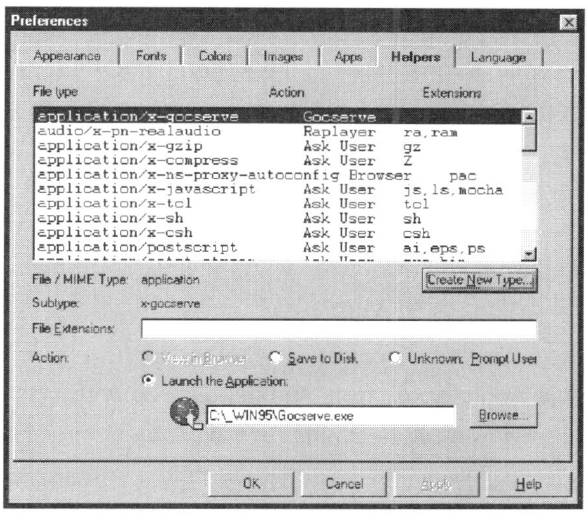

FIGURE 4.34

The Helpers tab can be overwhelming at first.

Another file type that you may encounter on the Web is the MPG (pronounced "em-peg") file format. MPG files display videos and sounds on your computer. Navigator does not support these files automatically, so you'll need a helper application to handle them. Fortunately such a program, VMPEG, is available on the Internet for download.

The Helpers tab includes a large scrolling list of names of many file types you may encounter as you surf the Web. These file types are listed using a naming standard known as *MIME (multipurpose Internet mail extensions)*. Although the MIME specification was originally created for files being sent via e-mail, these file types are not limited to mail.

MIME file type definitions are sent by the Web server before a file can be downloaded to your computer so that Navigator can prepare for its arrival. If you're requesting a MIME file type that Navigator already understands, such as JPG, Navigator tells the server to go ahead and send the file. If it's a MIME type that Navigator doesn't understand—but a helper application is configured to handle it—Navigator opens the helper application. The helper application receives the file via Navigator and handles it (for example, it plays a movie). If a helper application isn't set up, Navigator displays a message telling you that it has encountered a file that it doesn't know how to handle. At this point, you can cancel the transaction or download the file to your hard disk and run it from there.

Navigator recognizes each MIME file type by its file extension. In MIME nomenclature, for example, files with an EXE or BIN extension are classified as applications, with a subtype designation of "octet-stream" (otherwise known as an 8-bit binary file). If you scroll down the list, you'll see many types of files, some familiar and some unfamiliar. Usually, the MIME designations make sense. For example, GIF files are classified as images with a subtype of gif.

For each type of file it encounters on the Internet, Navigator has a default action you can find listed in the Action column of the list. For image/gif files, you can see that the default action is Browser. This means that GIF graphics will be displayed automatically by Navigator, within the browser window (sometimes referred to as a *native* action). For application/octet-stream files, the default is Ask User. This means that when you click a link to an EXE or BIN file, you will be asked what you want to do with the file (sometimes called activating an *external* application). See Figure 4.35.

Before you start to configure a helper application in Navigator, you must first obtain a helper application and install it on your system. Applications that enable you to view multimedia files are available from various sources, including books

TABLE 4.1 GRAPHICS VIEWERS	
Viewer Name	**Support File Types**
VMPEG	MPG/MPEG videos
WordPad	Rich Text Format (RTF) documents
Pkunzip	ZIP compressed files
QuickTime Viewer	QuickTime video
LView Pro	GIF, JPEG/JPG, TIFF, BMP
Paint Shop Pro	GIF, JPEG/JPG, TIFF, BMP
GhostView	PostScript

(like this one), software stores, FTP and Gopher sites, and Web sites. Table 4.1 lists some applications you may want to obtain or configure with Navigator.

In Table 4.1, you see that some helper applications support files which Netscape Navigator natively supports. That's OK. Many of those helper applications will support additional files that Navigator doesn't handle. One of these applications is LView Pro. This program supports GIF and JPG (which Navigator can display by itself), but it also enables you to view TIFF, BMP, and many other graphics file formats. These file types are common graphics file formats available on the PC platform. Some Web sites may include these types of graphics in their documents or repositories. The following steps show you how to use the

FIGURE 4.35

Navigator displays this message when it doesn't know how to handle a file type on the Internet.

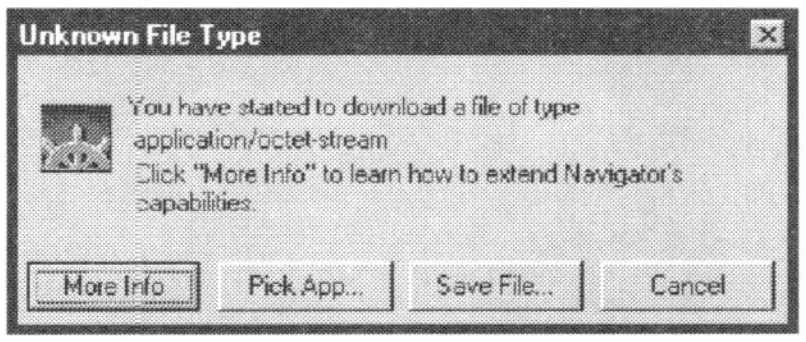

Helpers tab to configure LView Pro as a helper application (make sure LView Pro is installed on your computer first).

1. Click the Helpers tab.
2. In the list at the top, scroll down until you see the image/tiff entry. Click it. Notice in the File Extensions text box that the tiff and tif extensions automatically appear. These are the extensions for TIFF images that Navigator recognizes and that then cause the helper application to launch. The helper application loads the TIFF image and displays it.
3. Click the Launch the Application radio button. This tells Navigator to launch your helper application when it encounters a TIFF image.
4. Now you need to tell Navigator where on your computer to find the helper application. In the text box below the Launch the Application radio button, enter the full path and file name of the helper application. You can use the Browse button to find helper applications on your system. If you're using LView Pro, it should look similar to the following:

   C:LVIEWLVIEWP1A.EXE
5. Click OK to save your changes and to return to Navigator.

Now when you click a link to a TIFF image, Navigator automatically starts the helper application, LView Pro in this case, and lets you view and manipulate the image (see Figure 4.36).

Navigator lists many MIME types on the Helpers tab. For some file types, however, you'll need to add a new listing by creating a new file type. You can do that by clicking the Create New Type button on the Helpers tab. If you're familiar with Windows, you may notice in the list of MIME types in the Helpers tab that

FIGURE 4.36

LView Pro is one helper application that you can use to view graphics files that Navigator does not support.

some basic file types are not listed. One of these is a MIDI file format (MID).

If you want to add a new file type, open the Helpers tab by selecting Options, General Preferences and follow these steps:

1. On the Helpers tab, click the Create New Type button. The Configure New Mime Type dialog box appears.
2. In the MIME Type text box, enter a MIME type, such as audio. The following list are the seven MIME types you can use in Navigator:
   - Text
   - Audio
   - Image
   - Video
   - Multipart
   - Message
   - Application

   Any MIME type you set up must fit in one of the preceding types.
3. Enter a MIME subtype in the Mime SubType text box (see Figure 4.37). These are types such as x-wav, tiff, and so on. If you add an unofficial subtype, you need to place an **x-** before the name. In most cases, your subtypes will be unofficial and will contain the x- nomenclature. This doesn't mean you're adding a substandard MIME type—it simply means that the governing body of the Internet has not officially sanctioned it.

   In this case, type **x-MIDI**.
4. Click OK. You return to the Helpers tab.
5. You now need to specify the type of file extension associated with the new file type. In the File Extensions text box, enter the file extension, such as **MID**.

FIGURE 4.37

MIME types and MIME subtypes are used to help Navigator determine which application to launch when you encounter a file type on the Web.

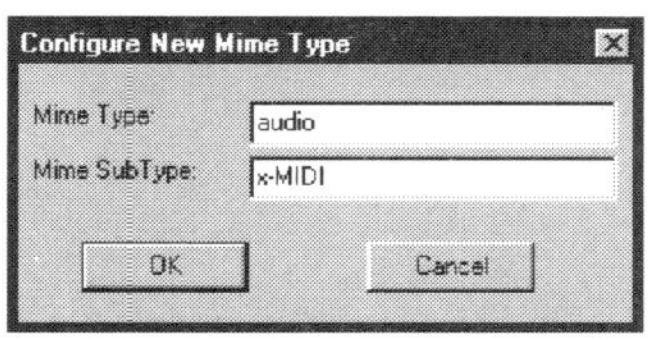

6. Click OK. You now can go back to the Helper tab and set up a helper application for that new MIME type (as shown in the previous steps).

WARNING

After you create the MIME type, you're stuck with it unless you want to edit your Windows 95 Registry or your INI file in Windows 3.*x*.

If you want to automatically save any file that Navigator doesn't understand, or if you want to assign that file to a helper application on your local hard disk, click the Save to Disk radio button on the Helpers tab. When you click this radio button, Navigator doesn't ask you what to do with the file; Navigator opens the Save As dialog box and you get to name the file and place it on your local system.

Understanding Netscape Plug-ins

One of the most innovative technologies in Netscape Navigator is its support of *plug-ins*. Plug-ins are applications that work in conjunction with Navigator to help the browser display certain file types. These file types are ones that ordinarily would be assigned a helper application (see the previous section), but which can now be supported automatically by Navigator.

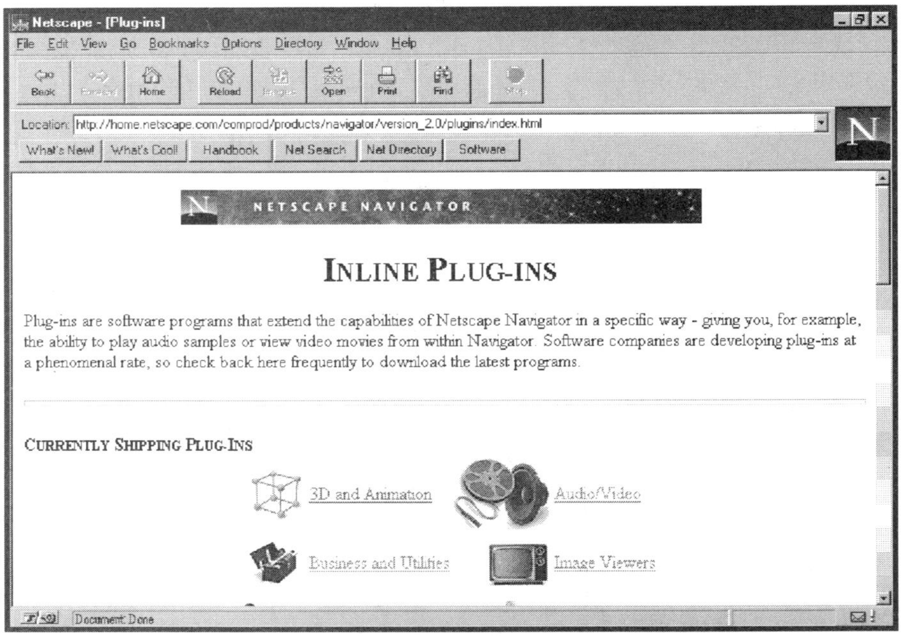

FIGURE 4.38

You can find a plug-in, which you can download from the Macromedia Web site, by visiting the Inline Plug-In page at Netscape's Web site.

The way plug-ins work is very simple. First, you choose a plug-in by visiting the following URL at the Netscape Communications site (see Figure 4.38):

> **http://home.netscape.com/comprod/products/navigator/version_2.0/plugins/index.html**

This page lists and briefly describes many of the plug-ins available online. Next, you link to the site where the plug-in you want resides, such as **http://www.macromedia.com**, and download the plug-in file. Some plug-ins are available for several types of operating systems, including Windows 95, Windows 3.*x*, Windows NT 3.51, and Macintosh. Be sure to download the correct one for your operating system.

When the download is complete, install the plug-in by following the instructions listed on the Web page where you obtained the plug-in. You might want to print those instructions in case you have trouble remembering how to perform them. Before you begin the install process, exit Navigator. If you don't do this, the plug-in won't work until the next time you start Navigator.

When the install is finished, restart Navigator. Now, when you encounter a file the plug-in supports, the file displays inside Navigator's main window. One of the hottest plug-ins is the Macromedia Shockwave plug-in, which plays Macromedia animation files (see Figure 4.39). Several sites now include small animations for advertisements or special features.

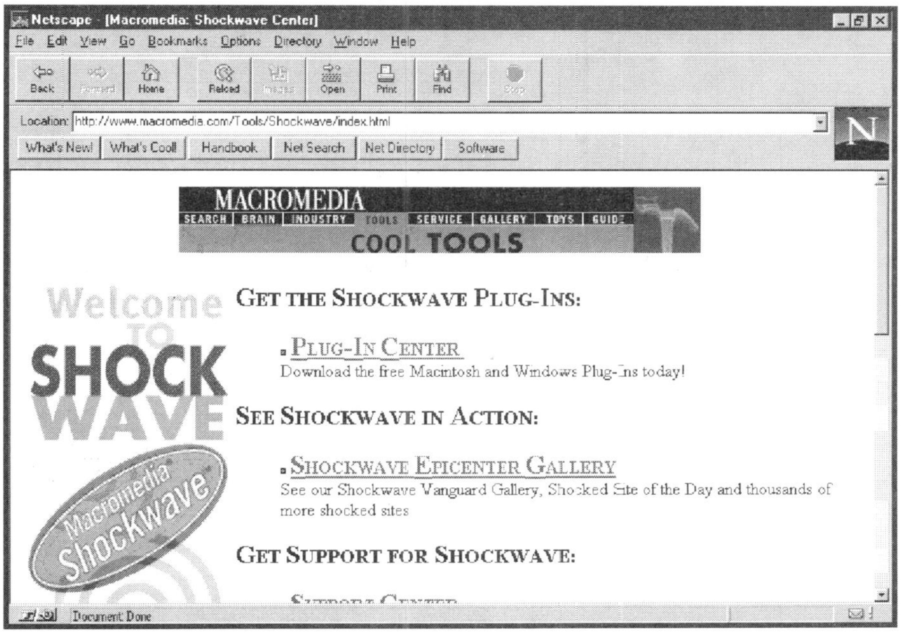

FIGURE 4.39

The Shockwave plug-in, which you can download from the Macromedia Web site, is one of the hottest plug-ins on the Web.

NOTE

The release of Microsoft Internet Explorer 3.0, which is due out in the summer of 1996, includes support for Navigator plug-ins.

Viewing Web Graphics

Now that you've spent some time on the Web, you've no doubt run into some graphics. Jump to any Web site and you'll probably encounter some type of image file, whether it's a small navigational icon that directs you to another page, an advertisement selling ISDN modems, or a promotional piece by Disney (see Figure 4.40). These are all graphics, and you should learn how to handle them to get the most out of your time online.

By default, Navigator tries to display all images it encounters in Web pages. This usually isn't a problem if you have a fast connection to the Internet. If your modem connection is 14.4 or 28.8, you may find it takes too long to download every image on every Web page. You can turn off the downloading of images by turning off the Auto Load Images command on the Options menu. When you do this, Web pages download with only text showing, which greatly increases the speed at which the page downloads.

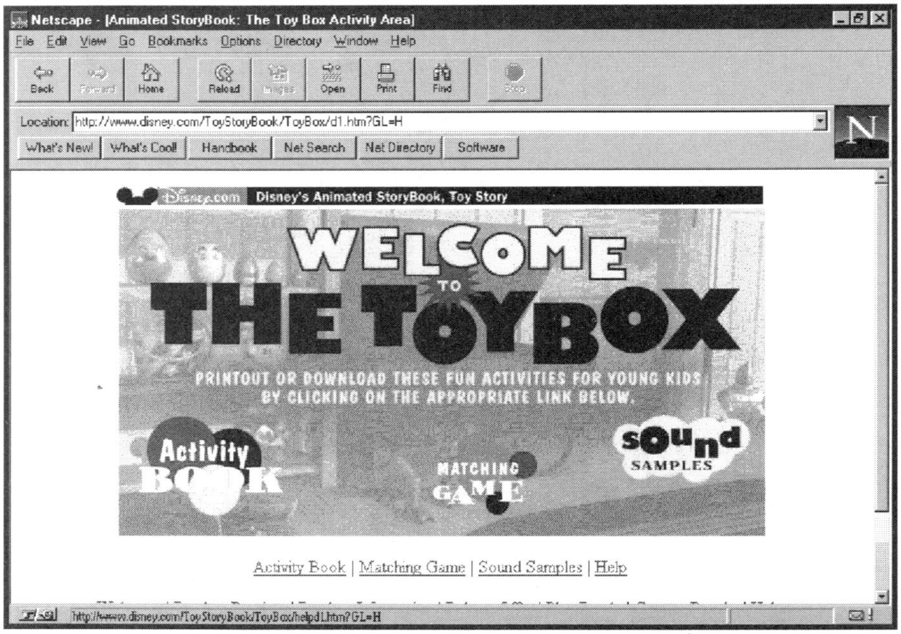

FIGURE 4.40

Many Web sites include graphics to advertise and promote their products and services, such as Disney's *Toy Story Animated StoryBook*.

This is a disadvantage, however, when a Web page includes images that are vital to the understanding of the Web page's content. If you want to temporarily turn on the images on a page, click the Images toolbar button. This forces Navigator to reload the current page with images displayed. When you move to new pages, however, images will not display until you turn back on the Auto Load Images command on the Options menu.

You can also use the Images tab on the Preferences page (choose Options, General Preferences) to control when Navigator displays graphics on Web documents. If you want to see the text on a page first, then have the graphics displayed, click the After Loading option on the Images tab. This lets you see all the text and, if you don't need or want to see the graphics on the Web, you can click Stop to prevent the download.

If you want to keep an image you see on a Web page, you can save it to your hard drive. In Windows 95, right-click the image and choose Save This Image As from the context menu. In the Save As dialog box, name the file and click the Save button. The file is saved to your hard disk.

Graphics Files Formats

Many computer graphics files are stored in *bitmap* format. Bitmap images are made up of tiny dots, called *pixels*, that are mapped to a palette of colors. When arranged in certain patterns, shading, and colors, these pixels, or dots, make up a picture. For example, if you look closely at a picture in a newspaper, you can see this same type of dot pattern that makes up the picture.

The number of colors in a computer bitmap depends on the number of bits used to define the color for each pixel. If you have an 8-bit image, the image can have 256 colors in its palette. 16-bit images can have up to 65,536 colors. On the high end, 24-bit images can have more than 16 million colors. When you encounter images that contain more colors, the file size increases (because the image has more bits) and the download time increases. Fortunately, most Web designers make their graphics files as small as possible (without obviously affecting their appearance) to optimize the user's download.

Many computer graphics file formats exist, but only three are supported by Navigator. These include GIF, JPG, and XBM formats. JPG may be shown as *JPEG*, depending on the computer platform that created the file. GIF and JPG files are the predominate file formats you'll find on the Web. The XBM file format is a monochrome bitmap file that's really a C programming language source file that displays images as numeric data in hexadecimal code instead of the binary code that GIF and JPG use.

JPG files are typically best suited for these type of images:

- Graphics with a large amount of colors (more than 256)
- Photographs

GIF files are typically best suited for these types of images:

- Graphics that have sharp edges, such as menus, buttons, and graphs
- Graphics that have a limited number of distinct colors, such as logos
- Black-and-white line art
- Images that are overlaid with text

Technically speaking, a GIF file is a 256-color image that is compressed using a compression technology known as LZW. A JPG image is a 24-bit file that is compressed by a sophisticated compression algorithm that reduces the file size by removing some of the picture detail to make the graphic file smaller. Depending on the compression ratio, a JPG image can lose so much of its detail and color in the attempt to reduce file size that a blotchy or unreadable image is the result. Most of the images you'll encounter on the Web, however, are reviewed by the Web page authors to make them reasonably viewable.

Using Helper Applications to View Graphics Files

You learned earlier about helper applications. Products such as LView Pro and Paint Shop Pro are ideal graphics helper applications because they can load and view a number of file types; they also enable you to edit and convert files. Table 4.2 lists the graphics file types recognized by Navigator in the Helpers tab.

The file types listed in the Helpers tab are not the only ones you'll probably encounter. In fact, of all the ones listed in Table 4.2, only GIF, JPG, TIFF, and BMP are likely to be found in large quantities on the Web. You're more likely to encounter files that are not listed automatically in the Helpers tab, but ones you may want to add support for. These include CGM, DXF, PCX, PIC, and WMF. If you work a lot with WordPerfect files, you also may want to add support for WPG files as well.

Progressive JPEG Files

Navigator supports a recently released JPEG standard, called *progressive JPEG*. Progressive JPEG is an image-compression method used to store the file in overlapping multiple layers. This gives the image a "venetian blind" look when you're downloading a Web page that contains progressive JPEG. This also enables

TABLE 4.2 NAVIGATOR GRAPHICS FILE TYPES

File Type	Description	File Extension
image/x-MS-bmp	Windows bitmap	BMP
image/x-rgb	RGB image file	RGB
image/x-portable-pixmap	PPM image	PPM
image/x-portable-graymap	PGM image	PGM
image/x-portable-bitmap	PBM image	PBM
image/x-portable-anymap	PNM image	PNM
image/x-xwidowdump	X Windows image	XWD
image/x-xpixmap	X Windows pixmap	XPM
image/x-xbitmap	XBM bitmap	XBM
image/x-cmu-raster	CMU raster image	RAS
image/tiff	Tagged Image Format	TIFF/TIF
image/jpeg	JPEG file	JPG/JPEG/JPE
image/gif	CompuServe GIF format	GIF

Navigator to retrieve the image quicker for you to view right away, although the image you see initially will be blurry and out of focus. As more of the image is downloaded, however, the image quality increases until the full image is on your system (see Figure 4.41).

This enables you to review the image as it's being downloaded with the rest of the page; you can make navigational decisions based on what you see. If the image you see isn't what you want, you can stop the download and return to a previous site. Or you can continue with the download to see the rest of the file.

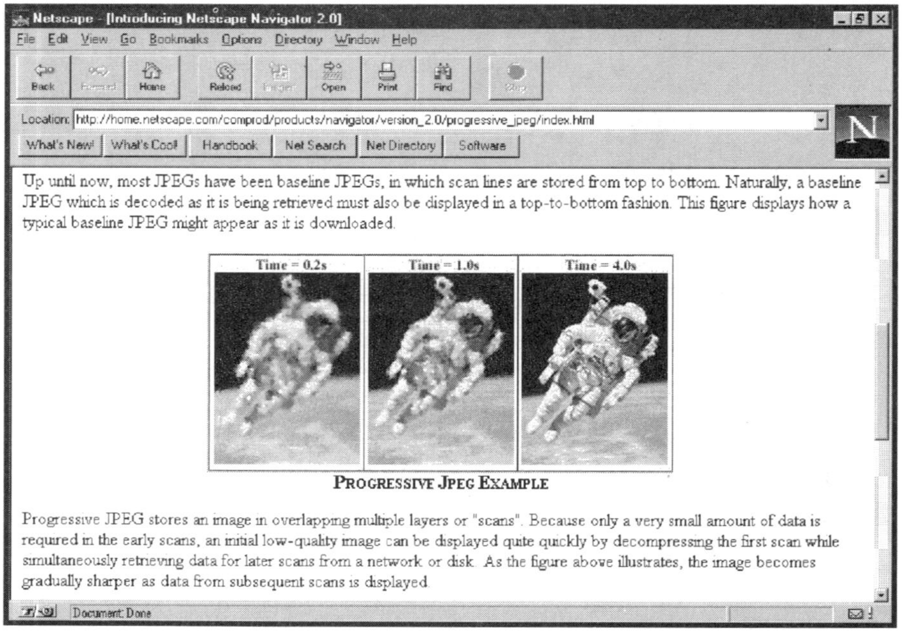

FIGURE 4.41

Here's an example of progressive JPEG files illustrated on the Netscape Communications site. Notice how the image gets clearer from left to right.

This technique is a great tool when you're visiting online art museums or tourism sites. If you're looking for a particular painting, such as Edward Hopper's *Nighthawks*, you may travel to several sites until you find the correct painting. Sites that use progressive JPEG images will let you quickly see part of each image as the pages download, and you can view each image without seeing the entire file come across.

NOTE

One misconception about progressive JPEG files is that they download quicker than normal JPEG files of the same size. This is only an illusion because you start to see something on-screen right away with progressive JPEG files, so your curiosity is satisfied quicker than when you have to wait for the entire file to download before any of it appears on screen.

Interlaced GIF files are like progressive JPG files. Interlaced GIF format is a type of GIF file that behaves like progressive JPG files but offer lower color depth. Like Progressive JPEGs, *interlaced* GIFs download and appear on screen a little at a time, creating a "wave effect," and also creating the illusion that they are downloading faster than a normal GIF would, although this isn't necessarily true.

GIF Animation Files

Another recent addition to the graphics you'll find on the Web are GIF animation files. GIF animation files are a series of images stored in a single file that can be played back as an animation. Because it's impossible to show an animation in this book, Figure 4.42 shows you an example of the sets of files used to create an animation (see **http://members.aol.com/royalef/gifmake.htm**).

GIF animations help solve a problem that some Web designers have experienced with most other animations. Typically, an animation is controlled by programs (called *CGI scripts*) that reside on the Web server. When a visitor links to that page, the *client* (which is the Web browser) requests the animation and the server sends it. This requires the server to stay busier than it would if it simply sent you the Web pages you requested initially. Also, the animation needs to stay relatively small because it has to be transmitted over the Internet. With GIF animations, the server doesn't need to stay connected after the Web page is sent to your machine. Your browser may continue to work as the animation runs, but the connection between you and the server is closed.

To see an example of a GIF animation, visit to the following URL:

> **http://home.netscape.com/comprod/products/navigator/version_2.0/gif_animation/index.html**

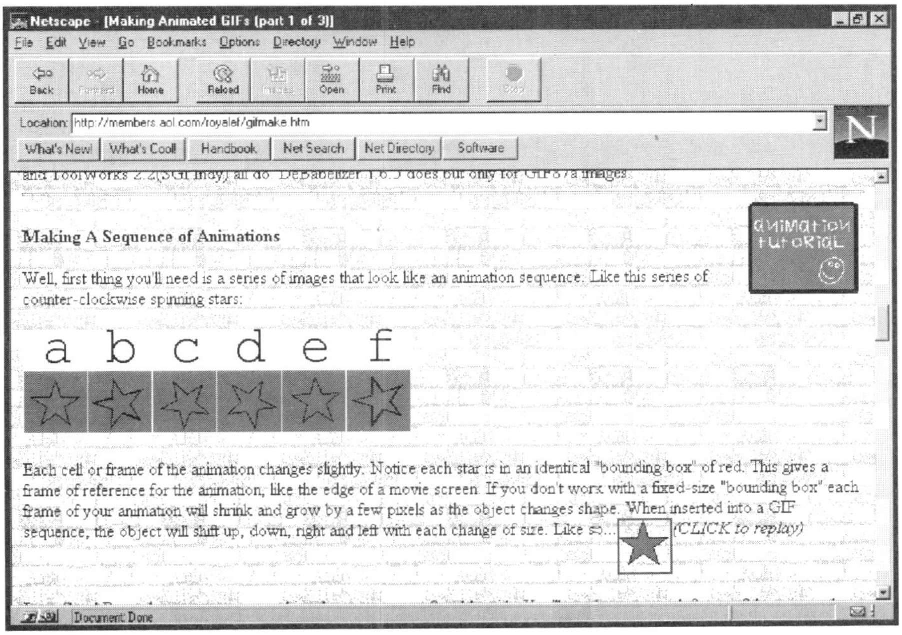

FIGURE 4.42

Animated GIF files are becoming popular on the Web.

Transparent GIF Files

One of the most popular types of GIF files on the Web is the *transparent GIF*. Transparent GIF files are used when the Web page author wants to allow the background of the Web page to show through the GIF image. Figure 4.43 shows the difference between a transparent GIF file and non-transparent GIF file. Notice how the transparent GIF seems to "float" above the page, whereas the other file has a gray background to it.

Navigator and Internet Explorer are two of the few Web browsers that support transparent GIF files. In Web browsers that don't support transparent GIFs, the background colors display in a rectangular fashion like the image on the left in Figure 4.43. This isn't a problem if the background of the Web page matches the image background, but it does have a profound affect on the overall look of a site if the image background stands out like this.

Using Web Forms

Some sites on the Web have fill-in-the-blank forms that require you to enter data of some sort. Forms can include blanks for you to enter text and numbers, and lists from which you select options, radio buttons, and check boxes. These are the same types of elements you find on Windows applications.

Figure 4.44 shows a typical form on the Web. To fill in a form, read the instructions (if there are any) and then start at the top of the form. Most forms require you to

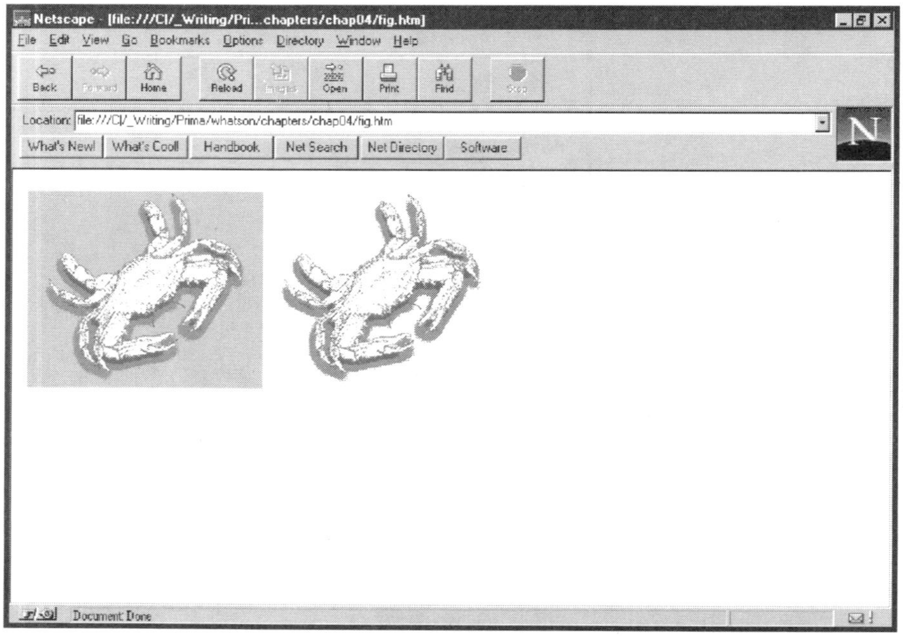

FIGURE 4.43

The example shown on the left is a non-transparent GIF file, while the one on the right is a transparent GIF file.

respond to all the questions and to fill in all the blanks. To move from one part of the form to the next, press the Tab key until you get to the bottom of the screen. If the form displays past the bottom of the screen, use the slider control on the side of the Navigator window to display the next portion of the form.

After you fill in the form, you must send the form to the Web site. You usually do this by clicking a button at the bottom of the form called Submit, Finished, or something similar (such as the Register Now! button in Figure 4.44). If you want to delete the information you just entered, there's usually another button called Reset or Delete All that cleans the form so you can fill it out again (such as the Clear Form button in Figure 4.44).

When you submit the finished form, a message may let you know that the document you're sending isn't secure and you have the option of not sending it. Although many forms you fill out and submit don't contain sensitive data, some do. These might be forms that include your name, address, phone number, and other personal information. Also, some sites require you to pay to enter the site, which can be handled by a credit card transaction. Remember: This information is not secure when sent over the Web! People with the proper skills can intercept the form and read your credit card number or other information. (You learn about online security in Chapter 12.)

One type of form you may use a great deal on the Web is a *search form*. You can find search forms at sites that enable you to search for documents or files on the

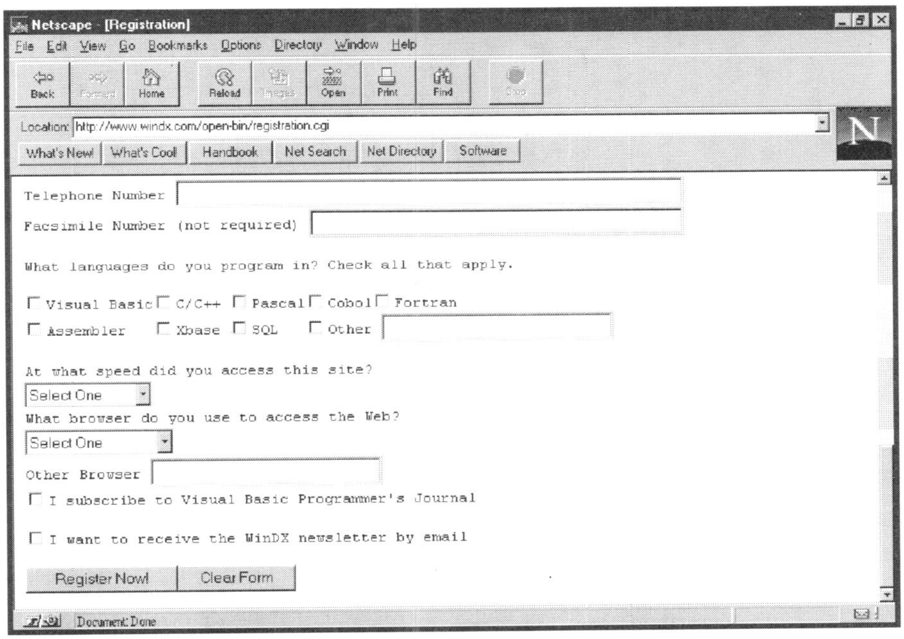

FIGURE 4.44

A typical form you might encounter on the Web asks for your name, address, phone number, and e-mail address.

Web or the Internet. The Yahoo! site is an example of a search form (see Figure 4.45). To find a site that contains information you want, enter a keyword or a short description in the blank text box and click Search. Yahoo! searches its database of Web sites looking for the item you're interested in and returns a list of sites. (In Chapter 10, you learn how to search for items on the Web.)

Viewing Tables

You'll often find tables of information on Web pages (see Figure 4.46). Unless you use a browser that doesn't support tables (most new browsers support tables), you'll see tables in Web documents. Except for the way tables appear on the page, there's no difference between a page without a table and page with one. You don't interact with it in any way.

Some Web pages include tables of lists, such as files you can download, pages you can jump to, or a table of contents of the site you're viewing. If there are links in a table, they behave exactly the same as links in regular text; just click the anchor text or graphic to jump to that URL.

Many Web authors use tables in their Web pages to help them organize and present information. In fact, many Web pages use tables that you can't see. Tables can have invisible borders (known as borders without width) so Web page authors can line up page elements to look more like desktop publishing documents.

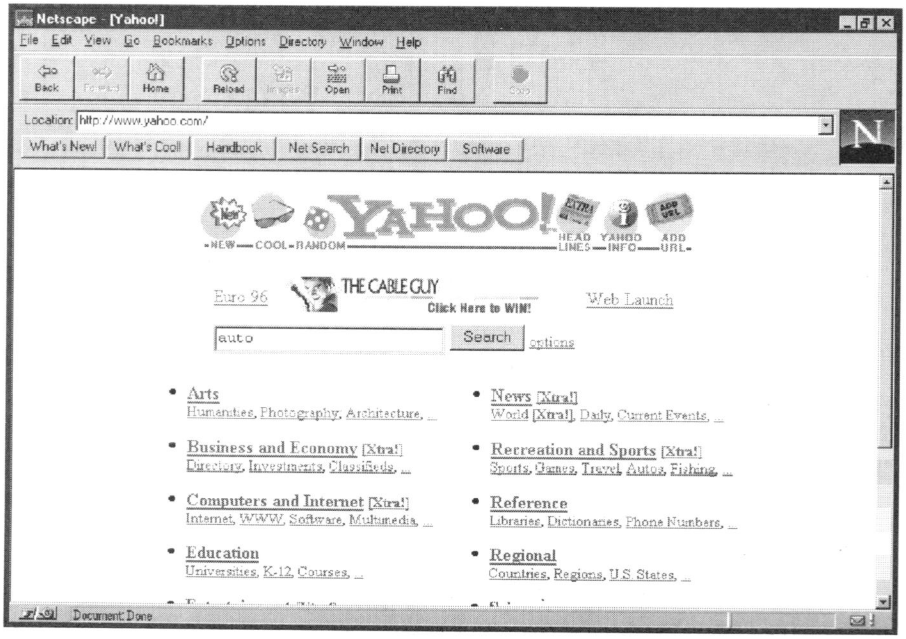

FIGURE 4.45

Search sites like Yahoo! usually use forms to enable you to query for information.

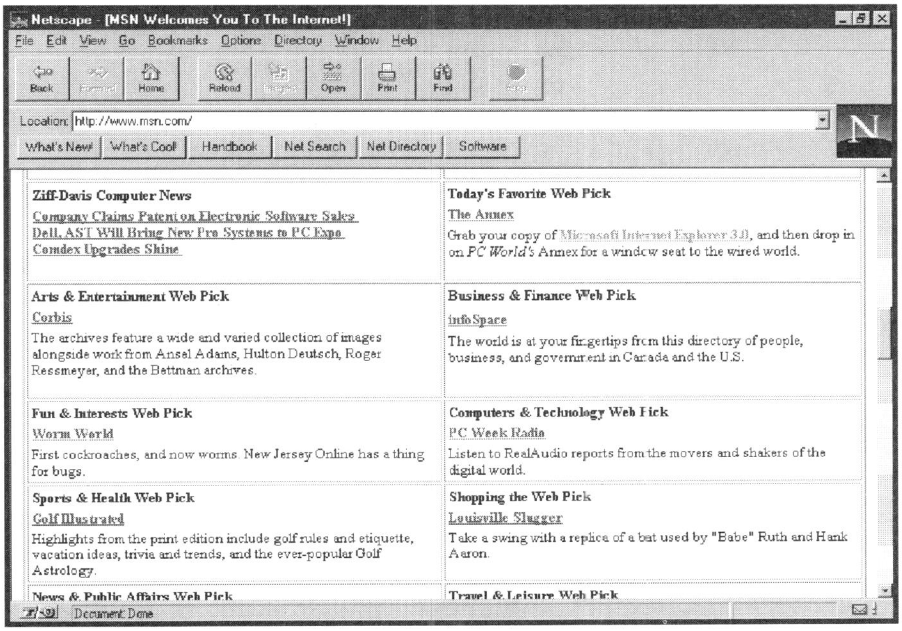

FIGURE 4.46

Tables are a nice way for Web page authors to display information.

Understanding and Navigating in Frames

Frames are newly supported features in Web documents that Netscape supports. Frames divide the Navigator window into sections so that each section can point to a different URL or list of URLs. Frames also appeal to Web designers and viewers because each frame is independent of the other frames on the page. Because of this, each frame can be designed to include scroll bars, to have a sizing handle, or to remain frozen.

An early implementation of frames included a table of contents that appeared on the left side of the screen. This table of contents was linked to specific parts of a reference document that displayed in a separate frame on the same page. In Figure 4.47, for example, the user can click each of the content items in the lefthand frame to display the document in the righthand frame.

The *active* frame is highlighted with a thin black border. This tells you which frame you have clicked or which frame has the focus, so you can know where a particular action will occur (such as the appearance of a new page or graphic). You might also need to refresh or reload a page inside a frame. To do this, click the frame to make sure it's active and then choose View, Reload Frame.

Because each frame has its own URL, you need to pay particular attention to the way in which you move around in frames. When you want to return to the previous page that displayed inside a frame, right-click in that frame and choose Back in Frame from the context menu. Similarly, choose Forward in Frame from

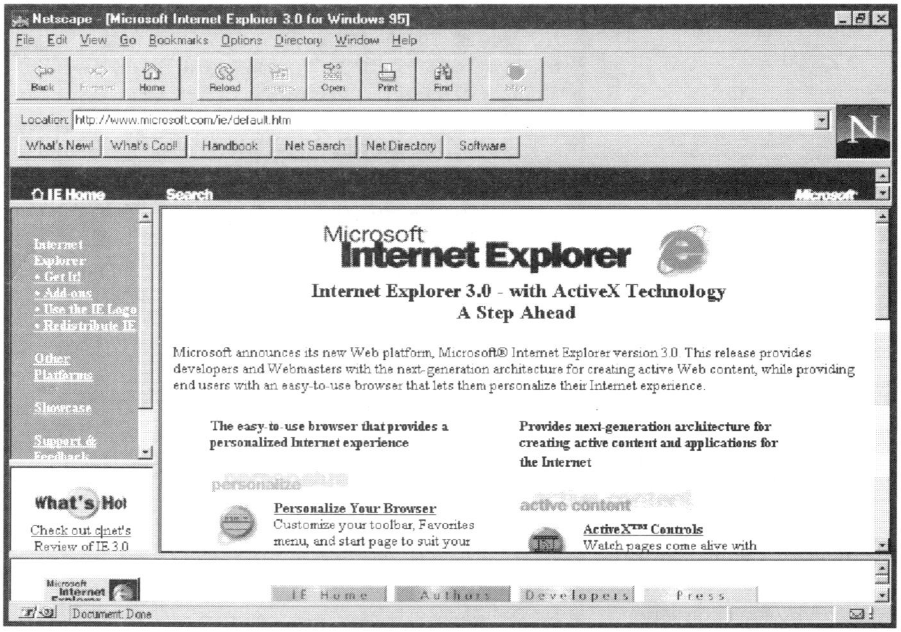

FIGURE 4.47

Many Web sites are including frames as a new way to present their information.

the context menu to move forward. If you want to return to the preceding Web document (the one you visited before coming to the current one with frames in it), click the Back button on the Navigator toolbar (or choose Go, Back).

Depending on how a frame is constructed, you may be able to resize it by dragging the frame's edge. In Figure 4.47, for example, you can resize each of the frames so that when you're looking for a particular story in the left frame, you can move the frame edge to the right. Conversely, as you're reading the story in the right frame, you can slide the frame edge to the left to give you more space to read the document.

Frames aren't limited to showing a table of contents. Many Web authors use frames as a way to "freeze" information they don't want to scroll off the screen as users interact with the Web page. Normally, as you scroll down a Web page, the entire document must scroll as well. This means that a Web author cannot show a copyright notice, advertisement, or other feature continuously while the user is visiting the site.

NOTE

Netscape introduced frames to the Web. Because of this, some other company's Web browsers don't support displaying frames. If you use another browser at times, you may not be able to use it to view frames.

Using Sound on the Web

During the past year, some of the most interesting advances on the Web have been related to audio delivery over the Internet. News agencies transmit live audio feeds or prerecorded hourly news reports. Coverage of sporting events shows up regularly on the Web, and rock and roll concerts are being *simulcast* online (they're broadcast over the Web at the same moment they're happening on stage).

Navigator doesn't support audio files by itself. You must use helper applications or plug-ins to hear what a site has to say. One of the helper applications you can use, called NAPlayer, is provided with Navigator. When you install Navigator, it automatically configures NAPlayer as the helper application for a couple of types of sound files. For other sound files, you need to acquire your own helper applications.

To listen to audio on the Web, you need to make sure your computer is configured to play the sounds you encounter. The primary piece to this puzzle is to have a sound card installed in your computer. Although each computer has a tiny system speaker included, it doesn't work to listen to sounds on the Web. You need a sound card such as a Sound Blaster 16 or similar device. If you purchased your computer in the past year or so, it probably has a sound card built-in already. Many computers are now "multimedia" machines that enable you to record and listen to sounds.

You also need speakers or headphones to connect to your sound card. Because the majority of audio files and sounds you'll encounter on the Web are of low quality, you probably don't need to invest a lot in speakers. If you plan on using these speakers for CD-ROM music, games or other multimedia programs, though, you might want to buy speakers with good sound quality. It's all up to you and your budget. But for the Web, all you really need is a set of $20 speakers and you're in business.

The final piece of equipment you'll need is the software that lets you play back the sound files. You'll learn more about this software as you read through this section. The following is a list of applications you can use with Windows 95; you can find many of these on the Internet as shareware or demo products:

- MIDI Jukebox 2
- TrueSpeech Internet Player
- Sound Gadget Pro
- Acoustic Player
- Real Audio Player
- Audio File Formats

Much like the way graphics formats come in different flavors, computer sounds come in different file formats. If you have Windows 95, you already have built-in support for WAV files and can install a utility that lets you play MIDI files. Table 4.3 lists the types of audio formats available on the Web.

Even though you're using Windows 95 or Windows 3.*x* to navigate the Web, you may encounter the file types in Table 4.3. The most popular sound types on the Web are AU and SND. Netscape 2.0 plays these sound files by using NAPlayer (see Figure 4.48).

There are also sound file formats that transmit in real-time over the Internet. This reduces the amount of time you have to wait to hear a sound file. Applications are available that allow you to listen to sound files as they're transmitted to your computer, instead of the typical way of downloading the file first then playing the file on your local machine. One of these packages is RealAudio. You can get more information on RealAudio at **http://www.realaudio.com**.

Using Other Internet Services

In Chapter 3, you read about a number of Internet services other than the Web. Although those services aren't as flashy and aren't as easy to use as the Web, some of them are still very popular and can be used to fill in the gaps that the Web leaves, such as e-mail, newsgroups, and chat.

This section looks at the Internet services in the following list. When a tool for a server is available in Navigator, that tool along with other ones are shown to help you understand how to integrate Navigator with other Internet services.

- FTP
- Telnet
- E-mail
- Gopher
- Chat
- Newsgroups

FIGURE 4.48

NAPlayer plays some of the sound files you can find on the Web.

TABLE 4.3 AUDIO FILE FORMATS ON THE WEB	
File Type	**Platform**
WAV	Windows wave
VOC	Sound Blaster
SND	Sun/NeXT
AU	Sun/NeXT
AIF/AIFF	Macintosh
MID/MIDI	MIDI music
MOD	Amiga, Atari ST
UL	US Telephony
IFF	Amiga

File Transfer Protocol (FTP)

Often when you're on the Web and are downloading a file, you may actually be using FTP. This is especially true when using a browser like Navigator or Internet Explorer. These browsers, like some others, support FTP without the need of another application.

The difference between a page of FTP resources and a typical Web page is that FTP information appears in a column on the left side of the page. Each file on the FTP site includes information about itself. This is the same directory information you obtain if you use a separate FTP utility (such as WS_FTP) to poll the file. This information includes the file name, the file size, and the date and time the file was saved. Also available in the FTP listing are the directories and subdirecotries at the FTP site.

You also see general information about the FTP server at the top of the page, including any announcements, warnings, policies, or site maintenance information about the FTP site. You might also see a related URL to a Web site with more information. This text appears in monospace font (`this is monospace font`) and is stored in a message text file on the FTP site. Next to each directory is a yellow folder icon. Files have small floppy disk icons. A paper icon indicates a text file, such as a README or INDEX file stored on the FTP server. Figure 4.49 shows an example of an FTP site accessed with Navigator.

To see the contents of a directory, click the hyperlink for that directory. This displays a new page in the browser window, with the current directory displayed at the top of the page. If you want to download a file, simply click the file and Navigator downloads it to your machine. When it's on your computer, you can use it like any other file on your system.

The URL format used to connect to an FTP site is ftp://ftp.*rest_of_url*. An example is **ftp://ftp.cac.psu.edu/pub/genealogy**, which is an FTP site devoted to genealogy information. Notice that instead of http://, which links you to a Web site, you use ftp:// instead. You enter this URL in the Location list box in Navigator, or choose File, Open Location and enter the URL. If the FTP server is an anonymous FTP site, Netscape attempts to log you in using anonymous as your username. If a site requires a password and specific username to gain access, you can enter the username as part of the URL, as follows:

ftp://username@ftp.rest_of_url

Press Enter after entering this. (Be sure to use your username for the preceding *username* parameter.) The next page that displays is a sign-in page where you must

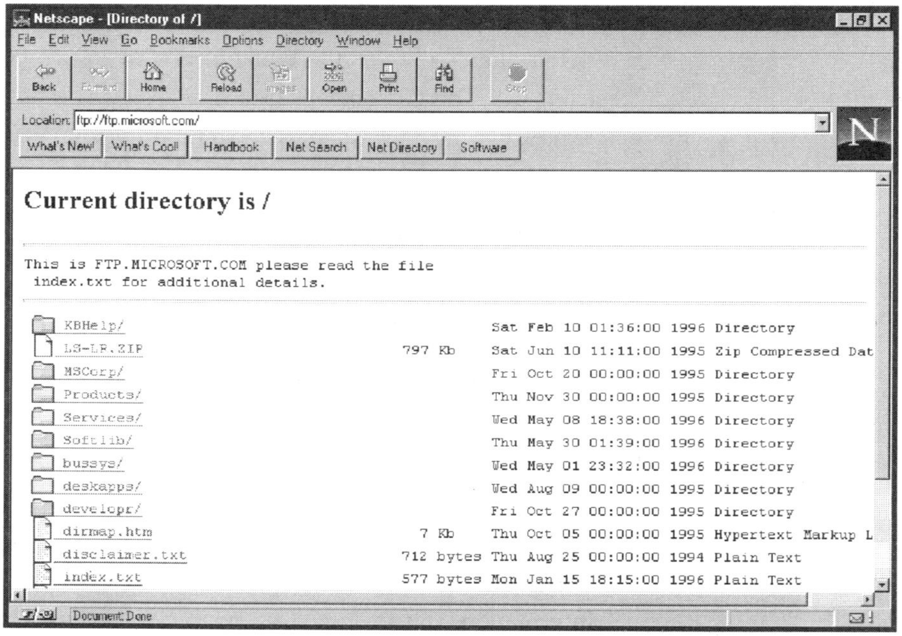

FIGURE 4.49

FTP sites (when accessed with Navigator) include hyperlinks to directories and files.

enter an assigned password to get access. If you don't enter your username in the FTP URL, you'll see a blank space to enter your username as well as your password.

You can upload a file using Navigator by connecting to an FTP site and choosing File, Upload File. In the Source dialog box, select the file to upload and click Open. If the FTP site allows you to upload files, the file is sent from your local computer to the remote computer. If you don't have proper permission to upload files, you'll receive an error message to that effect. If you think there's a problem, contact the administrator of the FTP site to get proper authority to be sent files from the remote server.

Usually, if you have to download or upload a number of files by FTP, you use a separate program, such as WS_FTP. WS_FTP lets you store multiple FTP sites with username and password information about each. This way, if you have several FTP sites that require you to use different usernames and passwords (which is usually the case), you can save these settings between each session so you don't have to remember them.

Another reason to use a program like WS_FTP is that you can download or upload multiple files. If you have to download several large files during an FTP session, it gets very tiring doing one file at a time. Likewise, if you have to upload several files at a time, it's nice to send several files in one batch. As your files upload or download, you can be doing something else.

Telnet

On the Apps tab of the General Properties Sheet (choose Options, General Properties), you can specify a few applications that support Navigator, such as Telnet applications. You use Telnet applications to establish terminal-based communications with other remote systems. Telnet is an old protocol that's still used by some services and isn't directly supported by Navigator. You can't use a Telnet service unless you have configured a Telnet application to work with Navigator.

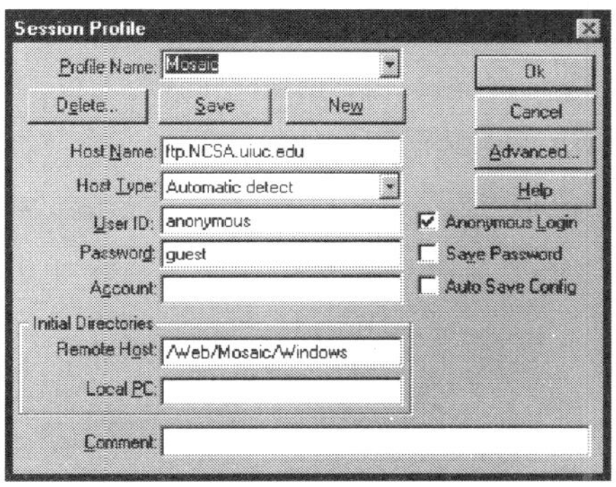

FIGURE 4.50

The Session Profile window in WS_FTP enables you to enter an FTP host name and connect to that server.

Installing WS_FTP

The following steps show you how to access an FTP site using WS_FTP:

1. Start WS_FTP to display the Session Profile dialog box (see Figure 4.52). To use WS_FTP, install it on your computer and start it. In the Session Profile dialog box, enter **ftp://ftp.microsoft.com** in the in the Host Name text box. This URL is for the Microsoft FTP site.
2. From the Host Type drop-down list, select Automatic detect. This tells WS_FTP to automatically determine the type of computer operating system you're logging into.
3. Check the Anonymous Login check box and enter your e-mail address or the word **guest** in the Password text box. The type of FTP site that allows you to login this way is known as an anonymous FTP site. Click OK.
4. The WS_FTP window appears. On the right side of the screen is the remote computer at the Microsoft site. The left side of the screen shows your local computer's files and directories.
5. Locate a file in the Remote System list to download and then click the transfer button in the middle of the window (it has a left-facing arrow).
6. The file copies to your computer system into the directory shown in the Local System list box. When the transfer completes, your system may beep. You'll also see a message at the bottom of the WS_FTP window that tells you the transfer was completed and successful. If there was a problem during downloading, you'll see a message to that effect as well.

After you finish downloading the file, click the Exit button to disconnect from the remote FTP site.

NOTE

If you use Windows 95, you can use its built-in Telnet application as Navigator's Telnet application. To do this, enter the path and file name of the Telnet program in the Telnet Application text box on the Apps tab. Usually, you can find the Telnet program in the Windows 95 program using the name TELNET.EXE, such as C:WINDOWS95TELNET.EXE.

Another Telnet application is Wintel for Windows. You can download this application at the following FTP site:

ftp://gatekeeper.dec.com/pub/micro/msdos/win3/winsock/wintelb3.zip

If you have a Telnet connection to an IBM mainframe, you'll need to use the TN3270 Application line and enter the path and file name of the TN3270 application you're using.

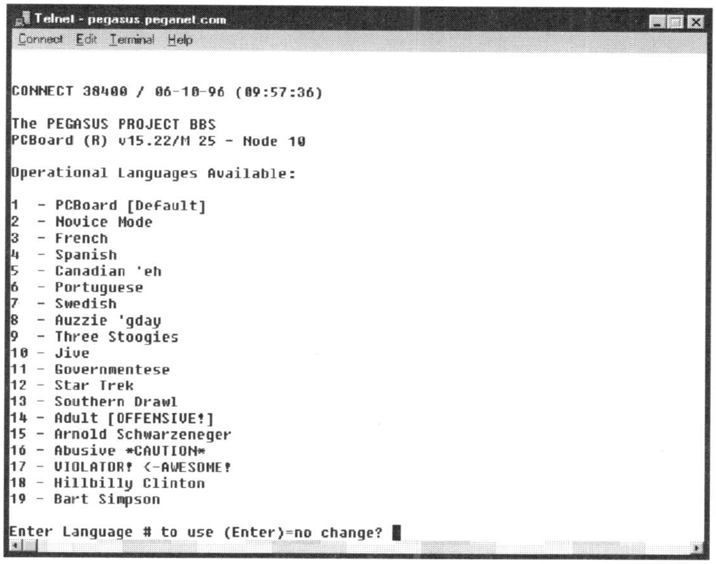

FIGURE 4.51

Although Telnet is not used that often on the Internet, you may still find yourself using it to access your e-mail or other Internet services.

Some people who don't have a direct connection to the Web use Telnet to access their e-mail or to surf the Web. Figure 4.51 shows a sample Telnet session. Except on very rare occasions or if you must access them for your work, you probably won't spend too much time using Telnet.

E-mail

For new e-mail users, the Navigator e-mail manager is a perfect way to introduce yourself to the world of e-mail. It's easy to use, relatively simple to configure, and has toolbar buttons that make creating, responding to, and sending messages very easy. New users will also like the window panes that separate folders, incoming mail, and the message body. You can resize these panes to view more or less information in a given pane, depending on your needs at the time.

When you establish an Internet account with a service provider, you receive a few pieces of information that will come in handy when you configure Navigator to receive and send e-mail. Before you can use the Navigator e-mail manager, however, you need to provide Navigator with information about your computer, your access provider (your ISP), yourself, and about how you want the e-mail manager to look on-screen.

There are general areas you need to configure when preparing Navigator to handle e-mail. These include the following:

- The appearance of e-mail messages in Navigator
- The encoding and queueing of your messages

- The manner in which the server stores e-mail until you download it
- Your username and password
- The manner in which e-mail manager organizes each message

You set your e-mail preferences in Navigator by choosing Options, Mail and News Preferences. This displays the Preferences dialog box, which contains tabs that correspond to the five settings previously listed. Although each setting is important, the Servers tab can be confusing. The following section walks you through setting up the information on this tab.

Setting Server Information

In Chapter 2, you learned how to configure the TCP/IP stack and dialer software that Navigator uses. You had to input some data that your ISP or network administrator gave you—namely, your account name and IP address. You need to get that information here to fill in the Servers tab of the Preferences dialog box.

The Servers tab is the most important tab you will fill out for your e-mail to work properly (see Figure 4.52). If you don't set this information correctly, Navigator won't be capable of accessing your ISP's mail server (the remote computer on which the ISP stores your mail until you retrieve it).

The following list describes the options on the Servers tab and how to use them:

- **Outgoing Mail (SMTP) Server.** Designate the Simple Mail Transport Protocol provided by your ISP in this text box. If your ISP did not provide you with specific SMTP information, try entering **MAIL**.

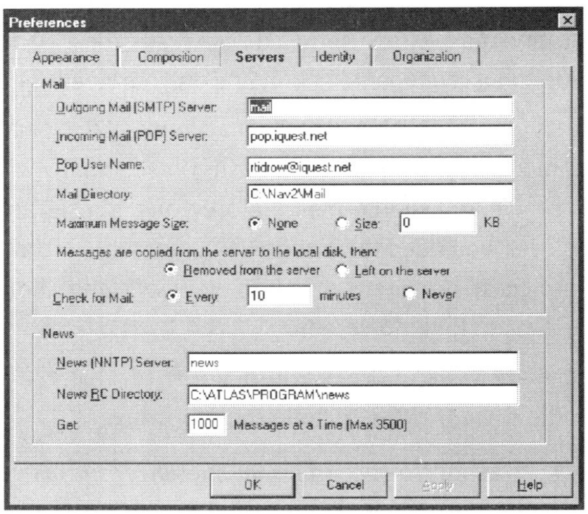

FIGURE 4.52

Use the Servers tab to configure the POP and SMTP servers you'll use to access and send your mail.

- **Incoming Mail (POP) Server.** Set the name of your service provider's POP3 server in this text box. Get this name from your ISP. Usually the name is *pop* followed by the domain name of your ISP, such as pop.iquest.net.

NOTE

POP (Post Office Protocol) is an e-mail system that configures the mailbox in your computer to be the primary mailbox rather; otherwise, the primary mailbox resides at your ISP. POP controls all incoming mail.

- **Pop User Name.** Add your username here. This is not your full e-mail address, only your username(usually, this is the information to the left of the @ symbol in your e-mail address). For example, my full e-mail address is rtidrow@iquest.net, so my username is rtidrow. If this strategy doesn't seem to work for you, contact your ISP for help.
- **Mail Directory.** This is the path to your Navigator mail folder, which stores incoming messages. The default setting should look something like C:NAV2NAVIGATORMAIL. If you want to store your incoming message in a different directory, enter the path here.
- **Maximum Message Size.** By default, None is selected, but you can click the Size radio button and fill in a number to indicate the maximum size (in kilobytes) for your mail messages.
- **Messages Are Copied from the Server to the Local Disk, Then.** You can configure Navigator to remove your e-mail messages from your ISP's server after you download them to your machine or you can click Left On The Server to leave your messages on the server. Be aware, however, that most ISPs periodically delete messages left on the server to free up space. You may want to leave your messages on the server if you're evaluating the Navigator e-mail manager while still using another e-mail client to read and send messages.
- **Check for Mail.** This option lets you configure how often Navigator checks for new mail messages while the e-mail manager is running. You can click Every and then enter a number in minutes. You also can click Never, which tells Navigator not to check for mail while the e-mail manager is running. If you click this radio button, you can check for mail manually by choosing File, Get New Mail.

After you establish these settings, click OK to save your configuration and to return to the Navigator browser window.

Using Navigator's E-mail Manager

When you use any e-mail package, whether it's Navigator, Microsoft Exchange, or Eudora Light, you can accomplish four basic tasks:

- Create and reply to e-mail
- Read e-mail
- Send e-mail
- Organize e-mail

After you configure the Navigator e-mail manager, you can start it by choosing Window, Mail in Navigator. Navigator displays the e-mail manager in a new, separate window. If you instructed Navigator to remember your mail password (in the Identity tab of the Preferences property sheet), then a window similar to the one in Figure 4.53 should appear on your screen.

If you elected to have Navigator prompt you for your password each time you start the e-mail manager, you'll see a dialog box asking for your password. Enter your password and press Enter or click OK. By default, Navigator looks for any

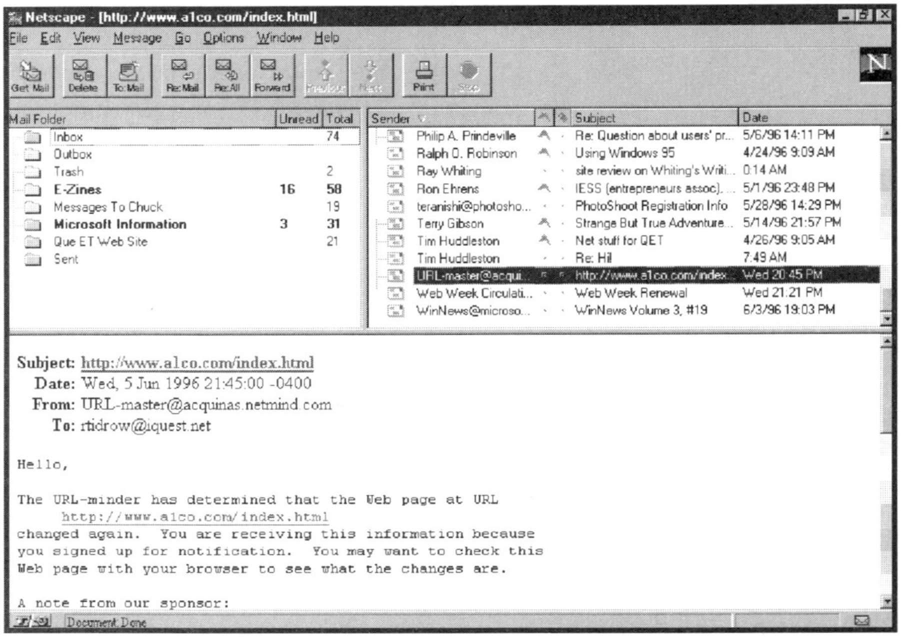

FIGURE 4.53

The Navigator e-mail manager window displays your mail folders, message headings, and currently selected mail message.

new mail messages you may have received and displays them in the e-mail manager window.

TIP

If you want to start the e-mail manager but work offline—that is, while not connected to the Internet—click the Cancel button to close the Password Entry Dialog box. If Navigator automatically remembers your password when you first start the e-mail manager, click the Stop button on the e-mail manager toolbar to work offline. When you work offline, you can create new messages, read and reply to messages in your Inbox, and organize and manage your messages, without paying for online time.

The upper-left pane of the e-mail window is the *mail folders pane*. This pane includes the names of the folders in which your mail is stored. By default, two folders are included: Inbox and Trash. The Inbox folder contains all the messages that Navigator downloads for you to read. The Trash folder is the folder that holds deleted messages until you instruct Navigator to delete them from your system for good.

If you configured Navigator to copy messages you send, Navigator creates a Sent folder to hold those copies.

The mail folders pane also includes the Unread and Total columns. The Unread column shows you the number of unread messages in a folder. This information is helpful if you want to know if you've read all the messages you've received without scrolling through the list of message in the message header pane. You can see the total number of messages you have in each folder by looking in the Total column.

NOTE

If you want to add your own folder to the mail folder pane, choose File, New Folder. In the Netscape User Prompt dialog box, enter a name for your new folder and click OK. Your new folder will appear above the Sent folder (if that folder exists) or at the bottom of the Folder list.

The upper-right pane of the e-mail manager window is the *message headers pane*. This pane lists the messages you have in the selected folder. Messages that have not been read are in boldface. By default, the Inbox folder opens when you start the e-mail manager, showing you all the messages you've received.

The message headers pane include the following columns:

- **Sender.** Shows the name of the sender who mailed you the message.
- **Flag.** Shows a small red flag icon when you have flagged a message. See the section "Managing Flagged, Marked, and Threaded Messages" for information on how to use this column.
- **Marked as Unread.** Shows a small green diamond icon when a message has not been read. After you read a message, the green diamond icon is replaced by a small gray icon. You can toggle between unread and read by clicking this column next to a message.
- **Subject.** Shows the message subject.
- **Date.** Shows the date you received the message from your mail server. This isn't the date the message was sent to you by the sender. For that information, you need to look at the Date line in the actual message.

Finally, the bottom pane is the *message text pane*, which displays the text of the message you're reading.

TIP

You can resize a pane by moving the mouse pointer over the thick bar that separates each window until the pointer changes to a double-sided arrow. Drag the window pane up, down, left, right, depending on how you want to resize it.

You can move around in each pane by using the scroll bars that appear in a pane when text, folders, or message headers scroll out of view.

Creating and Sending Mail

By now, you should be ready to create and send a message. This section shows you how and, in fact, it's fairly simple.

To compose a new message, click the New Message button or choose File, New Mail Message. The Message Composition window appears, in which you place a recipient address, message subject, and message text (see Figure 4.54). If you have a signature file, it will automatically display in the Message Composition

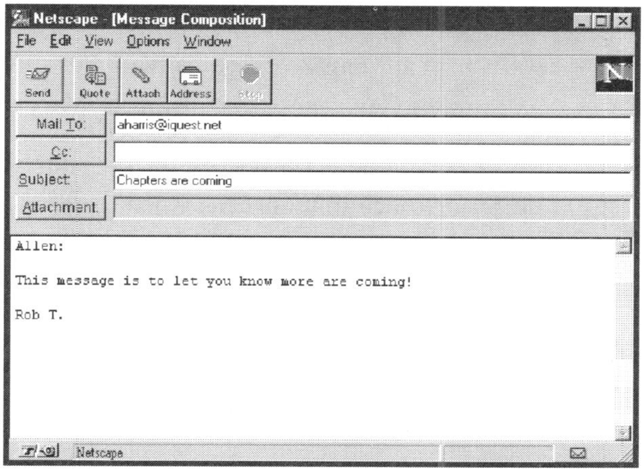

FIGURE 4.54

Use the Message Composition window to create new e-mail messages to send to colleagues, friends, and other recipients.

window. A *signature file* is a separate text file you can create that appears at the bottom of all of your e-mail messages. Usually, signature files are only four to six lines in length and include your contact information and sometimes a pithy statement about life. You also can attach a file to your message and send a carbon copy of your message to other recipients.

Use the following steps to create a new message:

1. Enter the recipient's e-mail address in the Mail To text box.

   If you have addresses saved in your Address Book, you can click the Mail To button and select a name from the Address Book window. Click a name or set of names (use the Ctrl key to select more than one name), click the To: button, and then click OK. This places all the names you selected in the Mail To field, separated by commas (but no spaces after the commas).

   It's important to remember that the address must be typed exactly as given to you. If the e-mail address is entered incorrectly on your end or if the e-mail address doesn't exist, it can't be delivered.

NOTE

You can save e-mail addresses in the Navigator Address Book. When using the Address Book, you need to enter a person's name and address only once rather than each time you create a mail message.

2. *Optional:* You can enter an address in the Cc: text box if you want to carbon copy your message to another person. This is handy if you send

messages to primary recipients and have secondary recipients who you want to read your message as well. Recipients on the Cc: list can read and reply to your messages just as primary recipients can.

You also can select a person in the Address Book and click on the Cc button to place that person's e-mail address in the Cc: text box.

TIP

To send a blind carbon copy (Bcc), choose View, Mail Bcc. This enables you to enter a recipient's address without others on your message list knowing you sent a copy to that person. You also can select a person in the Address Book and click the Bcc button to place that person's e-mail address in the Bcc: text box. You must first display the Bcc: text box by choosing View, Mail Bcc, however.

3. Enter a short description of the message in the Subject text box. This will be the header name that appears in the recipient's inbox. Make it short, but descriptive.
4. Start writing your message in the message list box by clicking in that part of the window, or by pressing the Tab key until the cursor appears in that pane.

   If you instructed Navigator to include a signature file on your messages, you'll see your signature file text a few lines down from the top of the message text box. You'll place your message text above the signature text. Any text below the signature text will probably not be read because most users tend to stop reading when they get to the signature text.

   For the most part, you can enter any characters in your message that are on a standard keyboard. You can also paste non-formatted text from the Windows Clipboard. To paste text from the Clipboard, use one of the following methods:

   Press Crtl+V on the keyboard;

   Choose Edit, Paste.

   Right-click on the message area and choose Paste from the context menu.

You can't place graphics, formatted text (such as bold or italic text), and so on in your message. If you want to send files that contain formatting, graphics, or are binary files (such as shareware programs), you need to attach these files to your message.

NOTE

Although you cannot directly place binary files in your message while using the Message Composition window, you can take advantage of Navigator's rich content capabilities. For example, you can send an attached file to another user and it will display in the message text list box as if it were the message itself. If you send a graphic file, the graphic will be displayed in the message text list box as a graphic. For this to work, the recipient must also be using Navigator's e-mail manage and have selected the View, Attachments Inline command. If the View, Attachments as Links command is selected, the attachment you send is displayed as an attached file to the mail message.

5. When you finish writing your mail message, click the Send button or choose File, Send Now. If you're online, Navigator will send the mail to your recipient over the Internet. If you're not online, Navigator displays your dial-up software (such as the Dial-Up Networking Connect To window in Windows 95) and informs you that you need to connect and log onto the Internet before you can send the message.

You can configure Navigator to line up (or queue) your messages and send them all at once. To set this in the Mail Composition window, choose Options, Deferred Delivery. When you're ready to send your messages, choose File, Send Mail in Outbox. This command doesn't appears unless you have selected the Deferred Delivery command.

Why do this? You'll want to do this if you compose your messages offline and queue them for delivery the next time you log onto the Internet. You also may do this if you have several messages to go out and you want to create them all before sending them, either for accuracy or so you don't have to wait for Navigator to send out each message before starting a new one.

Retrieving and Reading Mail

Each time you open the e-mail manager in Navigator, it automatically looks on your host mail server for any new messages. If you receive several e-mail messages a day, you may want to start the e-mail manager and place it in the background as it downloads your mail. To do this, just click another open window on your desktop or start a new application. This places the e-mail manager behind the other windows and lets you continue working.

Of course, after you receive an e-mail message, you'll want to read it. To do this, click the message header of the message you want to read in the message header pane. Your e-mail message appears in the bottom pane for you to read. You may need to maximize the mail window, resize the pane, or scroll through the message to read it completely.

To move from one message to another, you can simply click a new message in the message header pane, or click the Previous or Next buttons to display the messages before or after the one you're reading. You also can choose Go, Next Message or Go, Previous Message.

To save an attached file to your computer, click the hot link to the attachment in the message that contains it. If Navigator knows how to handle that particular file type, it will automatically process it. Usually, however, Navigator will display the Unknown File Type dialog box. Click the Save File button and save the file to your hard disk. After the file is on your hard disk, you can use it like any other file.

Using Mailing Lists

In Chapter 3, you learned about mailing lists. Most mailing lists are available to anyone who wants to subscribe to them. Usually, the hardest part of joining a list is finding if one exists for a specific topic you're interested in and then locating instructions on how to subscribe.

You can get a listing of mailing lists by sending an e-mail request to the following address:

mail-server@rtfm.mit.edu

In the body of the message, type

send /usenet/news.answers/mail/mailing-lists/*

Make sure you place the space after the word *send* and don't forget the asterisk at the end.

When you subscribe to any list, you'll be given instructions similar to the ones you just read. You must follow them exactly as shown or you will not be included in the mailing list. Mail servers (known as *listservs*) automatically handle your request and place you on the mailing list. These mail servers are computer programs that are designed to handle specific requests; they cannot guess to which mailing list you want to subscribe.

The following steps show you how to subscribe to a mailing list. This example shows how to subscribe to the Microsoft WinNews newsletter, an electronic newsletter that gets sent to all subscribers.

1. Enter **ENEWS99@MICROSOFT.NWNET.COM** in the Mail To text box in the Message Composition window in Netscape Mail.

   Be sure to send the message from the account you want to subscribe (some people use more than one e-mail account).

2. *Do not* fill in the Subject text box. This must be blank for your subscription request to work.

3. In the body of the message, type **SUBSCRIBE WINNEWS.**

When the remote computer receives and processes your message, it places you on the mailing list and you start receiving all the mail posted to that list.

One way to take advantage of mailing lists is to wait for a day or so before posting messages to the list. This way you can read some of the postings to understand policies, etiquette, and what types of people are on this list. Some mailing lists don't accept replies to them. These types of list (like the WINNEWS one in the preceding steps) are generally maintained by an organization or company that wants to disseminate a great deal of information in an organized, timely, and electronic way.

When you receive notification that you're part of a mailing list, the notification will have specific instructions on how to unsubscribe from the list. Keep these. You'll need them when you want the messages from that list to stop coming to you.

Gopher

Similar to FTP, Navigator includes support of Gopher sites on the Web (see Figure 4.55). You can also use a program like Hgopher to access Gopher resources. When you access a Gopher site with Navigator or a stand-alone Gopher application, you're presented with text-only display of information. You also are shown links on which you can click to display or download a file.

There a couple major differences between Gopher and the Web. First, you don't see entire pages until you select a specific document or file. Gopher is a series of menus that display titles of the files and documents. Gopher isn't a text transport protocol like hypertext transport protocol (HTTP). Instead, it's designed to deliver information in an organized way that FTP or Telnet cannot do.

Another difference is that it's relatively fast. One reason for this is that Gopher doesn't support graphics. There's just text. Another reason Gopher seems fast is

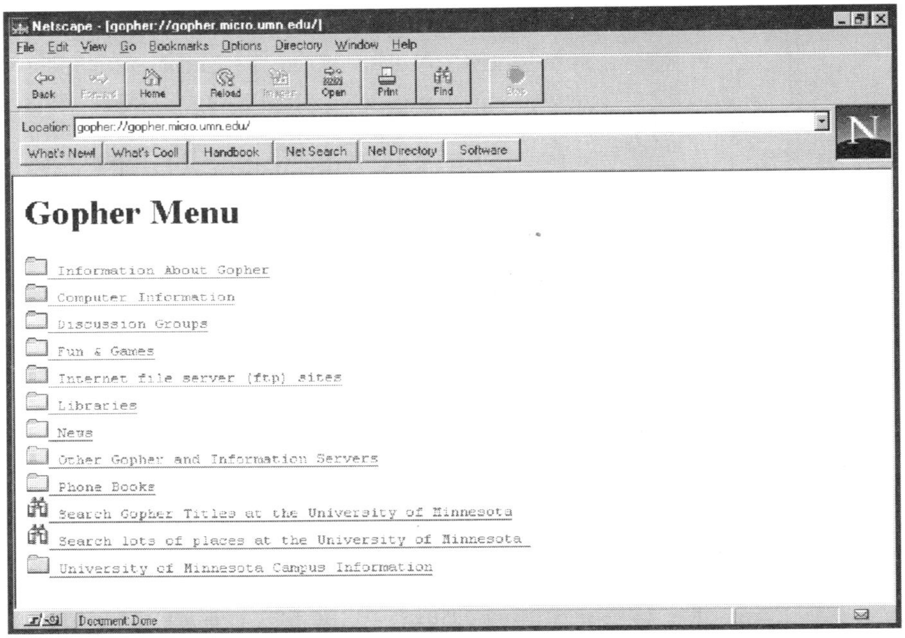

FIGURE 4.55

Gopher organizes content in menus, and enables you to click on links to view a document or graphic and to download a file.

because most of the people on the Internet are using e-mail, the Web, and FTP. This leaves gopherspace pretty empty.

Finally, Gopher doesn't support the capability to send forms back and forth. This means users who want to communicate with each other must do so using newsgroups, chats, or e-mail. If a Gopher site is open for any user, the Gopher administrator has no way of asking visitors to fill out a questionnaire or "guestbook." This is important if a site wants to keep a log of who's using their resources and for what reasons. On the other hand, many Web sites request user feedback to obtain demographic information, as well as suggestions for building a better Web presence.

To access a Gopher site using Navigator, enter the URL in the Location list box. Use the following syntax for Gopher URLs:

gopher://rest_of_url

Unless specifically part of the name, you do not have to include the word "gopher" after the slashes in the URL. When you enter a Gopher site, the files and links display on the left side of the Navigator window. Unlike FTP files, however, the document and file names in a Gopher menu can contain longer descriptions. This results in easier to read links to a file. Gopher menus use titles like "Glossary of Legislative Terms," "Legislative Rules - Assembly Rules," and "Text of Assembly Bill AB1624."

To find a Gopher site with information you need, one quick method is to use *Veronica (very easy rodent-oriented netwide index to computerized archives).* Veronica is a Gopher search tool that searches Gopher servers on the Internet and creates a database of all the documents and files on those servers. Users then can access a Veronica search page and enter search criteria.

To locate a Veronica server in Navigator, use the following steps:

1. Enter **gopher://gopher.micro.umn.edu** in the Location list box in Netscape. This takes you to the University of Minnesota Gopher server.
2. Scroll down the page and click the link called "Other Gopher and Information Servers." (It's about half-way down the page.)
3. On the next menu, click the link called "Search titles in Gopherspace using Veronica." This opens a menu with several search links. (Notice the binocular icons to indicate links to search pages.)
4. Click the link called "Search GopherSpace by Title words(s) (via NYSERNet)." This leads you to the Gopher Search page shown in Figure 4.56.
5. Enter your search criteria in the search text box and press Enter. A Gopher menu with the search results appears.

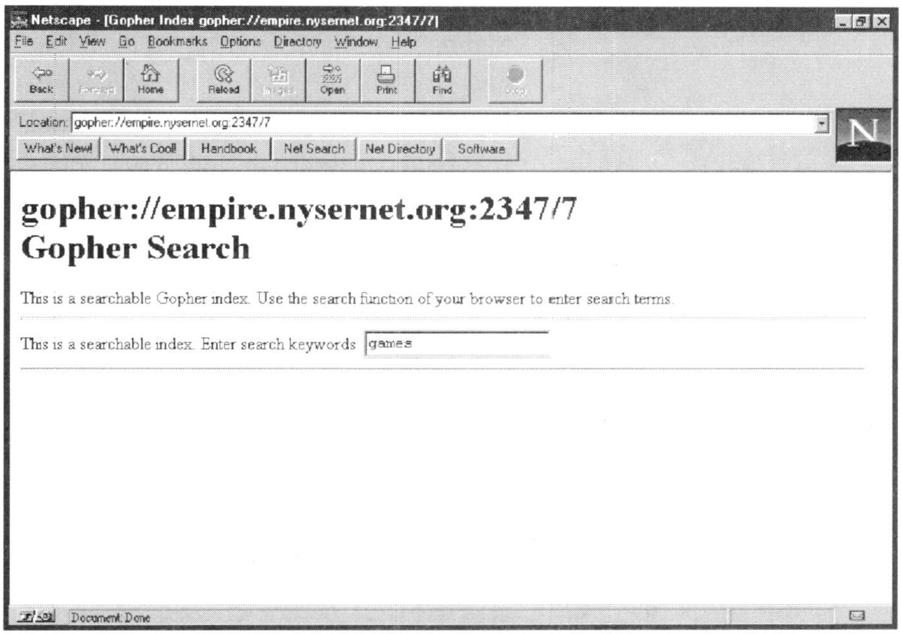

FIGURE 4.56

Use a Veronica search page to look something up while using Gopher.

NOTE

Another Gopher search tool is Jughead, *created by Rhett "Jonzy" Jones. Jughead stands for Jonzy's Universal Gopher Hierarchy Excavation and Display. Unlike Veronica, which searches the entire gopherspace, Jughead searches only on the server on which it is installed. Jughead searches that one server very extensively and gives back very precise search results for that server. On the other, Veronica uses a more comprehensive searching action for all of gopherspace.*

Chat

There are several stand-alone chat utilities that enable you to connect to *Internet Relay Chat (IRC)*. Unfortunately, Navigator does not support chat. This means you have to obtain an IRC application, such as Netscape Chat. This is an easy-to-use program that enables you to connect to and communicate on the IRC. Many of the techniques you use in this section with Netscape Chat can be used with other IRC applications.

When you start Netscape Chat, you see a dialog box similar to the one shown in Figure 4.57, the Server Connection dialog box. Enter your personal information (such as the on-screen nickname you'll use) and enter the IRC server to which you'll connect.

The following list describes each of the options on the Server Connection dialog box:

- **Name.** Lists the server name of the IRC server to which you want to connect. When you install Netscape Chat, it places the Netscape Communications IRC server (known as the Netscape Community System Chat Server) in the list. You can also enter a different server here. Netscape

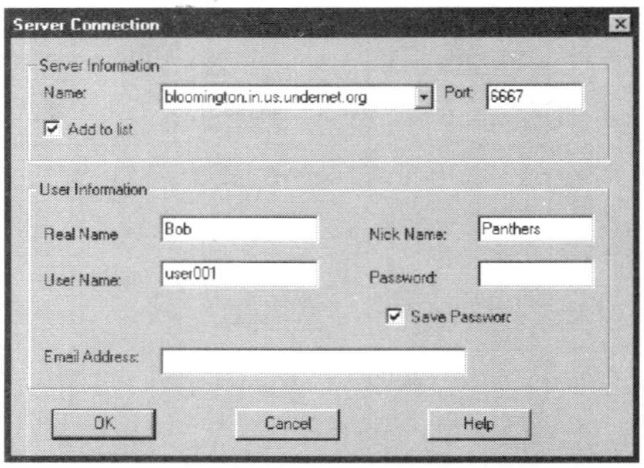

FIGURE 4.57

The Server Connection dialog box displays when you first start Netscape Chat.

Chat will save this name for you if you check the Add To List check box. After you add a name to the Name list box, you can select any of the entered server names from the Name drop-drown list. This saves you from reentering the same IRC server name each time you start Netscape Chat.

- **Port.** Shows the port number for the IRC server. Unless otherwise noted, this number is 6667. The port number is determined by your server or by the site administrator. Sometimes, you may need to enter 6668, 6669, or 7000 as the Port value. If none of these work, contact the site administrator for the correct port number.
- **Real Name.** Enter your real name in this text box. If you don't want other chat users to know your real name, enter a bogus one here. Although your real name doesn't appear on the main chat screen when you're connected to a server and have selected a channel, users can view a list of all nicknames and their associated real names.
- **Nick Name.** Enter an alias in this text box. This will be your on-screen name while you're in a chat session. Many users like to choose a nickname that reflects their personality, such as Gofer, Panther, Crawl, and Snoozer. You can enter any nickname here. If you connect to a server where someone else is already using the same nickname as you, you'll need to change your nickname before you can connect to that server.
- **User Name.** Most IRC servers don't require that this text box be filled in. Some, however, require a specific username for you before you can connect to that server. IRC servers that require a username will assign you one when you register with it—which is usually accomplished through e-mail. IRC servers that require usernames usually want to control the number of users logging into it, or want to have some control over the content and direction of conversations. This includes chats that are intended for business, training, or other focused conversations.
- **Password.** Includes the password to connect to the selected IRC server. Most servers don't require that you fill in this text box. If you need to enter a username for an IRC server, however, you probably will be given a password that must be entered before you are granted permission to connect. Check the Save Password check box to have Netscape Chat save a password for an IRC server. For now, you can leave this text box blank.
- **Email Address.** Lists your e-mail address. You need to input this manually, but can leave it blank if you do not want others to know your e-mail address.

TIP

If you don't want to be bothered by other users from a chat session, enter an alias in the Real Name field and leave the e-mail line blank. Many female chat users have complained about being bombarded with threatening messages after other users become aware they're female.

After you fill in the Server Connection dialog box, click OK to connect to the server you indicated in the Name text box. The Conversation Channels dialog box appears (see Figure 4.58). Chat lists all the channels associated with the IRC server to which you're connected. You need to select a channel before you can join in a conversation. The next section shows you how to do this.

If you enter a server to which you cannot connect, or if you've entered an incorrect name, Netscape Chat displays a message stating that an error has occurred in resolving the server host name. Click OK and click the Connect button on the Console toolbar to open the Server Connection dialog box. From the Server Connection dialog box, you can select or enter another server name.

Another problem you may encounter is connecting to a server in which your nickname is already being used by someone else. If this is the case, you'll see a message in the Console window that tells you that someone else is using the same nickname and that you'll need to change your nickname. To do this, you usually can click in the Notepad pane at the bottom of the window (the white part of the window), type the command **/nick**, and enter a new nickname. After

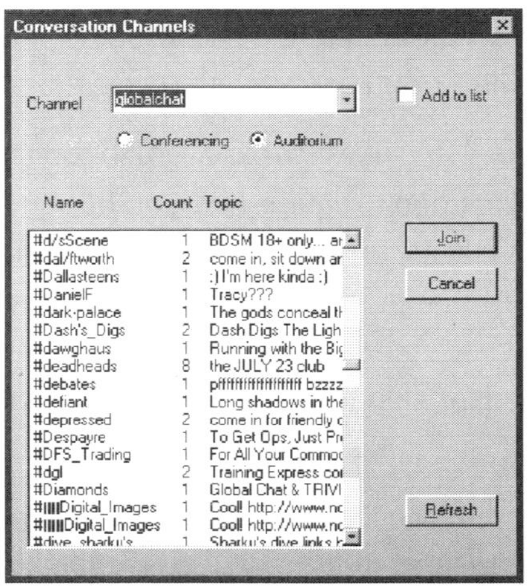

FIGURE 4.58

The Conversation Channels dialog box in Netscape Chat is where all the "action" is.

you enter a nickname, press Enter and the IRC server will either make the change or inform you that you need to choose yet another nickname. When you finally find a nickname that works, click the Group toolbar icon to display the Conversation Channels window.

Selecting a Server Channel

After you connect to an IRC server, you need to select a channel to join. The Channel drop-down list shows recently visited channels. If you see a channel in that list that interests you, click it to connect to that channel. You may experience problems with Netscape Chat if the channel name is not on the IRC server to which you're currently connected. Sometimes, if you click a channel that is not on that server, Netscape Chat will hang (cease to work) and you will need to restart.

You can see a complete list of the available channels on the connected server in the list at the bottom of the Conversation Channels dialog box. This lists the name of the channel, the number of currently connected users, and a short description of the channel topic (refer to Figure 4.58).

If you want to stay away from chats that have a large number of users participating, look for the Count column numbers to be fewer than 5 or 10. Many first-time chat users like to join conversations that are small because they're intimidated by overwhelming "crowds" of people in a channel.

If you want to see if any new channels have been added to the IRC server when you're in the Conversation Channels dialog box, click the Refresh button.

To select a channel to join, click the name of the channel and click the Join button. You also can double-click the name to automatically select the channel. When you select a channel, the Conversation Channels dialog box closes. The conferencing window displays, with the name of the channel in the title bar of the window. Figure 4.59 shows the Auditorium: #globalchat window.

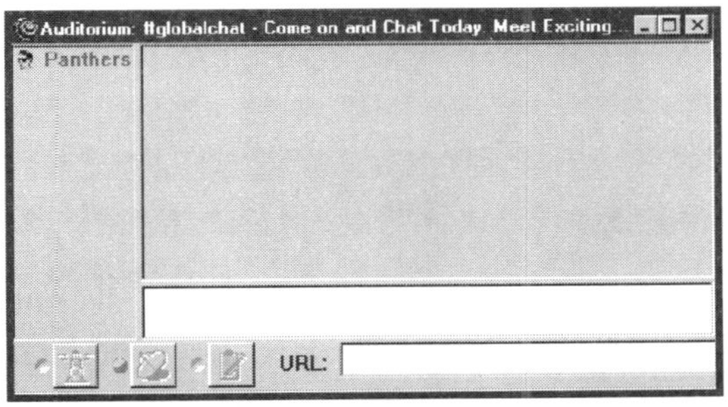

FIGURE 4.59

The name of the channel is displayed in the title bar of the Conference window.

Once You're Connected to a Channel...

Look at the Chat status bar at the bottom of the Netscape Chat window to see if you're connected to a server yet. If you aren't connected to a server, your current status will be Idle. After you're connected, the Chat status bar will change to indicate your new status, Server Connected.

The Console window is the window that appears behind a Conversation window. Usually, you won't see this window in full view unless you click it or you have a problem with the server after you're connected (such as using a previously reserved nickname).

In addition to some system messages that may display when you first connect to an IRC server, you also may see instructions, notices, or messages displayed in the Console window. Before selecting a channel, you may want to read these messages for more information about related servers, events, or chat sessions. The Bloomington, Indiana server, for example, even displays a fortune cookie message when you connect.

The Conferencing window displays a number of items. At the top of the window is the Chat menu bar and Chat toolbar. On the right side of the window is the list of participants currently tuned into the same channel. Although this area doesn't have an official name, you can think of it as the Participant list. These are the individuals with whom you will be chatting. This list is dynamic and changes as often as new users connect to the channel; it also reflects when a user leaves the channel. When someone leaves, their name disappears from the list.

TIP

If you want to chat with only one person while connected to a chat channel, you can whisper to him or her. To do this, click the person's nickname in the participant list and then compose your message in the Notepad pane. When you're ready to send the message, press Enter. Your message is seen only by the person to whom you are whispering.

Turn off the whispering feature by clicking the person's name again to deselect it. Now, any messages that you send are seen by everyone tuned into that channel.

The Transcript pane is where all the action takes place. This is where messages from you and other users are posted during the chat. As you enter and post new messages, you can see them displayed in the Transcript pane alongside other messages posted by other users. When many users are connected, there may be several conversations going on at once. In fact, you may be involved in many yourself. Pay attention to all the messages to ensure that you're catching everything in your conversation.

As messages appear in the Transcript pane, they scroll off the screen. You can use the scroll bar to scroll back to previously posted messages to catch up on anything you've missed or forgotten. You also may want to enlarge the Conferencing window to let you view more messages at one time.

You "talk" in the Notepad pane at the bottom of the Conferencing window. To talk, simply type in your question, comment, or response and press Enter. Your message shortly appears in the Transcript pane where everyone will be able to read it (unless you're whispering to a person). Before you send the message, you may want to read over it to make sure you typed in everything properly and spelled all the words correctly.

The bottom part of the Conferencing window is the URL toolbar. The URL toolbar contains the toolbar buttons that enable you to send and view URLs to other users who are using Netscape Chat. Most users on IRC (those who aren't using Netscape Chat) will not have capabilities to use these URLs.

Netscape Chat enables you to connect to as many channels on a server as you want. You may want to do this if one channel is particularly slow—but you still want to monitor it for activity as you look for more active or interesting channels. Don't confuse connecting to more than one channel as connecting to more than one server. You can connect to only one IRC server at a time. For most situations, however, you should not find this a limitation if you're interested in locating general chat sessions just to say "Hi" to someone.

Don't be surprised if you open several channels only to find the same type of chatting going on in all of them. Not to be overly pessimistic about chats, but I've found them to be surprisingly boring most of the time even if I have five or six channels active at once.

NOTE

Several new chat applications are coming out that let users select avatars. Avatars are characters that appear onscreen and are intended to portray you or your personality. At the moment, most widespread chat applications that support avatars are primitive or humorous. Microsoft recently release Comic Chat, which lets you pick from a few comical looking avatars (see Figure 4.60). When you start a chat session, your avatar joins others for an on-going comic strip in cyberspace. You can download Comic Chat at ***http://www.microsoft.com****.*

Newsgroups

Internet newsgroups are very popular. Even with the graphics, attractive text, and multimedia files on the Web, users are still attracted to the format of the newsgroups. Basically, newsgroups are electronic bulletin boards where users can read and post messages pertaining to different topics. Several newsgroup applications, called *newsreaders*, are available for Windows. Some of the most popular ones include WinVN, Forte Agent, and Netscape News. Netscape News is available with Navigator; you can access it in the Window menu, much like Netscape's e-mail application.

Reading an article in a newsgroup with Netscape News can be as easy as pointing and clicking. However, Netscape News enhances your viewing by providing some helpful features you may need along the way.

The Netscape News window supplies you with a comfortable interface for viewing and responding to newsgroup messages. You'll find that its interface is similar to the Netscape e-mail interface in a lot of ways. You can even read and post multimedia articles to newsgroups because Navigator is MIME-compliant.

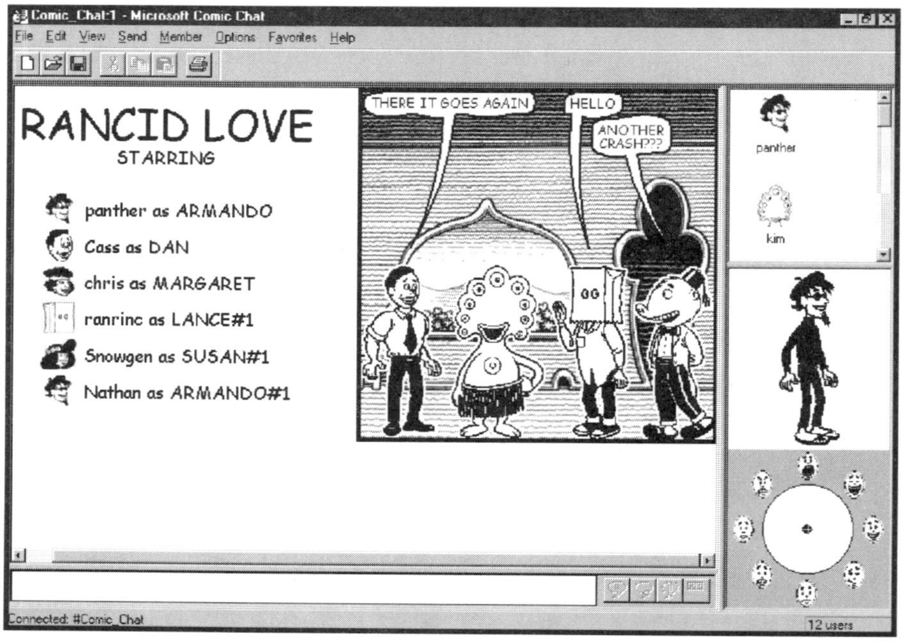

FIGURE 4.60

Comic Chat from Microsoft brings yet another perspective to online chats.

NOTE

Netscape News includes the capability to handle HTML news messages, as well as messages that include multimedia objects such as graphics. When you display a message that contains HTML content, such as a link to a Web site, you can click the link in the message pane and connect to that site via the Navigator browser window. You also can view a graphic file, such as GIF or JPG, that is attached to a newsgroup message. Many businesses and individuals create electronic newsletters and brochures that include information about their Web sites, services, and products, and they include an URL to their site which appears as a "hot link" in the newsgroup message.

Because reading messages is so easy, jump right in.

1. If it's not already open, open the Netscape News window by choosing Window, Netscape News.
2. Click news.announce.newusers in the News Server pane (on the left). It takes a moment for Netscape to retrieve the messages for that newsgroup—they appear in the Message Header pane (on the right).
3. Click any one of the message headers, such as Welcome to Usenet! (if it appears in your listing). The message text appears in the message pane. Your screen will look similar to Figure 4.61.

Read the introductory message information. You may be tempted to skip over the introductory information to the body of the message, but don't. You can't post a response effectively without knowing where to respond.

NOTE

You can subscribe to any newsgroup by clicking on the check boxes next to the newsgroups you want to join in the News Server pane of the Newsgroup window. To display only those newsgroups you have subscribed to, choose Options, Show Subscribed Newsgroup. By doing this you can reduce the number of newsgroups that display in the News Server pane to only those you've selected. If you want to display all the newsgroups on your news server, choose Options, Show All Newsgroups.

The message's subject is listed first, followed by the date of the posting and the sender's address. If the sender of the message provides "Respond To" information, the next line will show you where to respond to the message. Don't assume

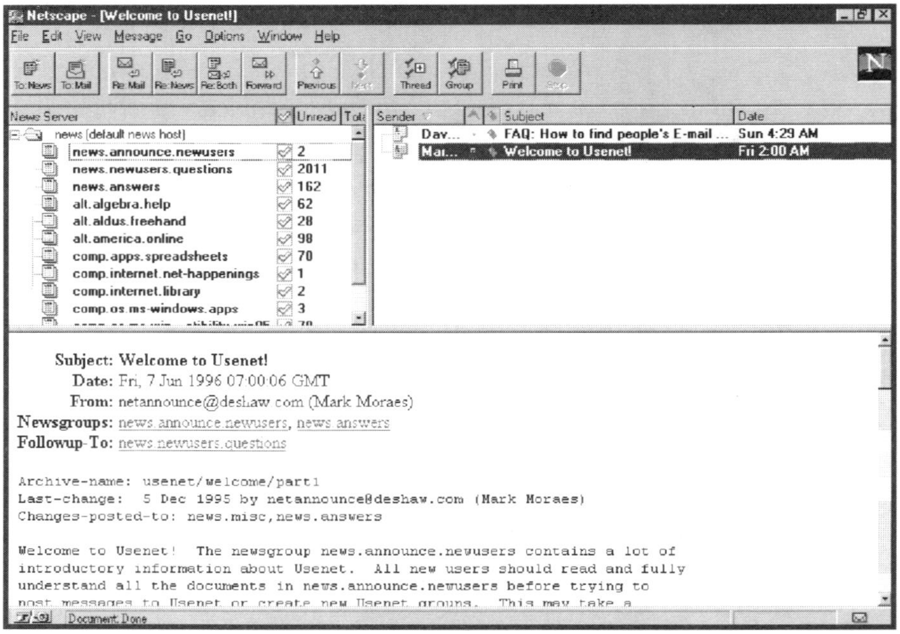

FIGURE 4.61

Reading a news article in Navigator is as simple as clicking a message heading.

that you will post your response to the newsgroup. If the sender of the original posting requests responses be sent by e-mail to him or her, do so.

The final introductory information shows links to other newsgroups and any follow-up links. If you're viewing one of the many messages posted to assist new users (as with this category), you may see further details before getting to the body text, such as information about the original author, the archive name, when the latest changes were made, and the newsgroups to which they were posted.

After the header information, you can read the message. Use the scroll bars to view portions of the message not currently visible. If you want to read another message in the same newsgroup, click it to display the message in the Message pane.

TIP

If you want to save the message to your hard drive, choose File, Save As. When the Save As dialog box appears, enter a path and file name for the file and click the Save button. Your file will be saved as an HTML file. If the message does not contain any original HTML formatting, the File, Save As command doesn't add any tags to the file. It simply saves the file with an HTM extension. If the original

message contains HTML coding, the message retains that code when you choose File, Save As.

Now that you've seen how easy it is to read messages in Netscape News, you can quickly navigate from one message to another using some of the options available on the Go menu:

- If you want to quickly read the next message in the Message Header pane, choose Go, Next Message. This will display the next message in the message pane, regardless of whether you've read the message or not.
- If you want to jump to the next unread message, choose Go, Next Unread.
- To jump back a message, choose Go, Previous Message.
- To read the previous unread message, choose Go, Previous Unread.
- Choose Go, First Unread to see the first message in the Message Header pane that you have not read. This feature is convenient when you frequent a newsgroup and you don't want to scroll through the long list of messages that you've already read.

TIP

If you're new to newsgroups, or even if you aren't, you should read all the postings in this starter set of newsgroups before branching out to the rest of the newsgroups. They provide valuable tips on advertising, how to find USENET groups, and Frequently Asked Questions (and their answers).

Message Threads

By default, related groups of messages are *threaded* in Netscape, making it easier to follow discussions. (A thread is a group of articles regarding the same subject that are grouped together in a newsgroup.) You may not have chosen to thread your mail messages—in which case, articles will be listed in the order you specified in the Preferences property sheet, regardless of their relationship to one another.

Netscape News displays messages in a hierarchical tree structure depending on how you elect to display them. For example, you can display the messages by subject. When you do this, messages that share the same subject will be grouped in the Message Header pane. The subject that has the oldest date in that list of messages will appear at the top of the group of messages. Below the top message are any responses to that message. In Figure 4.62, for example, the subject titled FAQ:rec.music.christian RADIO FAQ has one subordinate message. By using this hierarchical structure, you can quickly scan the Message Header pane for topics that have a lot of activity.

TIP

If you want to change the way the current messages appear in the Message Header pane, you can change the sorting method on the Organization tab of the Preferences property sheet. You can sort by date or sort by sender. You can also click the Sender or Date column at the top of the message header pane. When you do this, the messages are automatically resorted according to which column you clicked. Or, you can click the Subject column to have the messages resorted according to subject.

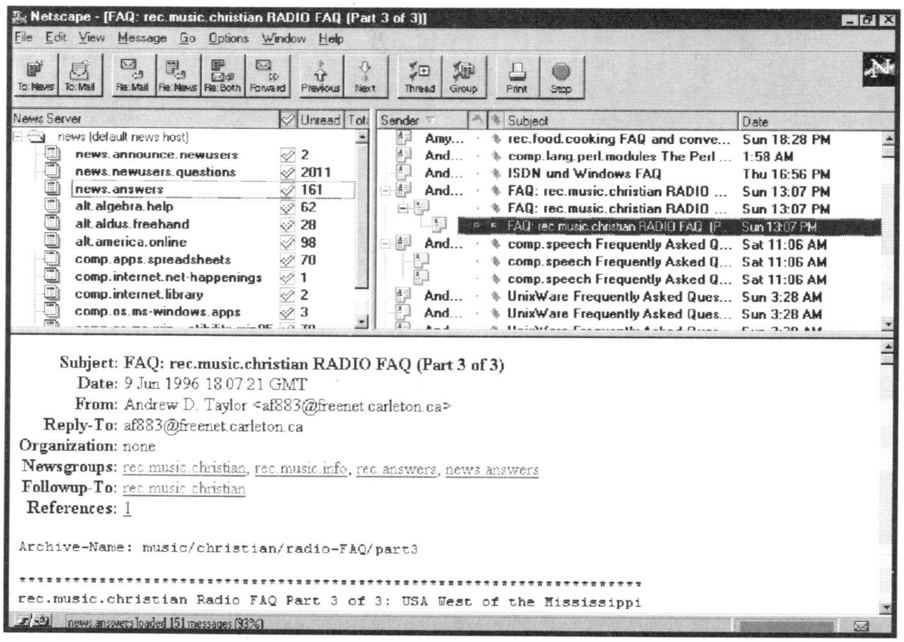

FIGURE 4.62

These messages are displayed in a hierarchical structure in the Message Header pane.

Another feature of the message header pane is the expanding and collapsing views of the message headers. To the left of the sender's name in the Message Header pane a plus (+) or minus (-) sign will appear if more than one message belongs to that thread. Click a plus sign to expand the thread to view additional messages in the thread. Conversely, click a minus sign to collapse the thread.

The View menu on the Netscape News window includes several sorting commands. When you choose View, Sort, a submenu displays with seven options. The Resort option resorts the message headers based on the last method you used to sort the headers. The Thread Messages option tells Netscape News to group threaded messages together. If you turn off this option, the collapsing and expanding features of the Message Header pane do not display. If you want to sort the messages in ascending order (from Z-A), choose the Ascending option. By default, messages are sorted in descending order (A-Z). You've already know how to use By Date, By Subject, and By Sender. By Message Number lets you sort the messages by their message number.

Posting a New Message

After you read the postings in a newsgroup and have a feel for the community, you might want to create a new message (that you feel will benefit the group), or you might want to respond to a message posted to the newsgroup. Consider these suggestions while creating your response:

- Plan what you want to say prior to creating your message. Never supply personal, confidential, or inappropriate information to a newsgroup. Be sure that your Subject titles express the intent of your posting in a concise way, and that your posting is relevant to the focus of the newsgroup. If you're passing along the thoughts of someone else's ideas or expertise, give the appropriate credit to that individual or source.
- Like e-mail, you create your new messages in the Message Composition window. You can use the following steps as a guide when creating a message to post to a newsgroup. (The newsgroup alt.newbies is used for these steps.) Still, you should read all the postings and familiarize yourself with the newsgroup prior to creating a posting.

Now, use the following steps to post a message:

1. In the Netscape News window, locate and select alt.newbies. Remember, to expand your alt category, click the plus sign to the left of the alt. newsgroup entry.

2. You might notice a posting with the Subject "1000 Apologies!!!!" In this posting, the author is apologizing for accidentally posting his initial posting numerous times by accident. Because this is a newbie (someone new to the Internet) newsgroup, most people are generous and will make the author feel comfortable about the matter. This should give you some comfort as you create and post your first message.

3. Take a moment to read the thread or locate another thread whose Subject interests you. After you read the latest posting, click the To: News button on the toolbar (or choose File, New News Message). A message window opens within your e-mail application, indicating the newsgroup to which you will be posting (see Figure 4.63). Always verify that this displays the correct newsgroup.

4. Enter the subject and a short message in the body. Notice that this window doesn't include a To: line. Netscape News assumes that you're posting a reply to the selected newsgroup. The method you use to send depends on which service you're using for e-mail. If you're using Netscape's e-mail utility, click the Send button or choose File, Send Now. If you're using Microsoft Exchange, click the Send button on the toolbar and your message will be posted and available to view shortly.

Posting a Response

Now that you're comfortable with sending a new message to a newsgroup, try posting a response in a thread. When responding to a posting, you'll still want to take all the suggestions into account as you did when creating a posting, but

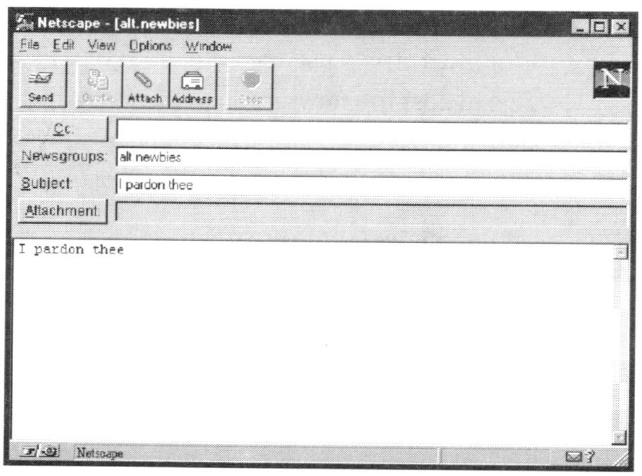

FIGURE 4.63

You create a newsgroup message the same way you do an e-mail message.

there are also other items to consider. Remember to check the follow-up instructions provided in the original article, and have it selected before you begin. Don't post a follow-up message to the newsgroup if the original posting tells you to respond to an e-mail address.

To post a response to a message, select the message to which you want to reply. The message will appear in the message text pane. Next, follow these steps:

1. Click the Post Reply toolbar button. The Message Composition window appears.
2. If you want to send a carbon copy of your reply to someone via e-mail, include that person's e-mail address in the Cc: text box. Don't change header group names or any routing information without referring to the change in the message body.
3. Create your response in the message area. If you don't want to include all of the original message, delete any text you don't want. If you're responding to a specific portion of the original article, include those portions of the original text in quotes in the message body.
4. When you're ready to post your message, click the Send button or choose File, Send Now.

Depending on the newsgroup and the news server to which you're connected, when you post a response or send a new posting to a newsgroup it may take several hours or even days before your message is posted. (Moderated groups may take longer than unmoderated groups.) If you're looking for a quick reply on a matter, such as an answer to a computer question, don't hold your breath. On the other hand, when your message is available in the newsgroup, you may be inundated with responses (or personal e-mail). Or, you might not receive any responses, which doesn't mean it was a bad question, only that no one knows the answer to it.

NOTE

If you get flamed, it was probably due to one of two reasons. First, you might have posted in the wrong newsgroup for that particular topic. Make sure you look around or ask if there's a FAQ file or message that details basic questions about the newsgroup, as well as answers to questions that have been posted there many times. In the alt.music.rush group, for example, don't ask if drummer Neil Peart has cancer. You're bound to get some flames telling you to read the FAQ.

The second reason you might get flamed is that you've entered a newsgroup that has immature people in it. Even if the title of the newsgroup makes you think it is for mature, sane people, it may not be. In these cases, ignore the flames and leave the newsgroup.

The following are some helpful hints when you're posting a response to a newsgroup:

- Don't use CAPITAL LETTERS. These are hard to read and they invoke anger in the reader. The reader may think you're shouting.
- Don't spam. If you do, you'll wake up the next morning with about a thousand e-mail messages in your inbox. It's not worth it.
- If you need to test how your postings look, go to the alt.test newsgroup, which is designed for this purpose. Don't send a message like "Does this work?" to a newsgroup.
- If you're female, you might want to use an alias or initials so users don't bombard you with "love" letters.
- Make sure you're in the right place when you post a message. Computer resources are finite, so don't clutter up newsgroups with inappropriate postings.
- Relax and have fun.

What's Next

Are you hooked yet? Have you forgotten what your kids look like or what color your car is? One of the downsides to getting connected to the Internet and the Web is that you may find yourself spending far too much time "surfing." This chapter showed you a lot of the basics of the Web, how to start Navigator, how to perform simple navigation tasks, and how to save a list of sites you've previously visited.

After you spend some time using the Web and the Internet, you may realize the ISP or commercial online service you use isn't the best solution for you. The next chapter is designed to show you how to find the best Internet provider for your needs. You'll find a comprehensive list of ISPs that may help you make that decision.

5

GETTING ACCESS TO INTERNET SERVICE PROVIDERS

Why is this chapter here and not at the beginning of the book? Although some readers will want to review this chapter before they've logged on to the Internet, many will want to read this chapter after they've spent time navigating the Internet (usually called *surfing the Internet).* This chapter is for both readers. If you're just now looking for an Internet Service Provider (ISP), this chapter will help you find one. It will help you understand the types of ISPs out there, where they are, and what services they provide. Moreover, this chapter helps you ask the right questions when you pick an ISP.

For readers who've spent time online already, this chapter is designed to help you evaluate your current ISP and determine whether it's the best one for you. If it isn't, you can find helpful hints on how to ensure a smooth transition to a new ISP, as well as find information on current ISP services and costs. (Chapter 2 covers some of the basics of what you need to obtain from your ISP once you find one.)

Although there isn't one best answer to picking the right provider or access company, there are some general rules you should consider. Cost is an important issue, so is technical support, free software and upgrades, and future support.

Emerging World of Internet Service Providers

In the old days of the Internet, finding a service provider was like looking for a telephone in the old west. You had to travel far and wide to find one—and when you found it, you didn't know whether it was going to work. Today, the problem of finding an ISP isn't as difficult. The difficulty is finding one that matches your needs, and is within your budget.

NOTE

Although there are more than 2,000 ISPs in this country, in addition to direct Internet access through a college or government link, there are some areas of the country that are not covered. In some rural areas and small cities, finding an ISP with local phone service may be difficult. One problem is that many ISPs are based in large cities. To offer services in smaller cities or to rural exchanges, the ISP must expand their businesses and open branch exchanges or access points in the smaller places. Economically, this doesn't always make good business sense unless a large subscriber base is available.

To get around this problem, some ISPs offer 800 numbers to dial to offset the long distance charges members entail when getting connected. If you live in an area without local Internet access, you might want to look into national ISPs that offer 800 number access. Some ISPs, however, charge a nominal fee for using 800 numbers, such as 10 cents per minute or a prorated amount. This isn't a problem if you get online to send and receive e-mail, which doesn't take very long. However, if you spend hours online, this fee adds up as quickly as a normal long-distance fee.

What ISPs Offer

Pick up any phone directory and look up online services under the Computers listing. You're bound to find one or two companies offering Internet access. In the listing, you may encounter terms and services you aren't familiar with. Before you call around for prices and support issues, it's a good idea to know what some of these terms mean. This way, you don't totally depend on the sales representative to explain technical issues to you. It also gives you a better idea of the questions.

The following list describes the type of information you might see in a typical ISP advertisement:

- **SLIP/PPP.** A SLIP or PPP connection is the preferred connection for users using a modem to connect directly to the Internet. SLIP (Serial Line Internet Protocol) and PPP (Point to Point Protocol) connections enable you to access all Internet services (FTP, e-mail, Gopher, and so on) as though you were on the Internet directly. This means you can have direct access to Web pages. Although a SLIP connection is a little faster than PPP, most areas have PPP connections because it works better with most Windows systems. SLIP/PPP accounts cost a little more than menu or shell accounts, but that's because you get more with a SLIP/PPP connection.

TIP

If you want a SLIP or PPP account, tell the ISP when setting up your account. Some ISPs have been known to set up users with shell accounts at first, only for the customer to become aggravated and change later to SLIP or PPP. Also, if you use Windows 95, you may want to ask for a PPP account because Windows 95 seems to handle PPP better than SLIP.

- **Menu or shell accounts.** These services let you access the Internet using a menu system. When you connect to your ISP using a menu or shell account, you first see a list of Internet options on your screen, such as FTP, Telnet, and Gopher. You might also see World Wide Web on the list, but it only enables you to see Web pages in text view (you don't see graphics or other multimedia objects). You need a SLIP or PPP connection to do that. Unless the ISPs in your area only carry menu or shell accounts, don't get one.

- **ISDN.** A high-speed connection to the Internet. *ISDN (Integrated Services Digital Network)* lines are high-speed digital phone lines that give you access up to 128Kbps, or about five times the rate as your 28.8 modem. ISDN actually has three lines, two 64Kbps and one 16Kbps. You can combine the two 64Kbps to get speeds up to 128Kbps. ISDN can be cost-prohibitive for many users, plus it may not be available to all customers in an ISP area. ISDN is also very difficult to configure, although new software (from companies like Microsoft and others) is attempting to make the connection easier. You also must purchase new hardware to replace your modem and have a special ISDN phone line installed in your home.
- **Dial-up.** A term used to describe using your regular telephone line to dial up and connect to the Internet with a modem. ISPs offer SLIP/PPP and menu (or shell) accounts for dial-up customers.
- **56K.** 56Kbps lines are dedicated Internet connections that stay connected 24 hours a day. Many businesses and other organizations use 56K lines because they're faster than modem connections and don't require users to dial-up the ISP each time they want to connect. Of course, with the speed and dedicated connection, customers end up paying high monthly rates for 56K connections. You may want to look for this type of service if you have a small- to medium-size business to connect to the Internet.
- **T1.** A very fast (1.544MB per second) dedicated connection to the Internet. Much of the Internet backbone is T1. T1 lines usually are used only by large businesses, organizations, and government agencies, and are very expensive. For home use, you won't need a T1 connection.
- **UUCP.** *UUCP (UNIX-to-UNIX Copy Program)* is the way many computers on the Internet communicate with each other. UUCP only supports e-mail and newsgroup transmissions; however, UUCP doesn't give full Internet access to users. If you want to use the Internet for Web, FTP, Gopher, and other Internet services, don't get a UUCP connection.
- **Home page design.** Some ISPs also offer Web page design to their customers, providing HTML, Java, CGI, or other programming skills. If you're interested in just surfing or browsing the Internet, you don't need

to worry about home page or Web page design. If, however, you need someone to help you establish a presence on the World Wide Web, look for services like this from your ISP.

- **Hosting.** *Hosting* is when your ISP allows you to publish or store Web pages on its server (see preceding bullet item). Many home and office users create and publish their own Web pages on the Web (see Figure 5.1). Although each ISP sets rates for this service, you can usually publish Web pages on an ISP server for $20 month for 10MB of information with restrictions on the number of *hits* you receive from other users. (A hit is when someone accesses your Web page.) Some ISPs include hosting as part of the regular membeship fee, so you may not need to pay anything extra to post some Web pages on your ISPs server. Basic Web pages are small (the one in Figure 5.1 is only about 8K including the graphics), so you can store several pages for a reasonable fee. Business accounts usually cost more, but are still in the $50 to $100 range.

How Many Modems Does Your ISP Have

It is important to ask your ISP what their *customer-to-modem ratio* is. This is simply the number of customers they have to the number of modems they have.

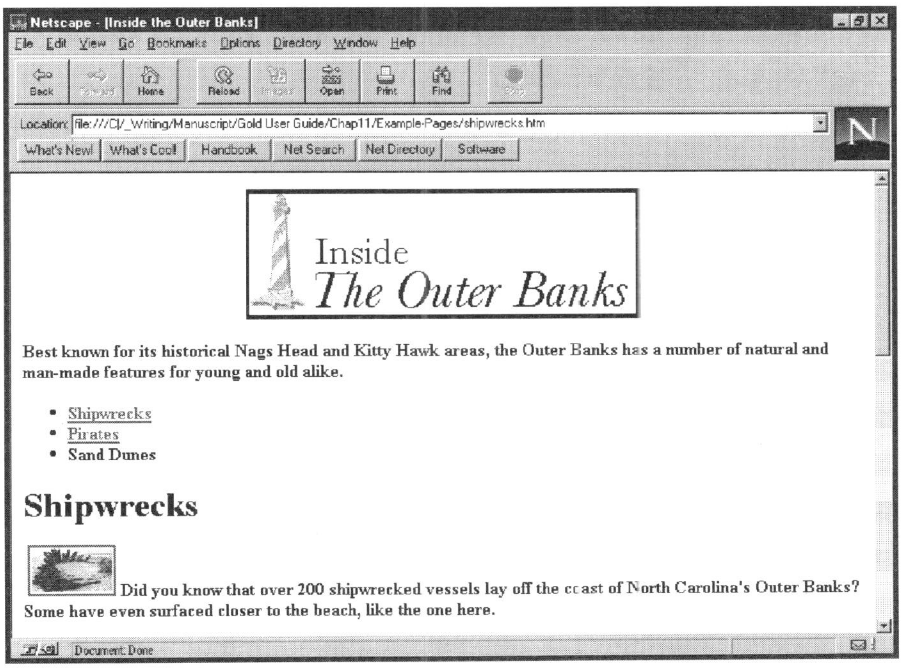

FIGURE 5.1

You can publish Web pages on the your ISP's Internet server for an additional monthly fee.

When you dial into an ISP, you connect to one of several modems in the ISP modem bank. Depending on the ISP, there may be 200 or 300 modems; large ISPs may have thousands of modems.

If you're lucky, each time you dial your ISP, you'll get through. Sometimes, however, all lines and modems at your ISP will be busy, especially at peak times of the day or week. The more modems an ISP has, the less likely you are to get a busy signal. A good customer-to-modem ratio is 8-1 or 10-1 (for every eight or ten customers, the ISP has one modem). Although it may seem that the odds are against you connecting with your ISP, remember that everyone isn't dialing into the Internet when you are. Ask your ISP when the peak times of the day are for them, and try to avoid those times.

As an ISP grows and more people get connected, you may experience busy signals more often. If you reach a busy signal often, you might want to call your ISP by phone and let them know you're having problems. You don't want to do this if you have one or two busy signals, but if you experience them over a few days or weeks, let them know. If the ISP hears from enough dissatisfied customers, the ISP may decide to upgrade the system. In some cases, this means adding more phone lines and modems without interfering with normal business operations. Other times, however, you may receive e-mail from your ISP warning you that the service will be down for maintenance for several hours or days. Usually, they do this at off-peak hours late at night or over a weekend.

Deciding on an Online or Internet Service Provider

There are three basic types of Internet Service Providers: commercial online services, national ISPs, and local ISPs. Commercial online services and national ISPs have dial-up connections across the country in most major cities. Cities with populations over 30,000 generally have one or more local access numbers to one of these services.

Choosing the right ISP is important; shop around before jumping right into the first deal. If you're in a rural area that offers only one or two choices, you don't have much homework to do. Just go for the one that has the best price and service. Readers in large metropolitan areas may have dozens of companies from which to choose. In some ways, having multiple choices is a nice luxury, because you can usually find a service to meet all your needs. On the other hand, having too many choices can overwhelm you and leave you worn out from shopping for the best service.

Access Numbers

Your first consideration when picking an ISP is telephone access. Make sure your ISP has a toll-free or local access number. You don't want to have to pay for long-distance charges in addition to ISP charges. Some ISPs or commercial online services distribute setup software that guides you through the setup process. Look out for installation software that automatically connects you to a long-distance number without warning you first. If this happens, look for an updated phone listing or call the ISP's sales or technical support line and ask whether they have a local number for your area. If they don't, look for an ISP that does.

One alternative to using a national ISP is to look at the big four or five commercial online services for Internet access. Many commercial online services are now ISPs. You can use CompuServe, America Online, The Microsoft Network, and Prodigy to access the Internet. One reason to choose a commercial online service instead of a local ISP is access to national phone numbers. If you travel, you'll want to make sure you can access e-mail, newsgroups, and other Internet services without the expense of long-distance charges. Some local ISPs do offer toll-free numbers, but many don't. Commercial online services have local access numbers in most medium- to large-size cities. This means you can dial a local number from a hotel room or client office to reach one of these services. If you don't have the local access number, you can simply download a list from the service and store it on your laptop as a text file or directory list.

NOTE

You learn more about choosing a commercial online service in Chapter 9. Many of the same strategies for choosing ISP services covered in this chapter also apply to commercial online services.

Easy Installation and Free Software

An advantage to using a commercial online service instead of a local ISP is that online services usually make the process of configuring your computer for Internet access very easy. Commercial online services provide you with easy-to-use installation software that configures your computer for both Internet access and direct access to the online service. For example, CompuServe's WinCIM setup screens help you establish CompuServe as your ISP (see Figure 5.2).

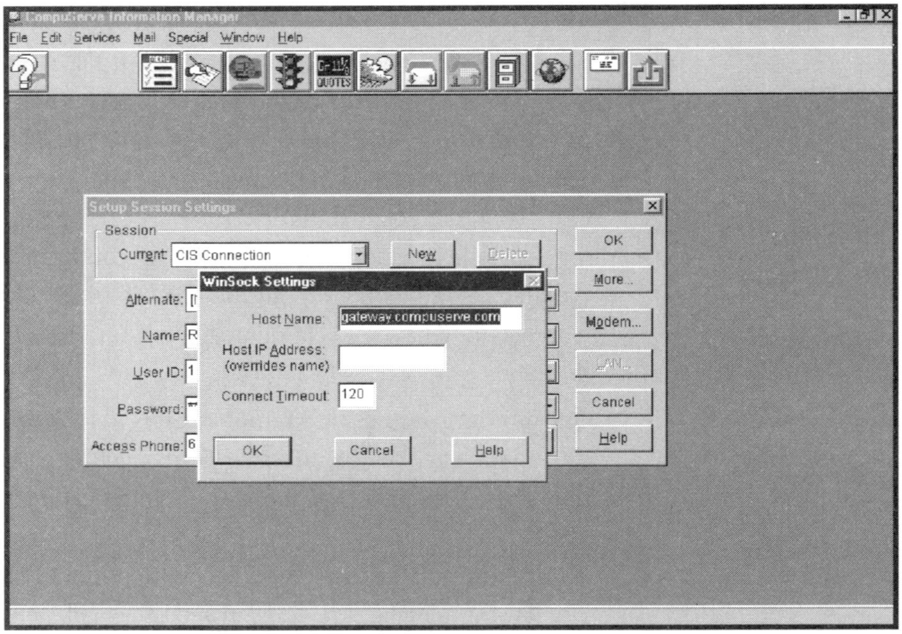

FIGURE 5.2

Commercial online services, like CompuServe, generally have user-friendly software to get you connected to the Internet.

On the other hand, some ISPs include a suite of Internet tools to help you get online. Generally, you get the following tools:

- A Web browser, such as Navigator or a Mosaic-clone
- An e-mail package, such as Eudora Lite or Pegasus
- A newsreader, such as Free Agent or WinVN
- Gopher, such as Hgopher
- FTP, such as WS_FTP
- Telnet, such as Hytelnet
- Chat, such as WSIRC or Netscape Chat
- A Winsock application, such as Trumpet Winsock. You need a Winsock application for your Web browser to work on the Web.

Some ISPs also include a setup procedure that walks you through configuring your operating system for TCP/IP support. With this software, you should receive written instructions on how to install and use the software. If you don't receive documentation from the ISP, look for README.TXT or help files included with each application.

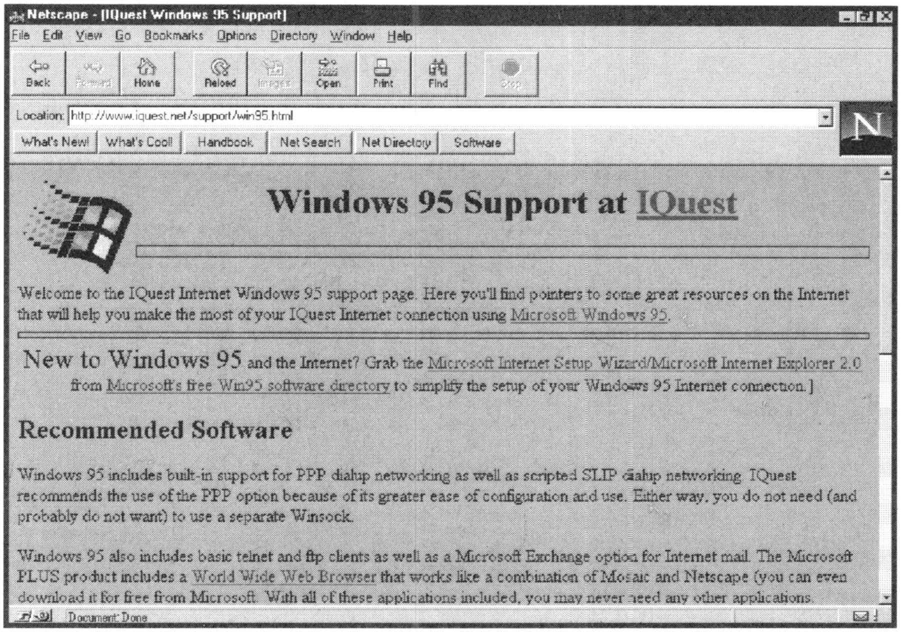

FIGURE 5.3

Many ISPs offer links to popular and useful software you can download from the Internet.

Another service many ISPs offer is a list of software you can download from the Internet. Usually, an ISP has a Web page with short descriptions and links to these software repositories (see Figure 5.3).

Technical Support

Some ISPs may lack sufficient printed documentation or technical support if you run into problems. Printed documentation (as opposed to electronic documentation) is important to have if your system malfunctions during setup. Also, a common problem is when the ISP only offers technical support through their Web site. What if you can't get online in the first place, or if the ISP's Web site is too busy or not functioning?

Having competent technical support staff available when you need them is important. Look for an ISP that offers 24-hour, seven-days-a-week technical support. Unless you access the Internet during the workday, most of your support problems will come in the evening or weekends.

NOTE

Ask your ISP for a FAQ (Frequently Asked Questions) *file. Most ISPs create and update a user-friendly document that gets posted and routed to their customers to help them solve common problems. Depending on the size of the document, you may want to make a hard copy printout of it and file it for future reference. The following is an example of a FAQ listing:*

My modem doesn't respond. What should I do?

Sometimes a modem doesn't respond because it isn't connected properly to your computer. If it's an external modem, double-check all connections and make sure the modem is plugged in. Next, make sure your communications software is installed and the port settings to your modem are correct. Finally, try rebooting your machine to reset the modem.

In addition to the days and times that technical support is available, technical support also should be free. Many of the problems you encounter online can be rectified quickly by someone who knows what they're doing. Before you call, however, make sure you're prepared and have a profile of your system handy, including the following items:

- **Type of computer.** Know your system processor size, how much memory you have, and the amount of available hard drive space.
- **Modem.** Write down the type of modem (internal or external) and the baud rate (usually 14.4 or 28.8).
- **Operating system.** Are you running Windows 95, Windows 3.11, or Windows for Workgroups 3.11? If you're running Windows 95, your desktop looks like the one in Figure 5.4. If you're running Windows 3.*x*, you can find out the version by choosing Help, About Program Manager in Program Manager. In the About Program Manager window that appears, look for the Windows version number and write it down (see Figure 5.5).

In addition to the system information, create a summary of the problem you have. If you receive any error messages on screen, make a screen print of the messages or write down the complete message to give to the technical support person. You should also summarize the events leading up to the error, such as if you were in the process of receiving e-mail or if you were downloading a file from a Web site.

NOTE

To make a quick screen print (an electronic copy of what you're viewing on screen) of a message, press the Print Screen key on your keyboard. This makes a bitmap image of the screen and places it on the Windows Clipboard. Next, run an image viewer, such as Paint (called Paintbrush in Windows 3.x), and choose

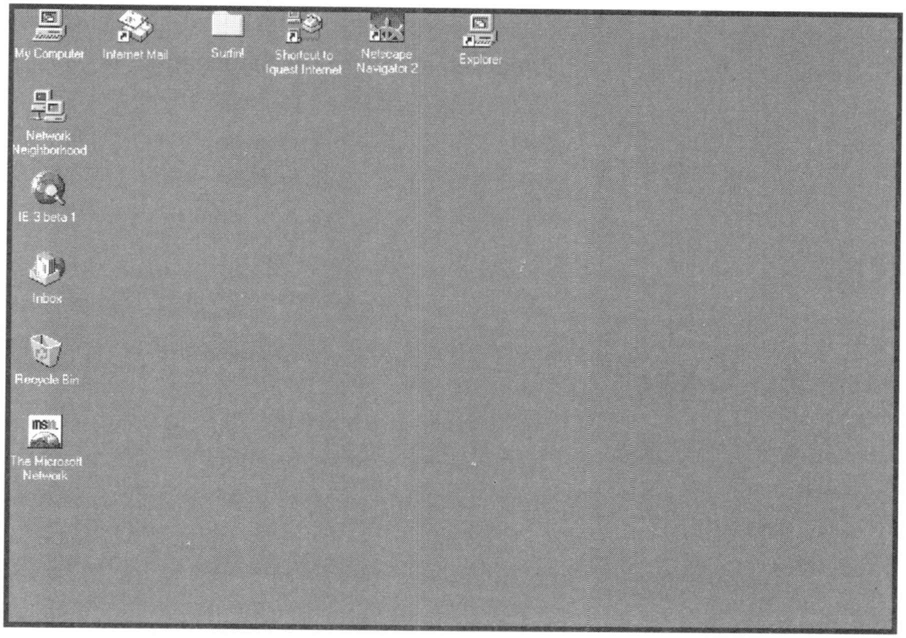

FIGURE 5.4

If you're using Windows 95, the desktop looks similar to this one.

Edit, Paste to paste the copied image into the application. Finish by saving the image to a file on your hard drive.

A service many ISPs have, particularly local ones, is e-mail technical support. With this service, you can send an e-mail message to the technical support representative and (usually within 24 to 48 hours) you'll get a response. This assumes, of course, that your e-mail application is working. Many business users subscribe to two or three services (such as a local ISP and CompuServe) to have a backup in case one service is down for the day or all the lines are busy.

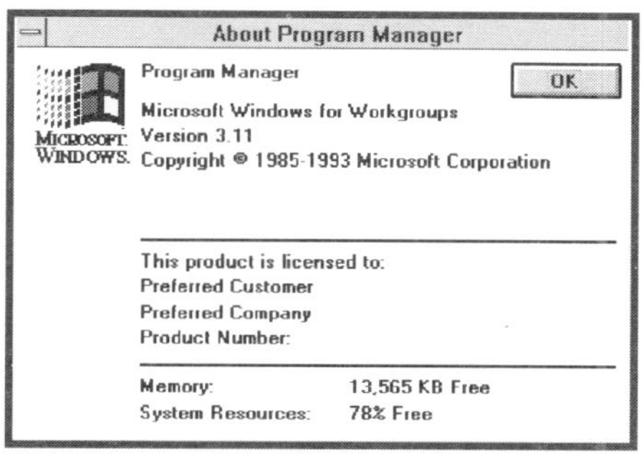

FIGURE 5.5

You can find the version number of the Windows 3.x system by looking at the version line toward the top of the dialog box.

When you send e-mail to a technical support person, be sure to include your e-mail address, full name, telephone number, and a detailed explanation of the problem. It's a good idea to include your system information as well. This way the technical support person won't have to send an e-mail message back to you requesting this basic information. When including your telephone number, be sure to include when the best time to call you is (such as early morning, early evening, and so on). Keep in mind that your message probably isn't the only one this person receives, so make it as easy as possible for that person to reach you.

Online Costs

If you plan to spend more than 8 to 10 hours a month on the Internet, your best bet is to look for a local or national ISP instead of a commercial online service. Commercial online services generally have basic monthly rates between $4.95 and $9.95. This rate includes a number of online hours each month. Any additional hours you spend online cost extra. Most services charge between $1.95 and $2.95 for additional hours. Plus, some commercial online services have content and service areas that are considered premium, such as news services or magazine areas. Premium areas cost extra on top of the monthly service charges.

Local or national ISPs that offer only Internet access, on the other hand, don't charge for premium services and usually have better payment structures for users who want 15 to 20 hours of service a month. Typically, these ISPs charge $15 to $20 a month for 20 hours of service. Any hours you spend online in addition to the set amount are charged at an additional rate, such as $1.50 to $2.95 per hour.

Access Speeds

Most ISPs and commercial online services offer access speeds up to 28.8Kbps. Some smaller markets may be limited to 14.4Kbps, so shop around until you find the fastest one. If you have a 28.8 modem, but your connection is only 14.4, you won't have a problem. A 28.8 modem can adjust itself to a slower speed. On the other hand, you can't access a 28.8 connection with a 14.4 modem. It doesn't work that way.

When you connect with your ISP, don't be alarmed if your connection isn't at the highest speed. Line noise, traffic, and modem software will sometimes cause your connection to be slower than the speed at which you want to connect. If you're connecting to your ISP's 28.8Kbps connection with a 28.8 modem, you may get a connection that's only 24Kbps or lower. One way to optimize your online speed is to look for a fast TCP/IP stack to install on your system. If you're using the built-in Windows 95 stack or a shareware product, you may find that they're slower than third-party stacks, such as Frontier Technologies' Super TCP/NFS product.

TIP

One way to get the fastest connection speed when using Windows 95 is to limit the number of networking protocols installed. If you're running Windows 95 and are not part of a LAN, make sure you disable all networking protocols except for TCP/IP. (If you're on a LAN, you may need these other protocols so don't remove them and disregard this tip.) You can see which protocols you have installed by clicking the Start menu and choosing Control Panel, Settings. Double-click the Network icon. On the Configuration tab of the Network dialog box, look for settings like NetBEUI and IPX/SPX-compatible protocol (see Figure 5.6). Select the protocol(s) to remove and click the Remove button. After Windows removes the protocols, reboot your computer to make the changes take effect.

Sample ISP Questionnaire

To help you make the most of the time you spend qualifying and searching for the right ISP for you, the following questionnaire consolidates many of the suggestions found in this and other chapters. You might want to make a photocopy this questionnaire for each ISP you review and write down responses for each of the questions. Then, as you evaluate your choices, you'll have a handy guide to help narrow your choices.

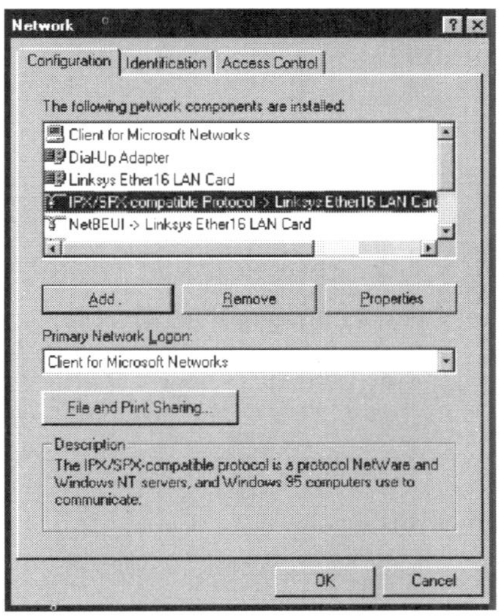

FIGURE 5.6

You can view the networking protocols installed on your Windows 95 machine by opening the Network dialog box.

General Information

Local access telephone number: ______________________

Toll-free access telephone number (such as 1-800): ______________________

Connection speeds: ______________________

Technical support telephone number: ______________________

Technical support hours: ______________________

Technical support e-mail address: ______________________

Special software provided: ______________________

Billing Information

Monthly service fees: ______________________

Billing procedures (credit card or direct billing): ______________________

Sign-up fees, if any: ______________________

Number of hours included in monthly fee: ______________________

Cost of additional hours: ______________________

Online Information

Web site address (URL): ______________________

Address for online documentation or FAQ files: ______________________

Address for repository of shareware or freeware programs: ______________________

____

Service Information

E-mail address: ______________________

Password(s): ______________________

News server information: ______________________

Space provided for own Web page, if applicable: ______________________

Procedures for uploading own Web pages, if applicable: ______________________

____

Software Information

World Wide Web browser: ______________________

E-mail application: ______________________

Newsgroup newsreader: ______________________

FTP application: ______________________

Telnet application: ______________________

Gopher application: ______________________

IRC chat application: ______________________

Utilities, if any: ______________________

Additional Information

How to find out how much time you use during the month: ______________________

____

Procedure for canceling membership: ______________________

NOTE

Use Table 2.4 in Chapter 2 to help you fill out specific setup and configuration information from your ISP. That table includes items for IP address, domain name, and other critical system information.

Changing ISPs

Does your current ISP satisfy you? Are you happy with its service? Do you want a second ISP to handle business accounts? These are all questions that users need to ask themselves before changing ISPs.

When you change ISPs, it isn't as simple as changing your shirt. This is because your ISP determines your e-mail address. As you learned in Chapter 3, your e-mail address contains your username (such as tcruise) and a domain name (such as iquest.net). The domain name routes any e-mail message sent to you to that domain, which is your ISP's Internet e-mail server.

Unlike the U.S. Postal Service, the Internet doesn't have a service to re-route your mail if you decide to move. Just like when you move to a new home or apartment and your mailing address changes, your domain name changes when you change ISPs. If your current ISP is Iquest Inc., for example, your e-mail address may be something like tcruise@iquest.net. You might then decide to switch your ISP to Netcom. Now, your e-mail address would be tcruise@netcom.com, assuming of course you could still use tcruise as your username. That particular username may already be used by another member, or the ISP may use different naming conventions.

When someone sends you e-mail at your old address, the message may get lost in cyberspace. This is like the dead-letter stack at the post office, except no one sees that your message is trying to get to you. Sometimes the sender receives a return message stating that the original e-mail message is undeliverable. But this may occur only if a domain name cannot be found on the Internet, such as if the mail server is down at your ISP or the sender incorrectly spelled the domain name. Usually, when you cancel an account with your ISP, your name is removed from the server and no record of you (or what your new address is) is on the server. (This may also occur if you don't pay your bill and your ISP cancels your account automatically.)

Before you change your ISP, be sure to give yourself a few days or even weeks to send out change of address notices. Not only is this a courtesy to those on your address list, but it ensures that your contacts can reach you in the future. If you use e-mail as a business tool, this change of address message can mean the difference between landing a contract or losing one. Not to mention the irritation your clients or potential clients go through when they can't rely on your e-mail connection.

In the change of address message, you'll want to include the date of activation, the new e-mail address, the old (or current) e-mail address, your phone number, and your full name. Don't assume everyone knows who you are by just your e-mail address. Also, the subject of your e-mail message should say something to let recipients know it contains address information. For example, you might use "Change of e-mail address" as the subject, or "Notice: E-mail address correction," or "E-mail address change." This way recipients who don't read all their mail will open your message and note the change. Some users get hundreds or thousands of messages a day and read only those they have time for or those that have subject lines of interest.

NOTE

The following is a sample change of address note you can use to send to people in your e-mail address book:

To: List
From: Sender
Re: Change of Address Notice

To All:

Effective September 1, 1996, please note that my e-mail address will change from tcruise@iquest.net to sconnery@netcom.com. If you have any questions or need additional information, don't hesitate to call me at 555-5555.

Another issue you need to consider when changing ISPs is how much time you've used during the current month. Most ISPs bill you for a specific number of hours whether you use them or not. If you decide to cancel your account with an ISP and have not used up those hours yet, ask if they can prorate your final bill to include those hours you haven't used. If they won't credit you these hours, consider going online and using those final hours to access sites or download files. If you don't use them, no one will.

Finding Online or Internet Access Providers

The following is a list of national ISPs and their contact information. Most ISPs have Web sites you can access for updated information. This assumes, of course, that you have an Internet connection already and can access the Web.

Most of the ISPs listed have more than one pricing plan, so you should contact each to get an updated pricing list and other information. Most ISPs also have special business and student rates.

Due to the competitive nature of ISPs, the prices and services shown in the following list may change by the time you read this book. For that reason, be sure to contact an ISP your interested in using and inquire about its rates and services. You'll probably find in most cases the rates have dropped or the number of hours included in the base rates have increased.

America Online (AOL)
800-827-6364
703-918-2062
http://www.aol.com
Monthly fee: $9.95
Hours: 5
Additional hourly cost: $2.95

Arrow Crab Internet
702-786-5900
http://aci.net/
Monthly fee: $19.95
Hours: Unlimited
Additional hourly cost: None

AT&T Worldnet
800-967-5363
http://www.att.com/worldnet/
Monthly fee: $19.95
Hours: Unlimited
Additional hourly cost: None

CompuServe
800-848-8199
614-457-8600
http://www.compuserve.com
Monthly fee: $9.95
Hours: 5
Additional hourly cost: $2.95

Concentric Network
800-939-4263
408-342-2800
http://www.concentric.net/
Monthly fee: $19.95
Hours: Unlimited
Additional hourly cost: None

Earthlink Network
800-395-8425
818-296-2400
http://www.earthlink.net/
Monthly fee: $19.95, with $25.00 startup fee
Hours: Unlimited
Additional hourly cost: None

Global Enterprise Services
800-358-4437 ext. 7325
http://www.jvnc.net/
Monthly fee: $35.00, with $29.00 startup fee
Hours: 20
Additional hourly cost: $2.50

Global Network Navigator (GNN)
800-819-6112
510-883-7220
http://www.gnn.com
Monthly fee: $14.95
Hours: 20
Additional hourly cost: $1.95
Note: GNN is a division of America Online (AOL)

Imagine Communications Corporation
800-542-4499
http://www.imagixx.net/
Monthly fee: $60/quarter
Hours: Unlimited
Additional hourly cost: None

IBM Internet Connection
800-455-5056
http://www.ibm.net
Monthly fee: $4.95
Hours: 3
Additional hourly cost: $2.50

internetMCI
800-955-6505
http://www.mci.com
Monthly fee: $9.95
Hours: 5
Additional hourly cost: $1.95

MCI Communications
800-471-6675
http://www.campus.mci.net/account.htm
Monthly fee: $12.00, plus $10.00 startup fee
Hours: 60
Additional hourly cost: $0.95

MCI Internet 2000
800-550-0927
http://www.mci.com
Monthly fee: $19.95
Hours: Unlimited
Additional hourly cost: None

The Microsoft Network
800-386-5550
http://www.msn.com
Monthly fee: $19.95
Hours: 20
Additional hourly cost: $2.50

Netcom
800-353-6600
408-983-5950
http://www.netcom.com
Monthly fee: $19.95
Hours: Unlimited
Additional hourly cost: None

Primenet
800-463-8386
602-416-7100
http://www.primenet.com/
Monthly fee: Varies by area code ($20.95-$25.95)
Hours: 150
Additional hourly cost: $1.00

Prodigy
914-448-8000
http://www.prodigy.com
Monthly fee: $9.95
Hours: 30
Additional hourly cost: $1.00

PSINet InterRamp
800-774-3031
717-770-1701
http://www.interramp.com/
Monthly fee: $29.00, with $9.00 startup fee
Hours: 29
Additional hourly cost: $1.50

PSINet Pipeline USA
703-904-4100
http://www.usa.pipeline.com/
Monthly fee: $19.95
Hours: Unlimited
Additional hourly cost: None

SolGate, Internet Access Inc.
800-419-4484
316-264-8386
http://www.solgate.com/
Monthly fee: $18.00
Hours: Unlimited
Additional hourly cost: None

SpryNet
800-777-9638
206-957-8000
http://www.sprynet.com/
Monthly fee: $9.95
Hours: 7
Additional hourly cost: $1.95

The WELL, Inc.
415-332-9200
415-332-9355
http://www.well.com/
Monthly fee: $24.95 (Premier plan)
Hours: 20
Additional hourly cost: $2.00

UUNet Technologies
703-206-5600
http://www.uu.net/
Monthly fee: $30.00
Hours: 25
Additional hourly cost: $2.00

WOW! from CompuServe
800-943-8969
http://www.wow.com
Monthly fee: $17.95
Hours: Unlimited
Additional hourly cost: None

You can also find local ISPs in your area by looking in the Yellow Pages or local newspaper advertisements. Many ISPs advertise on local television and radio stations, and team up with marketing and advertisement agencies to promote their services and business.

Another way to find hundreds of ISPs while on the Web is to search for them on the Yahoo! searching engine at **http://www.yahoo.com**. Enter the keywords **ISP**, **Internet Service Provider**, or **Internet Access**. These searches will yield a number of links to local and national ISPs.

NOTE

The following are a few good Web sites that offer comprehensive lists and more information about ISPs:

- *Providers of Commercial Internet Access (POCIA):* ***http://www.celestin.com/pocia/index.html***
- *c|net's The Ultimate Guide to Internet Service Providers:* ***http://www.cnet.com/Content/Reviews/Compare/ISP/***
- *Mecklermedia's The List:* ***http://thelist.com*** *(see Figure 5.7)*

The Internet is always changing and so are the companies that provide Internet access and services. Keep this in mind when you select an ISP. Although many soothsayers are predicting the demise of local ISPs (and have been for the last two years), many local ISPs are offering outstanding services to their customers. Local ISPs are vulnerable to larger national ISPs, as well as to cable and regional telephone companies, so don't be surprised if an ISP you choose goes out of business suddenly. In fact, there are horror stories of ISPs pulling the plug overnight without warning customers. For customers relying on Internet e-mail or hosting services, this can be a nightmare.

National ISPs are not immune to business problems either. With the state of commercial online services changing monthly, plus takeovers and mergers happening every few weeks, expect some of the national ISPs to go out of business

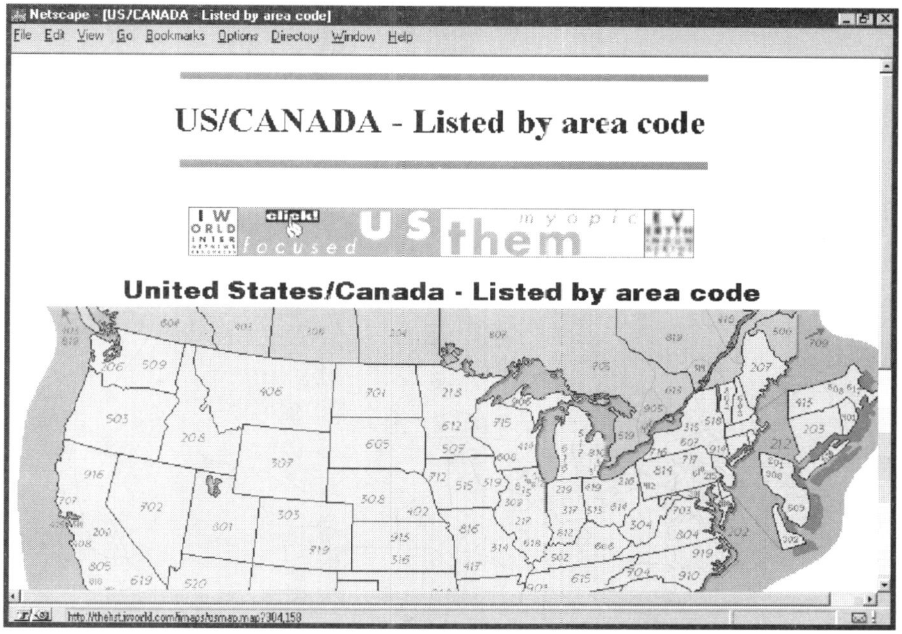

FIGURE 5.7

Use The List to find ISPs by country, geographic area, area code, domain name, and other search criteria.

or to drastically change their business model. A few national ISPs are finding it difficult to compete at the local level when regional telephone companies start providing services, particularly high-speed access services.

What's Next

Before you sign up with the first Internet Service Provider you find, shop around a little. Call a few local ISPs to find out their costs and services before heading to the national level; thus, you can compare the national ISPs to the local ones. The primary question for any ISP, is does it have a local telephone number for you. You don't want to find a great monthly deal with an ISP only to find out that you must pay a long-distance phone charge on top of the monthly ISP fee.

The next chapter begins Part III, "Commercial Online Services." If you're interested in finding out about the big commercial online services before you make a choice about an ISP, read that Part. If you have already found an ISP, you might want to skip ahead to Chapter 10 now, which shows you how to search for information online.

PART III

COMMERCIAL ONLINE SERVICES

6

AMERICA ONLINE

Call it "the vision thing." It was a trait born in abundance in the early days of America Online. Today, the truth about joining the online world is evident, but back in 1985 it represented a bold cultural and technological gamble. That was the year a company called Quantum Computer Services (known as America Online, Inc. today) unveiled its vision of a future in which people and resources came together online: *an interconnected world.* It was visionary because while personal computers, the primary medium of access to online services, had begun to come of age as business tools, their future as standard complements of the home and family was dramatically uncertain.

Would home computers be used strictly for business tasks, such as managing the checkbook and preparing reports? Would their prices come down, their power come up, and their usability increase to the point that families could use them for professional, educational, and recreational tools? Would vital software developers, used to the big margins from mainframe software sales, involve themselves in lower-profit home computer software? Would users need to become computer-literate to exploit them? Or would computers become people-literate to enable access by anyone?

The vision team at Quantum surveyed the landscape; more reasonable people would have gone into another line of work. "Online" was anything but a byword. The Internet back then was used by a few thousand people, mostly military and academians. The World Wide Web didn't exist. The graphical Windows operating system hadn't been introduced. IBM's personal computer was a four-year-old, underpowered, essentially stand-alone business implement. There was no frenzy about the "information superhighway." There was little in the wind that promised online revolution, yet the vision nagged at them...*an interconnected world.*

America Online was born out of a stubborn belief that the need to unite people and information resources electronically was inevitable. But it took AOL several years to become an overnight success. By 1989, it still had only a few thousand users. It was primarily a medium that enabled users to exchange electronic mail (e-mail), locate software, and research subjects that had files accessible online. The online revolution was more like an underground electronic guerrilla movement, but the infrastructure—and user interest—were coming together. By the early '90s, AOL's maverick visionaries were looking like prophets.

AOL Today

Today, AOL is the largest commercial online service in the world. With more than five million subscribers at the time of this writing, it's twice as successful as its closest competitors, and adds tens of thousands of new subscribers each

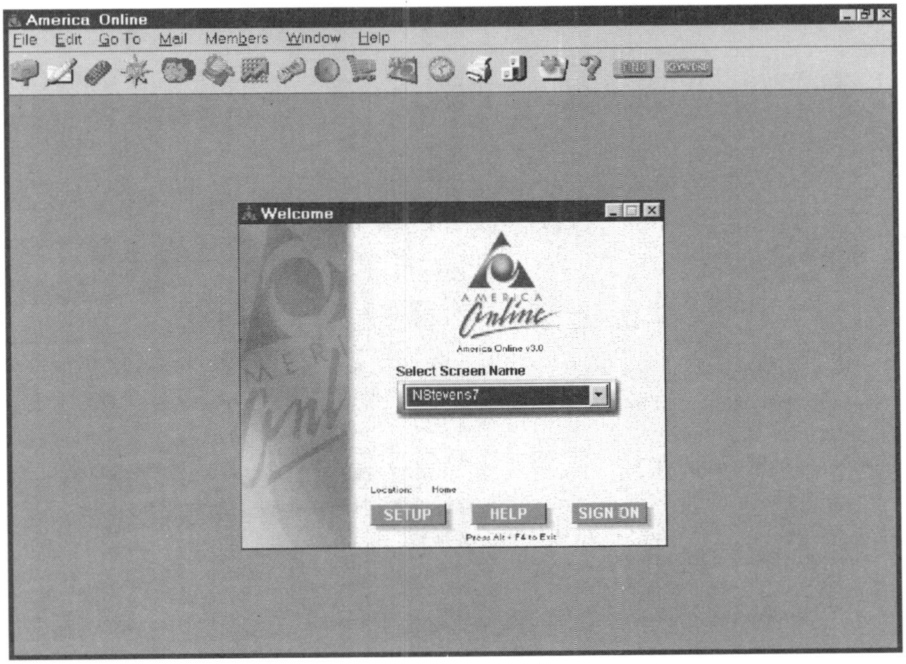

FIGURE 6.1

From the initial Welcome window that appears when you first set up AOL, going online even for novices is designed to be simple. The entire one-time setup, conducted by a wizard, takes only a few minutes.

month—in spite of the competition described in this book. Everything the vision team at AOL ever imagined has evolved, and more. Originally conceived as a family-oriented service, AOL for its first few years appealed to a more technical crowd, largely because that was who had and used computers at home at that time. But the service never lost its vision as a family medium, and today stands as the simplest-to-use, most age-independent service available anywhere (see Figure 6.1).

A Focus on Simplicity

America Online has succeeded in large measure because it has made entry into cyberspace simple and easy. This section discusses how simplicity has been integrated into everything from setting up your account to utilizing the Internet. Also noted are the efforts put into keeping AOL's content current via relationships with worldwide information sources.

AOL has managed to design simplicity into almost every aspect of its service. From the graphical Channels window to addressing e-mail, from using chat rooms to providing details of files you might wish to download, AOL is careful never to venture into technical jargon or convoluted procedures (see Figure 6.2). This staple has been one of AOL's enduring strengths and is undoubtedly a principal reason for its runaway popularity.

FIGURE 6.2

America Online boasts a range of channels, from news to entertainment to sports to kids' forums, that appear similar to its competitors. One big difference is the intuitive interface on each destination site—no tutorials required.

AOL hasn't allowed its preference for simplicity of use to keep it from being a serious provider of all kinds of information, including technical, current events, and reference. Within its family-oriented context, AOL recognizes a spectrum of channels that appeal to various ages and interests.

AOL also has taken an aggressive approach to expanding its subscriber base through affiliations with a number of major organizations. It has combined forces with ABC News to produce a dynamic news forum containing breaking stories from around the world (see the section "Today's News" later in this chapter). Because of consumers' interest in having a complete service that includes news access, this has been one of the more hotly contested areas for commercial online service providers (for example, The Microsoft Network forged an alliance with NBC News to do the same thing).

Linking to the Internet

Another hot button for consumers has been access to the Internet. AOL has responded to demand for Internet access by striking up partnerships with some of the dominant players on the cyberspace scene. It has joined AT&T Corporation to provide online services for AT&T's WorldNet Internet access service. This move could give AOL an inside track to the 89 percent of U.S. households that don't currently have online services.

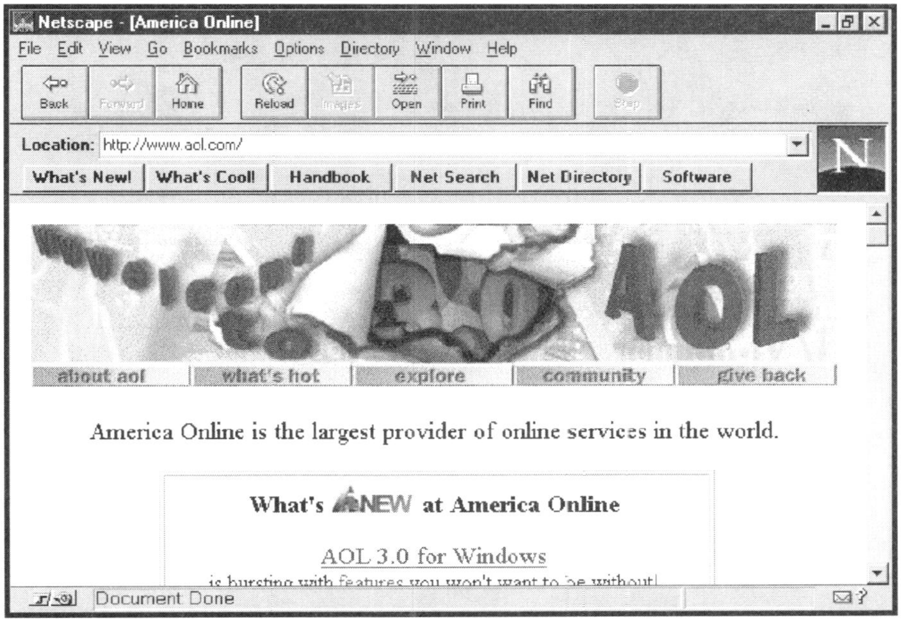

FIGURE 6.3

AOL is adopting the highly functional and popular Netscape Navigator Web browser for users who want access to the Internet and World Wide Web.

AOL also enhanced its position in the Internet world through a partnership with Netscape Communications Corporation, the developer of the popular Web browser Netscape Navigator 2.0 (see Figure 6.3). Netscape, even before aligning itself with AOL, had captured more than 80 percent of the world's Web browser market, and perpetually led the way in browsing features since its introduction in December 1994. It's the *de facto* standard in businesses, universities, and homes worldwide. AOL's alliance with Netscape means that AOL is dropping its own Web browser in favor of the familiar and functional Netscape Navigator.

Partnering with Microsoft

Another breakthrough in AOL availability recently involved burying the hatchet with Microsoft Corporation. AOL had been engaged in a year-long battle over Microsoft's inclusion of the The Microsoft Network software with each copy of Windows 95. Under the agreement signed by AOL and Microsoft, Microsoft will now include copies of AOL in each release of Windows 95 (in addition, of course, to The Microsoft Network). This new availability is bound to increase AOL's reach into households and businesses.

Strategically, AOL is well positioned to maintain its leadership in the online services market. The alliances with major corporations involved in online services and the Internet assure that AOL will be in a position to be both widely available and technologically advanced.

AOL's Channels

Computers & Software	Digital City	Entertainment	Games
Health & Fitness	The Hub	International	Kids Only
Learning & Culture	Life, Styles & Interests	Marketplace	MusicSpace
Newsstand	Today's News	People Connection	Personal Finance
Reference Desk	Sports	Style Channel	Travel

AOL Features

AOL has incorporated a range of more than a thousand forums, features, facilities, and destination sites in its services lineup. You can access all of them from the 21 primary categories listed on the main menu called *Channels* (refer to Figure 6.2). There isn't room in this book to discuss every destination you can reach, but we will take a look at some of the 21 major categories of services and AOL provides.

Today's News

Think of this as your morning paper. Today's News is a compilation of major world and national events, assembled in sections you're accustomed to: Business, Entertainment, Sports, Weather, and so on (see Figure 6.4). Both headline text and graphic images provide links to the articles (Figure 6.5). The entire section is updated every day, so many subscribers use it as their primary news medium.

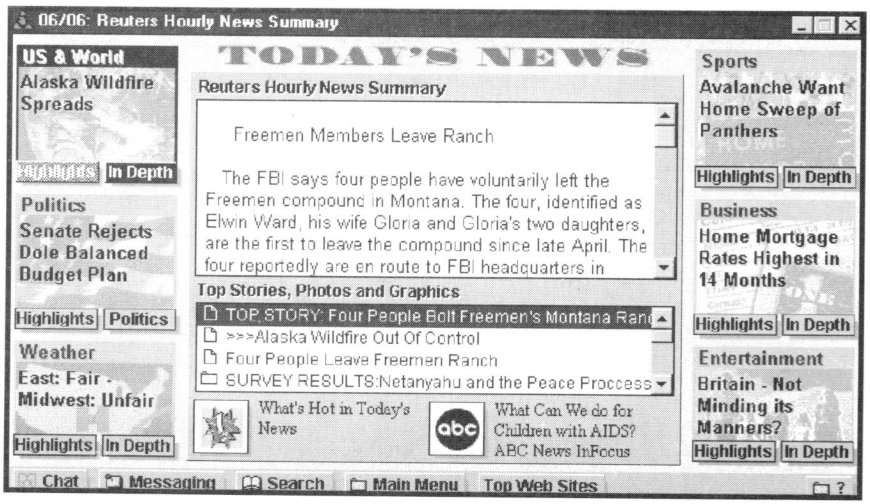

FIGURE 6.4

News is laid out like a magazine's table of contents. Each graphic is a clickable link to the story it represents.

FIGURE 6.5

From US & World, you can click hot headlines in the list box, read the *New York Times*, talk politics, or visit the Internet's news sources.

AOL has a news-gathering relationship with ABC News to help assure a consistent worldwide excellence in its journalism resources. Today's News contains scores of articles, which means not all of them can be shown on screen. If you want to find information on a subject not listed, you can locate it in the National News Photos and Graphics folder. Or, you can type the subject in a keyword line in the Search News dialog box and ask AOL's search engine to locate the stories that discuss it. Weather reports show graphical illustrations of national and regional weather conditions, including forecasts. AOL's link to the Internet's news resources—including major newspapers and news magazines—gives Today's News the feel of a "virtual newsstand" where little news is out of reach.

Personal Finance

Personal Finance is like a financial support group; this feature helps people organize and optimize their financial resources and activities, such as investment portfolios. Personal Finance distributes financial news via reports from journals such as *BusinessWeek Online* and *Investor's Business Daily*, assesses products through *Consumer Reports*, and examines potential investments using Hoover's Company Profiles and Fidelity Online (see Figure 6.6). It boasts a What's Hot section to look at promising investments, a research facility that enables you look into certain investments, and direct access to investment information on the Internet.

Life, Styles & Interests

Life, Styles & Interests is a network of gathering places for vocations, avocations, and occasional whims. Organized by categories (such as Food, Genealogy,

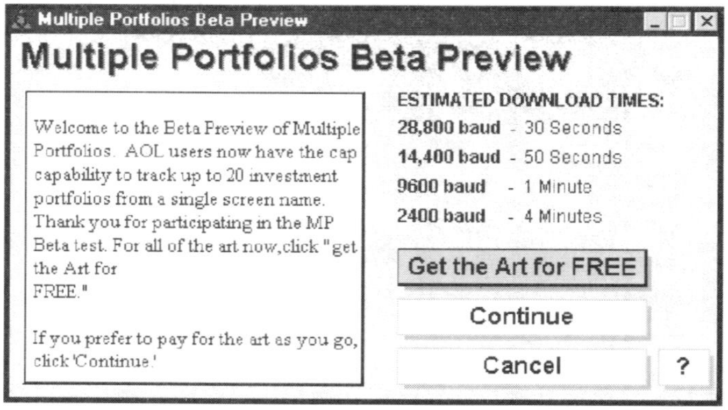

FIGURE 6.6

From Multiple Portfolios Beta Preview, you can download extensive information from up to 20 investment portfolios you would like to track.

Pets, Real Estate, Religion, Aviation, and so on), Life, Styles & Interests provides links to people and resources (see Figure 6.7). If the club, group, or information you're seeking doesn't reside on AOL, you can link to many other locations on the Internet. And like any good club, the links include those to chat rooms, where you can discuss your interests, activities, and passions in real time with other people who share them.

Computers & Software

The common denominator among AOL users is that they all use a computer to access the service. So it isn't surprising to learn that the Computers & Software channel is one of the most frequently accessed sites on AOL (see Figure 6.8). It's also one of the best-stocked sites, with literally hundreds of links to areas of interest. Computers & Software contains a spectrum of news sources, product evaluations, specific technology analyses (such as Communications & Networks, Games & Entertainment, Business, Desktop Publishing, and Education), as well

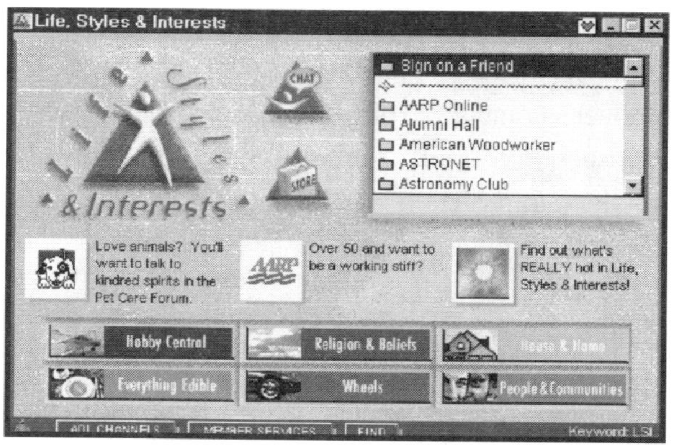

FIGURE 6.7

Chat rooms, newsgroups, and live conferences are part of the Life, Styles & Interests site.

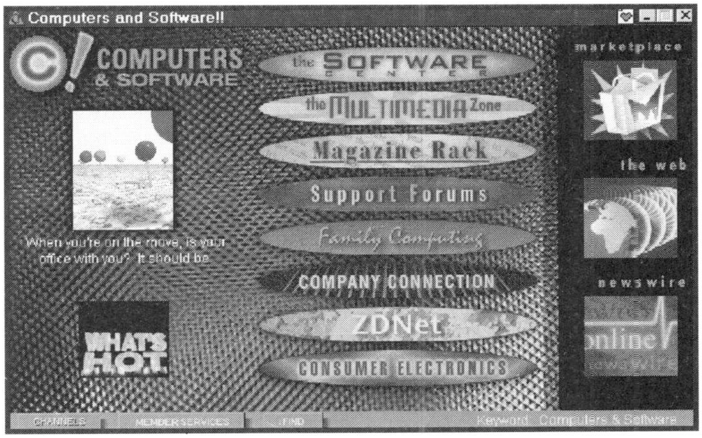

FIGURE 6.8

If you're looking for available software, the Computers & Software site offers a search engine in which you can choose the type of software you want, search for it, and download it right to your computer.

as links to both general and subject-dedicated chat rooms. One of the hottest sites is an original one from AOL's early days—the software library where you can find and download software for your computer, including games, personal and business applications, and utilities. This channel provides assistance to AOL users via AOL-specific chat rooms, bulletin boards, and member assistance. It also boasts fully-staffed support from a variety of computer, software, and electronics manufacturers.

Travel

If you're into the mobile life, the Travel site links you to a variety of pages designed to put you on the road—or in the air or on the water—and lets you share discoveries in chat rooms with other wandering souls (see Figure 6.9). You can

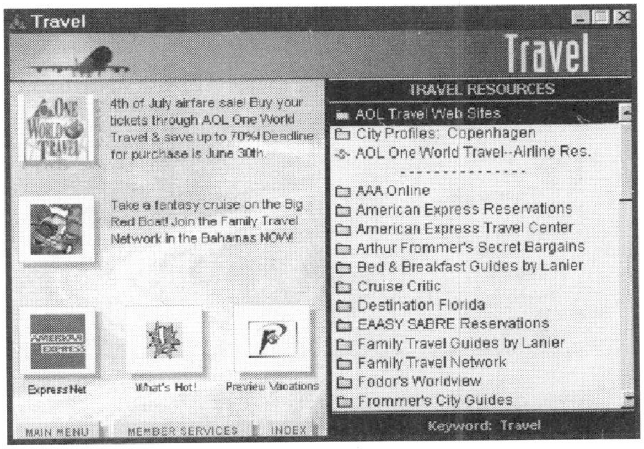

FIGURE 6.9

The Travel Resource directory puts you in touch with travel journals, reservations systems, city guides and maps, and the Travelers' Corner, where you can chat about adventures with other AOL travelers.

make reservations with major airlines, check out bed and breakfast inns, review destinations in the Weissman Travel Reports, and take virtual tours of domestic and international hot spots. You can even reserve rental cars and hotel rooms right from your keyboard, comparing rates along the trip.

Marketplace

So shopping is your passion? Online shopping is a relatively new experience, but AOL's Marketplace has gathered a fairly broad range of merchants who have set up virtual stores for you to browse in (see Figure 6.10). You can check out *Consumer Reports* analyses of many products, order flowers for a loved one, hunt for bargains, scour features of new cars, and pay online for many of the products you find. You can also sell your own merchandise by placing classified ads.

NOTE

While there has been some trepidation about using credit cards for online purchases, the commercial services such as AOL offer extremely secure transaction environments. The card numbers are sent over a dedicated network of AOL computers, as opposed to the random stops and varied platforms one encounters on the Internet. But while AOL and the other services offer the most secure transactions, even the Internet conducted $300 million in commerce last year and never reported one major credit card theft incident.

FIGURE 6.10

If the AOL Marketplace doesn't have the goods you're seeking, it can link you right to a shopping network on the Internet.

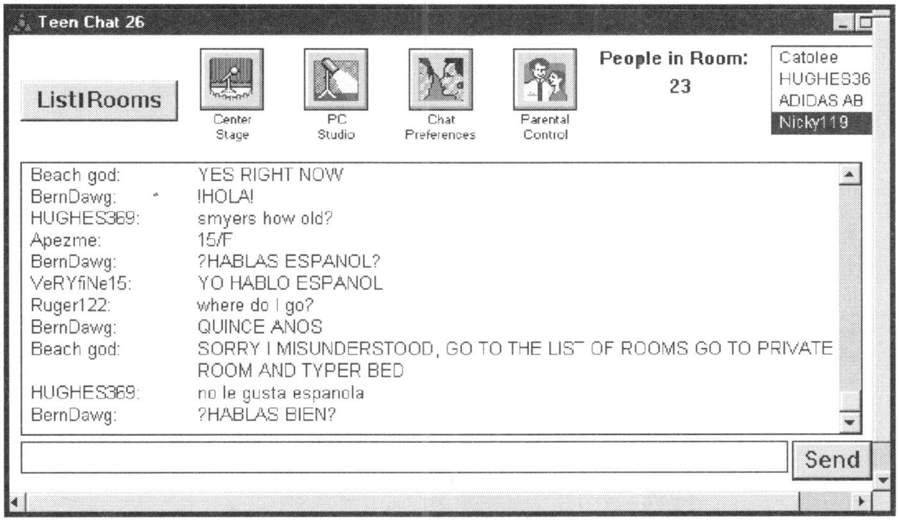

FIGURE 6.11

Even multilingual chats, such as the one here in the Teen Chat room, are found on AOL's People Connection. If you want to screen some chat rooms from younger members of the family, the Parental Control button at the top of the screen lets you block them.

People Connection

AOL has always taken great pains to maintain a human connection amid its plethora of communications, computers, and flying electrons. The best online hangout on AOL is the People Connection site, where you can join a variety of chat rooms, attend conferences, interact with celebrities, make new friends, develop professional acquaintances, find other AOL members, and generally do things interactively with other people (see Figure 6.11). By using chat technology, where you can use your keyboard and computer screen to send and receive responses from other people in a chat room, you can carry on a conversation that's just a second short of being in real time.

Newsstand

News and reference information is central to the success of any online service. In the Newsstand site, AOL took an extremely aggressive approach in organizing a virtual newsstand to complement its Today's News site (see Figure 6.12). The result is an electronic compendium of news and reference journals that's far too large to list here, but includes general news chronicles (such as *Time* and the *Chicago Tribune*), an array of specialty publications (such as *Backpacker Magazine* and *Bicycling Magazine*), business journals (such as *BusinessWeek*), the ABC News site, feature publications (such as *Atlantic Monthly*) and many more. When you link to each one, you get a scrolling table of contents. Click the feature you

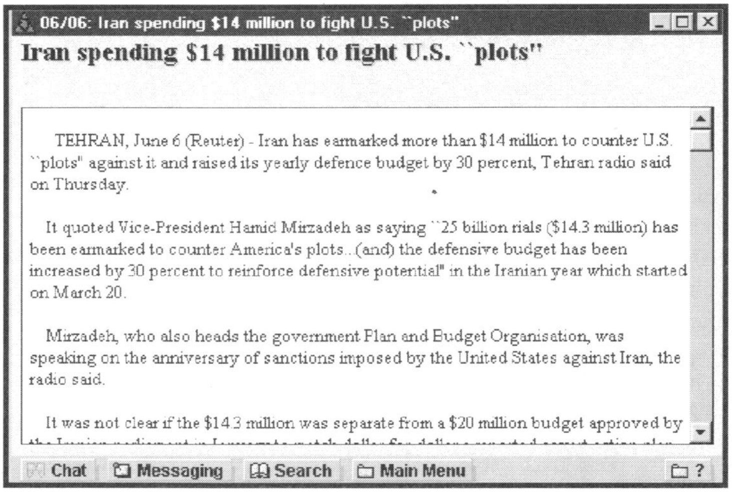

FIGURE 6.12

There are tons of journals to read in AOL's Newsstand, and they're available before the print versions ever reach subscribers.

want to read and it opens in a window. You can find columnists, subjects, scores, graphics, and tables.

Entertainment

AOL's Entertainment site is a gateway to movies, books, television, games, chat, and politics (for those who find politics entertaining). It contains the standard fare of movie reviews and celebrity gossip columns in addition to live chats with celebrities themselves (see Figure 6.13). Entertainment provides concert schedules and locations, a little humor from Comedy Central, a cartoon network, advice on the performing arts for aspiring singers, dancers, and actors, and of course, the latest news from Hollywood.

FIGURE 6.13

The Entertainment site is a mecca for both the fans of performing arts and the artists themselves.

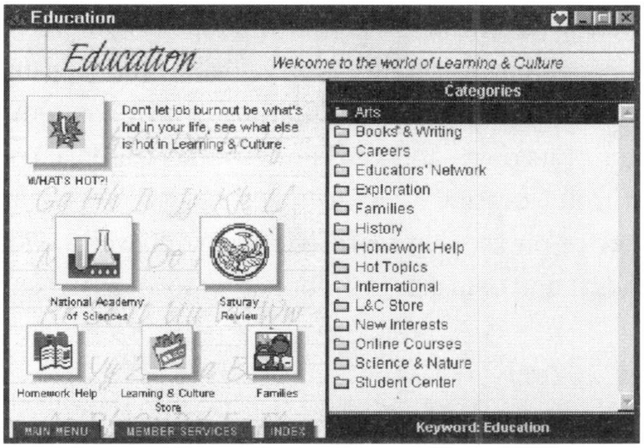

FIGURE 6.14

AOL's Education site provides a variety of forums where students can hone their skills and increase their knowledge at their own pace, with or without the watchful eye of an instructor.

Learning & Culture

Anyone who has ever struggled to a library in the middle of a snowstorm to research homework assignments will appreciate the value of doing the grunt work from your keyboard at home. AOL's Education site offers reference and advice on doing projects, and it provides courses and tutorials on a variety of subjects (see Figure 6.14). You can also visit the Smithsonian, read Scientific American, check out the Career Center, look over the college boards, and much more. Teachers even have their own forums to go one-on-one with each other and students.

Reference Desk

The perfect complement to the Learning & Culture site, AOL's Reference Desk is your link to an array of resources on AOL and the Internet (see Figure 6.15).

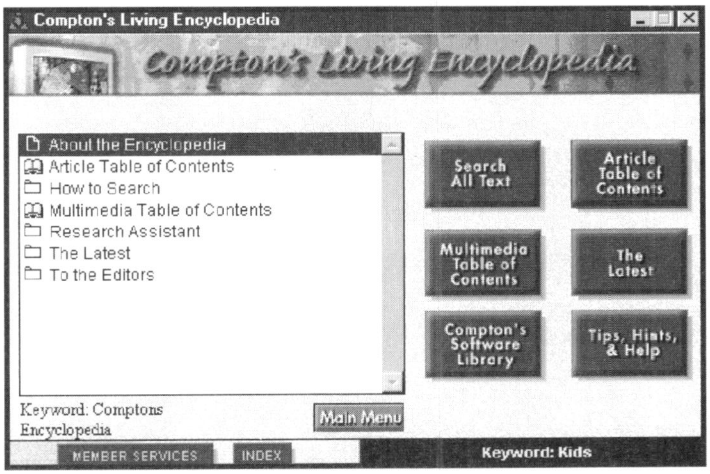

FIGURE 6.15

Compton's Encyclopedia is one of the many reference sources you can search by keywords and phrases.

What makes it handy is that it condenses those resources into an organized compendium, which saves you valuable searching time. AOL has a team of people who constantly scan the Internet—which has tens of thousands of reference sites of its own—and adds links to the reference compendium. If you still have difficulty locating references, you can use AOL's search engine. Just enter a keyword or phrase that represents what you want to locate, and the search engine finds it and delivers the information to your screen.

Internet Connection

As discussed earlier, having access to the Internet is imperative to get the most benefit from the online experience. All of the commercial services now offer this access, and AOL is among those that provides direct hypertext links from its own pages right to pages on the Internet. AOL's Internet Connection site (see Figure 6.16) makes interacting with the technically complex Internet about as easy as it can get—much easier than the Internet itself makes it. The Internet Connection links you to newsgroups, e-mail (though you can get AOL's e-mail from any AOL page), Web page development tools, chat rooms, Internet search engines (such as WebCrawler), and Internet tutorials for beginners.

Sports

AOL's Sports site follows the model of the Entertainment category; it links you to scores, articles, references, player and team profiles, the latest sports news, discussion groups, and interactive chats with sports stars themselves (see Figure 6.17). The Sports site is categorized to make it easy to locate information

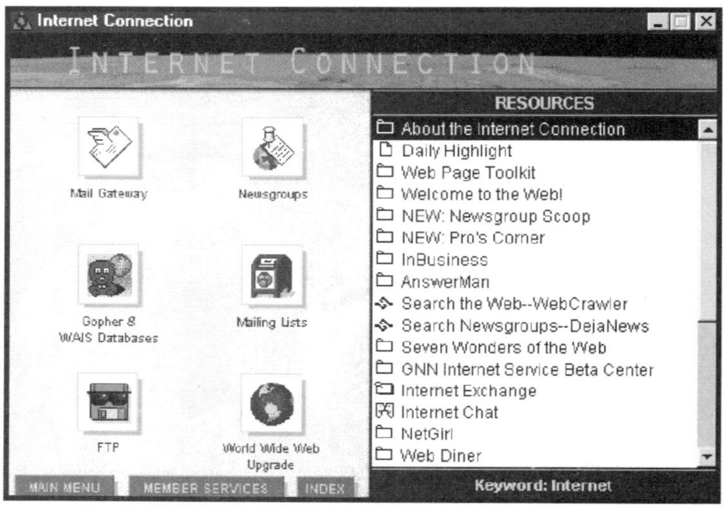

FIGURE 6.16

The Resources list box on the Internet Connection links you instantly to information about the Internet as well as the Internet itself.

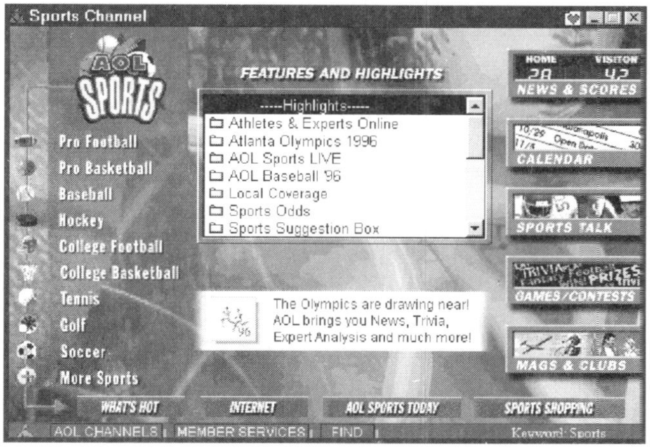

FIGURE 6.17

From surfing to mountain biking to ABC Monday Night Football, AOL's Sports destinations deliver information for both spectators and participants.

about your favorite sport. You can scroll through the list box of the latest headlines (double-click a selection to display the article), and the Top Web Sites for sports are only a couple of clicks away. AOL makes a nice attempt to cover not only mainstream sports, but those off the beaten path as well. There also are games, trivia contests, and press conferences for major events.

Kids Only

AOL's strong drive to make online services a family affair gave birth to Kids Only, a site where children can learn, interact, explore, and conquer any fears they might have of a computer keyboard (see Figure 6.18). The destination sites range from fun stuff—Cartoon Network, DC Comics for Kids, and Games—to ABC's *Kidzine*

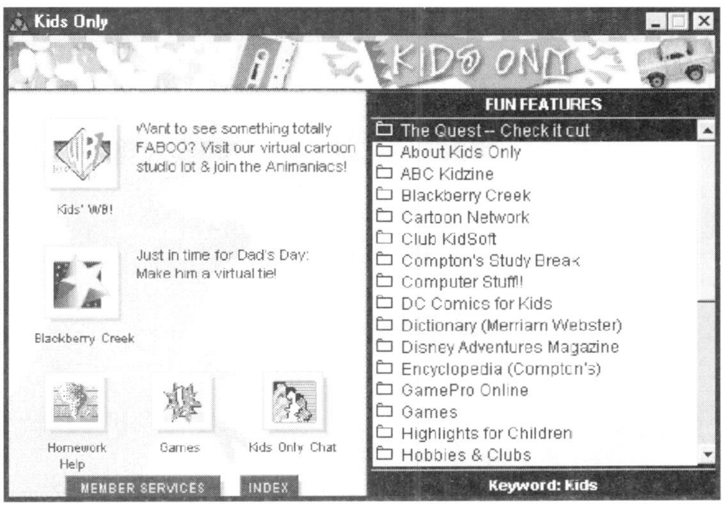

FIGURE 6.18

Through Kids Only, children can read cartoons.

magazine, Compton's Encyclopedia, Homework Help, and Kids Only chat rooms. If the kids are into hobbies and clubs, Kids Only links them to online organizations such as the *Star Trek* club or the Astronomy club. Kids Only is a nicely maintained, completely overseen safe haven for children to learn and grow.

AOL's Communication and Interaction Services

AOL provides what can be considered the standard complement of tools and services for an online service today: E-mail, Internet access, file transfer capability for sending and receiving documents and so forth, access to newsgroups and bulletin board systems (BBSes), and chat technology. The difference is that AOL makes them simple. For people who haven't used e-mail before or whose only exposure to it has been through the sometimes complicated addressing schemes needed on the Internet, AOL reduces the exercise to a couple of mouse clicks . The toolbar at the top of the America Online window assures that you're only a click away from services such as e-mail. To send a message, just click the Post Office button (see Figure 6.19).

E-mail is one of the most useful (and sometimes addictive) applications of online services. You can send e-mail to companies you want information from, people you meet in chat rooms, business colleagues, and online friends. No zip code is off limits. You can mail to people who use AOL, and even to people who use other commercial online services or the Internet. Literally millions of e-mail messages are mailed around the world every day, usually arriving within seconds of being sent. AOL's simple-to-use e-mail isn't going to discourage use, either. If you want to make your text snazzier, there are even text formatting tools right in the Compose Mail window. Simply follow these steps:

1. Type the recipient's member ID in the To: list box.

FIGURE 6.19

AOL's Post Office gives you a simple mail menu from which you can compose, send, receive, print, schedule, and review mail; you can also send faxes, edit your address book, and much more.

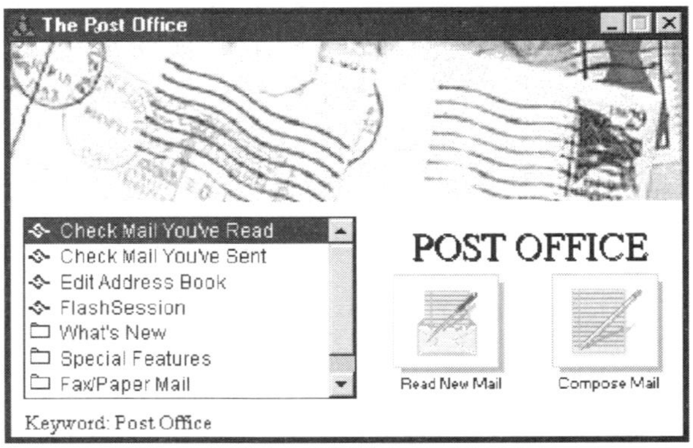

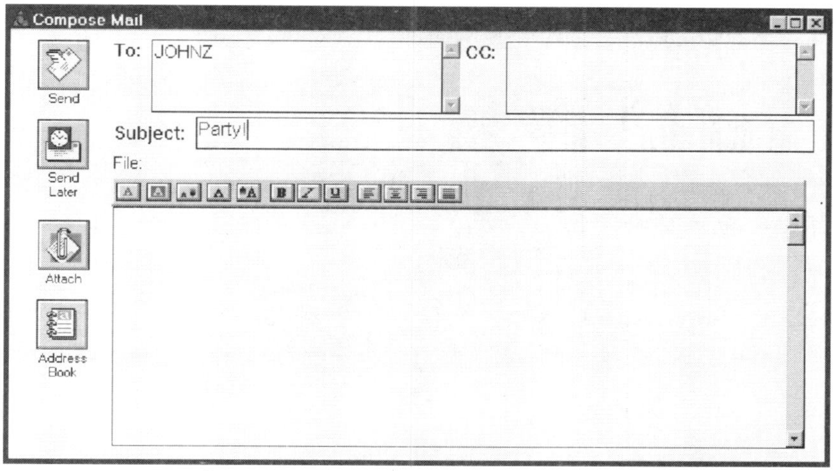

FIGURE 6.20

E-mail messages on AOL can be sent to other AOL members, but also to subscribers to other online services as well as Internet users.

2. If you want to send a copy to someone, type their member ID in the CC: list box.
3. Type the subject you're writing about in the Subject: text box.
4. Compose your message and click the Send button (see Figure 6.20).

TIP

If you want to attach a file (such as a formatted document), click the Attach File button in the left margin and select the file from the Online Downloads dialog box. The file will be sent with the message.

AOL's shortcomings in the e-mail realm are ones that might or might not be considered important, depending on the types of messages you send. Most other services (and most Internet e-mail software) do not provide them either. You can't insert objects, such as video clips, into composed text. And you can't embed HyperText Markup Language (HTML) links in the composed message, which would enable a recipient to click the link and jump to an Internet site whose address is embedded in the link (although Netscape Navigator's e-mail client has this facility, and Navigator will soon be part of AOL).

These are, however, relatively recent advances in e-mail technology, and are by no means the primary way people send messages. In all likelihood, AOL will enhance its e-mail service to do these things. Until then, you can send formatted files, including graphics files, via file attachments.

FIGURE 6.21

Hot topics and new features appear in the Welcome window at sign on providing instant links to AOL's fresh destinations, services, and fields of interest.

Any worthwhile online service is eternally a work-in-progress. It's never finished in the sense that it's as good as it will ever get. To that end, the forums, features, and facilities of AOL are constantly evolving. It's easy to keep up with these new forums via a page known as the Welcome window, a visual greeting you receive when you sign on (see Figure 6.21). On average, AOL has three to six new destination sites and services every month, so even if you're an experienced AOL user, you'll want to check out the latest online options.

Summary

When Quantum Computer Services unveiled the AOL prototype in 1985, it was with no guarantees that an interconnected online world would ever approach reality. But AOL's bet paid off in that it allowed the company to entrench itself with the earliest users. Those users provided the first feedback about what they wanted next in online services, and AOL demonstrated that it was listening. The result has been that AOL has led the way in providing interesting and practical forums, varied fare for kids and adults, and light and casual sites as well as technical and in-depth ones. With its industry-leading five million subscribers, AOL is well positioned to utilize the information they provide to stay on top of the online services market.

Certainly, AOL will maintain the simplicity of use that has become its hallmark. AOL will probably add the functionality—some of it extremely sophisticated, such as support for video, 3-D images, and virtual reality—that now is emerging in the online world. And you'll probably be able to access it with a mouse click or two. AOL could benefit from adding these features, along with beefing up its international site links (it's mainly an America-focused service, though you can communicate worldwide) in the way that The Microsoft Network has started to. But at 11-years-old and counting, no one knows the concept of a work-in-progress better than the management at America Online. If the number of subscribers is any indication, no one does it better.

7

COMPUSERVE

All online services, including America Online, Prodigy and CompuServe, have certain things in common. Each offers you ways to talk to other members and send e-mail to people through a connection to the Internet. Each has information services you can search and online versions of popular publications like *People Magazine* and *The New York Times*. Typically, you're provided with a highly graphic, easy-to-use software, and search, file management, and communications features.

However, each online service provides these and other features in slightly different ways. This chapter gives you an overview of CompuServe: You learn about the environment, tools, and features that make up one of the most popular online services in the world today.

An Overview of CompuServe

CompuServe was one of the first commercial online service providers to come into existence back in the early 1980's. Today, it has more than four million members, and claims that it has more than 3,000 products. These products range from magazines to information services with databases of articles you can retrieve and online stores.

If you ask people who've used several online services what makes CompuServe different from its competitors, you'll probably be told that it tends to be more oriented towards the businessperson. While America Online, for example, is strongly geared toward the home user and families, CompuServe tends to offer more in the way of business profiles and professional associations. This generalization is probably true, but only to an extent. Even though CompuServe has a strong business focus, it hasn't neglected to include features that allow parents to control their childrens' access to certain areas. CompuServe has services and forums that are appropriate for and entertaining to children and teens. However, it doesn't offer a division of services just for children in its Explore CompuServe categories as some services do (see Figure 7.1).

CompuServe differs in its user interface: CompuServe is less graphically oriented than some of its competitors. CompuServe has simpler icons and textual lists of choices instead of cleverly drawn buttons and images you can click (see Figure 7.2). Graphic files typically take several seconds to load on your computer which makes using some of the more graphically-oriented services, like America Online, slower than CompuServe in most instances. If you're serious about doing research online, you're probably not interested in waiting for little pictures to appear on screen as you look for what you need. For that reason (and others)

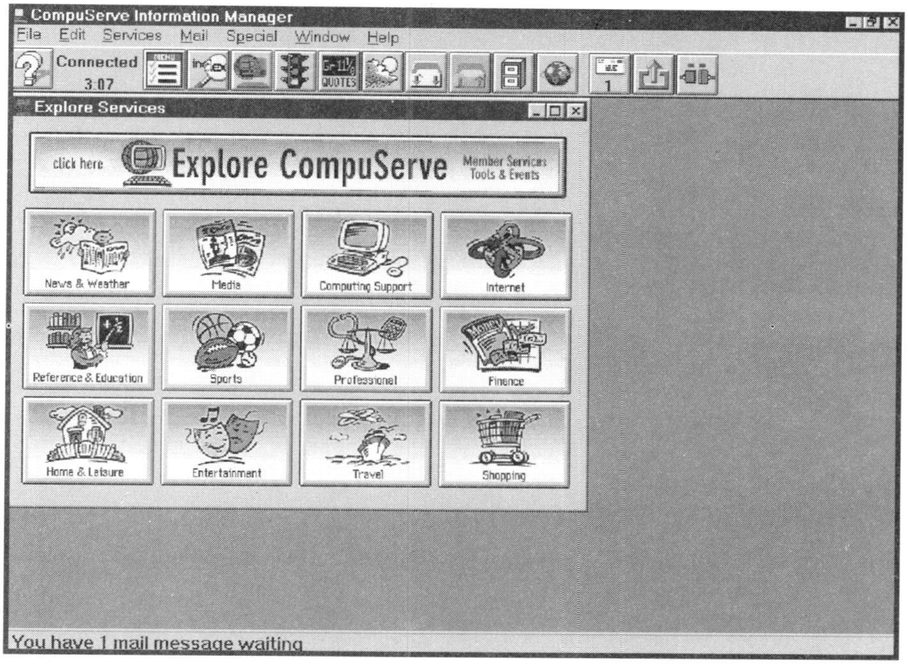

FIGURE 7.1

The Explore CompuServe list of topics is one of the first things you see when you enter CompuServe.

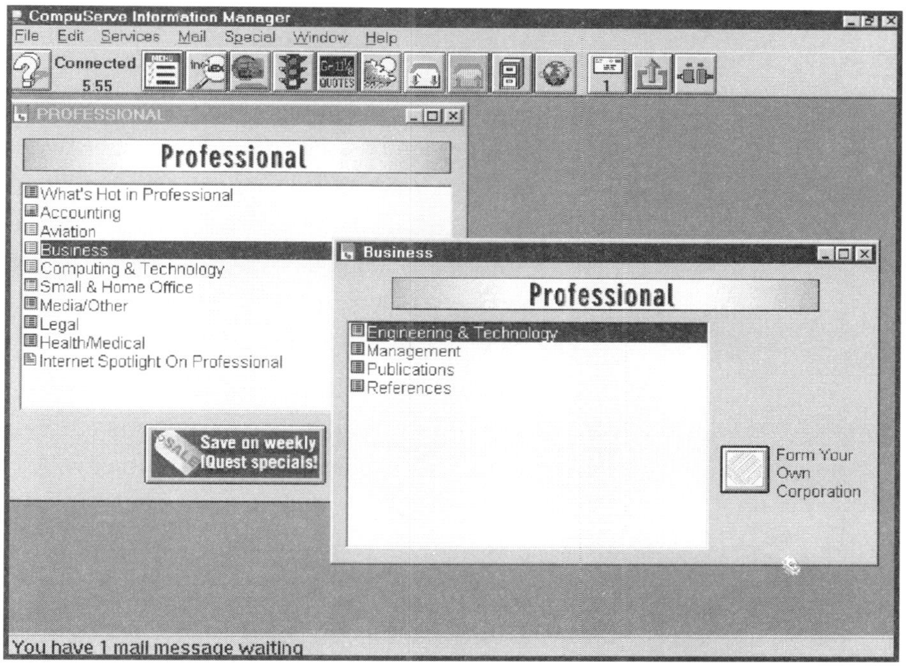

FIGURE 7.2

To find services, you often make choices from one list and then another list until you find what you need.

even though it has entertaining aspects, CompuServe does tend to appeal to those who want to get work done, rather than be entertained.

NOTE

At the time of this writing, CompuServe had announced a new version 3.0 of its Information Manager software. This new software interface is likely to offer a more graphical environment. The figures in this chapter were taken of WinCIM 2.0.1. Although the actual screens you will see if you use the new version may differ from the figures in this chapter, the basic structure and type of features CompuServe offers are likely to remain similar.

What's Available

CompuServe offers its own services, connections to services such as huge databases or stores, areas where members can congregate and exchange messages or files, online conferences, and an Internet connection. To understand how all of these services are organized and how to get to them, take a look at the CompuServe interface. The CompuServe Information Manager software (the Windows version is called WinCIM) presents various tools you can use to move around in the CompuServe environment.

Exploring the WinCIM Environment

WinCIM, like most online service software, is provided free of charge to CompuServe members. Once you're a member, you can spot announcements in CompuServe's What's New window of periodic software updates which will tell you how to download the software. If you're not yet a member, you can obtain the software from CompuServe by calling 800-848-8199; ask for an Introductory Membership Kit. Be sure to specify which computer operating system you use (such as Windows or Macintosh).

After you have the software, installing it is simply a matter of running a setup file and following the instructions presented to you. Even though you'll be given free online time initially, you will need to provide billing information, such as a credit card number, so your account can be set up.

TIP

Settings for running a CompuServe session should automatically be correct when it's installed. However, if you have a problem connecting or if you change the way you

FIGURE 7.3

CompuServe allows you to make modifications to how you access the service through the Session Settings dialog box.

want to connect (for example, if you get a new modem), choose Special, Session Settings. In the Setup Session Settings dialog box, you can adjust your User ID, your Password, the phone number for local Access to CompuServe, and your Modem settings (see Figure 7.3).

◆ ◆

After you successfully install the software, the Connect to CompuServe dialog box appears (see Figure 7.4). To connect to the service, click the Connect button.

The following sections take a brief look at some of the tools and types of features available when you first enter CompuServe.

The CompuServe Opening Window

Figure 7.5 shows what your screen looks like when you first connect to CompuServe. This main area of the CompuServe Information Manager window is where CompuServe displays other windows for its services. By default, there are two windows on screen when you connect: What's New (FREE) appears on top and lists current events and new CompuServe features or events, and the Explore Services window in under the What's New window and lists categories of services. Refer to Figure 7.1 to see the Explore Services window clearly.

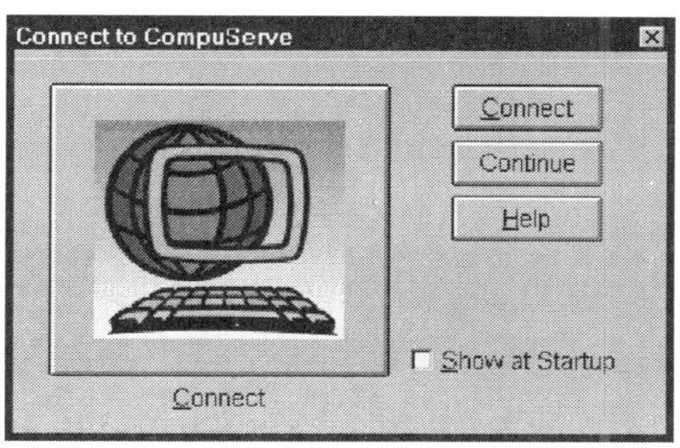

FIGURE 7.4

You can also open this dialog box by choosing File, Connect.

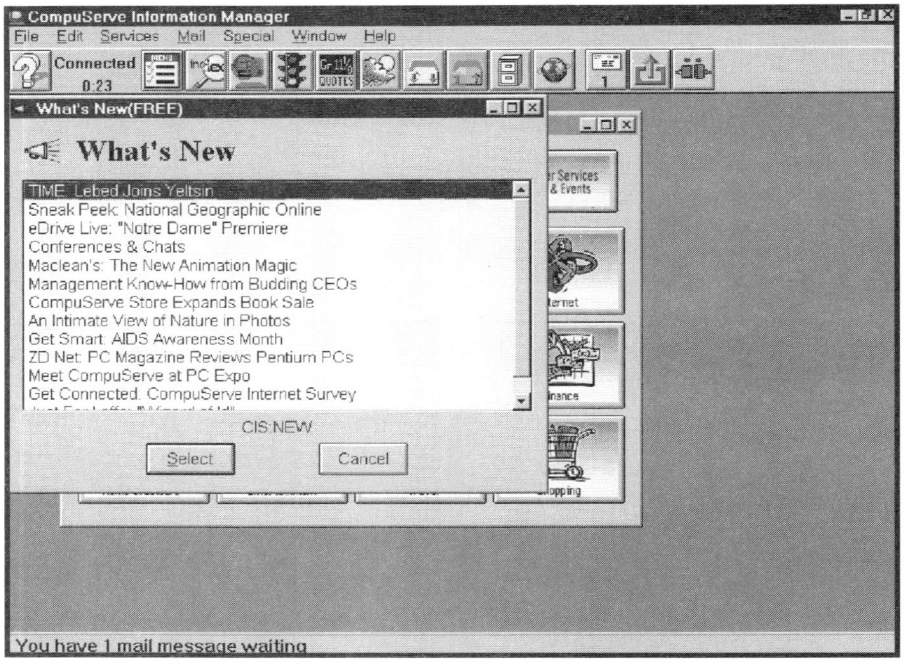

FIGURE 7.5

When you first open CompuServe, the service lets you know about current events and new features in its What's New window.

At the top of the window there is a menu and a customizable toolbar made up of buttons you can click to perform tasks. Usually, clicking a button displays a list or opens a dialog box from which you can make choices. Table 7.1 lists the default buttons on the toolbar and their purposes.

Many of the functions on the toolbar are also available through menu commands. Basically, the menu commands break down this way:

- The File menu has commands for opening, saving, and printing.
- The Edit menu provides commands for cutting, copying, pasting, and performing other editing functions.
- The Services menu takes you directly to specific major services and search features, such as Go and Find.
- The Mail menu commands help you create and receive mail messages.
- The Special menu commands let you customize session settings by establishing your preferences and making modifications.
- The Window menu allows you to arrange windows on screen.
- The Help menu gives you additional information about different options in WinCIM.

TABLE 7.1 COMPUSERVE TOOLBAR BUTTONS

Button	Name	Function
	Help	Invokes the WinCIM Help system
	Favorite Places	Opens a window that lists the CompuServe services you visit most often
	Find	Opens a dialog box where you can search for services by typing a search term
	Explore	Opens the Explore Services window
	Go	Opens a dialog box where you can type a Go word to take you directly to a particular service
	Quotes	Opens a customizable stock portfolio you can use to check on current stock prices
	Weather	Opens a service to get weather reports by location
	In Basket	Opens your incoming mail basket
	Out Basket	Opens your outgoing mail basket
	Filing Cabinet	Opens a list of folders containing copies of mail you've sent or saved and files you've downloaded
	Internet Browser	Takes you to software to search the Internet
	Get New Mail	Opens a window listing any new mail
	Exit	Disconnects from CompuServe and exits WinCIM
	Disconnect	Disconnects from CompuServe but does not exit WinCIM

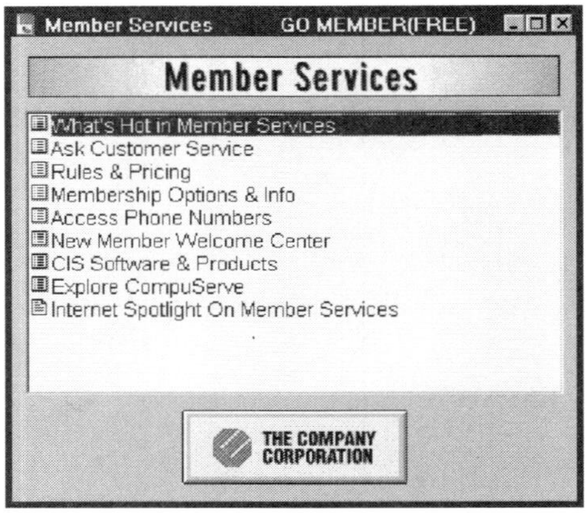

FIGURE 7.6

Look for Go words in some window title bars, such as GO MEMBER here.

Using Go

Online services typically have a feature that takes you directly to a particular area of interest. They do this by assigning an address to each windows. In CompuServe, this address is called a Go word. Some windows have the Go word printed right in their title bar, so you can make note of it if you want to go there again. For example, the Member Services window in Figure 7.6 tells you that it's Go word is Member.

To use the Go feature, click the Go button in the toolbar (the stoplight), or choose Services, Go. The Go dialog box appears (see Figure 7.7). Type the Go word in the Service text box and click OK. CompuServe takes you to that area, which can save you from plowing through layers of windows and lists.

Some Go words are pretty obvious (like Member to get to Member Services and Billing to get information about your account); others aren't so obvious. You can get a searchable list of Go words by typing **Quick** in the Service: text box of the Go dialog box. In the dialog box that follows you can type a search term, such as the topic "Pets," and CompuServe will list all the services and their Go words that fit that topic.

Using Find

Go words are fine if you already know the correct word. But, just like those times when your mother told you to look up a word you didn't know how to

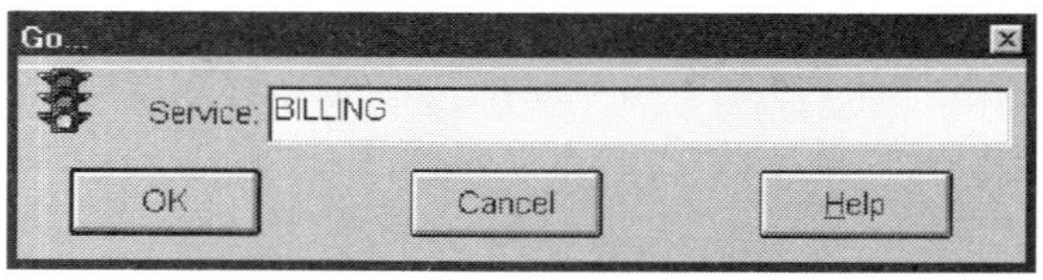

FIGURE 7.7

If you know a service's Go word, click the Go button.

FIGURE 7.8

If you want to find an assortment of services that relate to a topic, try the Find search feature.

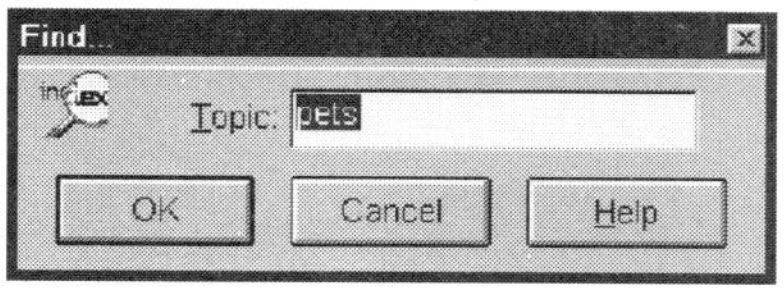

spell in the dictionary, there are times when you don't know where to begin. It's times like these that you'll use CompuServe's Find function. Basically, Find lets you type in a word—a topic, phrase, or name—and lets CompuServe search for any matching services.

You open the Find dialog box by clicking the Find button in the toolbar (the button that has a magnifying glass and the word Index on it). The Find dialog box appears (see Figure 7.8).

Type a topic, word, or phrase and click OK. CompuServe will provide a list of any services that have contents matching that general topic. You can then go to that topic by double-clicking it in the list.

How CompuServe Organizes Services

The Explore CompuServe window divides available services into several categories:

- News & Weather
- Media
- Computing Support
- Internet
- Reference & Education
- Sports
- Professional
- Finance
- Home & Leisure
- Entertainment
- Travel
- Shopping

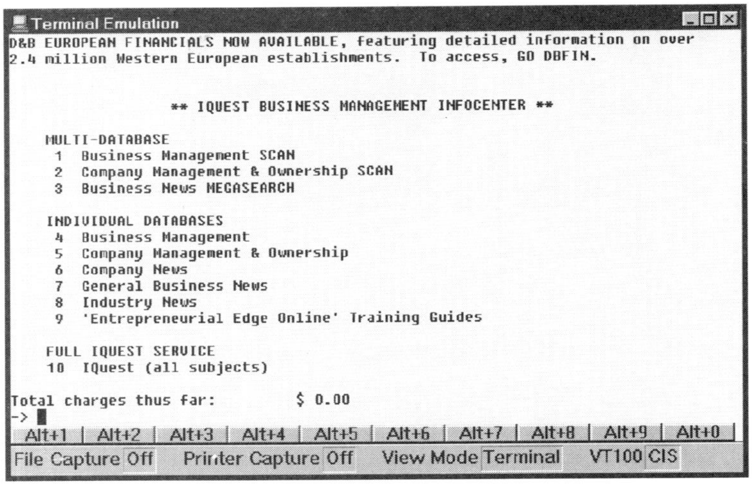

FIGURE 7.9

Many information services display a terminal emulation (or straight text) interface.

To explore a category, simply click its button in the Explore Services window, then click a choice in the list that appears. In some cases, you continue clicking items in subsequent lists until you narrow down to the service you want.

In each category, you'll find a variety of types of services:

- There are likely to be information services that are actually search features connected to huge databases maintained by companies like IQUEST (which searches several major databases when you initiate a search). Figure 7.9 shows the main search menu of IQUEST. You can use these information services to research topics and print or save reports.
- There are several publications including magazines, newspapers, and newsletters you can download graphics files from and read or print copies of articles (see Figure 7.10).

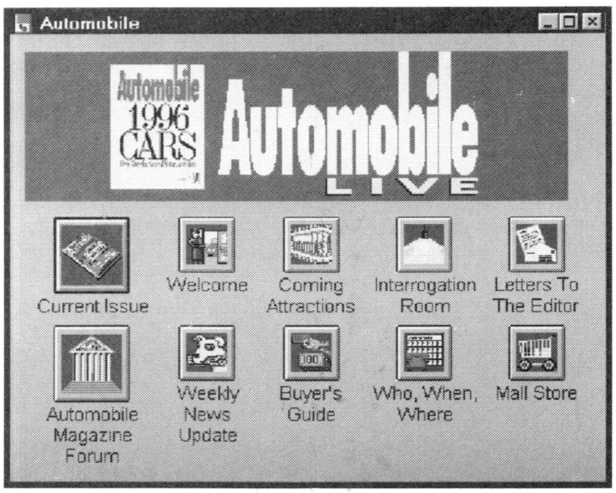

FIGURE 7.10

Automobile magazine's site is typical of the variety of features you'll find in an online publication.

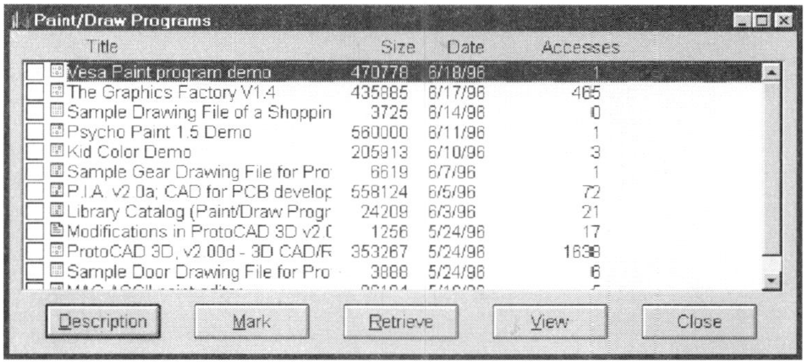

FIGURE 7.11

Forum message boards list a file by size, date uploaded, and how many people have accessed it.

- You'll find *forums* in most categories. These are special interest areas that consist of libraries of message boards. These areas contain messages and files posted by other CompuServe users, all related to a particular topic. For example, the Graphics Support Forum shown in Figure 7.11 is devoted to those who enjoy using computer graphics. Look here for files that others have uploaded containing free graphics images, shareware, or software utility programs.
- There are stores where you can buy products or services. These stores are collected together in the Shopping category, but you can also access them throughout other categories of services (see Figure 7.12).
- There are two areas for meeting people and attending live discussion events. You'll see items mentioning conferences or special events throughout category lists. Some of these items will take you to a description of a live event in CompuServe's auditorium (see Figure 7.13). Auditoriums host

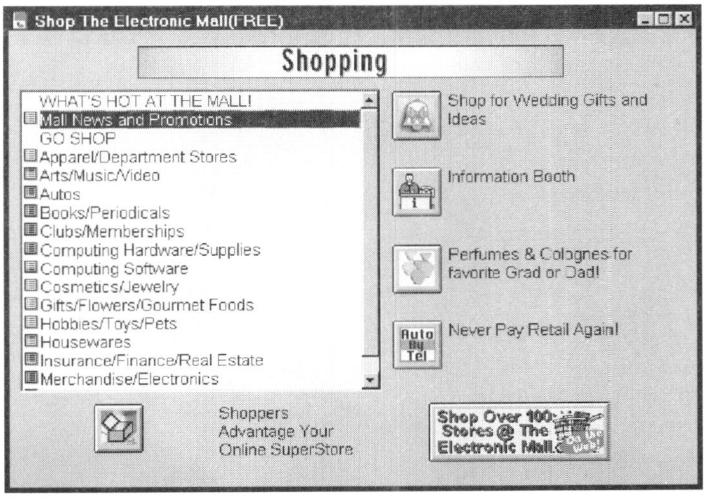

FIGURE 7.12

You can buy almost anything online in The Electronic Mall.

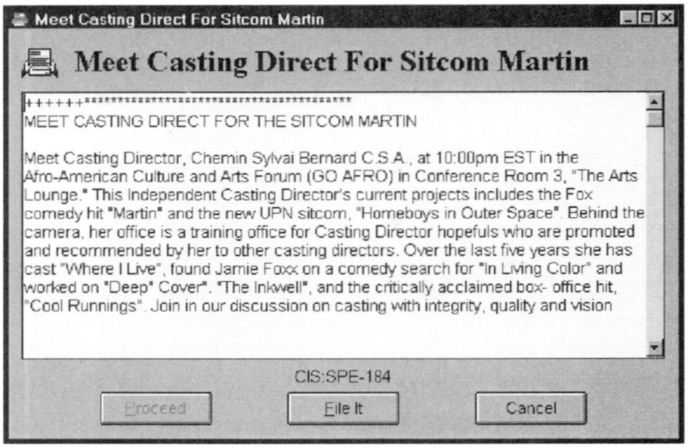

FIGURE 7.13

In the CompuServe auditorium you can "talk" with famous people by submitting questions through a moderator.

famous guests or experts who hold live discussions with CompuServe members.

- The Convention Center is the other place for live interaction (see Figure 7.14). You can enter conference rooms where you participate in live discussions with other CompuServe members who share your interests. Voicing your opinion is as easy as typing your own comment in the bottom pane of the window and then pressing Enter.

TIP

Remember, you can go directly to these services using Go words or the Find feature. Also, access to a service might be found in more than one of the Explore Services categories.

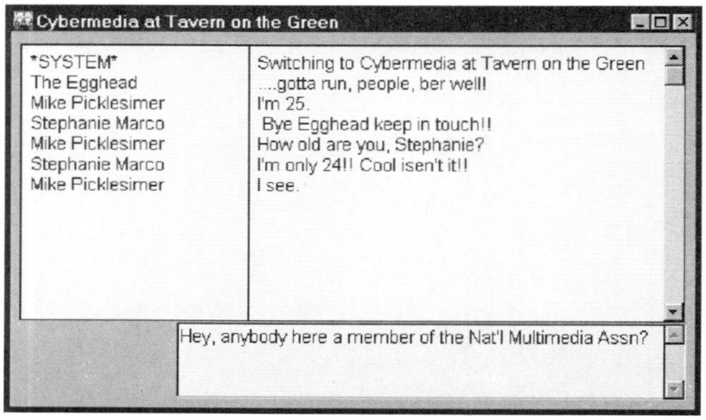

FIGURE 7.14

Follow the discussion and add your own comments in the Convention Center rooms.

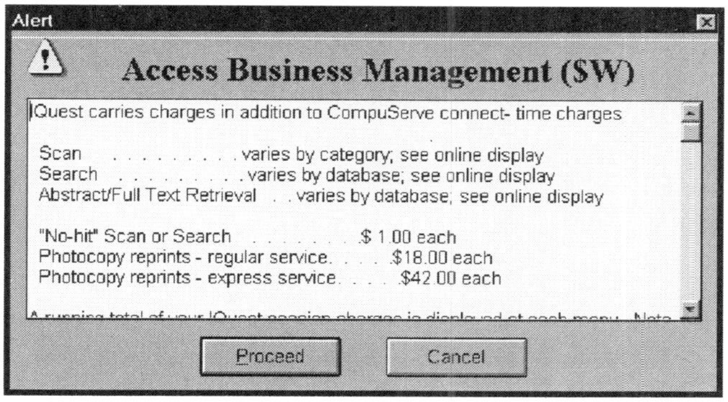

FIGURE 7.15

Be alert to Alert windows like this—they tell you that you're about to incur additional charges.

What CompuServe Costs

One important area where online services differ is in their pricing. Basically, CompuServe has two pricing schemes: *Standard* and *Super Value*. The Standard plan charges $9.95 a month for five hours online. The Super Value Plan charges $24.95 for 20 hours a month. Any time spent online beyond these hours costs $2.95 per hour under the Standard Plan, and $1.95 per hour under the Super Value Plan.

CompuServe also has several premium services. These involve an additional charge regardless of the payment plan you use; these services are usually associated with a task, such as creating and printing a data report. If, for example, you run a credit report on a company through the TRW Credit service, you would be charged a few dollars for that report. Premium services have a $ symbol next to their names on lists, and a window similar to the one in Figure 7.15 will appear to alert you to the charges before you enter the service.

Using E-mail with CompuServe

E-mail is one of the most useful features of online services and the Internet. It's easy to use CompuServe's e-mail feature to create and receive mail, and send files to other CompuServe members, or to members of other online services via the Internet.

NOTE

Files sent to another CompuServe member go to them without a hitch. However, files you send to someone across the Internet may need to be encoded in special ways. Some online services, like America Online, automatically encode and decode file attachments for this purpose. At this time, CompuServe does not. You can use any common encoding program, like WinCode, to code files so they can be sent as text through the Internet. You may want to be sure that the recipient of the file has the same coding software to decode it when it's received.

Receiving Mail

When you connect to CompuServe, a woman's voice announces whether you have new mail (if you have a sound card and speakers installed). In addition, the Get New Mail button on the toolbar (it looks like a little envelope) will have a number on it indicating the number of new messages. To get your mail, just click the Get New Mail button. The list of new messages appears (see Figure 7.16).

To read a message, just select the message, then click the Get button. The message window appears as shown in Figure 7.17. In messages which come across the Internet there's a rather lengthy, cryptic heading before the actual message. Just ignore this: it's Internet talk for how, when, and where the message got from there to here.

Sending Mail

To compose your own mail message, choose Mail, Create Mail. The Create Mail window appears (see Figure 7.18).

To address your message, click the Address button. The Recipient List window appears (see Figure 7.19). You can store addresses of people with whom you regularly communicate in the Address Book. When a name is in the Address Book, you just copy it from the Address Book list to the Recipients list to address your message. Or, you can type the recipient's name and address and choose the address type in the text boxes at the top of the window.

After you type the subject of your message and its contents, you send the message immediately by clicking Send Now, or send it later by placing it in the Out

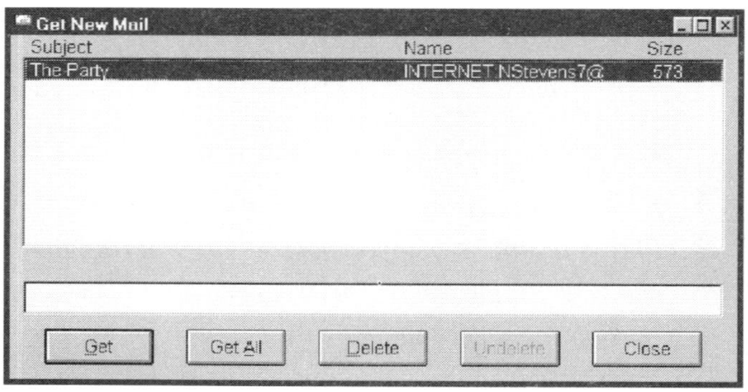

FIGURE 7.16

The subject, the name of the sender, and the size of new messages appear in the Get New Mail window.

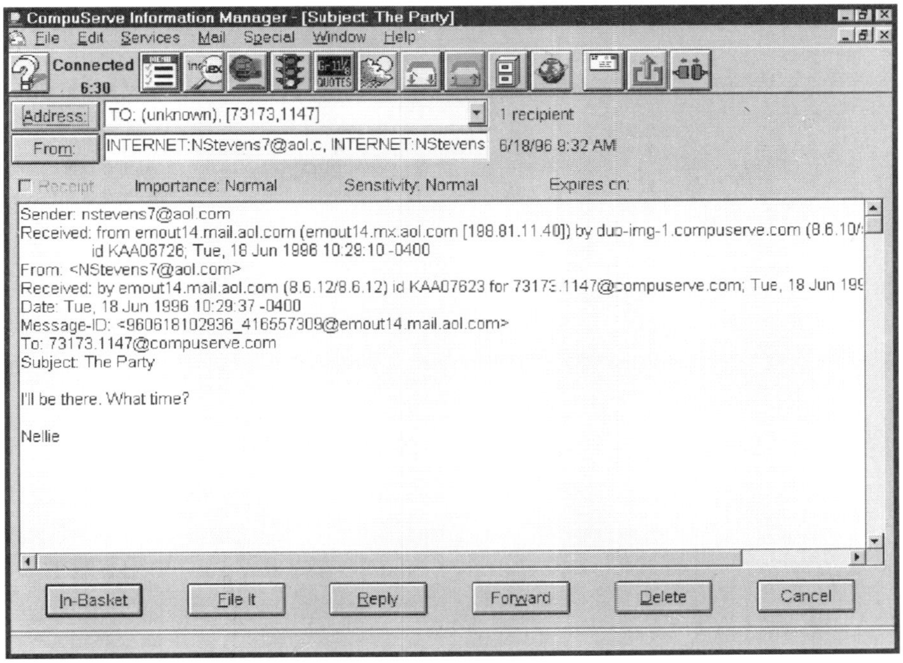

FIGURE 7.17

The buttons at the bottom of this window allow you to save, reply to, or delete the message.

Basket (refer to Figure 7.18). If you want to attach a file to your message, just click the Attach button and locate the file you want to send.

CompuServe's Internet Connection

Many people today choose to access the Internet through an online service like CompuServe, rather than through an Internet Service Provider. This choice depends on how much you will use the Internet. The cost of accessing the Internet through CompuServe or any of its competitors is higher than through a service

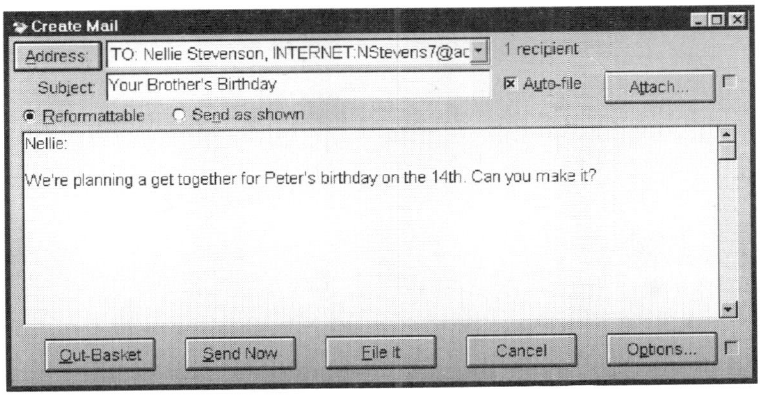

FIGURE 7.18

You can create a message and attach a file using this window.

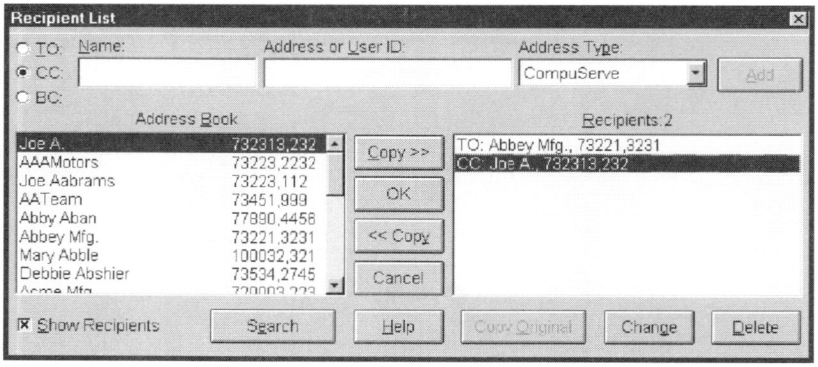

FIGURE 7.19

You can choose as many recipients as you want when you address your message.

provider. This is because most providers offer unlimited access for a flat fee. CompuServe applies any time spent on the Internet in the 5 hours you get for your monthly membership fee on the standard pricing plan; after that first 5 hours, CompuServe charges by the hour for access. CompuServe does offer tools, such as Web Central, shown in Figure 7.20, and Home Page Wizard, shown in Figure 7.21, to get around the Internet and to create your own Web page. There is also access to many popular browsing programs, such as Netscape Navigator, through CompuServe.

CompuServe offers the following features for interacting with the Internet:

- Access to discussion groups called USENET newsgroups.
- File downloads using FTP software.
- Access to the World Wide Web with a browser and lists of popular Web page destinations.

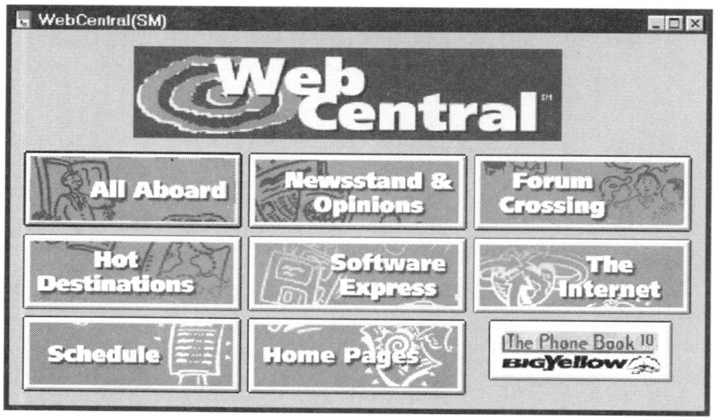

FIGURE 7.20

Web Central offers browsing and lists of hot destinations to get your Internet experience going.

FIGURE 7.21

The Home Page Wizard walks you through the creation of your own World Wide Web home page.

- Internet forums where CompuServe members can post messages relating to Internet interests, such as those who want to publish on the Internet or new users of the Internet.
- Internet Q&As, which provide answers to frequently asked questions about using the Internet.

Summary

CompuServe offers a variety of services and features that are especially useful to those who want to conduct business or perform online research. CompuServe's tools and services are designed to make research, communication, and online learning easy. CompuServe's access to the Internet, although somewhat more expensive than what's offered by Internet Service Providers, comes with features that help you find your way around the Internet in an organized efficient manner.

8

PRODIGY AND OTHER ONLINE SERVICES

Once the largest commercial online service, Prodigy is attempting to position itself as one of the primary national Internet Service Providers (ISP). This chapter looks at Prodigy's World Wide Web presence, as well as its proprietary network and content areas.

Along with Prodigy, CompuServe, and AOL, there are also several other online services that may interest you. In this chapter, you learn what these services offer and how to access them.

Prodigy

Prodigy Services Company is owned by IBM and Sears and has been one of the top three commercial online services since its debut in 1990 (see Figure 8.1). Although it lags behind America Online and CompuServe in content features and membership, Prodigy usually is the first online service to provide innovative and cutting-edge features, such as Internet and World Wide Web access. It was also one of the first online services to offer Internet e-mail for its regular online service members.

There are two ways you can use Prodigy. First, you can access proprietary content and services. Prodigy offers original content, such as news, sports, software support, and business information. Some of the services you get include chats, e-mail, and software downloads. The other way you can use Prodigy is as your ISP. Prodigy's

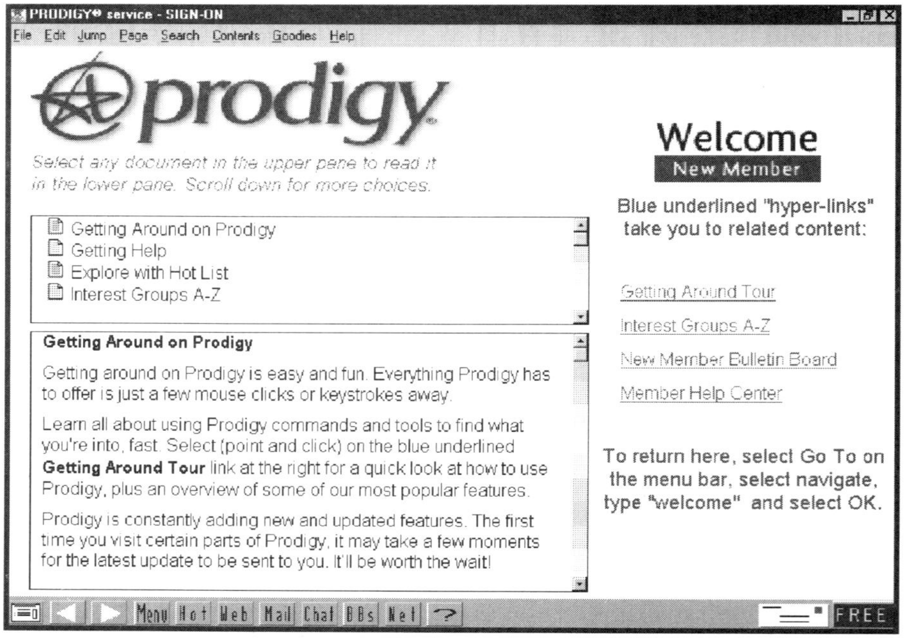

FIGURE 8.1

Prodigy offers both a dedicated online service and an Internet service (AND).

AND (Access Net Direct) connects you directly to the Internet at one dollar per hour, without a monthly service fee or minimum usage requirements.

The following sections show you how to use both of these Prodigy services.

Accessing Prodigy's Online Service

When you log into Prodigy you see the main menu (see Figure 8.2). From here, you can select one of Prodigy's main categories: Highlights, Interest Groups, or Learn About. When you select one of these choices, Prodigy shows you a detailed list of topics within these categories. You also can use Prodigy's Jump words to go from one area to another area on Prodigy, to an Internet service, or to a USENET newsgroup. The Jump word for the Microsoft Winnews area, for instance, is **support**. (You can find additional Jump words in the Prodigy Help tool under the JumpWords topic.) For now, click one of the links, such as Business/Finance.

NOTE

On the left side of the window, Prodigy displays daily highlights you can click to immediately access them. Daily highlights include news, music information, holiday reports, and so on. This area is similar to the front page of your local newspaper; it shows you the top stories or events of the day.

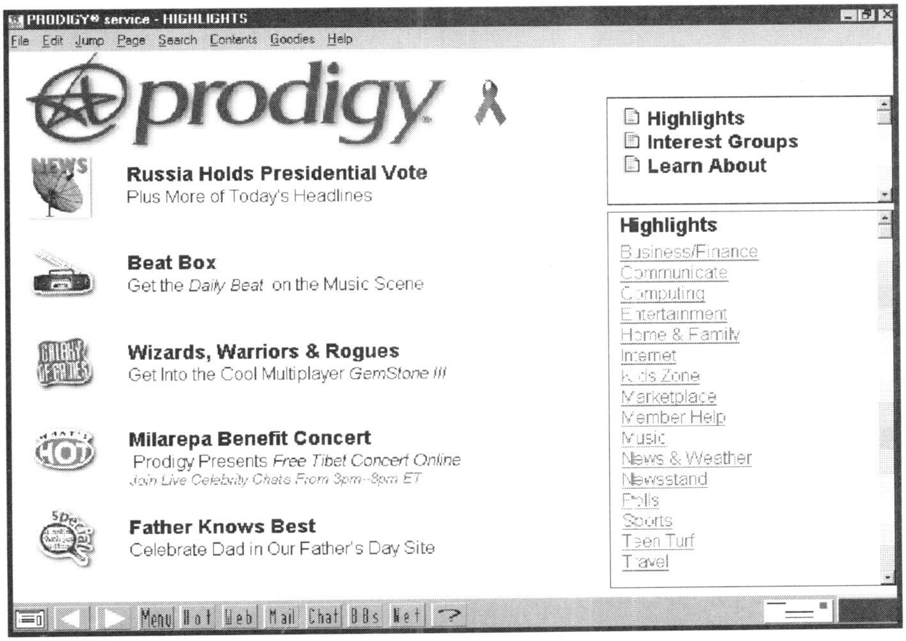

FIGURE 8.2

The Prodigy main menu is where you begin your online journey.

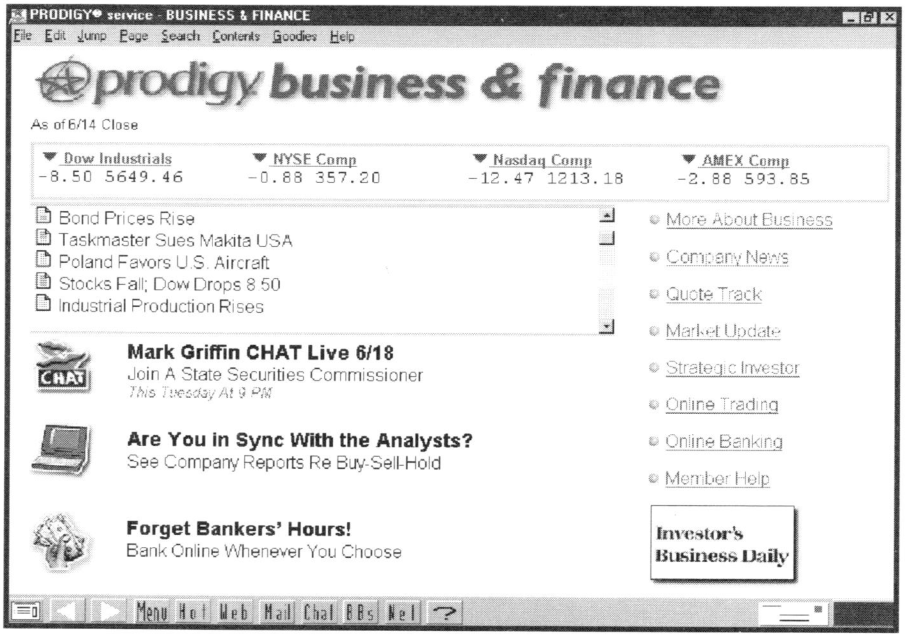

FIGURE 8.3

You can read the latest stock and business information while using Prodigy.

Figure 8.3 shows you the Prodigy's Business and Finance site. One feature Prodigy prides itself on is the stock reports it offers. You can read the Dow Industrials report, New York Stock Exchange Composites, NASDAQ Composites, and American Exchange (AMEX) Composites by clicking one of the links at the top of the Business & Finance page.

If you select the Nasdaq Comp link, for example, you see a screen with NASDAQ volumes, advances and declines, and latest activity (see Figure 8.4). To find a specific stock, click the See Also button and click Stock at a Glance. You can then enter a stock symbol or find one using the Find Symbol button.

Other business information you can access from the Business & Finance page includes company news, banking information, and daily business news highlights. If you want to find more business information, click the More About Business link to open the More About window. From here, you can find related Web pages, news and information services, and newsgroups devoted to business.

To return to the Prodigy main menu, click the Home Base button (the far left button on the toolbar). If other members of your household are using this same account, they can set up different home bases as well.

You use the toolbar at the bottom of the Prodigy screen to navigate through other parts of the service as well. The left and right arrow buttons enable you to move back one screen or to the next screen in a multi-page story or section. These buttons are not always available; they turn from white to black to let you

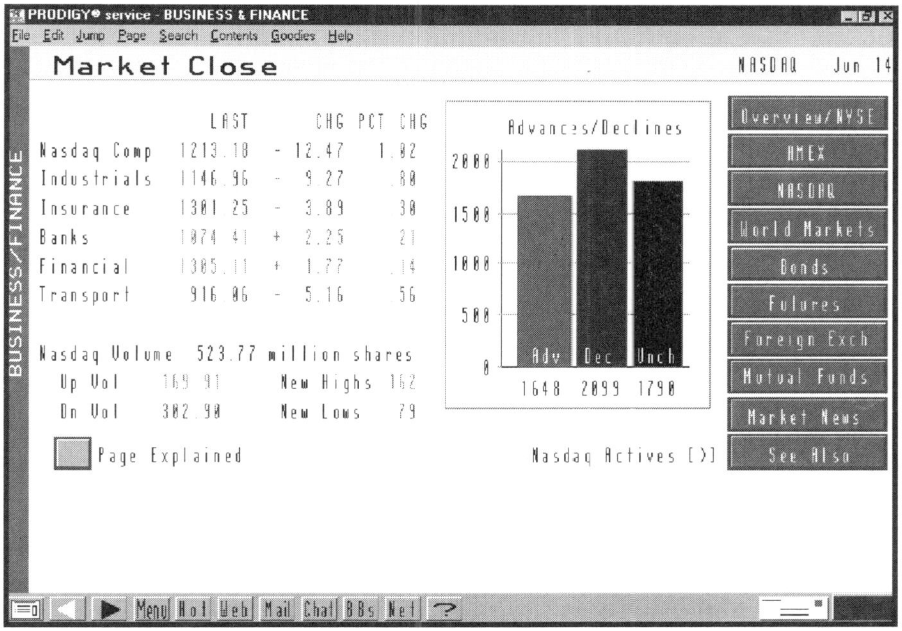

FIGURE 8.4

You can see individual stock reports using Prodigy's extensive tracking and reporting tools.

know when you can use them. The Menu button enables you to return to the last menu you selected a choice from. This may be the main menu, or the menu of a section like Business & Finance.

NOTE

You can use Prodigy's Contents menu to select one of the 10 main areas on Prodigy. These areas include the following:

- *News/Weather*
- *Business/Finance*
- *Sports*
- *Communications*
- *Entertainment*
- *Kids Zone*
- *Shopping*
- *Computers*
- *Travel*
- *Member Help Center*

To store your favorite sites on Prodigy, you can create a hot list, which you can display by clicking the Hot button. Prodigy lets you store up to 20 hot spots on this list. To create this list, click the Hot button to open the HotList dialog box and click the Add GoTo Word button (see Figure 8.5). In the Add GoTo Word dialog box, enter the complete GoTo word and click OK. Your new GoTo word displays in the HotList dialog box.

NOTE

You might notice the pre-defined GoTo words in the HotList. These were placed there automatically when you installed the Prodigy software. To delete one you don't want on this list, click it and click the Remove button. This deletes the item from the HotList.

Also, if you aren't sure what the GoTo word is for, click the A-Z Index GoTo word and click Go. This displays all of Prodigy's areas, with their associated GoTo words.

Another toolbar button is the Web button. When you select this button, the Prodigy Internet page displays. You can read about how Prodigy enables you to navigate on the Internet and Web using Prodigy software. You also can find help on general Internet and Web terminology and services. You might, for

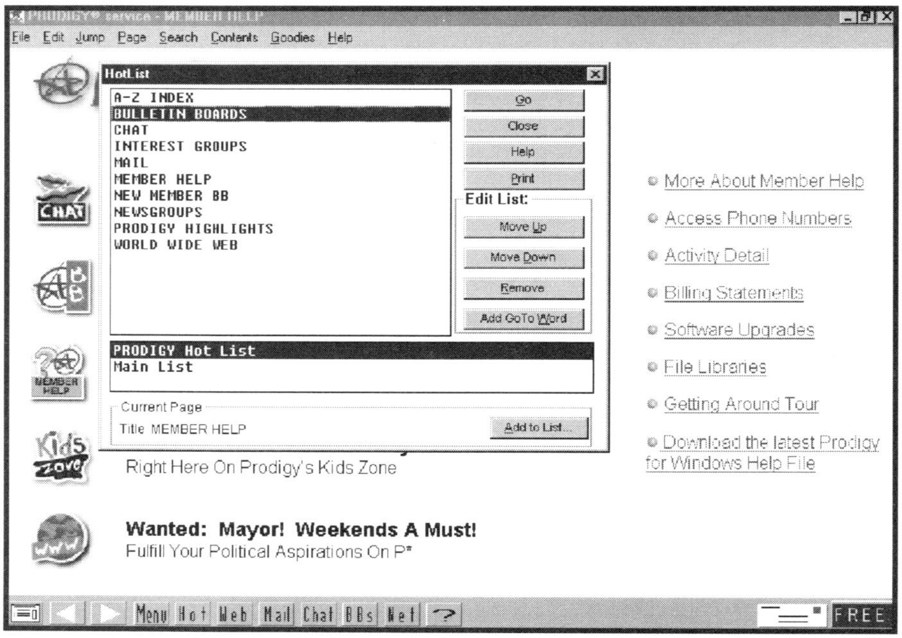

FIGURE 8.5

The Hot List is an easy way to collect favorite Prodigy sites and jump to them quickly.

example, want to read information on how you can speed up your Web session or how you can retrieve a file using FTP or Gopher. (The next section, "Using the Internet with Prodigy," shows you how to use Prodigy to access the Web and other Internet services.)

The toolbar button next to the Web button is the Mail button. Prodigy enables you to send e-mail to other Prodigy members, Internet e-mail users, and to other online service members, using their Internet e-mail address. The Prodigy e-mail software enables you to receive, read, and compose messages (see Figure 8.6). A nice feature of the Prodigy mail software is its capability to attach file attachments to your messages. This means you can send a binary file to another Prodigy member without encoding the file first for transmission. At this point, however, you cannot send attachments to an Internet address unless you convert the files to MIME using a UUENCODE tool and then send the file as a text file. Prodigy allows you to send up to 10MB of files and a maximum of three files per e-mail.

Prodigy wouldn't seem like a real online service if it didn't provide a way to communicate with other members in live forums. By clicking the Chat toolbar button, you can access the Prodigy Chat area. To begin a chat session, click the Select/Change Nickname link. A Chat Nickname dialog box appears, in which you enter a nickname for yourself. Nicknames are 3 to 12 characters long (starting with a letter) and enable you to join chat sessions without using your real name.

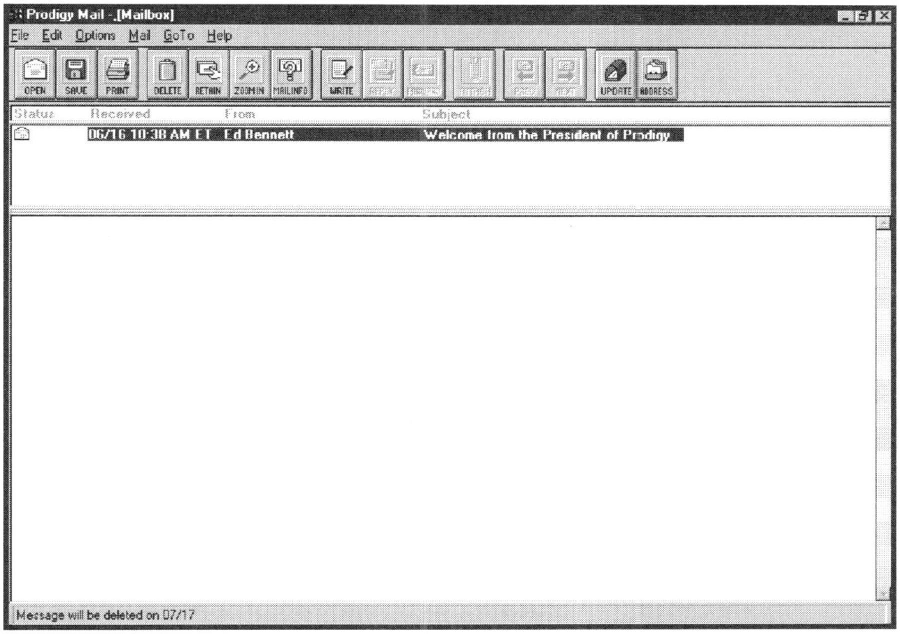

FIGURE 8.6

Prodigy offers enhanced e-mail software, which lets send messages and attached files to mail recipients.

NOTE

Using nicknames is an easy way to disguise your name and family members' names so users online cannot tell who you are. Although this may sound like an extreme step to take for anonymity, don't forsake it—and educate your children on using it. Too many users prey on unsuspecting young users while online. Users should never post member IDs, passwords, credit card information, real names, phone numbers, or addresses while online.

After you enter a nickname (you may need to enter several until you find one not already in use), click the Chat toolbar button again. You can then click the Begin Prodigy Chat link to open the Area and Room List dialog box (see Figure 8.7). Select a chat area, room type (Prodigy, Member, or Auditorium), and the room name. You can see the number of users active in a chat room in the Chat/Max/Passwords column in the Room Name list. The number of members in a chat room appears on the left of this column (such as 3/25). This means there are three members in the room, and the maximum number that can join is 25. The Passwords column is empty to indicate no password is required to join this chat. Find a room and click the Go To Room button. For special events and specific chat topics, watch the main menu for upcoming chats.

WARNING

Although Prodigy has specific guidelines against the use of profanity, "grossly repugnant material," and threats, you still may encounter topics and conversations that violate these guidelines. You should warn your children about these areas and keep them out of as many of them

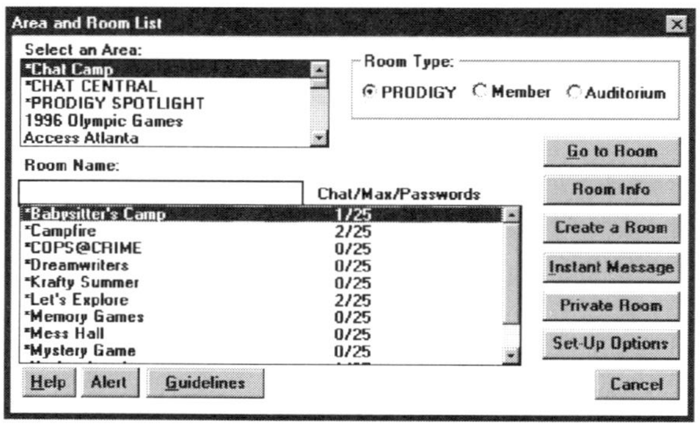

FIGURE 8.7

Prodigy chats offer you a number of topics, including art, business, politics, and wrestling.

as possible. If you're easily offended by opinions and sometimes discriminatory comments, stay out of chat rooms that appear to discuss these topics. To read about Prodigy's chat guidelines, click the Guidelines button in the Area and Room List dialog box.

Because Prodigy enables you to assign up to six members to one account (you plus five other people), you can block certain members from accessing the Chat area. Do this by clicking the Access Control link on the Prodigy Chat page. Next, click the Select Names button and select the names of the members you want to block from Chat. As a recommendation, you may want to block children and young teens from the Chat area to ensure they're not exposed to uncensored or adult-oriented content.

Similar to Prodigy Chats, you can post and read messages on the Prodigy Bulletin Boards (BBs). Bulletin Boards on Prodigy are similar to CompuServe message forums and USENET Newsgroups. Prodigy offers a number of bulletin boards, including the following:

- Adoption
- Auto racing
- Books and writing
- Country music
- Genealogy
- Movies
- NFL (National Football League)
- Science fiction
- Wine, beer, and spirits

When you access a Prodigy Bulletin Board you can select topics by clicking on the Choose a Topic button (see Figure 8.8) and then selecting from a Topic List. Topics are similar to subject lines in e-mail messages. They let you know the type of information discussed in the message thread. If you don't find a topic of interest, you can contribute your own by selecting the Write a Public Note option once you've selected a bulletin board. If you use the Bulletin Board feature a lot, you can customize it so you read only those notes and topics you haven't read yet. This makes it easy for you to enter a bulletin board and get the latest messages without reading through the entire topic list.

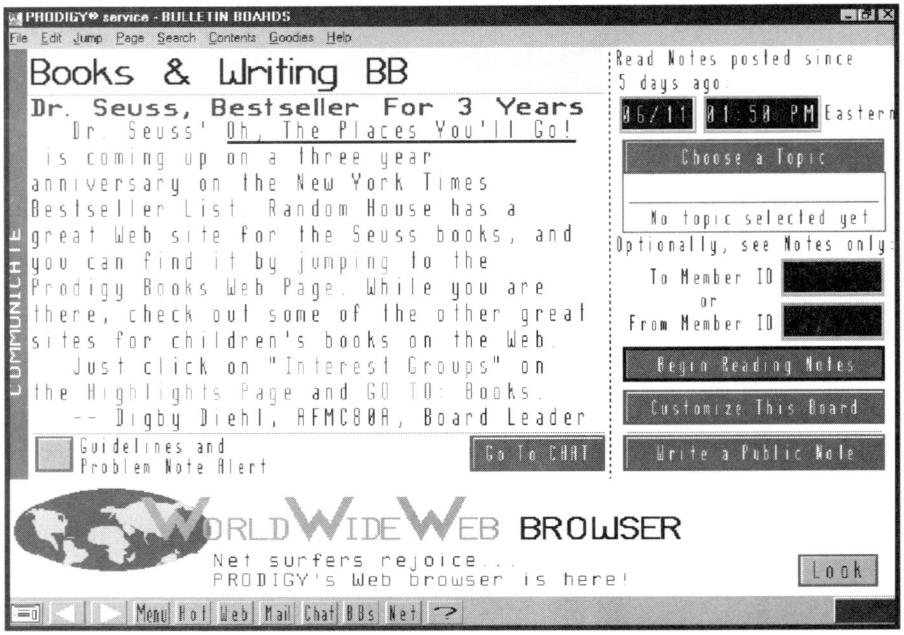

FIGURE 8.8

If you prefer a bulletin board exchange instead of real-time chat sessions, check out the Prodigy Bulletin Board area.

The last two buttons on the toolbar enable you to jump to the Prodigy USENET newsgroup service and to the Member Help section. You can read about the Internet access in the following section.

By clicking the question mark button, you jump to the Member Help page. Here, you can obtain help on navigating Prodigy, get detailed billing information, download the latest Prodigy software, and read about using Microsystem's Cyber Patrol software to block children from accessing certain areas (although Chat and newsgroups cannot be blocked at this time). Cyber Patrol, which is a retail software product, is free to Prodigy members. You can download it from the Prodigy Member Help page.

Using the Internet with Prodigy

Although Prodigy offers many unique areas on its proprietary online service, you may want to join Prodigy to be able to access the Internet and World Wide Web. When you click the Web or Net toolbar buttons, you can enter the Prodigy Internet areas. From these areas, you can find out more about the Internet as well as launch the Prodigy Web browser without disconnecting from Prodigy and re-dialing a different access number (see Figure 8.9).

From the Prodigy Web Browser Home Page, you can access a number of services, including the following:

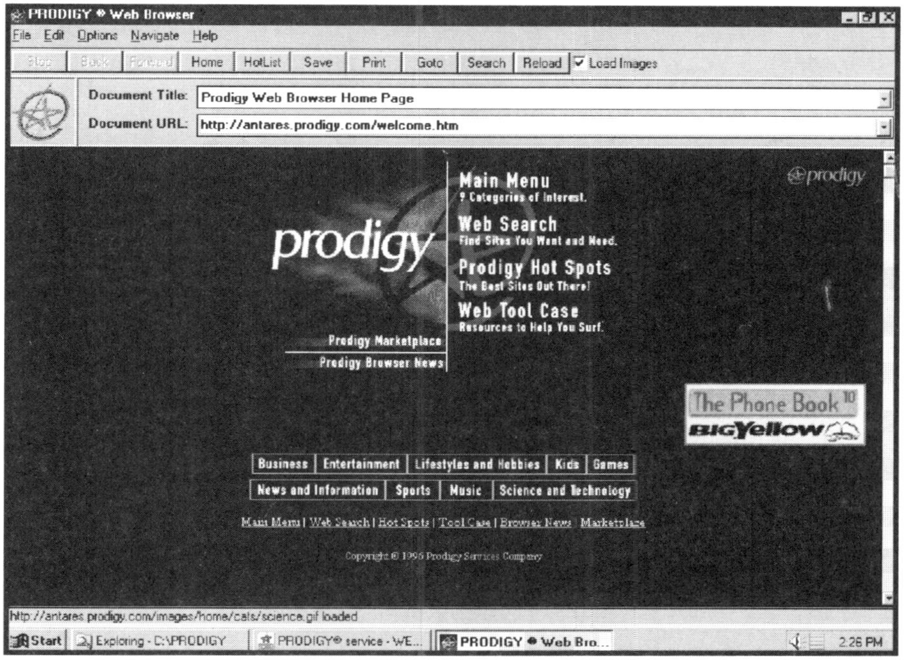

FIGURE 8.9

Prodigy's Web browser enables you to access the World Wide Web from within Prodigy.

- **Business.** Includes information and links relating to investments, real estate, mutual funds, careers, and more. The Working from Home link is a great link for people who use or want to use their homes as their offices.
- **Entertainment.** Use this link to read about movies, science fiction conventions, television, books, and more. The Ch@t Soup link connects you to Prodigy's celebrity gossip site (**http://www.chatsoup.com/**) under the same name as the link.
- **Lifestyles and Hobbies.** Here you can find out more information on topics as diverse as adventure travel, beer, puppetry, and Ukrainian culture. The Photography section includes photographs you can download, contests, and a soon-to-be-released Prodigy member photo album (see Figure 8.10).
- **Kids.** Point your children in this direction. They can learn games, join in activities, and chat with other kids and teenagers. You also can access the Girl Scouts Resource Center.
- **Games.** You can find multiuser games here, which let you play against other Prodigy members in real time. Some of the games included are checkers and Duke Nukem 3D.

FIGURE 8.10

Prodigy's Photography section includes more than 500 photographs you can download.

- **News and Information.** Get up-to-the-minute headlines from the Associated Press, as well as information on a variety topics ranging from America and distance learning to schools online and weather.
- **Sports.** Stay informed of the latest sporting events using Prodigy's Sports page (see Figure 8.11).

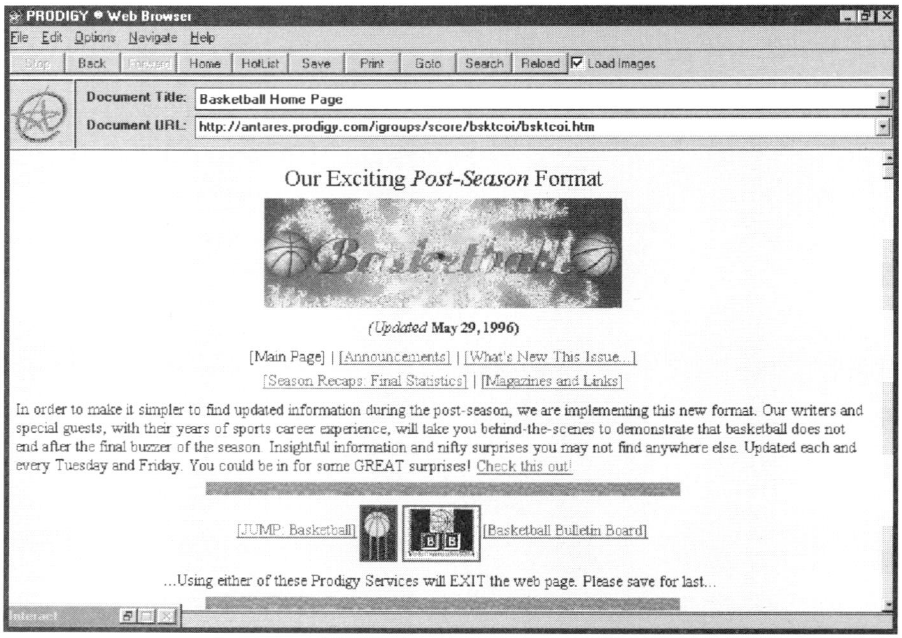

FIGURE 8.11

Prodigy's Sports area includes up-to-date sports news, opinions, and message boards.

- **Music.** Prodigy's Music site includes tour information, behind-the-scenes gossip, and links to several sites devoted to groups and performers.
- **Science and Technology.** You can find out information on different scientific, computer, and medical topics from Prodigy's Science and Technology site.

You aren't confined to the sites Prodigy lists; you can access other Web sites by entering their URLs (Web addresses) in the Document URL: list box and pressing Enter. If you're not sure where to go, you might try the Web Search site available from Prodigy's Home Page. Here you can search the Web using popular search tools like Yahoo!, Infoseek Guide, Excite, Lycos, and Alta Vista (see Figure 8.12).

TIP

You can close the Prodigy Web browser by choosing File, Exit from the browser menu bar. If you want to also end your Prodigy session, choose Exit and Logoff Prodigy from the File menu.

In addition to the Web, you can view USENET newsgroups using Prodigy. Newsgroups are similar to the Prodigy Bulletin Boards; they enable you to post and read messages related to specific topic and interest areas. Newsgroups are

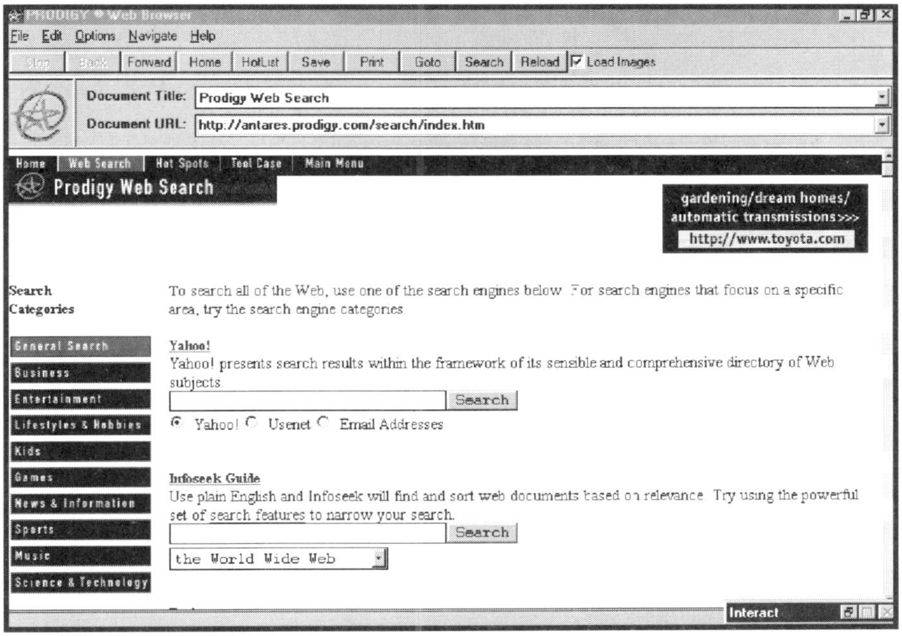

FIGURE 8.12

Use Prodigy's Web Search site to search the Web for interesting sites to visit.

part of the Internet. There are more than 10,000 newsgroups you can access through Prodigy. These are a few:

- **alt.parents.teens.** Includes discussions about raising teenagers in the '90s.
- **alt.architecture.alternative.** Devoted to discussions about alternative architecture issues, such as solar energy, innovative design, and building materials.
- **comp.os.ms.windows.95.** Information, questions, and helpful suggestions about Windows 95.
- **misc.legal.** Includes discussions about legal resources, issues, and of course, free advice.
- **rec.games.video.** Devoted to discussions of video games, such as games for Sega Genesis and Nintendo systems.
- **soc.couple.wedding.** Includes discussions on preparing weddings: from hiring photographers, disc jockeys, and florists, to how to keep your in-laws out of your business.

NOTE

You must become a full member to access USENET newsgroups with Prodigy. If you originally signed on using the free usage credits, you must use the Member Access options to register as a full member.

Although most newsgroups don't have a moderator or someone in charge to regulate them, you're required to understand and abide by certain regulations and etiquette. These general rules are known as "netiquette" and are discussed in Chapter 12.

Other Online Services

There a few other commercial online services, but most of them are heading to the World Wide Web to offer their content and services. Three of the primary services recently to announce their transition to the Web include Genie, The Microsoft Network, and AT&T Interchange.

Genie

The Genie Online Service is a subsidiary or General Electronic. Genie currently offers a Web site and proprietary online service. Although Genie has fewer services and less content than CompuServe, AOL, and Prodigy, you may find something of interest. One area you may want to look into is the Genie Villages on the Internet (see Figure 8.13). Genie Villages offer Internet users a way to join in discussions and round table events like those found on CompuServe forums without connecting to a proprietary online service.

You can access the Genie Villages by entering the URL, **http://vivos2.village.com/villages.html** in your Web browser. Genie Villages include a number of topics and disciplines, such as the following:

- Computer Village
- Romance & Women's Fiction Village
- Science Fiction
- Game Fans
- Singles Village
- Fantasy Village
- Reading Village
- Finance Village
- Needle Arts Village

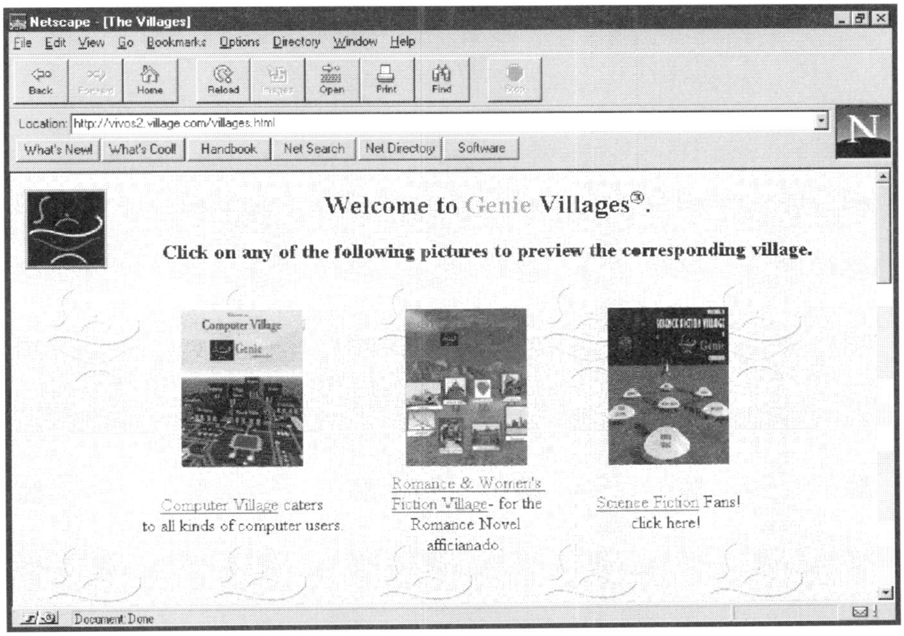

FIGURE 8.13

The Genie Villages area provides a place on the Internet for users to gather to discuss professional and personal topics.

To access the Genie Online Service (see Figure 8.14), you need to obtain Genie's free navigation software from the World Wide Web, or use a communications program to dial into and download the software directly from Genie. The URL to obtain the software on the Web is **http://www.genie.com/about.html**.

If you aren't connected to the Web or want to use your communications program to access Genie, start your communications program (such as HyperTerminal in Windows 95) and use these settings:

- Half duplex (local echo)
- 300, 1,200, or 2,400 buad
- 8 data bits, no parity, 1 stop bit or, 7 data bits, even parity, 1 stop bit
- Dial 1-800-638-8369
- At the U#= prompt, enter **JOINGENIE**, press Enter, and enter **DEB225**.

NOTE

You can view a comprehensive list of Genie access numbers at the following Gopher site:

gopher://gopher.genie.com:70/00/genie/access

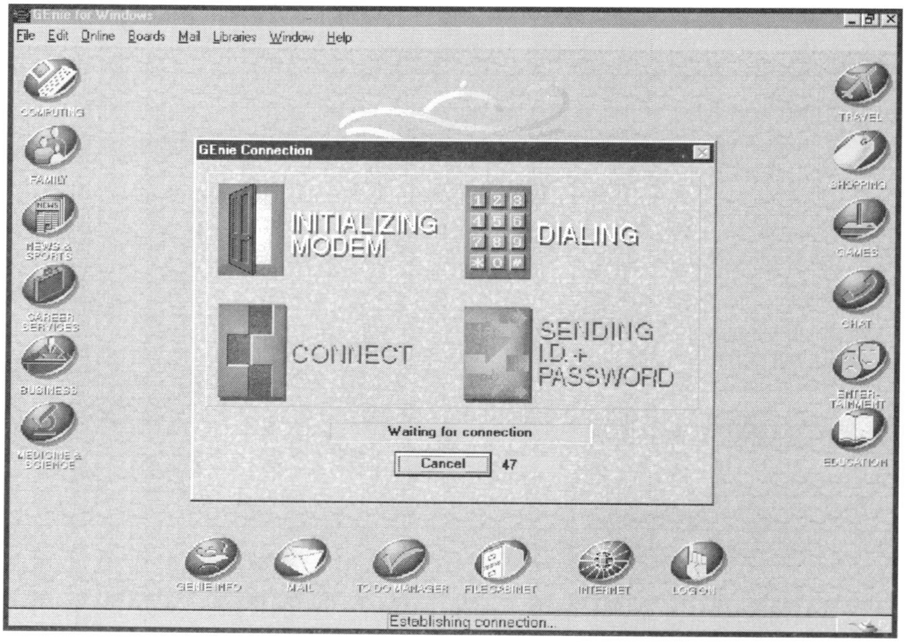

FIGURE 8.14

Genie offers users a nice interface to interact with its services.

Genie's online service has several areas users can use, including the following:

- Computing
- Family
- News & Sports
- Shopping
- Games
- Education
- Entertainment
- Medicine & science

Genie also includes interactive chat areas, e-mail, Internet information, and travel information.

The Microsoft Network

Another online service making the transition from a proprietary online service to the Web is The Microsoft Network (MSN). Currently, to become a member of MSN, you must have Windows 95 and use The Microsoft Network icon to sign up.

Some of the features of MSN include integrated e-mail with the Microsoft Exchange client, daily news, software support, general interest areas, chat areas, and software downloads. The MSN Today screen displays updated news and daily events (see Figure 8.15). You can click images or text to jump to items. You

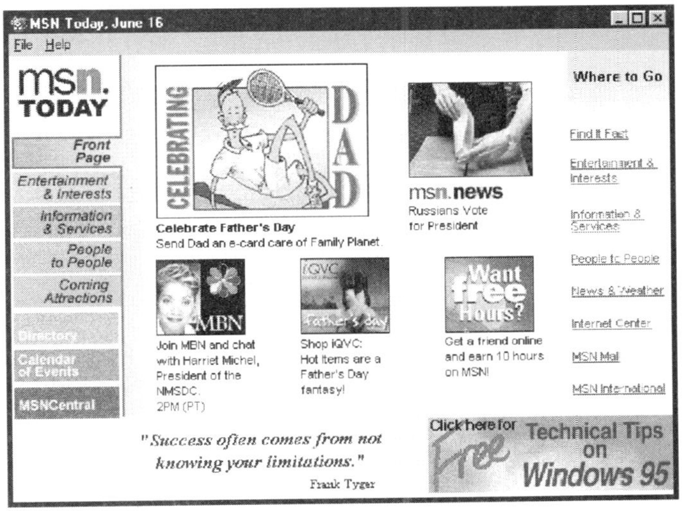

FIGURE 8.15

The MSN Today screen is updated daily.

also can use the MSN Central page to access MSN's main areas. The following list describes these main areas:

- **MSN Today.** See daily news, special links, and information on upcoming events.
- **E-mail.** Click this button to launch Exchange and receive your e-mail. If you have e-mail waiting for you when you connect to MSN, you receive a message telling you.
- **Favorite Places** You can save your favorite MSN places in one folder so you can quickly jump to them.
- **Member Assistance.** Get membership information, tutorials, and account information from this area.
- **Categories.** MSN organizes its content and services into categories, such as Sports, Education, Computers, and Internet. You can see all of the MSN listings by clicking the Categories button.

Currently, Microsoft is working to move the content of The Microsoft Network to the World Wide Web. In the near future, look for the MSN commercial online service to be discontinued with only Web services being offered by Microsoft. One such area where Microsoft is making a strong showing on the Web is by offering a Web site for users to customize as their home page (see Figure 8.16). You can set up a customized page that displays the following items:

- Your favorite Web sites
- Search utilities, such as Yahoo!
- Up to five stock quotes
- Sports scores, including NBA, NFL, MLB, PGA, and more
- Daily Web picks, such as computer sites, business and finance, and shopping picks
- World, national, and business news
- Science and technology news
- Weather information and maps

You can use the Microsoft Internet Explorer Web browser to access MSN from the Web. You have to disconnect from your ISP (if you're connected to the Internet using an ISP) and reconnect to the Internet using MSN as your service

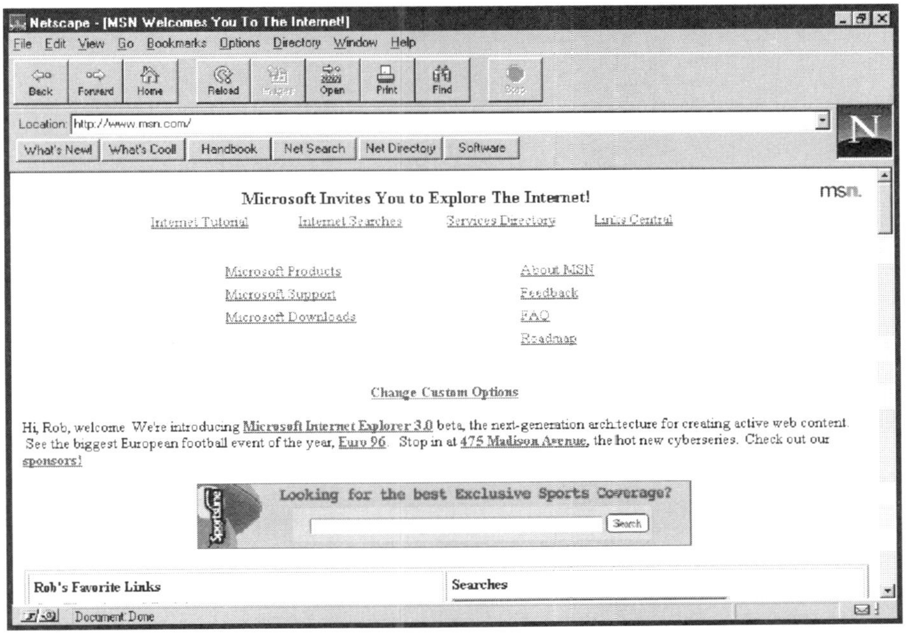

FIGURE 8.16

Many users start their Web journey from the MSN home page on the Web.

provider. Once connected, your MSN account is charged for the time you spend on the Web and MSN service.

AT&T Interchange

By the end of 1996, the AT&T Interchange online service will be entirely Web-based. Currently, its content is being merged to the Web and is offering services for business professionals. The first Web-based service AT&T announced is Lead Story, a Web site that provides links to news and events from a number of sources. Lead Story includes analysis, background material, and original content to give users in-depth information about a topic.

The premise of Lead Story is to provide busy professionals with a central area to access a breadth of news and information (see Figure 8.17). This way users don't have to go out looking for it themselves; AT&T brings it to them. A recent issue included stories on automobiles, car safety issues, striking McDonnell Douglas workers, and the MCI Sports Center in Washington.

If you're interested in using AT&T Lead Story, point your browser to the URL below. There's no fee to use Lead Story, but don't get upset by the small advertisements that flash on your screen.

http://www.bnet.att.com/leadstory/index.html

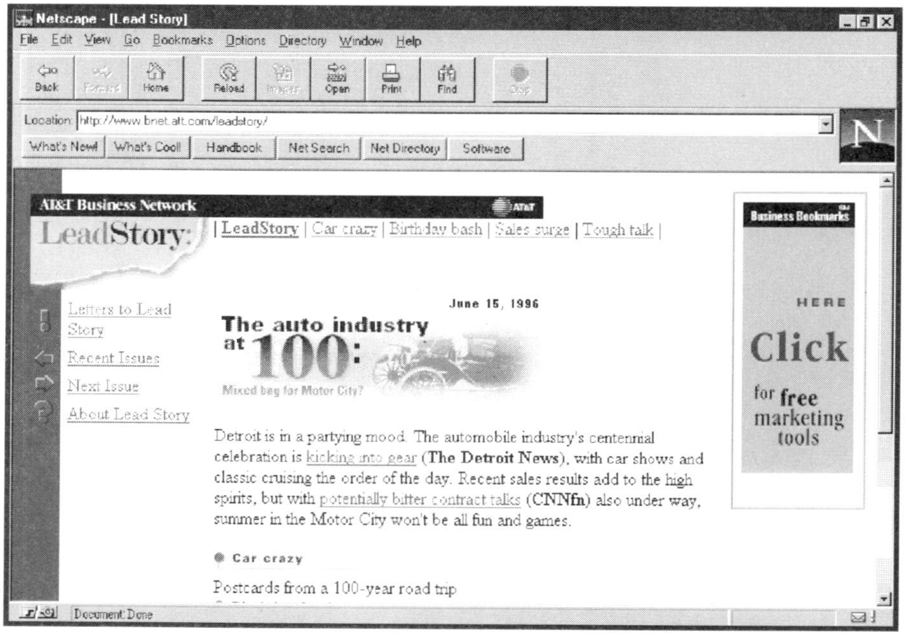

FIGURE 8.17

AT&T's Lead Story Web site offers busy professionals a quick way to obtain a look at major issues of the day.

On the other hand, if you're interested in the AT&T Interchange service, you cannot become a member of it. AT&T has stopped accepting software orders for the service. You might want to join another service, such as CompuServe, if you're looking for an online service with a large quantity of business and professional information.

NOTE

If you're a current member of AT&T Interchange, you can cancel your membership (you'll need to this year anyway) by calling 1-800-299-9699. You must cancel by telephone.

What's Next

Although most commercial online services are phasing out and moving toward the Web, you can still find some quality content on some of them. Prodigy and The Microsoft Network seem to be making a great effort to provide users with original content and services on the Web, much like their proprietary services have done. Others, such as Genie and AT&T Interchange, are making great strides to create new business opportunities on the Web.

The next chapter shows you how to use the information you've received in the last three chapters to pick the right commercial online service for you.

9

CHOOSING A SERVICE OR PROVIDER

In the last three chapters, you read about the major commercial online services, some of the features they offer, and how to use them to access the Internet and World Wide Web. Without connecting to all of them and trying them out, it might be difficult to choose just the right one for you. This chapter will help you determine which provider offers the best services to fit your needs.

After looking through this chapter, you should feel encouraged to use the free hours of online time each service offers to take them for a "test drive." One service cannot satisfy all users. If you're a beginner, you might find CompuServe difficult to navigate. Or, you might want more software vendor support than America Online offers. If you aren't satisfied with any of the commercial online services, you might want to opt for full Internet access (described in Chapters 3 and 5). The key is to keep looking for a service if you are not completely satisfied.

Online Services Feature Set

The following sections describe some of the most common tasks you'll perform and services you'll use while online. Although there are several commercial online services available, these sections compare only the big three: America Online, CompuServe, and Prodigy. (If you're looking for an Internet Service Provider that isn't a commercial online service, see Chapter 5.)

News, Weather, and Sports

Going online is great for users who can't live without having news updated as it happens—or at least when other news agencies receive the stories. One of the most used features of online services is news. Most online services offer hourly headline news from major news agencies, including Reuters News Service and Bloombergs (see Figure 9.1).

Some services let users sample headlines and partial stories for free. A premium rate or additional fee is added to the user's account to access the entire story. Another feature is to let users read complete news stories and then download related stories for more complete coverage of the news event.

Of the commercial online services, America Online probably has the easiest to use interface for news (see Figure 9.2). It includes buttons you click (US & World, Weather, Sports, Business, and Entertainment) to access news stories in those areas. You also can find news stories from *The New York Times*, *Time*, *Business Week*, and ABC television.

Don't let the interface of the CompuServe News area discourage you. After you use it a few times, you won't notice that it can be cumbersome and you'll appreciate the news services you can access. You can get *U.S. News and World Report*,

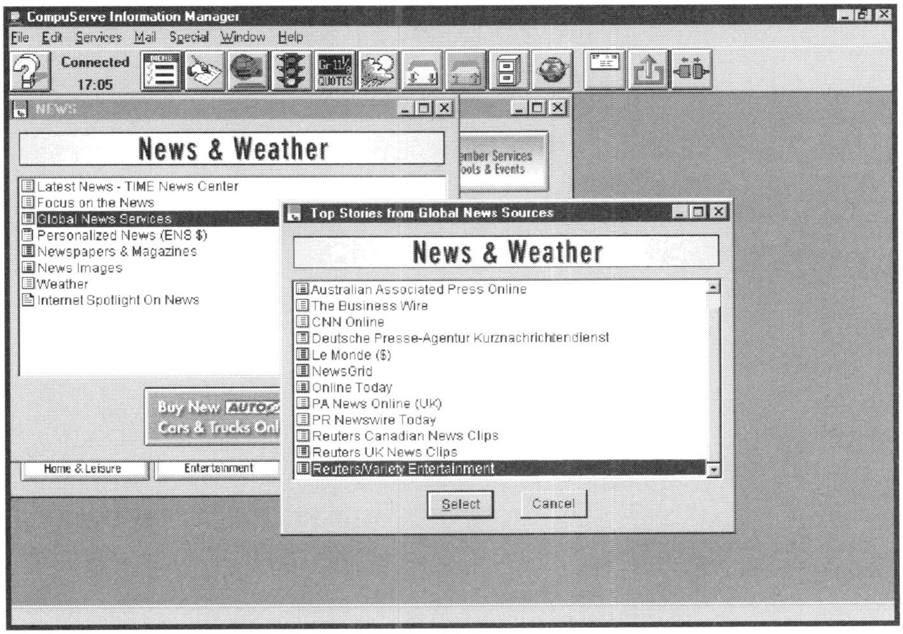

FIGURE 9.1

Online services, like CompuServe, offer many news sources.

Rolling Stone, *AP Online*, and various newspapers from around the world. The *AP Online* service updates every hour, so you can read the latest news coverage throughout the day.

Prodigy offers adequate news updates on its Highlights page, and has Web links to *AP Online* via its Web browser (see Figure 9.3). Prodigy also has a fantastic stock reports and composites area.

Recommendation: America Online

Business and Professional Resources

Many online users rely on commercial services and the Web to help them get ahead in business and professional worlds. Commercial services provide many

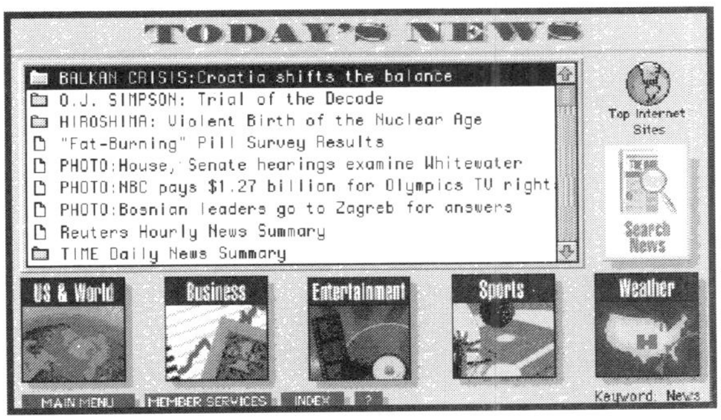

FIGURE 9.2

AOL has an easy-to-use news interface and plenty of content to satisfy even the hungriest news junkie.

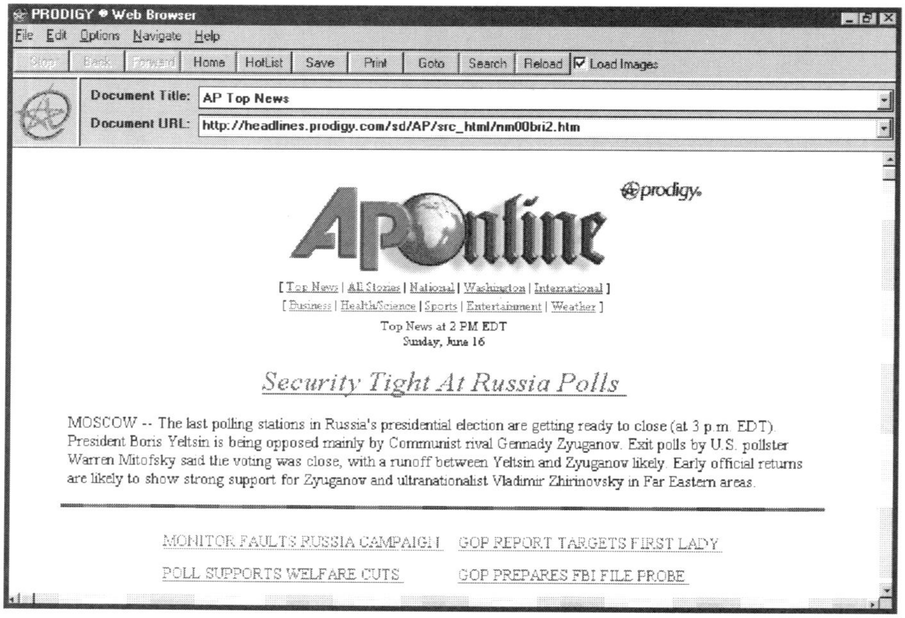

FIGURE 9.3

Prodigy gives you daily AP Online news feeds.

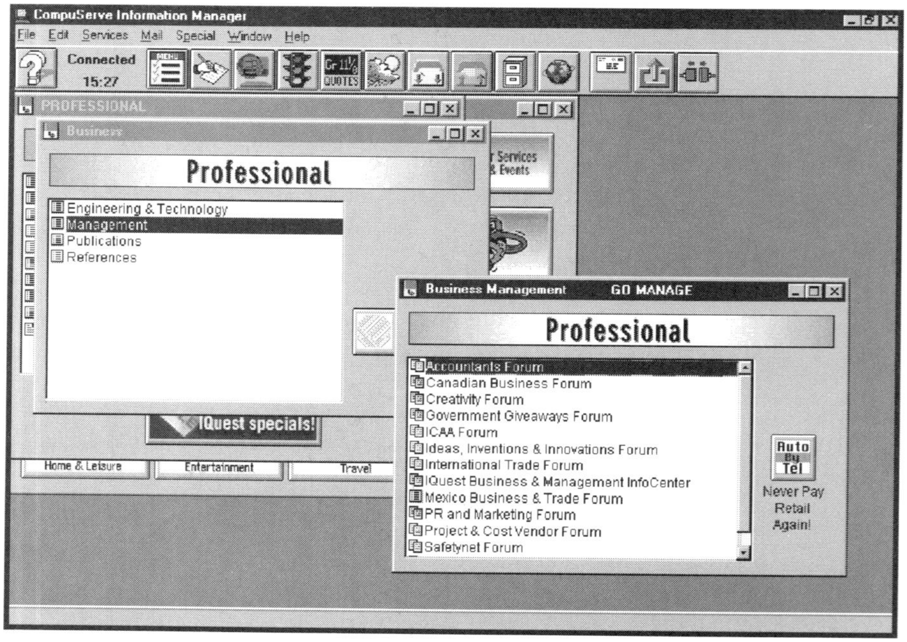

FIGURE 9.4

CompuServe is an excellent resource for business and professional information.

services and forums for members to exchange information, share ideas, download software, and stay informed in their career areas.

Without a doubt, the preferred online service for business and professional users is CompuServe. CompuServe's Professional area includes topics such as aviation, computers, writing, publishing, education, law, medicine, and more (see Figure 9.4). Several forums are devoted to members looking for information on starting a new business, working at home, or changing careers.

America Online and Prodigy have limited resources for members looking for business and professional resources. You can, however, use Prodigy to locate financial information, such as stocks and investment information.

Recommendation: CompuServe

Travel

If you want to add to your traveling pleasure, use CompuServe's or America Online's resources to make reservations and pinpoint likely destinations. All three online services provide access to the easySABRE online ticketing service, but Prodigy lacks some of the detailed information and some of their guides are out of date.

CompuServe includes areas for members to make hotel, car, and airline reservations (see Figure 9.5). You also can read restaurant reviews and get updated

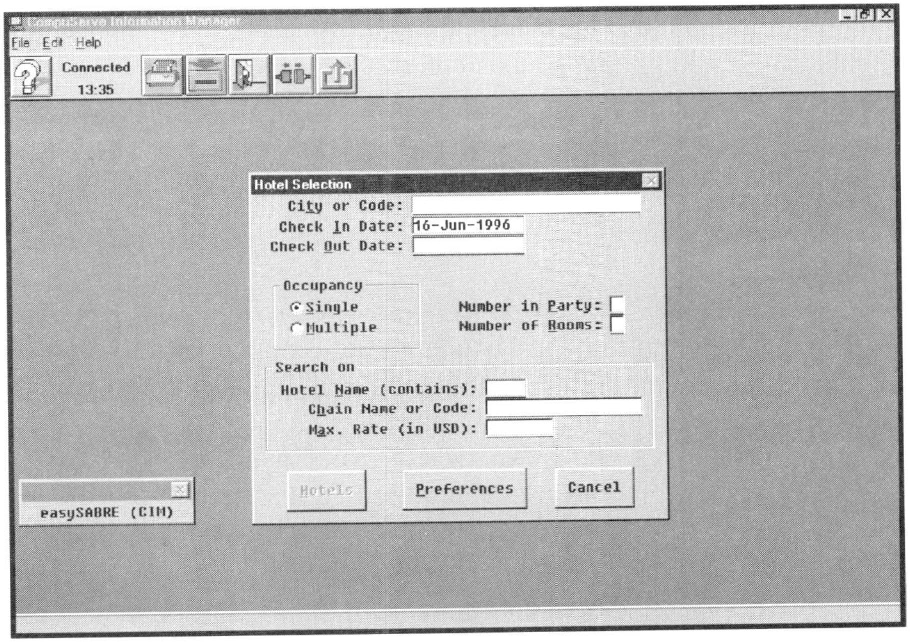

FIGURE 9.5

The easySABRE ticketing service lets you purchase airline tickets, reserve automobiles, and make hotel arrangements while online.

State Department advisories, travel-related message boards, and weather updates. By clicking the Travel button on CompuServe's Explore Services screen, you can pick What's Hot in Travel, International Travel Services, Map Services, How To Get There, and other items.

If you really want to do your travel planning online, check out America Online's services. With AOL, you can access more than 30 travel areas, including the following:

- American Express' ExpressNet
- *Travel Holiday* magazine
- Bed and Breakfast USA

Recommendation: America Online

Internet

All three online services let you access the Internet and World Wide Web from their regular services. The differences between the services are usually in the types of browsers you can use with your normal account. Both CompuServe and AOL have announced support of the Microsoft Internet Explorer, but will give members the choice of using any Web browser, particularly Netscape Navigator 2.0. Prodigy, however, requires users to use their proprietary Web browser, which behaves very similar to previous versions of NCSA Mosaic.

If you want to connect to the Web using CompuServe, you must access their service using a Winsock connection (this establishes a TCP/IP PPP connection to the Internet) available with CompuServe's NetLauncher and WinCIM 2.01 software. CompuServe also enables you to access FTP sites for file downloads, USENET newsgroups, and Telnet remote logins. The CompuServe Mosaic browser now being distributed is a nice browser for new Internet users.

TIP

To set up Winsock support, check the Use Winsock check box on the Setup Sessions Settings dialog box.

In Prodigy, you can access the Internet and World Wide Web by using the Web and Net toolbar buttons. Prodigy lets you access the Web, FTP, and USENET newsgroup services (see Figure 9.6). As a Prodigy member, you can download Microsystems' free Cyber Patrol software to restrict users from accessing certain Web sites. Currently, Cyber Patrol does not work to block out newsgroup sites.

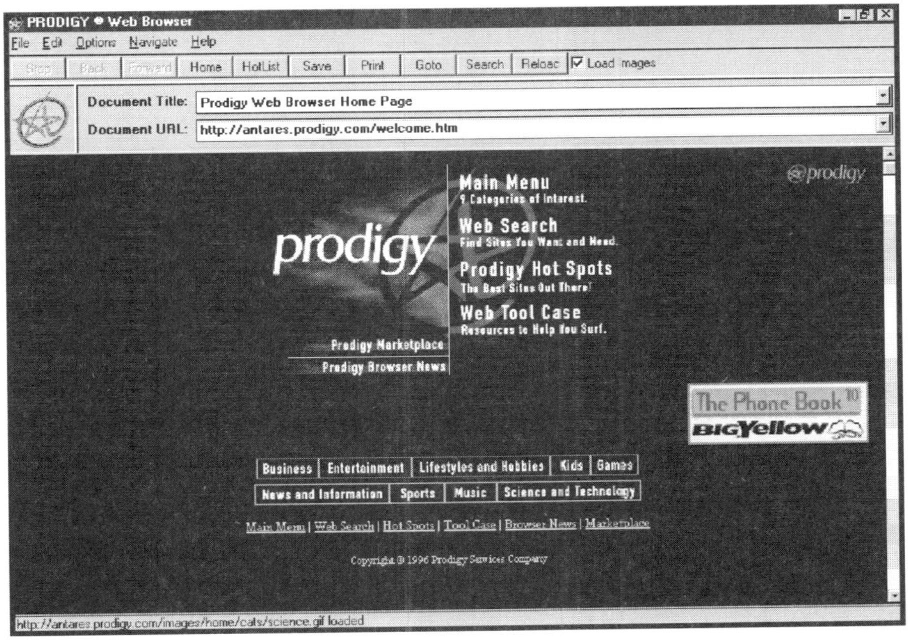

FIGURE 9.6

You can use Prodigy to access World Wide Web sites directly from its online service.

With AOL, you can access the World Wide Web, FTP sites, Gopher and WAIS databases, and USENET newsgroups. Although AOL makes it fairly easy to navigate the Web using its own browser, many users have experienced difficulty viewing Web pages on some sites. AOL offers some remedies and tips to get around these problems at their Web site, **http://www.aol.com**.

NOTE

Some online services offer their members personal Web page posting. With CompuServe, you can download a Web page authoring tool called Home Page Wizard, *which enables you to create and then publish a Web page on CompuServe's Our World Web site (see Figure 9.7).*

Recommendation: CompuServe for ease of use, and Prodigy for breadth of Internet coverage

Computer Technical Support

Eventually, you're going to experience some kind of technical problem. If you're lucky, it will be something minor, like sluggish computer performance. When

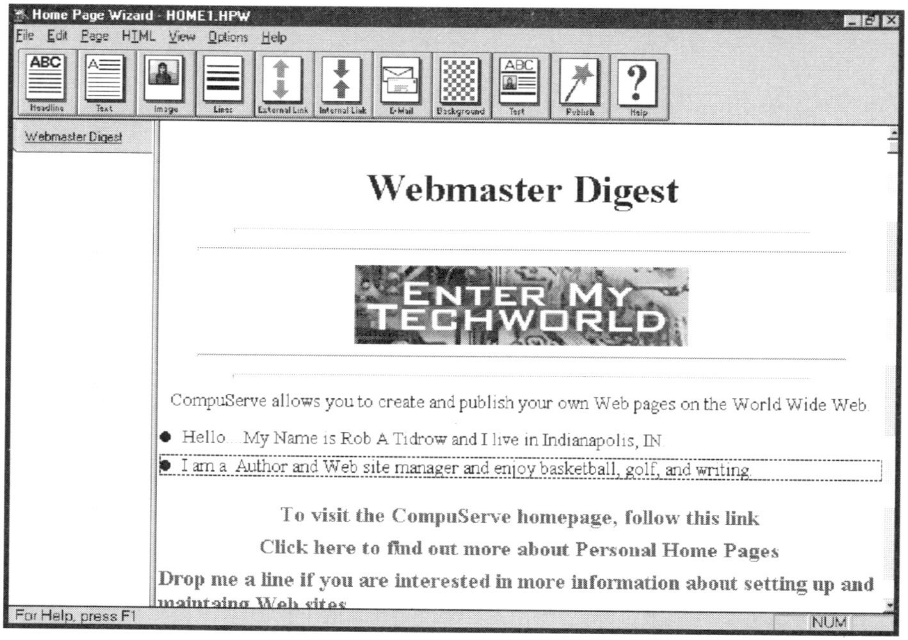

FIGURE 9.7

It's very easy to create and publish a Web page on CompuServe using the Home Page Wizard.

these problems occur, one of the best places to obtain support is from online services. There are two kinds of support: vendor supported forums and message areas frequented by users.

In the former case, software and hardware vendors set up technical support sites on places like CompuServe and AOL. Through this medium, customers can send technical support questions about the products and services directly to the vendor. The vendor then replies by direct mail or posts a public message for others to see in case many people experience the same problems. Hundreds of vendors use these methods to communicate with their customers, including Adobe, Novell, Amiga, and Intuit (see Figure 9.8).

The other way you can receive technical support is by obtaining information and help from fellow members. Through message forums, users can post messages and replies to messages to help solve problems with software and hardware. One topic that receives a lot of questions is Windows 95 in the GO WINDOWS CompuServe forum. There you can find information on installing hardware, troubleshooting peripheral problems, and where to find the best utilities for certain tasks.

Although AOL has improved its support areas, CompuServe still reigns as the most comprehensive online source for technical support and help. Prodigy also

FIGURE 9.8

Can't solve a problem you're having with one of your applications? Use CompuServe and AOL to search for vendor support areas to receive excellent technical support.

offers some technical support, but mainly on its Web site through its Science and Technology page.

Recommendation: CompuServe

Online Services Checklist

Table 9.1 is a checklist of features common to all online services with each feature evaluated. Although these ratings are subjective, they do give you an idea of how each service rates and which ones you may want to try out.

Obviously, there isn't one best answer for which online service you should choose. If you're looking for a commercial online service to help you get acclimated to the online world and the Internet, you should consider America Online because of its ease of use and extensive resources and software. On the other hand, if you want business information and computer support, CompuServe may be your best bet.

Several users have subscriptions to two or more online services. By doing this, they can ensure they have adequate resources for research, technical support, and in the event they have problems with one service, such as with sending e-mail, they always have a backup service to use. Of course, each additional service you subscribe to means additional membership fees, even for services you don't use.

TABLE 9.1 CHECKLIST OF ONLINE FEATURES			
Feature	**CompuServe**	**America Online**	**Prodigy**
E-mail	Can send binary files to other CompuServe members; text files to Internet addresses.	Can send binary files to other AOL users; MIME compliant files to Internet addresses.	Can send binary files to other Prodigy members; text files to Internet addresses.
Internet Services	Web, USENET, Telnet, FTP	Web, USENET, Gopher, FTP, WAIS	Web, USENET
Web Page Hosting	Yes	Yes	No
Chat	CB Simulator	Chat areas (outdated interface, but active)	Chat areas are very active
Multimedia	Separate CompuServe CD; many graphics and sound files for download	Animation, graphics, and audio files	Graphics and audio files
Connection Speeds	14.4Kbps and 28.8Kbps in most large cities	14.4Kbps and 28.8Kbps in most large cities	14.4Kbps and 28.8Kbps in most large cities; Web access at 14.4Kbps
Migration to Web	In progress with Microsoft (code name "Normandy")	Some content on Web, but mainly information pointing to AOL online service	Original content and links to related sites. Providing Internet access with AND (Access Net Direct) at $1.00 hour
Computer Information	Very good	Good	Fair
Business and Professional	Very good	Good	Fair, but their Web site is getting stronger
Travel	Good	Very good	Good

TABLE 9.1 CHECKLIST OF ONLINE FEATURES (CONTINUED)			
Feature	**CompuServe**	**America Online**	**Prodigy**
News, Sports, Weather	Good	Good	Good
Children	Fair	Very good	Good
Ease of Use	Good	Very Good	Poor

What's Next

In this chapter, you learned how CompuServe, America Online, and Prodigy compare. You may choose an online service based on this discussion, or you may decide the cheapest service is all you need regardless of the features and services available.

The next chapter shows you how to use online services and the Internet to search for information. You learn about intelligent agents, searching tools, infobots (information robots), and how to access files using FTP and other Internet tools.

PART IV

PUTTING THE ONLINE WORLD TO WORK

10

SEARCHING FOR INFORMATION ONLINE

In a book titled *Discover What's Online*, few lessons are more important than learning just *how* to discover what's out there. Finding things—people, businesses, and information—is the primary reason any of us joins the ranks of cybernauts. This chapter will examine search features on the commercial services and the Internet, though much of the text will be devoted to the latter. The commercial services are almost intuitive in their organization, and their search tools are simple to use. The Internet is neither intuitive nor simple, though it's getting better all the time.

About Online Searching

When you contemplate the excitement of finding things in cyberspace, it's useful to remember the old maxim about wishes: *Be careful what you wish for, or you will surely get it.*

What many of us wished for in the early days of personal computing was to have a window to the world on our desktops. A link to the world's greatest libraries; insight into the minds and works of great teachers, inventors, and philosophers; doorways to businesses, civic organizations, and political information; and instant access to jokes, tutorials, and people.

The good news is that we got it—and more. The online world delivers all of that as well as things we *didn't* contemplate. We can find and explore travel destinations, download previews of movies, play interactive games, and shop to our credit limit. We can talk to doctors, fix our cars, and call friends who can talk back to us from our computer screens. Someday, we'll probably vote online. (The term "political hack" will acquire a whole new meaning.)

The bad news is that we got it *and more*. It's the "and more" that makes finding things online an adventure.

In the online world, you'll find more information than you have ever encountered in your life—and it grows by the day. There are more than eight million interconnected sites and their documents on the World Wide Web alone. There are more than 10,000 newsgroups devoted to specific subjects. There are more than 14,000 downloadable files at Gopher and FTP sites ready for your perusal. Each commercial online service, such as The Microsoft Network (MSN), has more than a thousand destination sites. There are about 40 million subscribers hooked into it all. And the nagging truth about this wealth of information? It's way too much.

For one thing, there are uneven quality control problems. The commercial services such as CompuServe, America Online, and MSN have a leg up on the wild and woolly Internet. They have some control over their destination sites, and those deemed unworthy are kept out. While this level of approval doesn't guarantee the quality of the information, it at least eliminates conspicuous charlatans and infoquacks. The Internet is a different story.

Anyone who can learn HyperText Markup Language (HTML) and set up a page on the Web can say pretty much what they want. If they're clever about getting their site listed with Internet search engines, a lot of people will end up visiting their sites and finding chaff instead of wheat—or worse. The prime example, of course, is to go to an Internet directory such as Yahoo! and enter the keyword "sex." You'll be presented with a list of sites to visit that will range from profound discussions about sexual dysfunction and its therapies to—well, you can imagine.

But having said all of that, going online is one of the most effective ways on Earth to find information. It will continue to get both better and worse in that both good and bad information will be more plentiful. Fortunately, that information is increasingly being organized into accessible pockets that are easy to find. And the search technologies that aid you are getting more sophisticated in their detective work. Much of your success depends on three things:

- What information you want
- Which online medium you're using to find it
- How effectively you use online search techniques

Even the Internet, with its sprawling size and needle-in-a-haystack look, is growing usable—though venturing on to junk is inevitable. Because no one owns the Internet, there's no central control to determine information quality, and no central directory of what's there (unlike the commercial services' offerings). Some of the Internet directories, fortunately, are starting to be a little more selective in the sites they list. This is mostly spawned by threats from lawmakers to start regulating Internet content if such things as pornography are made available to children. But this deals more with material that's possibly illegal to transmit than it does with establishing volumes of high-integrity information.

Still, so much of what is out in cyberspace is good that it merits putting up with the junk to find it. The following sections contain some ideas for finding anything online.

How the Internet Differs from Commercial Online Services

Searching for information in cyberspace can be maddening if you don't understand the basic structures and tools of the medium. The commercial online services have one great advantage over the Internet in finding information: coherent organization (see Figure 10.1).

An Online Search Mini-Glossary

These are a few definitions that will help you understand the art and science of searching online.

crawler. A software program that roams the Web looking for candidates for new pages to add to the search engine database. Crawlers are also known as *robots* or *spiders*.

directory. A simple, category-based search tool if you're interested in general topics, such as "motorcycles" or "cancer." After you get to a topic, you can further refine your search by viewing more specific categories within the more general ones, or using specific keywords to search.

FTP. This stands for File Transfer Protocol, which are specifications for downloading or uploading files.

hits. Refers to the number of matches found for your search inquiry. It's also used to describe the number of inquiries made to a given site.

keyword. This refers to a word or words on which a search is based. The search engines scan sites and documents for those that have these keywords in titles or text. Some advanced "intelligent" search engines offer you sites based on what they interpret as related words.

metasearch engines. Search tools that simultaneously enter your keyword(s) into several search engines and directories, then show you what each one found.

robot. Software programs used by search engines to roam the Web and find new pages to add to search engine databases (also referred to as "crawlers" and "spiders").

search engine. These are often exotic search tools used to locate specific information contained in text or titles covering sometimes hundreds of thousands of sites and millions of document pages. They can be Internet-based search engines, such as Lycos or InfoSeek; site-specific search engines, such as SoftInfo (**http://www.icp.com**), which searches a database of 16,000 software products; and commercial service search engines, which can locate specific information inside commercial services such as CompuServe or America Online.

spiders. Software programs used by search engines to roam the Web and find new pages to add to search engine databases (see "crawler" and "robot").

URL. Universal Resource Locator, which is the specific technical address of a site on the Internet or Web. It usually appears with the prefix "http://www."

Commercial online services are organized in descending tiers. Starting with general category buttons, such as Travel, Recreation, Entertainment, Sports, Shopping, Computers, Newsstand, Reference, and so on. You can burrow further into each category by clicking successive icons. For example, if you click Sports, you go to a page that contains a series of sports-related topics, such as

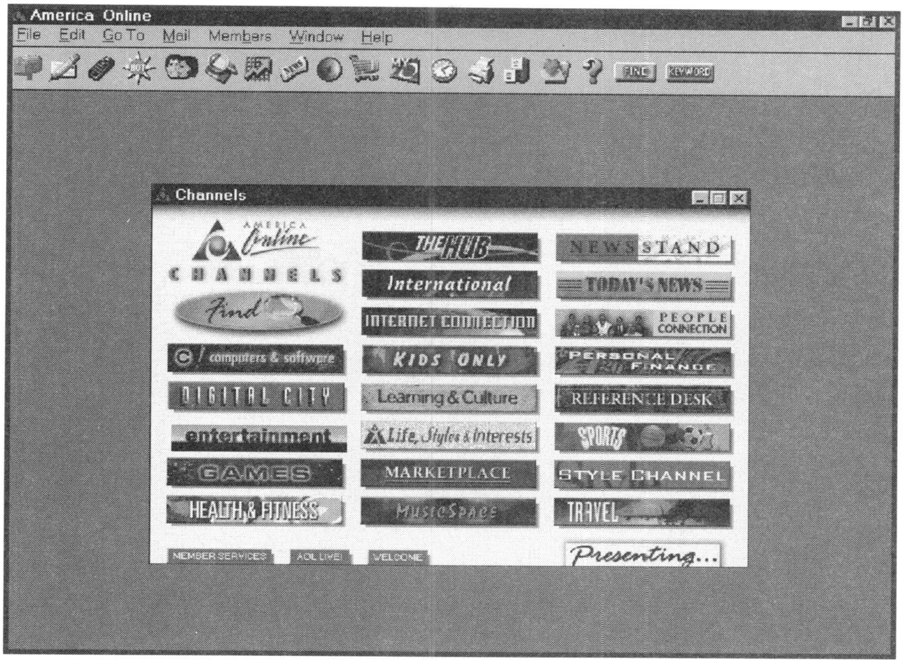

FIGURE 10.1

The logical organization of the commercial online services' offerings enable you to locate almost anything quickly.

Baseball, Football, Indoor Sports, Water Sports, Sports Magazines, Sports Fitness, Motor Sports, Sports Medicine, and so on. If you open the Baseball subcategory, you will get into even finer detail about it: Box Scores, League Statistics, Hall of Fame, Press Conferences, Profiles, Interviews, and so on. Some of the burrowing can get quite extensive. The Microsoft Network, for example, has 17 general categories with more than a thousand logically structured subcategories and destination pages.

NOTE

If what you're seeking isn't apparent from the listed categories, the commercial online services have keyword search functions that enable you to enter a word or words describing what you want, and then go off to find it for you.

This sort of logical organization makes it relatively easy to find things on commercial services. The commercial services also benefit from the fact that all that each service offers resides on one computer network. This makes searching a commercial service's offerings simpler and more comprehensive than on the Internet. For example, if you can't figure out from the main categories where you want to search, you can search using keyword search functions. In these, you can just enter a keyword or words (that describe what you're seeking) into a text box. The search tool then goes into every site and tells you where it finds a match. Also you will always end up at a real destination when you click on the services' carefully maintained destinations; occasionally a search on the Web will land you on a dead end.

If simplicity, organization, and ease-of-use are the strengths of the commercial services, size is the strength of the Internet. The Internet has millions of sites and Web pages, while the commercial services each have about a thousand. There is a higher percentage of meaningful destinations among the services offerings because of quality review and maintenance policies; but there actually are more great sites on the Web, if you know how to find them. In the matter of searching for things, however, the Internet's size is also a liability. With no central directory of what's on the Internet, finding a specific document can be like mining a ton of pitchblende to get a gram of radium.

The good news, though, is that search tools (called *directories* and *search engines*) are changing the face of Internet searching. A few years ago, you had to know a site's URL before you could access it. Today, there are more than 70 search tools on the Internet that will find those sites for you. Even though there's no central directory of Internet sites and documents, these tools are able to help you search billions of words that have been indexed, and then take you right to the ones that match your query.

Using Search Tools on the Internet

The Internet presents search problems that don't apply to commercial online services. It is by far the most expansive network in the history of mankind, and it is growing every day. But enterprising programmers—call them search entrepreneurs—have joined the fray to try to bring some sanity to the search process by developing Internet *search directories* (see Figure 10.2). These are pages on the Internet that enable you to move to a specific category you want to explore. On these pages, you define search criteria, usually by entering a word or words into a text box, and the directory searches a database containing information about millions of documents residing on the Internet.

When the search is complete, you see a list of the documents. Many contain summaries of what the pages contain; all contain hypertext links that enable you to simply click the document title and go to the document itself.

Directories do a good job of categorizing subjects at a high level. For example, one of the most popular directories is Yahoo! (**http://www.yahoo.com/**), which has broken subjects into 14 categories, such as Arts, Computers and Internet, Education, and so on. You can click one of Yahoo!'s category headers and jump

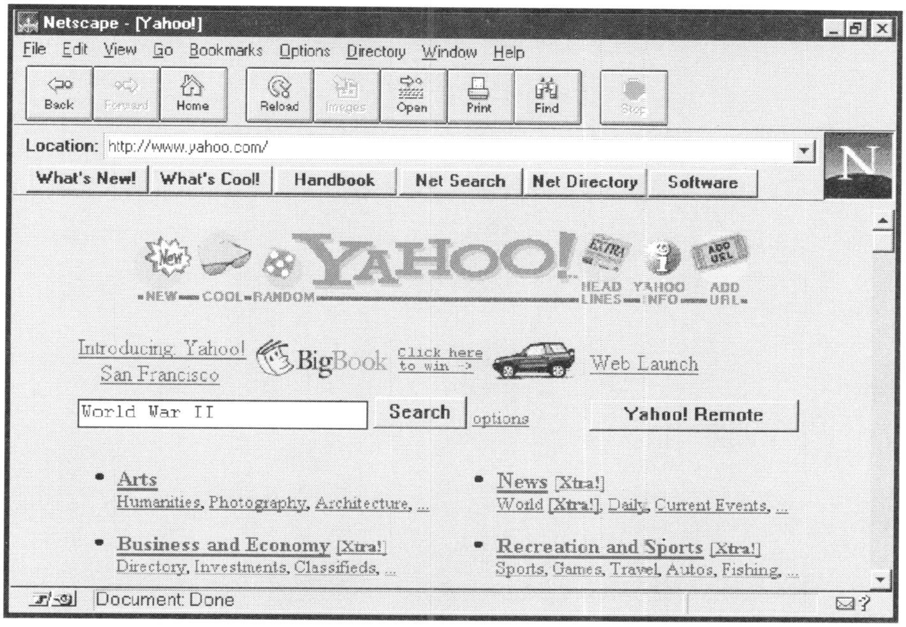

FIGURE 10.2

Yahoo!, which lists more than 80,000 Web sites, Gophers, FTP pages, and USENET newsgroups, lets you search by categories.

right to that category; or if you're unsure just where your subject might be located, you can enter keywords into the search box and click Search. A few moments later (depending on how expansive a list the directory acquires for you), the list of hypertext sites appears on screen (see Figures 10.3 and 10.4). Then you just click and go.

Niche-Specific Directories

Yahoo! covers a vast portion of the Internet's sites. Other directories are confined to their niches, such as model airplanes or pet funerals. After you locate them, you can easily find anything on their sites—including information you can't always find using a generic Internet directory. Often, you use Yahoo! or a similar directory to locate the niche site, then use the niche site's directory to find the most specific information.

To return to the example of finding software, you can use Yahoo! to track down a fairly large number of companies and products just by peeling back category layers. But some of the niche-specific search engines are dramatically better suited to locating specific information on something like computer software.

For example, the Technology Information Centre KnowledgeBase—known as TICK (**http://www.tickit.com**)—specializes in searching for information on technology-based products. It has tens of thousands of products listed in its database, all categorized for quick access (see Figure 10.5).

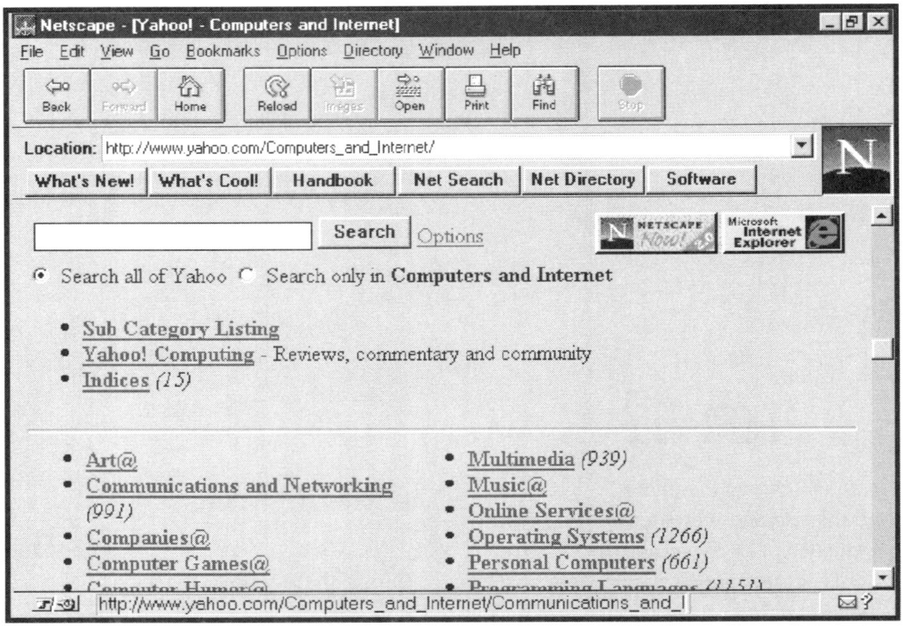

FIGURE 10.3

If you're looking for software, just click Yahoo!'s Computers and Internet category. It takes you to related categories...

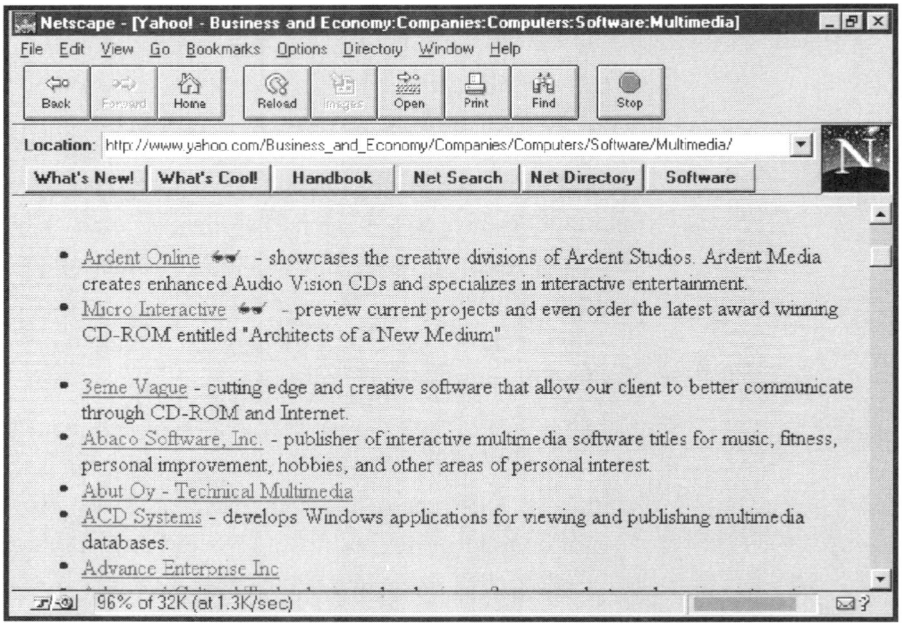

FIGURE 10.4

...until you find the type of software, or software company, you're looking for.

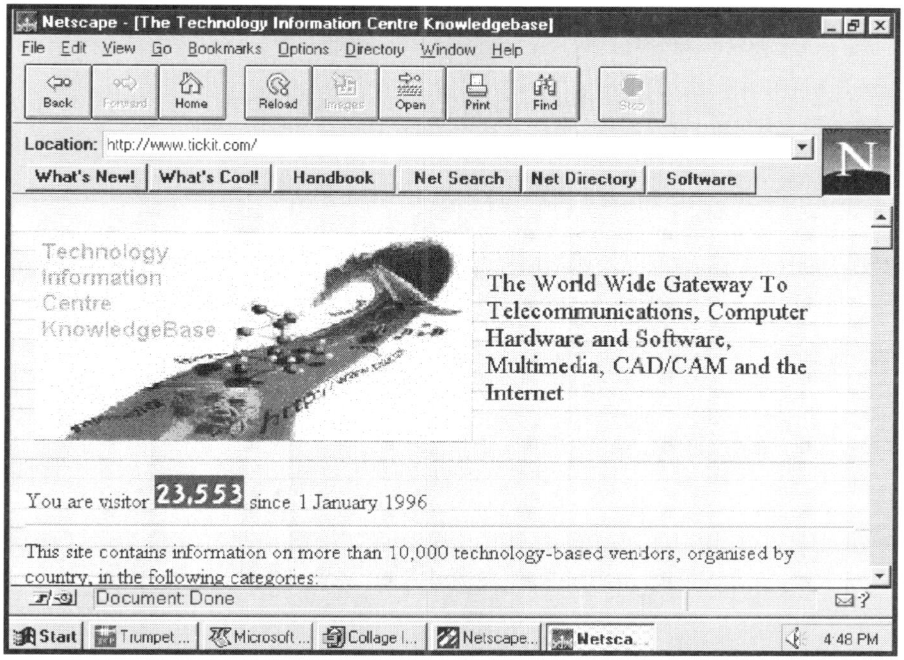

FIGURE 10.5

TICK enables you to search for thousands of products and companies in its niche, technology—more than a generic Internet search directory can provide.

Of course, outside the realm of technology and its suppliers, TICK isn't a practical search tool. That's where you need to use the generic Internet search directories.

Using Keyword Searches

While Internet search directories tend to have logical category structures, it can still be difficult to locate exactly what you want because of category limitations or just vagueness. This is where the *keyword search* capability comes in hand.

Keyword searches are exactly what they sound like: You ask the search engine or directory to find a page based on a word or words that are likely to appear in its text or title. They usually work one of these ways:

- They search *summaries* of documents that were found by a crawler and stored in a database. This is the technique used by generic Internet directories and search engines.
- They search *entire* documents using what is called full-text searching. These are more likely to be found on site- or niche-specific search engines and directories.

It's impractical for Internet-wide generic directories to do full-text searches. While it would produce more thorough results, it would take far too long, and the costs of storage and maintenance would be prohibitive.

Keyword searches are a little bit art and a little bit science (see Figure 10.6). Entering the wrong words will get you the wrong answers. So will entering words that are a little bit off. If you search on the word "bike" when what you want is "motorcycle," you will get a fraction of the hits you would have gotten with the correct word instead of the colloquial one.

The "science" of keyword searching—a form of searching that anyone who comes online will want to master—lies in the software and computers of the search engines you use. The "art" of it lies in the words you select. Here are some general guidelines to follow when performing keyword searches:

- **Be specific.** More hits doesn't mean better hits. If you know enough about the subject to be precise, be so.
- **Move backward toward generalities.** If the specific word search doesn't reveal anything, work backwards using more general search criteria. For example, begin with "black widow spider habitat." If you don't get any hits, try "black widow spider." If you still don't get any hits, try "spider."

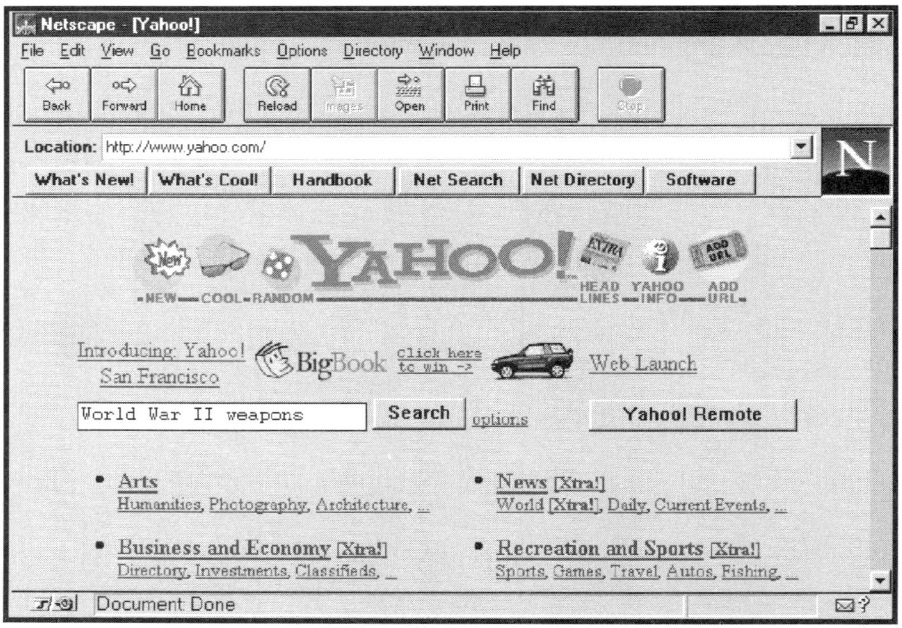

FIGURE 10.6

Conducting your keyword search amounts to putting the right words in the text boxes you will find on most search engines and directories. The art is selecting the right words to search on.

- **Use concepts when needed.** If you want to experiment with fried chicken cooked different ways, don't just search on "fried chicken," try "fried chicken recipes."
- **Spell words correctly.** Because they're computerized, search engines are precise in the words they look for. If you misspell a search word, you're out of luck—unless the database entries are misspelled too.
- **Look for variations of words.** Take the time to look for different expressions of the same thing. If you want house painting, search on "house painting," "house-painting," and "housepainting."
- **Think of synonyms.** If you want "skydiving," search for it—or search for "parachuting."
- **Pay attention to capitalization.** Most search engines are not case-sensitive; that is, they don't care if you capitalize or not. They don't want to ignore a capitalized hit just because it begins a sentence or is in a title. A good rule is: If it's regularly capitalized, capitalize it; if not, don't. But check each search engine to be sure of the rules.
- **Read your hits.** The hits you get sometimes contain the key to better search words. Look them over and search on the ideas they give you.

TIP

Search engines and directories usually have their own rules, operators, and delimiters that can help you be much more specific in your searches. These tell you how to phrase your search, and how to use words such as "and" and "or." Some use operators, such as "not," to help you eliminate unwanted hits. (For example, if you want to search for a kind of rock, you can eliminate some pages by indicating "not acid not music.") The search engines also tell you what words and constructions you can't use in each instance. In some cases, they recommend certain word usage. Except for the most complex search engines, these instructions usually are simple to understand, and it's worthwhile to read them. The designers of the search engines know how to optimize searches based on their specific content, and using their suggested techniques can do marvels for finding answers.

Finding Internet Directories

Table 10.1 lists some of the directories you can find on the Internet. Most of these are generic directories in that they aren't tied to searching everything on a specific site, but merely to finding the site itself. After you get to a site, you can find a site directory to locate more specific information.

Using Internet Search Engines

While Internet directories are useful for their categorical structure, they usually aren't the ultimate search solution—especially for finding obscure references. The deeper you go into your search, it's more likely that you'll need a *search engine* to help you track the information you want.

There are dozens of search engines on the Internet, with widely varying capabilities. After you get accustomed to using them, try out as many as you can find. You'll narrow your favorite search engines to a short list in no time.

Using a search engine is similar to using the keyword facility in a directory. The keywords you enter are sent to huge databases where crawlers gathered information about sites and indexed it according to a given engine's criteria. They usually seek out the URL, the title of the page, the words in the headings, and a summary paragraph of text (either the first paragraph or keywords throughout the text).

When your keywords are presented to the search engine, it scours the database for matches and presents you with a list of sites (see Figure 10.7). All of the sites have a title and descriptive text. You can jump to the sites by clicking the hypertext links. Most search engines rank the hits they return in descending order of quality: 98 percent means the site probably contains what you want, 50 percent means (in most cases) that it's a shot in the dark.

TIP

The databases of most Internet search engines and directories are composed of what are called HTML titles. When the robots begin searching the Internet for new additions to the databases, it is the title—and often some representative text—that they seek out. If you create your own Web page, you can stimulate interest in your site by making sure your HTML title is a captivating one.

While the rule still applies (number of hits doesn't equal quality), you will find that search engines with a massive index have a lot of power and appeal. Among

TABLE 10.1 INTERNET SEARCH DIRECTORIES

Search Directory	Address
Clearinghouse for Subject-Oriented Internet Resource Guides	**http://www.lib.umich.edu/chhome.html**
Galaxy	**http://galaxy.einet.net/**
The Global On-Line Directory	**http://www.gold.net/gold**
Magellan	**http://www.mckinley.com/**
NetCenter	**http://www.netcenter.com/netcenter/ whats-new/whats-new.html**
Point Communications	**http://www.pointcom.com**
Pointers to Pointers	**http://www.homecom.comglobal.pointers.html**
Starting Point	**http://www.stpt.com/util/submit.html**
The Yellow Pages	**http://theyellowpages.com/feedback.htm**
Web Voyager	**http://webspace.com/~wvoyager/**
Whole Internet Catalog	**http://nearmet.gnn.com/wic/index.html**
Yahoo!	**http://www.yahoo.com/**

the best are Lycos (**http://lycos.cs.cmu.edu/**), InfoSeek (**http://infoseek.com**), and Excite (**http://excite.com**). Lycos has achieved tremendous popularity by having one of the busiest crawlers in cyberspace, which adds new URLs to the index every hour of every day (see Figure 10.8). Lycos and Excite have more than 1.5 million indexed Web pages. Another search engine, called Open Text (**http://www.opentext.com:8080/**), is also among the more distinguished. It has indexed almost as many pages as Lycos and Excite, but instead of indexing keywords and titles, it indexes entire pages. This means you can search for

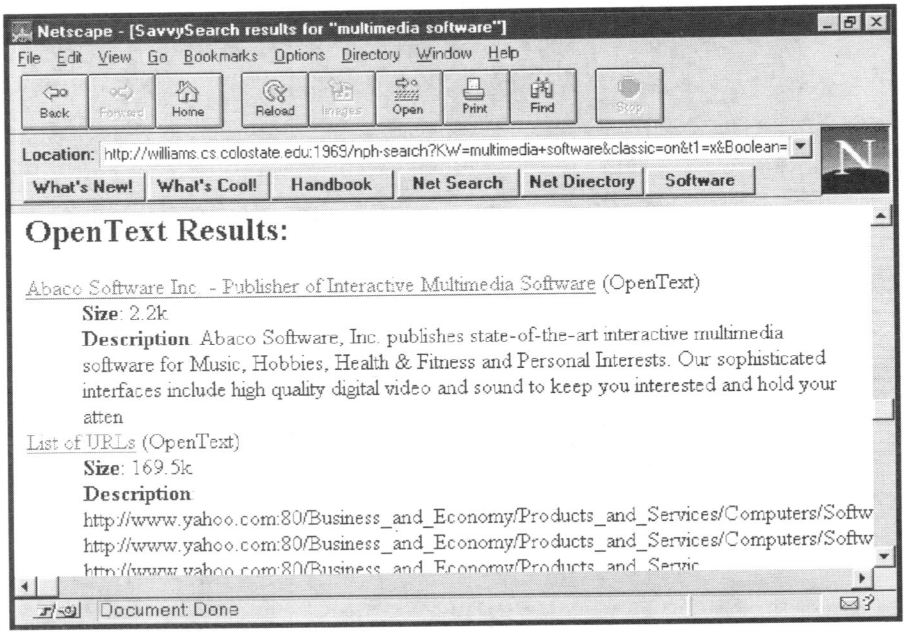

FIGURE 10.7

The information you get from a search engine displays both the title of the page and, in some cases, keywords or sample text taken right from the pages themselves.

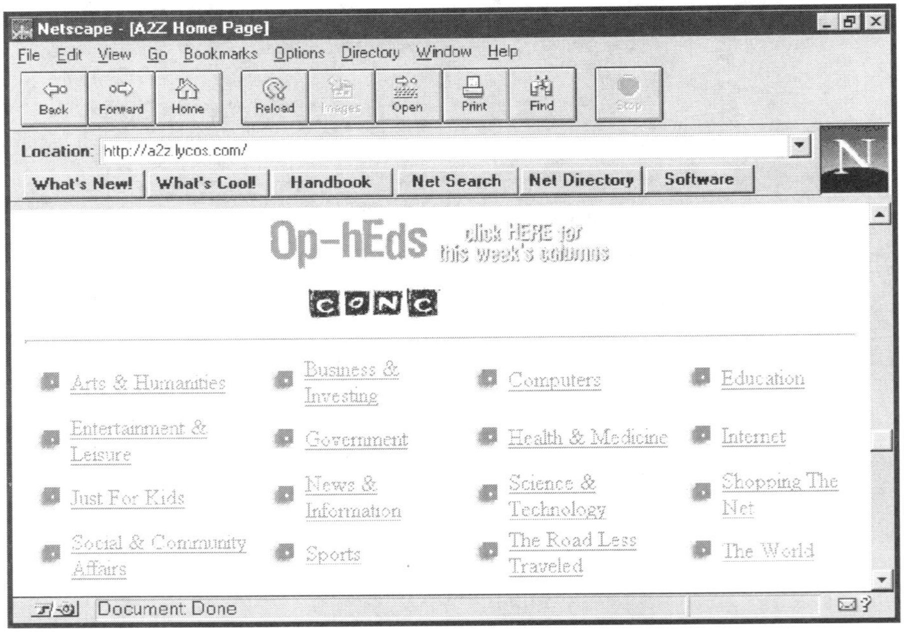

FIGURE 10.8

With more than 1.5 million indexed Web pages, Lycos has a broad scope and simple search criteria to aid in locating a topic.

TABLE 10.2 INTERNET SEARCH ENGINES	
Search Engine	Address
Aliweb	**http://web.nexor.co.uk/public/aliweb/aliweb.html**
CUI's W3 Catalog	**http://cuiwww.unige.ch.w3catalog**
Excite	**http://www.excite.com**
InfoSeek	**http://www.infoseek.com/**
Inktomi	**http://inktomi.cs.berkeley.edu/**
Lycos	**http://lycos.cs.cmu.edu/**
New Riders Yellow Pages	**http://www.mcp.com/newriders.wwwyp.index.html**
Nikos	**http://www.rns.com/cgi-bin/nikos**
Open Text	**http://www.opentext.com:8080/**
WebCrawler	**http://webcrawler.com/**
WWW Worm	**http://www.cs.colorado.edu/home/mcbryan/wwww.html**

phrases instead of words. For example, "Quoth the Raven—Nevermore!" will get you to a text of Edgar Allan Poe's famous poem.

Even when your search engine has delivered the hits—which could number in the hundreds—your search isn't done. On a 400-hit query, perhaps only the first 20 or so contain truly relevant information. (It could also mean your search words were too broad.) After you jump to the most promising sites, you might also find that those sites lead to even more detailed information on the subject you're trying to locate—to sites that might not be included among your hits. Take a moment when visiting hits to check out their trails to new sites.

Finding Internet Search Engines

Table 10.2 lists of some of the Internet's best search engines and where you can find them.

Using Metasearch Engines

Metasearch engines are like a search conductor, with regular search engines and directories as the orchestra. They take your keyword(s) and ask a range of search engines, such as those in Table 10.2, to search all of their respective indexes for your query. They then report back to you and list the results of the individual searches. Metasearches can take a full minute or more, as opposed to 10 to 30 seconds for most searches. If you have a search that generates a huge number of hits, the list of hits might be abbreviated to just the respective search engines that found them; then you just have to jump to that search engine to see the results already displayed (see Figure 10.9).

Metasearches are useful for many searches, but have a drawback for others. They don't enable you to use the search tools (operators, delimiters, and so on) that you can employ on the individual search engines. For highly focused searches, search tools are valuable, so a metasearch engine is better confined to more general queries.

SavvySearch (**http://www.cs.colostate.edu/dreiling/smartform.html**) is one of the most popular metasearch engines on the Internet. It's easy to use, it

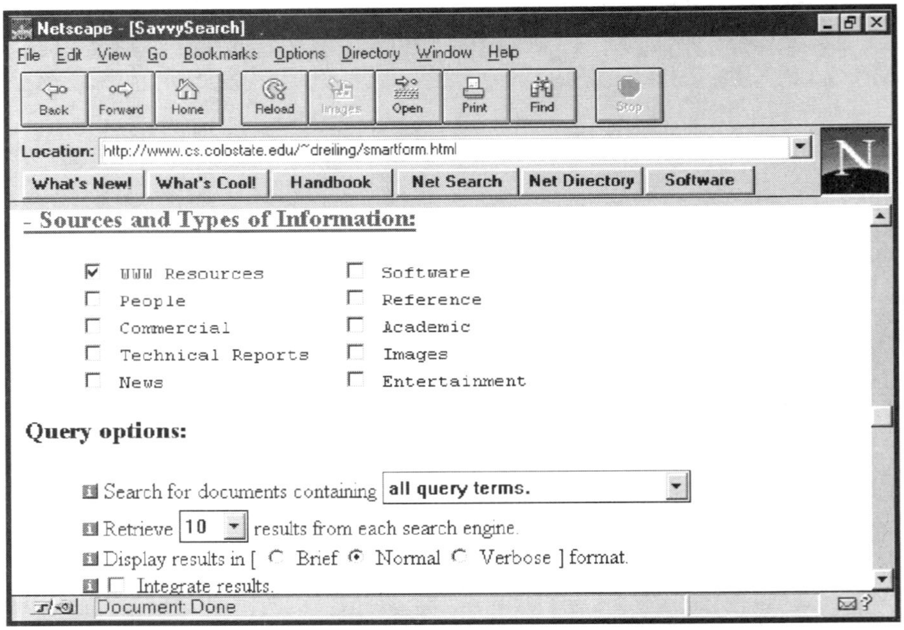

FIGURE 10.9

Metasearch engines, such as SavvySearch, do not present all of the detail you get in individual search engine output, but provides links to all of the discrete search engine sites they engage.

TABLE 10.3 METASEARCH ENGINES

Metasearch Engine	Address
All-In-One Search Page	**http://www.albany.net/~wcross/all1srch.html**
CUSI	**http://web.nexor.co.uk/susi/cusi.html**
Fun City Web Search	**http://www.funcity.com/search.html**
HyperNews	**http://union.ncsa.uiuc.edu/HyperNews/get/www/searching.html**
InfoMarket	**http://www.infomkt.ibm.com/**
Internet Sleuth	**http://www.intbc.com/sleuth/sleuth.html**
LinkSearch	**http://where.com/ls/LinkSearch.html**
MetaCrawler	**http://www.cs.washington.edu/research/projects/ai/metacrawler/www/home.html**
SavvySearch	**http://www.cs.colostate.edu/~dreiling/smartform.html**
Searchers	**http://gagme.wwa.com/~boba/search.html**
W3 Search Engines	**http://cuiwww.unige.ch/meta-index.html**
Web Search	**http://www.biddeford.com:80/~soaring/**

engages the greatest number of search engines, and it presents easy-to-read results. SavvySearch also enables you to search for FTP files to download by engaging Archie, and it engages Deja News to help you find newsgroups.

Finding Metasearch Engines

Table 10.3 lists where you can find some of the popular metasearch engines on the Internet.

Finding FTP Files

There are thousands of *FTP files*—those that can use *file transfer protocol* to be downloaded. They range from free software to multimedia clips to lengthy text files for research. Finding FTP files can be more challenging than finding other information on the Internet. But if you need to locate FTP files, one of the best ways is to use Archie.

There are different kinds of FTP sites, and some are more difficult to use than others. A couple of years ago, finding specific files on FTP sites was tough. Site administrators of FTP directories often just listed the filenames—without descriptions—and unless you knew the precise name of the file, you had to guess which one to download. Archie was designed to create a centralized index of files that are available on *anonymous FTP sites*—sites you can enter, download a file to your computer, and not be required to register with the FTP site. For example, anyone can download Netscape Navigator 2.0 (and other software) from **http://www.netscape.com**. Just follow the prompts to the software you want.

The Archie database indexes more than a thousand anonymous servers and a total of more than 2.5 million files (see Figure 10.10). If you use Netscape Navigator, you can conduct Archie searches by going to the central index at **http://pubweb.nexor.co.uk/archie.html**. This site explains Archie servers and directs you to *mirror sites*, which contain the Archie database but are physically closer to your computer.

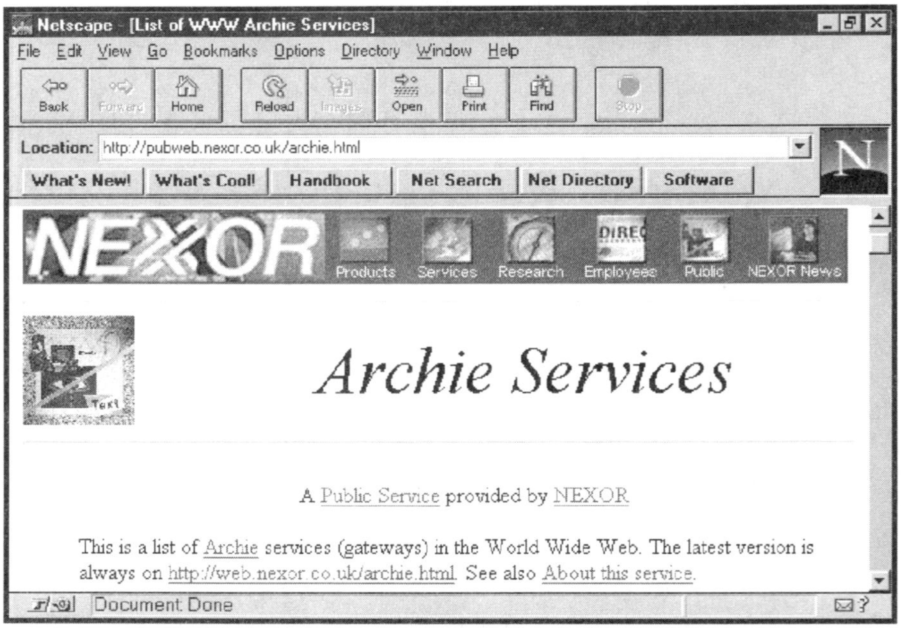

FIGURE 10.10

The main Archie index points you to Archie servers on the World Wide Web.

Normal Archie searches are precise, case-sensitive, and generally a little more complicated than standard searching. But there are multiple Archie search forms that you can choose for your search. They range from complex ones that include naming a range of identifying parameters to simple keyword search forms that aren't even case-sensitive. You'll find Archie indexing to be fairly understandable, though it can occasionally be vague. It's still the best act in town when it comes to logically finding files to download.

After you find an FTP file you want, check out your download options. Most files can be downloaded right from your browser. Other files are so large that it's a good idea to look into specialized FTP software. Check out FTP software such as WS_FTP, a useful freeware program you can get over the Internet or from your ISP. While many of the smaller files you locate can be downloaded without WS_FTP, the time it takes to download the bigger ones can be enormous. You usually see a message on screen that indicates how large the file is and how long it will take to download. Choose the option that makes sense.

Searching with Commercial FTP

The majority of downloadable FTP files reside on the Internet, but there are tens of thousands more files on commercial services. In particular, America Online has an extensive library of FTP software that you can easily find and download to your computer (see Figure 10.11). There's a lot of duplication of FTP files: many businesses that make files available on the Web often put them on the commercial services as well.

TIP

You will want to use "mirror sites" to download your FTP files whenever possible. These are sites that contain files identical to the primary site, but which are dispersed geographically around the country or the world. They are established for two reasons: To remove the heavy load from the primary site's servers, and to provide a shorter access link to your computer. When you see a list of mirror sites, you will also see their locations. Try those physically closest to you first.

The programs in AOL's Software Center (one of the service's best features) are available free of charge to AOL members. They include practical applications, such as database programs and business software, as well as games, audio clips,

FIGURE 10.11

AOL's Software Center has a wealth of downloadable software for members. The search engine it uses to help you locate software is one of the friendliest anywhere.

and images of all kinds. You can download interesting programs, test them, then keep or discard them. AOL members often end up with a dozen or more resident pieces of software from the AOL Library.

AOL's FTP libraries are somewhat simpler to operate than the Internet's FTP sites (though neither is difficult). This is because AOL operates entirely in its own network of computers, while the Internet FTP transfers must be done over a complex hodgepodge of servers and platforms. To get to AOL's Software Center, just click the appropriate icon or press **Command+K**. In the Search dialog box that appears, type **File Search**. The Criteria dialog box appears, stating your search options, including criteria such as software type (desktop publishing, games, business, and so on). You can do a search that covers the entire database, or you can limit it to software that has been added in the last month.

If the search categories don't describe what you're seeking, there's a Keyword box at the bottom of the Software Search screen that enables you to enter words that describe characteristics of the software you want.

Finding Newsgroups

If you're like most cybernauts, you'll end up exploring newsgroups. There are more than 10,000 newsgroups on the Internet. Newsgroups are essentially online clubs for information exchanges, news postings, help, and advice. Joining a newsgroup usually only requires that you "subscribe;" that is, send an e-mail indicating that you want to join. They range from software user groups to political discussion panels to fervent admirers of Bart Simpson. In other words, something for almost everyone.

There are several ways to sort through this wealth of forums. You need a software tool called a *newsreader*. The Netscape Navigator 2.0 (or later) browser and Microsoft's Internet Explorer include newsreader clients. If you use an earlier version of Navigator or another browser that doesn't have a newsreader client, you can get one (such as News Xpress) by downloading it from an FTP site. News Xpress and other newsreaders are also available free from most ISPs.

After you have a newsreader, you need to find newsgroups. If you have a lot of time on your hands, you can just download all 10,000 of them and see which ones you want to join. Otherwise, you might want to focus your search. One of the best ways to do this is to use Deja News, a search service designed expressly to help people find newsgroups of interest to them (see Figure 10.12).

If you have Netscape Navigator 2.0 (or later), you can go to Deja News by clicking the Net Search button on the main Navigator screen. If not, go to **http://www.dejanews.com** to get access to the search form.

Don't worry about capitalization—Deja News isn't case-sensitive. Deja News automatically assumes there is an "or" between multiple words—keep that in mind if you enter more than one keyword. To keep your hits to a manageable size, you can designate the number of responses you want. For example, if you're

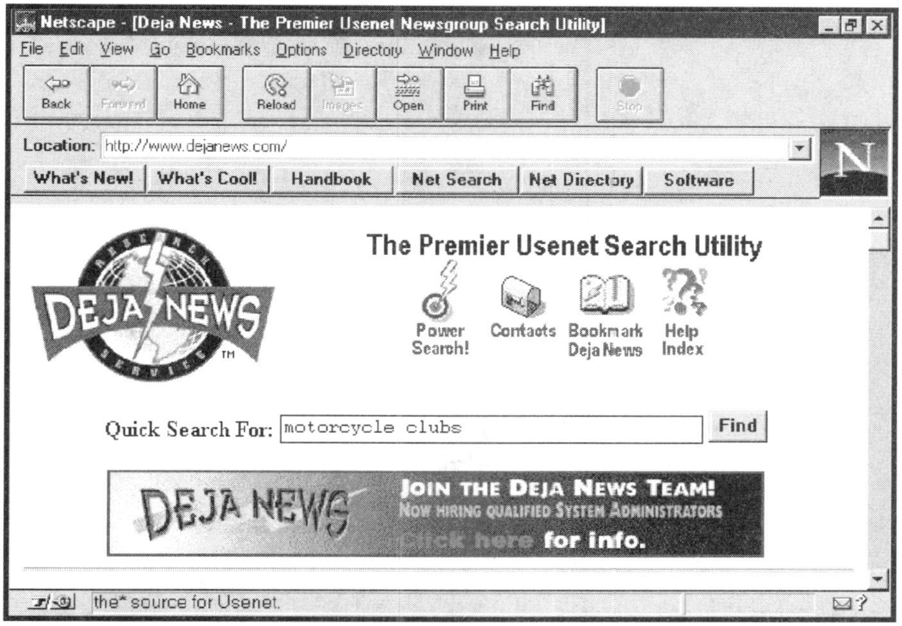

FIGURE 10.12

Deja News keeps tabs on all of the Internet's newsgroups, and enables you to search for ones of interest just by entering keywords into a search form.

looking for "computer" or "software" newsgroups, both have a large number and you could end up visiting a lot of useless ones before you found what you really want. Just as specificity is important in using other search engines, it is equally important here.

Finding People Using the Internet

Here's a million-dollar secret that private eyes and missing-person specialists wish I wouldn't tell you about: **http://www.switchboard.com**.

That's the address of one of the Internet's best search sites for tracking people. Private eyes can charge hundreds or even thousands of dollars for something they can do in 30 seconds at Switchboard; they check 90 million names, addresses, and telephone numbers to find out where someone lives.

In addition to that, Switchboard contains names, addresses, and phone numbers (often including fax and e-mail numbers) on 10 million businesses in the U.S. (see Figure 10.13). You can know as little as a word in the company name, and Switchboard can start tracking it down.

Most Switchboard searches take about 30 seconds if you entered data in all of the text boxes (first name, last name, city, and state). If you have only the first and last name, you might have to wait a couple of minutes.

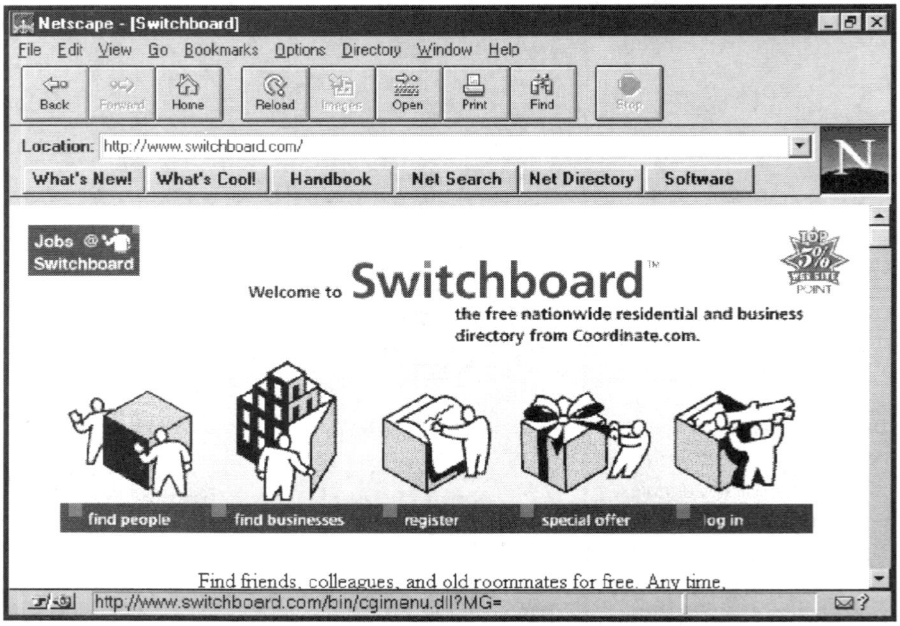

FIGURE 10.13

Whether you're a private eye, class reunion coordinator, or someone looking for an old friend, Switchboard likely has your search target's name, address, and phone number among its 90 million entries.

Switchboard probably isn't a site you would visit every day, but it's invaluable when you need to find someone. Private numbers aren't listed, so don't think you can use it to call Madonna. You can go into your own listing and make revisions and additions. For example, you can add your fax number and e-mail address, as well as correct any misinformation that might exist in the Switchboard entry. But the real beauty of Switchboard is that, like most search services on the Internet, it's free to use and it can deliver knockout results.

If you're interested in the universe of 1-800 numbers, AT&T was kind enough to create an index to almost all of them. The AT&T Internet Toll-Free 800 Directory (**http://www.tollfree.att.net/dir800/**) provides a search engine that will locate numbers by location or subject matter.

Finding People Using Commercial Services

The Internet has Switchboard to track down people, but that isn't the only way to do it. The commercial online services also offer people-finding search engines. Their only drawback is that they're confined to other members. So, if you're a Microsoft Network member and you want to search for the e-mail address of a CompuServe member, you're out of luck.

The nature of the commercial services, however, is that most of the interaction that takes place in their forums is done among members, so the limitation is usually a moot point. For example, if you're visiting a chat room in America Online and find that someone chatting there is interesting enough to check out further, you can highlight their member ID and open a Member Profile window to see who they are, where they're from, and what their e-mail address is (see Figure 10.14).

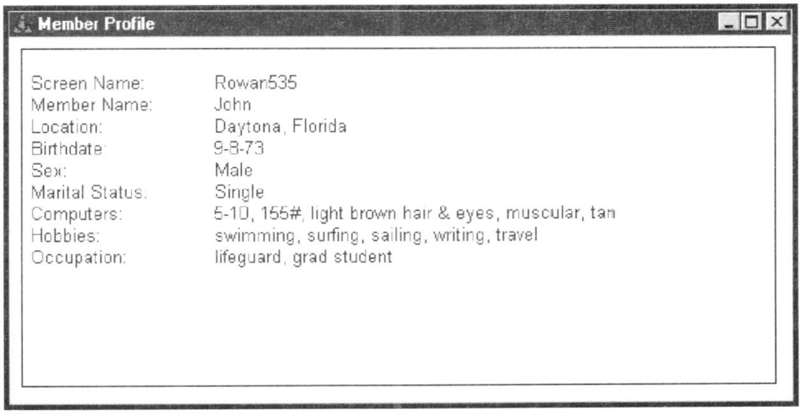

FIGURE 10.14

In AOL, you can search for more information about members by clicking their member ID and displaying their profile (something every member has and every other member can see).

If you just want to check out someone in AOL whose name you know, you can go to Member Services and open the Members directory. You can get a member's profile—there's much less anonymity in the commercial services world than on the Internet. You can ask the system to check if a member is currently online anywhere. If they are, the software will inform you which forum they're in. If it's something like a chat room, where people gather, you can join them.

Like America Online, CompuServe and The Microsoft Network both have member search facilities that enable you to learn more about their respective members. None of these search services provides the specific address of a member, but you can almost always get the city, state, and country. If you want, you can go to the Internet's Switchboard from there.

Remembering Your Searches

So you don't have to re-search a topic or remember complicated URLS, set up your own index of search engines and favorite destinations. Fortunately, there's some handy technology to help you. The most common name applied to this technology is "bookmarking." It works a little differently (but not much), depending on which of the Web browsers or commercial services you use. The concept is generally the same: Land on a neat page, click Add Bookmarks (or the appropriate button), and that URL is automatically added to a Bookmarks list. When you want to recall it, just open your Bookmarks folder and click the selected name (see Figure 10.15).

A great tool for Internet users is SmartMarks (see Figure 10.16). Developed by First Floor, Inc., SmartMarks is an advanced system that organizes your bookmarks, and monitors them. SmartMarks informs you when a bookmark's content or address changes.

TIP

You can download a free copy of SmartMarks by going to the Netscape home page at **http://home.netscape.com/**. Then click on Netscape Products at the bottom of the page to find the download site. Or you can go directly to **http://home.netscape.com/comprod/netscapeproducts.html** to locate the list.

SmartMarks saves you tons of searching time by coming fully-loaded with more than 300 popular destinations, including search engines and directories. These

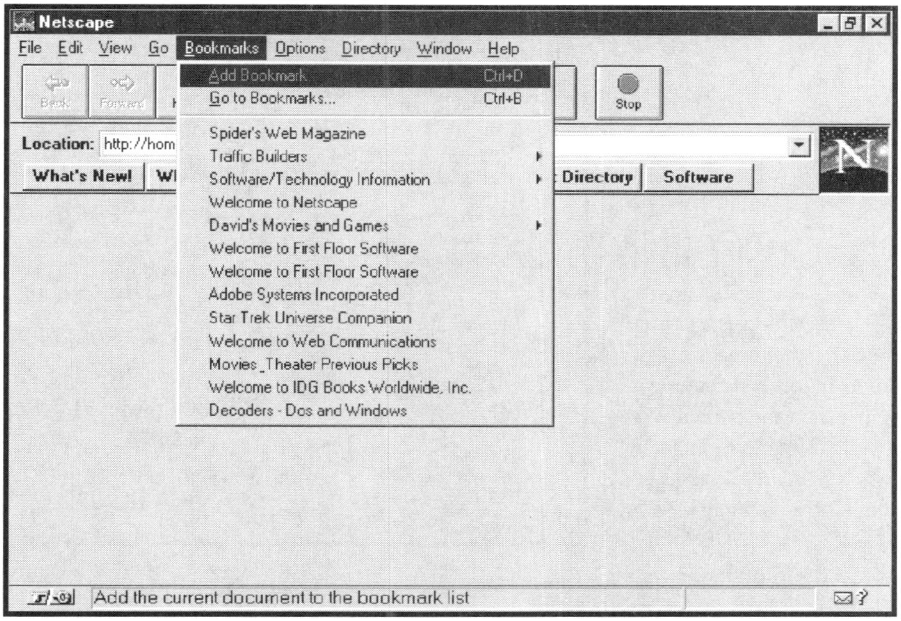

FIGURE 10.15

You can Add Bookmarks any time you land on a page you want to visit often. In Navigator just choose Bookmarks, Add Bookmarks.

destinations are organized into folders such as Arts, Health, Business and Economy, Computers and the Internet, and so on. As you locate new pages, you can add them to an existing SmartMarks folder, or you can create a new folder if the page you've found doesn't fit a category.

Behind the scenes, SmartMarks keeps an electronic eye on sites you designate as important. The software runs with Navigator, and comes up whenever you open it. But it can also run independently, if you choose. So, if you come across a site that has dynamic information (such as a stock market readout or breaking news), you can instruct SmartMarks to look in on it and tell you if the content or address has changed. SmartMarks would be a good deal even if it weren't free.

Commercial services all have bookmarking features to help you recall neat pages you've found. Like the Bookmarks and SmartMarks commands, adding a site to your favorite pages list is usually no more than a two-click activity. And the commercial services have one edge over even a tool as sophisticated as SmartMarks: They can index sites in the services themselves as well as on the Internet, while SmartMarks is confined to the Internet only. For example, if you're working in The Microsoft Network and want to visit a place on the Net, you just click Favorite Places and double-click the icon that represents your destination site. MSN then automatically loads the Internet Explorer browser and takes you to that site on the Net.

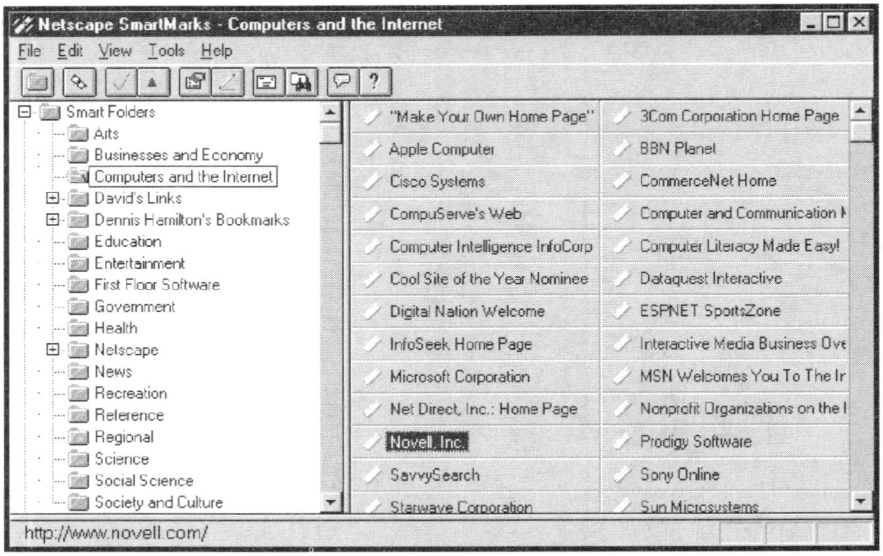

FIGURE 10.16

SmartMarks is a hot tool that organizes your bookmarks and comes with more than 300 popular Web destinations, including search engines and directories, already listed in its folders.

Searching for Online Shopping

Unfortunately, there's no easy answer if your goal is shopping on the Internet. It's a wild and somewhat untamed electronic mall. But the direction of online shopping is unmistakable. In 1995, about $300 million in commerce was conducted in cyberspace. It's a sizeable number that's going to grow a lot in the future; there are more people coming online, more businesses setting up virtual storefronts and opening for business, and more security in online financial transactions. Today, you can buy everything from software to automobiles to real estate online. Tomorrow...?

The simplest places to shop in cyberspace are the commercial services' malls, such as MSN Mall on The Microsoft Network. One of their great advantages over the Internet is that they have shopping sites neatly categorized. Yet the commercial services' don't have as many businesses set up in their malls. In the last year, however, all of the commercial services stopped fighting the Internet as a competitor and embraced it as a collaborator. Thus, they now have not only their own shops, they also provide direct links to many Internet-based shops, thus making the total offering more complete.

Click America Online's Marketplace and you can take an electronic stroll through auto dealers, flower shops, bookstores, software merchants, and classified ads (see Figure 10.17). Its 2Market service is a gift shop where you get high-quality

FIGURE 10.17

AOL's Marketplace isn't as big as the Internet's, but like other online service malls it represents a secure environment for shopping electronically—and it contains links to top Internet shopping sites.

visuals and descriptions of merchandise (it also comes on a CD if you want to shop offline and save running up a connect-time bill). MSN Mall presents pretty much the same options, as does CompuServe. The shopping malls of the online services are not large in terms of the number of merchants, though they have thousands of products. Their advantages are convenience, slick presentation, and a nice sense of transaction security.

The big mall is the Internet. There are thousands of merchants now online, but locating them isn't always easy. There's no complete centralized directory of Internet merchants, although the All-Internet Shopping Directory (**http://www.webcom.com/tbrown/**) is probably the best place to start. There are also some smaller niche-specific indexes that can help. A lot of merchants are just floating out in cyberspace, so finding them can be a matter of conducting a search along the lines of the keyword SavvySearches discussed earlier in this chapter.

The All-Internet Shopping Directory lists hundreds of virtual outlets, catalogs, and malls (see Figure 10.19). The mall listings can lead you to most of the destinations you'll want. But you can also do a lot of searching in the catalogs. You will find catalogs you can order from, as well as catalogs you can read. The hottest place to check out catalogs is the Mall of Catalogs (**http://www.csn.net/marketeers/mallofcatalogs/**), where you can look through hundreds.

You should also check out the Shopping2000 Home Page (**http://shopping2000.com/shopping2000/index.html**). Is this the future of online shopping?

Create Your Own Shopping Mall

Because there are thousands of merchants on the World Wide Web, you might want to consider creating your own shopping mall index. After all, no one else has your particular interests, so it's unlikely that you'll even find a niche directory that encompasses every place you like to shop.

By far the best way to do it is to use the SmartMarks software described earlier in this chapter (see "Remembering Your Searches"). You can create a folder (call it "Bill's Sports Mall" or "Jan's Electronic Outlets") and add merchants to it as you come across them. You can build a directory that includes your favorite virtual shops and other niche-specific search engines that might be of use to you (see Figure 10.18).

If you don't have SmartMarks, you can use Netscape Navigator's standard Bookmarks feature (a similar feature is included on all other Web browsers). In Navigator, you can create folders to put common links under a single general heading. It doesn't have the snappy look of SmartMarks or the capability to detect changes in content, but it's still a way of organizing your mall.

All of the commercial services also have a bookmarking feature you can use to establish your own mall. As you search for merchants, just add them to the Favorite Places folder (in The Microsoft Network). If you get enough sites, create a folder for your mall. When you're ready to shop, double-click your folder and your mall opens before you. MSN, AOL, and CompuServe folders allow you to include their own merchants as well as those on the Internet.

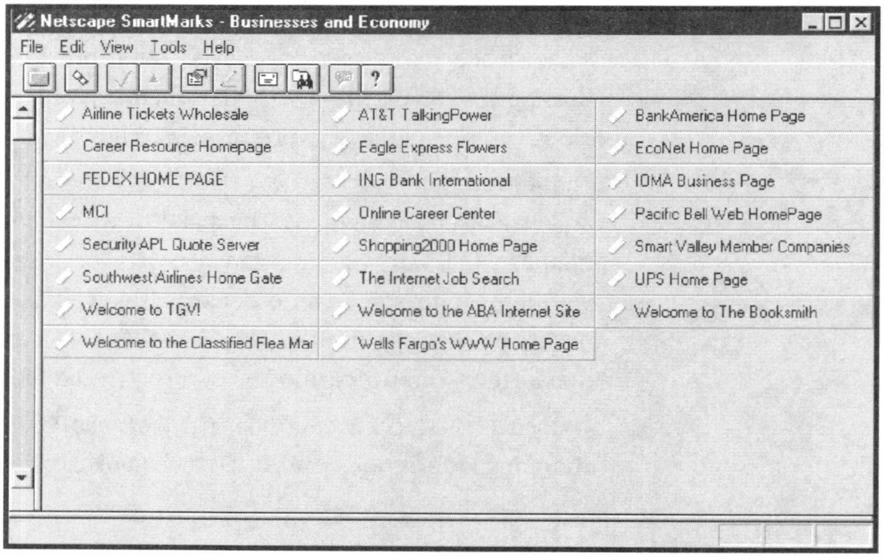

FIGURE 10.18

In the profile boxes that SmartMarks provides with every entry, you can designate specifics such as whether this shop accepts credit card orders, how they ship merchandise, how long it takes, and so on.

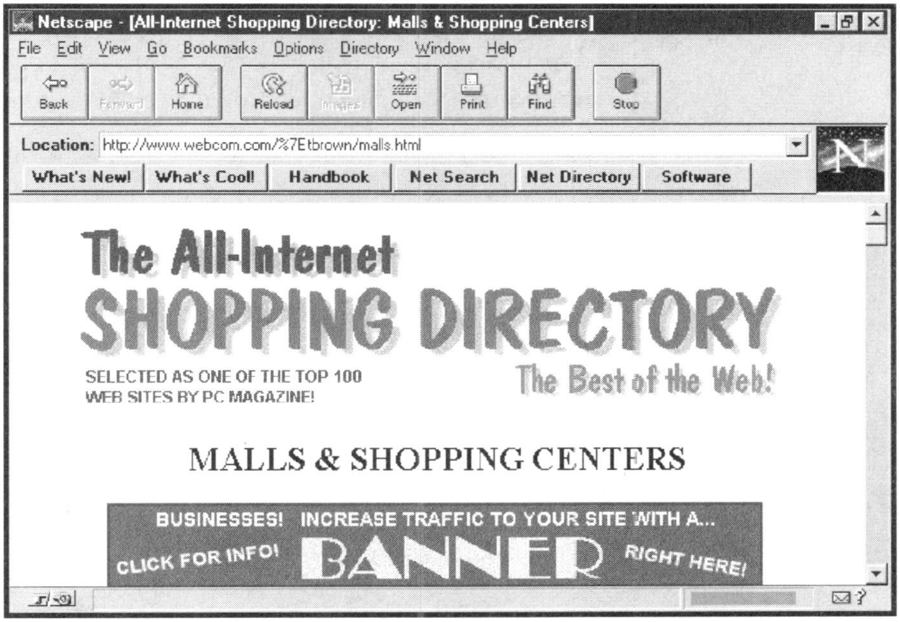

FIGURE 10.19

The most comprehensive central directory of malls is the All-Internet Shopping Directory, which directs you to stores, malls, catalogs, how-to-shop online information, and more.

Finding Software and Computers

The common denominator among cybernauts is that they have all access to computers. The Internet is the largest user group in the history of the world. With more than 30 million Internet users and more than 10 million additional ones subscribing to the commercial services, there's bound to be a lot of searches for information about computers, software, modems, chips, cabling, printers, communications, and anything else that falls under the banner of "computing."

Thankfully, nowhere else in the world is there more help, companies, products, tutorials, documentation, and advice available than in cyberspace. There are more than 300 USENET newsgroups devoted to computer technology subjects. There are software malls and directories. Every technology provider in existence has some form of residence on the Internet. The commercial online services have their own computer-dedicated chat rooms, BBSes, automated e-mail help lines, hotline telephone numbers, and context-sensitive online help.

But how do you sift through everything to find exactly the help you need?

The commercial providers, as usual, make it easy to find their help lines, computer malls, and chat rooms. Computers and related technology are such dominant subjects in cyberspace that they all reserve a major front-page category button for the subject. Just click the Computers button and follow the links to the information you want.

The Internet, again, is both bigger and tougher. But there are sites and search directories that can help you track down what you want. Here are some of the major sites for finding software- and computer-related information:

Technology Information Centre KnowledgeBase **http://www.tickit.com**

SoftInfo **http://www.icp.com/softinfo/**

Software Net **http://www.softwarenet.com**

Apple Computer **http://www.apple.com**

IBM Corporation **http://www.ibm.com**

The Netcenter **http://www.netcenter.com**

Computer Literacy Made Easy **http://zeb.nynaes.cornell.edu/z/Cimlit.html**

The World Wide Web Virtual Library **http://www.w3.org/hypertext/Datasources/bySubject/Overview.html**

There are hundreds of guides to computer information on the Internet, and you can reach them via the search directories and search engines. Yahoo! (**http://www.yahoo.com**) delivers nicely categorized lists of computer and software suppliers, though it isn't as complete an index as the Technology Information Center KnowledgeBase or SoftInfo. The latter maintains a database of 16,000 software products from 5,000 vendors, and includes full-text searchable files of each product, not just titles.

Where to Search for...

Of course, this chapter cannot list every site you might ever want to search, but to help orient your Internet compass, the following sections list some interesting sites to check out.

Business and Careers

Career Resource Homepage **http://www.rpi.edu/dept/cdc/**

Online Career Center **http://www.occ.com/occ/**

The Internet Job Search **http://www.wpi.edu/Depts/Library/jobguide/what-now.html**

The ABA Internet Site **http://www.abanet.org.**

The Classified Flea Market **http://www.cfm.com/cfm/**

Entertainment

BookWeb **http://www.spiders.com/bookweb/**

The Information Superlibrary **http://www.mcp.com/**

Warner Brothers Records **http://www.iuma.com/Warner**

Children's Literature Web Guide **http://www.ucalgary.ca/dkbrown/index.html**

Internet Entertainment Network **http://husbandloverspy.com**

Music Sites Index **http://www.euro.net/music.html**

The Hollyweb Online Film Guide **http://www.ingress.com/users/spease/hw/hollyweb.html**

The Internet Movie Database **http://www.cm.cf.ac.uk:80/Movies/**

TV Net **http://www.tvnet.com**

Government

The Federal Web Locator **http://www.law.vill.edu/Fed-Agency/fedwebloc.html**

FedWorld Beta Home Page **http://www.fedworld.gov/#usgovt/**

U.S. Tax Code Online **http://www.fourmilab.ch/ustax/ustax.html**

The White House **http://www.whitehouse.gov**

U.S. House of Representatives **http://www.house.gov**

Library of Congress **http://lcweb.loc.gov/homepage/lchp.html**

Legislative Information on the Internet **http://thomas.loc.gov/**

Health

Breast Cancer Information **http://www.nysernet.org/bcic/**

Health & Fitness **http://www.coolware.com/health/info.html**

Health & Nutrition **http://akebono.stanford.edu/yahoo/Health/Nutrition**

MedWeb **http://www.cc.emory.edu/WHSCL/medweb.html**

Pharmaceutical Information Network **http://pharminfo.com**

The Medical Education Page **http://www.primenet.com/gwa/med.ed/**

World Wide Web Virtual Library: AIDS **http://www.actwin.com/aids/vl.html**

Sports

ESPN Sports Zone **http://www.espnet.sportszone.com/**

Summary

Without question, the key to making the online experience fruitful and fun is the search. The tools we use, the skills with which we use them, and our ability to organize information we find all play pivotal roles in making our time in cyberspace count. Conversely, if you don't become at least semi-skilled in searching cyberspace—whether with the Internet or the commercial online services—has the potential to deliver you nothing but eye strain and frustration.

This chapter discussed some search directories, search engines, niche-specific searches, and how to find people, merchants and much more. Listed here also are a range of search sites to visit.

The best activity you can possibly undertake is to get in and try out the directories and search engines with specific goals. Determine a subject you want information on, then follow the advice given here—as well as explore on your own.

The cyberspace world is the most dynamically growing entity in the history of computing. The prediction here is that it is not going to stop anytime soon, if ever. It will become integral, even indispensable, to our businesses, communication, education, and entertainment. Yes, there will be a lot of junk, particularly on the Internet. But there also is a wealth of wondrous sites on the Net. As time goes by, better search tools will enable us to bring some sense of organization to the chaos. In just the last two years, search tools have dramatically improved the ways we find and organize information. But the best is yet to come.

11

ONLINE ACTIVITY PRIMER

Aimlessly surfing the online world may be fun, but after a while you'll want to get more out of your online experience. There are dozens of practical ways you can use what's out there to get things done.

In Chapter 10, you learned how to search for topics online. Those skills are some of the most useful you can acquire for actually doing things in the online world. This chapter takes those skills and suggests ways to use them in four areas:

- Locating people
- Buying and selling things
- Planning your travel
- Finding a job

Locating People

With the whole world jumping on the Information Superhighway, it's getting easier and easier to find people, businesses, and organizations. Some have an online presence in the membership directory of an online service; others have their own Web site. Most of us have contact information available online simply because we have a phone number and our name pops up in searches of online phone directories.

Beyond finding a particular person, you can also look for groups of people who share a particular interest with you. You can even look up your great great grandfather in a genealogy forum. So, let's get started looking for people online.

Using Phone and Address Directories

The commercial online services and the Internet have directories you can search using a variety of criteria. Some of these are specialized directories, such as the American Business Information Yellow Pages shown in Figure 11.1. This directory helps you find company contact information, including a score for the company credit rating.

Other directories are more general and include individuals, organizations, and businesses. For example, the ProCD National Telephone Directory Search allows you to search all phone directories in the U.S. (see Figure 11.2). Several services on the Internet contain international listings of addresses. This broader scope may be a reflection of the truly global nature of the Internet, and the fact that the Internet is not run by an American company, as are CompuServe, America Online, and Prodigy.

Typically, you'll find lists of such directories in reference categories in online services. On the Internet, use the search feature of your browser, and enter keywords like "phone directory" or "addresses." You can find fax number

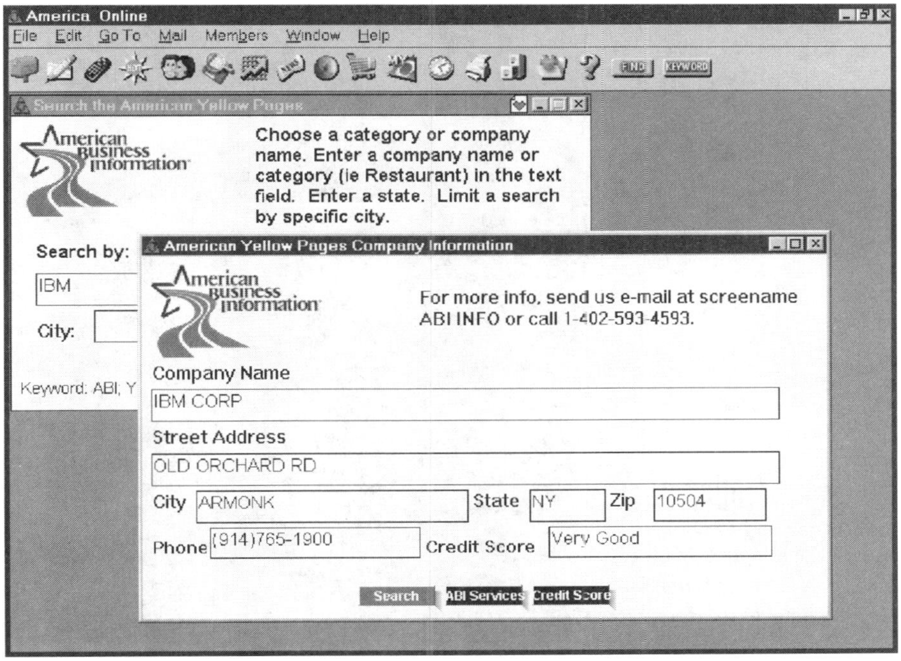

FIGURE 11.1

You can search by company name and location in the American Business Information Yellow Pages.

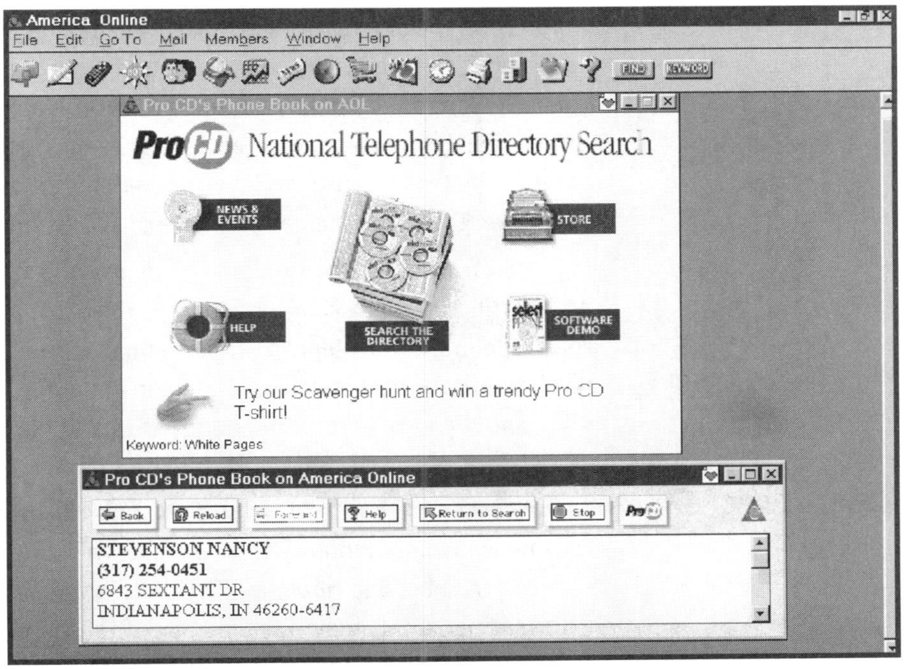

FIGURE 11.2

This searchable directory found me...but at my old address.

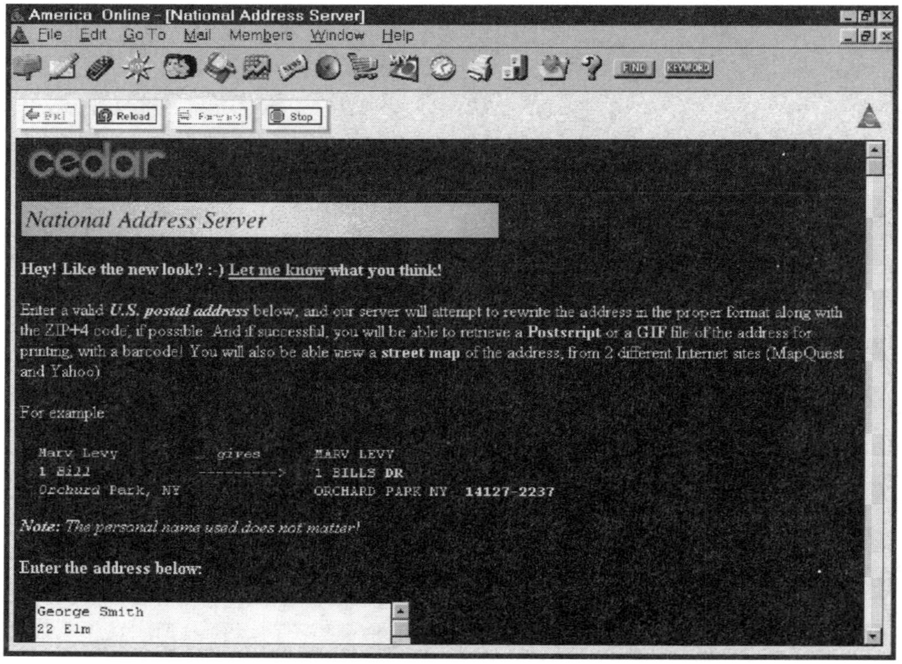

FIGURE 11.3

The National Address Server finds the best match for whatever information you know.

directories, e-mail addresses (for example, **http://www.worldemail.com** offers fax and e-mail listings), and special-interest mailing lists.

After you find a directory, the method used to search it is pretty straightforward. You typically fill in fields with a name and as much information as you have about the state, city, zip, or area code of the individual or organization you're looking for. You may be asked to choose a region of the country to perform a search or choose by category. For example, a search form might ask you to enter the type of business if you're searching a business directory. The more you know, the better chance you have of succeeding at your search.

If you aren't sure of the spelling of the person's name, try using the National Address Server. Enter your best guess at the name and address. You can enter a rough spelling of the name, a variation on the street name, and no zip code, and it will return the best match it can find. In figure 11.3, I entered the street address 1 Bill, and the service returned 1 Bills Drive and the correct zip code.

Locating Members of the Online Community

Anyone who joins an online service creates a listing for himself or herself in the service's membership directory. Typically, some kind of a profile is associated with that person. If they want, members can fill in these profiles with details about their interests and hobbies (see Figure 11.4).

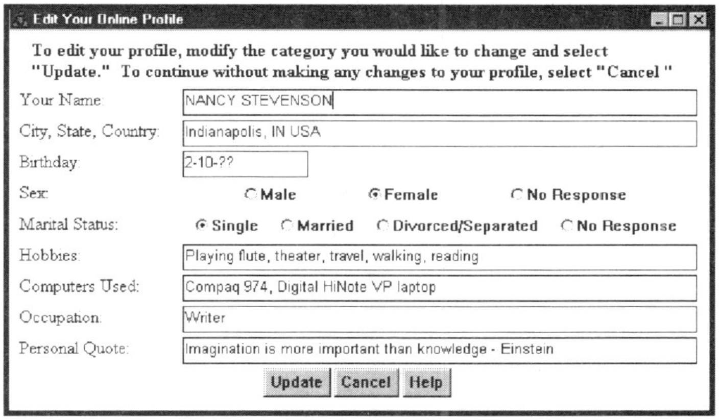

FIGURE 11.4

I filled in my America Online member profile, but members may add less detail than this if they want.

You can search the membership directory of the particular service of which you are a member with the simple search tools provided by the service. Most services have menus called Members or Member Directory. You can search for a particular person by name, or enter more general information (such as an area of interest or city or state) to search for groups of members who have that term in their profile.

On the Internet, you can find indexes of Internet addresses such as the one in Yahoo! (**http://yahoo.phone.com**) and directories of discussion groups to help you connect with groups of people who have common interests. The Liszt Directory of E-Mail Discussion Groups (**http://www.liszt.com**) shown in Figure 11.5 is one example. There are also indexes listing Web sites and USENET newsgroups that you can search to find organizations online. There are even specialized location services, such as one that lists celebrities and allows you to get their addresses—for a fee.

Genealogy Online

Not everyone you want to find is among the living. How about checking out your ancestors with online resources? You can search online services under categories like home and family to find genealogy forums and software. You can post messages in genealogy forums looking for long lost family connections, or find software utiltiy programs or online services like the Family Tree Maker Online to record the various branches of your family tree (see Figure 11.6).

On the Internet, there are genealogy discussion groups as well as services that help you find lost relatives or friends (see Figure 11.7). Who knows, someone might be looking for you!

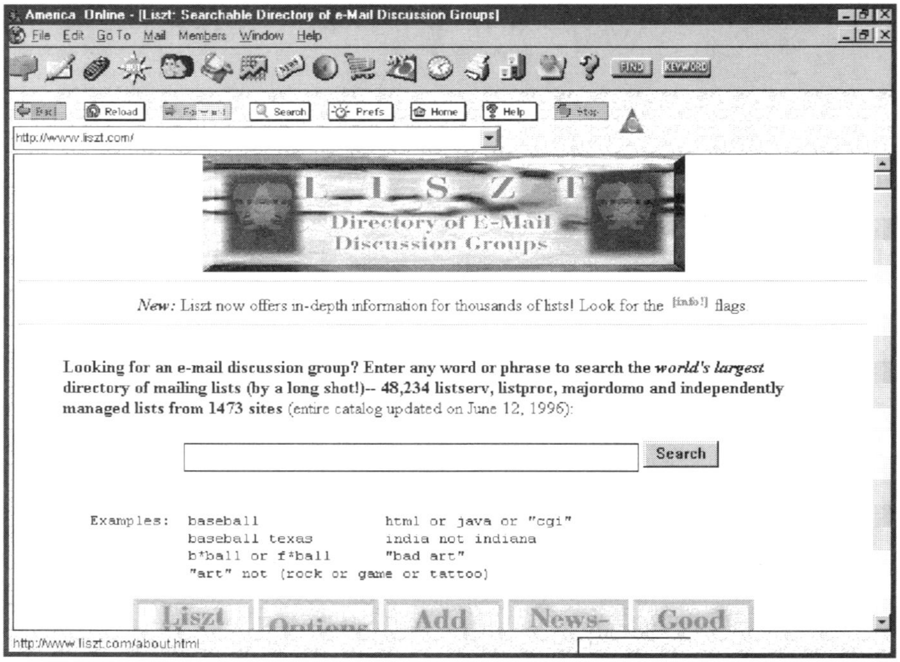

FIGURE 11.5

This directory helps you find discussion groups for people with common interests.

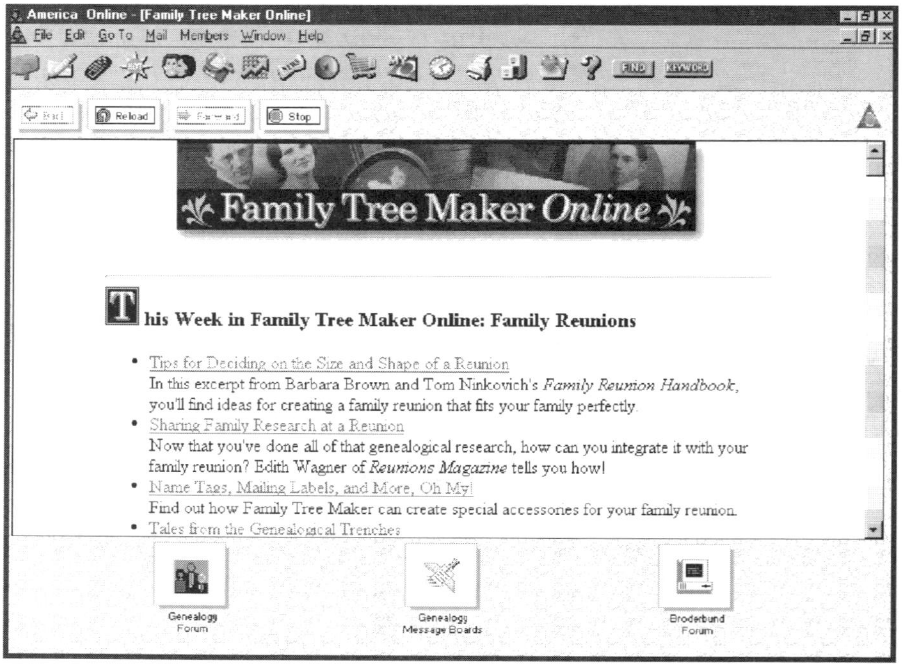

FIGURE 11.6

You can find the Family Tree Maker Online in the Genealogy Forum on America Online (keyword: genealogy).

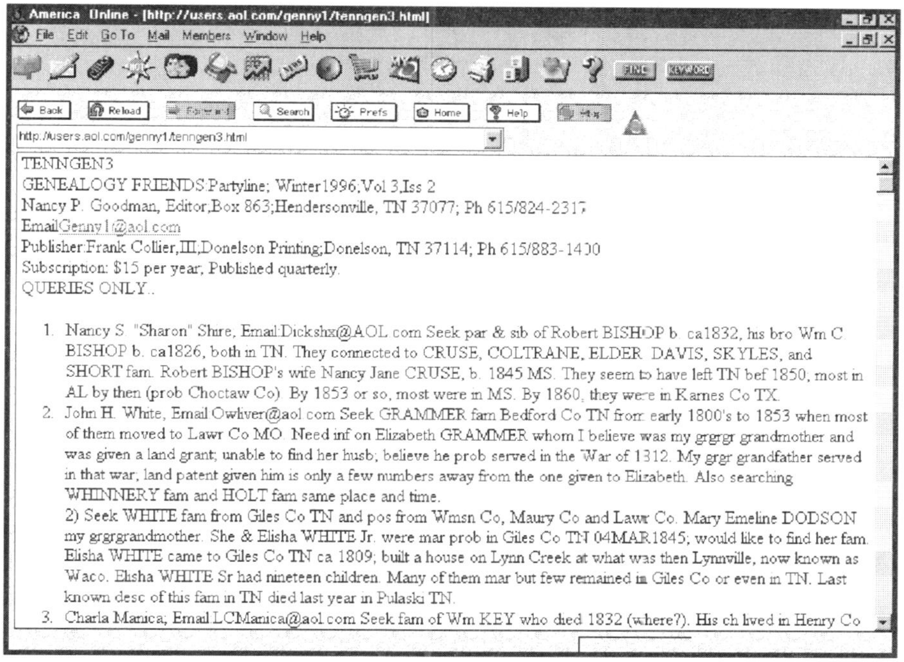

FIGURE 11.7

More and more information about people—living and dead—is being added to the Internet, making locating people easier than ever.

Buying and Selling Online

Commerce online is an area of concern to some people for several reasons. Because most segments of society are represented online, the criminal element is unfortunately present. There have been numerous scams to part people from their money, and incidents of online fraud. However, one of the greatest areas of concern—providing your credit card number to someone online—isn't really a problem if you follow a few simple rules. In fact, having a clerk in a store read your credit card number and expiration date over a phone to get authorization is probably much more dangerous than typing your number into a form and sending it online to place an order at an online store.

In this section, you learn about some of the ways you can buy things online, and the rules for smart online shopping.

Places to Shop

There are a few basic types of places you can shop at online:

- Online stores, run by companies like The Shaper Image or Avon.
- Classified ads where anyone can post an ad for (almost) anything.

- Company Web sites, which could be run by a megacompany or by one guy with a computer.

Typically, you'll find the online stores of companies you recognize through the online services. AOL, CompuServe, and Prodigy all have shopping malls with collections of stores and simple interfaces for ordering (see Figure 11.8). Each of these services has approved these companies for inclusion on their service, and holds them and you to certain regulations for shopping online. This kind of shopping is one of the safest of online transactions.

Ordering from one of these stores is simply a matter of browsing the ads for merchandise, like the one from the American Express ExpressNet store shown in Figure 11.9, and filling out an order form. You're usually offered several opportunities to cancel or to change an order before it's actually placed. Information about any extra charges, such as shipping costs, is usually presented in a very straighforward manner in every store's policies document.

Commercial online services and the Internet offer classified ad services. Although the online services will monitor their classifieds and bounce any ad with offensive or illegal content, there's no way for them to check the honesty or policies of those who place the ads. Internet classified ads are less likely to be controlled. The problem with any classified service is that you're doing business with someone you can't see and don't know. Money and merchandise must change hands at some point, and you have to find ways to ensure that if you mail a check, you get what you paid for.

One solution I discovered is a service called TradeSafe, shown in Figure 11.10. This is a kind of clearinghouse for buying and selling online. You find something

FIGURE 11.8

You'll find many companies you're familiar with in places like the AOL Marketplace and CompuServe's Electronic Mall.

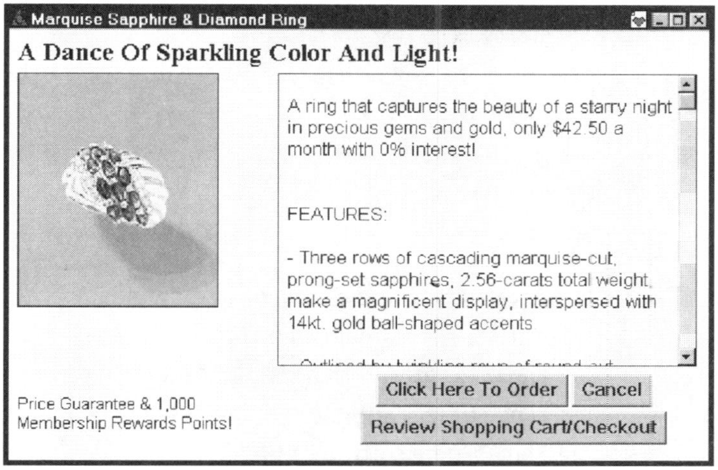

FIGURE 11.9

It's not exactly like browsing the aisles at K-Mart, but you can usually find a picture of products to get an idea what they're like before you buy.

you want to buy, say a collectible antique doll from someone in Indianapolis, and submit the transaction to TradeSafe. The payment goes to them, and they notify the seller to send the goods after they payment clears. There's a 24-hour inspection period; if the buyer isn't satisfied, TradeSafe returns the payment on return of the item. Look for more safeguards like to this to come into existence as the Internet becomes more a part of mainstream economic life.

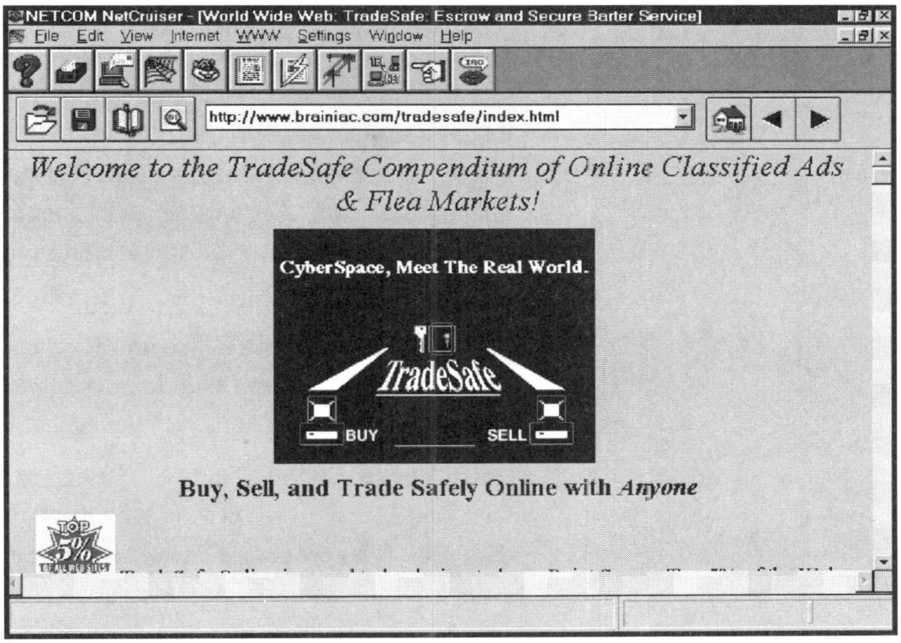

FIGURE 11.10

A safe place to trade makes responding to an online ad much easier.

TIP

It's not a bad idea to check an area like Consumer Digest, which has a presence on both America Online and CompuServe, to educate yourself on products before you buy.

Finally, you may find companies or individuals with Web sites where they offer software or books that can be ordered online. Others will simply provide product and ordering information online so you can order by phone or mail. These can range from reputable companies who are familiar to you, to individuals selling a small-time software utility.

If you're interested in selling instead of buying, you'll need to avail yourself of classified ad services, or create your own Web page (which is pretty easy to do). The thing to remember if you do create a Web page is that that's only half the battle: The other half is placing pointers online so people can find your page. You can do that by getting your site listed in Internet indexes, or by asking others to place HTML links to your site in their own related site.

The Do's and Do Not's of Online Shopping

As stated at the beginning of the chapter, shopping isn't that risky if you know a few rules. Here they are:

- **Know who you're dealing with.** You're safest with well-established companies, but you can also find out more about less well-known companies by checking their credit rating in a business directory or by asking them for business references or contact information of satisfied customers. If you're dealing with an individual, simply getting their address and phone number and checking them for accuracy can be a good idea. Call the phone number they give you and see if it's really them at the other end.
- **Read policies carefully.** Classified ad services and online stores have policies that govern things like how long an item will take to reach you, shipping costs, warranties, and return fees. Classified ad services' policies will tell you what you as a seller can and can't put in an ad you post.
- **Get a confirmation number.** If you place an order online with a credit card, most stores provide a confirmation number so you can trace the order if the product is late in arriving or if problems occur after the order is placed. Some online services even offer you the option of sending

the confirmation number to you as an e-mail message, which saves you the trouble of writing it down.

- **Remember that online stores typically don't carry the breadth of brands you can find in real world stores.** For example, an electronics vendor might have two or three models of a CD player, while an electronics store might carry 10 or 20 models. Consider using online searches in combination with visits to local stores to find just the right item for your needs.
- **Online stores don't necessarily offer the best price, especially when you add shipping costs.** Again, comparison shop with print catalogs or a trip to your local store to see if you're getting a good price. The convenience of getting your shopping done quickly online is worth something: Just don't pay too much for the privelege.
- **If something sounds too good to be true, it is.** Don't believe offers that are too good, advice about hot stocks or even innocent-seeming testimonials from other online users. Do your research and use your common sense.
- **If somebody buys something from you, ask for a cashier's check or money order.** By the time you cash a regular check and it bounces, that someone could be very long gone.

Planning a Trip Online

Because the travel industry is, of necessity, such an online beast, the infrastructure of computerized reservations systems has been in place for years. Now many of those services, such as American Airlines' easySABRE, are available to you and me.

Today, you can search for hotels, rental cars, and train and airline information. You can narrow those searches using a variety of criteria, such as price range, whether you can brings pets, hotel chain, or size of car. You can even specify a kosher meal and window seat when you make a plane reservation. You can join travel clubs and services, such as AAA, whose online service welcoming window is shown in Figure 11.11. These clubs often offer discounts or special packages that save you money as well as time.

Because you can't print your own tickets from your computer (yet) if you make a reservation online for a plane, train, or cruise, you'll either have to have a ticket mailed to you or get yourself to a local ticketing source within a few days

FIGURE 11.11

The automobile club, AAA, helps travelers with information, maps, and special offers.

of making the reservation. Other services, like car rental agencies or hotels will guarantee your reservation with a confirmation number in exchange for credit card information (see Figure 11.12).

NOTE

Some airlines are testing paperless ticketing, where you receive a confirmation number but don't receive a paper ticket to board a plane. If these experiments are successful, watch for this to impact the way online airline reservations work.

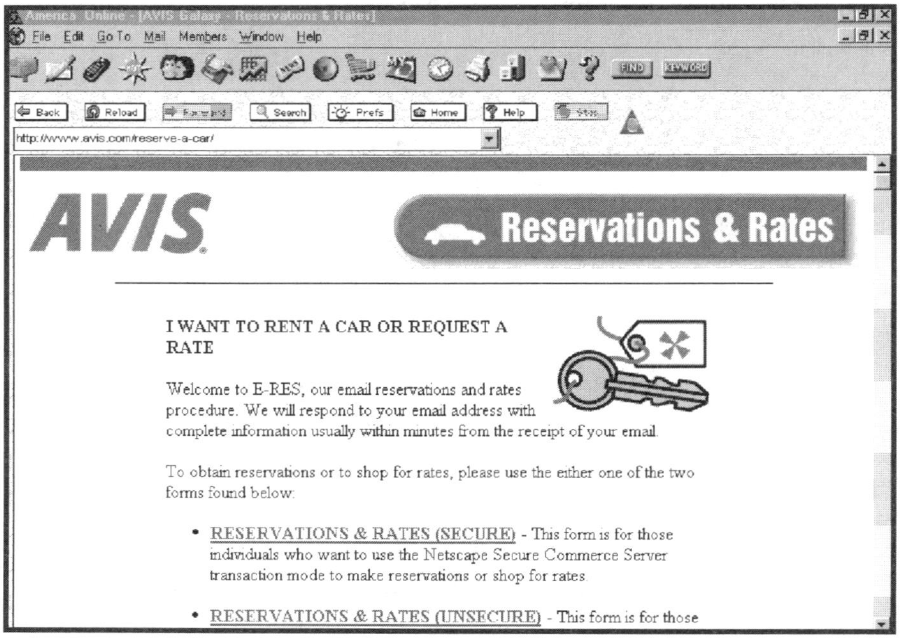

FIGURE 11.12

Reserve your next rental car with Avis online.

Making a Reservation

To give you an idea of the type of information you can find to help you make travel reservations, take a look at American Airlines' easySABRE reservation service, which you can access on CompuServe. This particular service requires that you join and obtain an account number and password to use it, but it is a free service. Others, like WorldSpan Traveller (also on CompuServe and also free), do not have any requirements to use them.

When you enter easySABRE, you're offered a selection of travel services, including air travel, hotel reservations, and car rental. When you select air travel, you're asked to fill in the information you can see in the Destination window in Figure 11.13. After filling in the departure city, date of travel, arrival city, and number of passengers, you can then choose to see flight or fare information. You can see the flight information for a jaunt to Madrid in Figure 11-13.

You can get information about connections, what aircraft your flight will use, seat availability, and airlines. By clicking the Detail button, you can get even more information, such as what meals will be served.

Clicking the Fares button displays price information about the highlighted flight, as shown in Figure 11.14. You'll get several variables as determined by the fare basis. Fare basis relates to the class of travel (first, business, coach, and so on) and any special requirements, such as advance purchase. Be sure to check the

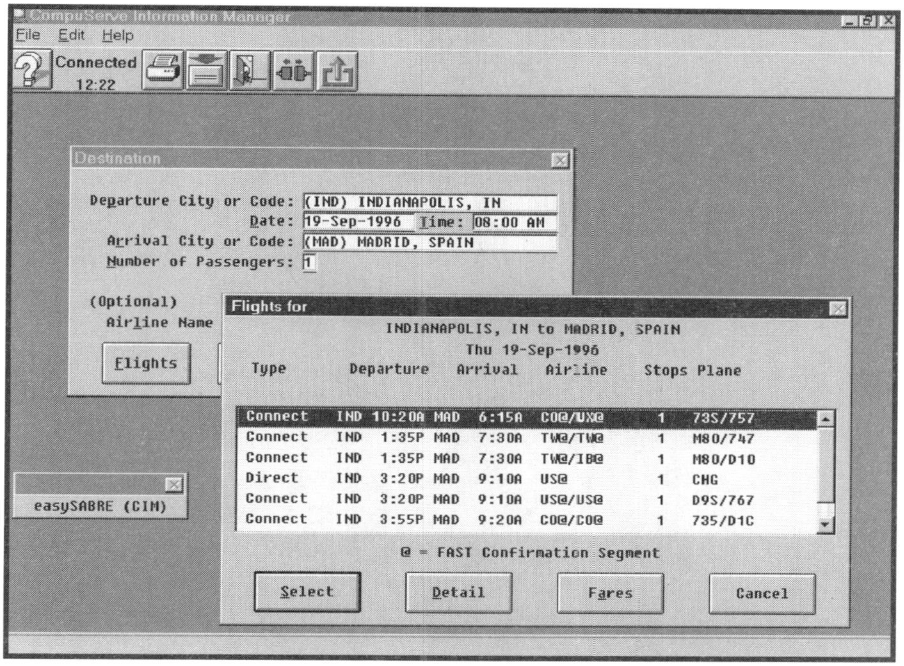

FIGURE 11.13

It's a good idea to learn some of the codes that appear on these screens if you plan to book travel online on a regular basis.

requirements for a particular fare by clicking the Rules button. If you do place a reservation, you can also take advantage of frequent flyer miles by entering that information in your traveler profile.

NOTE

Online flight listings are not comprehensive. Be aware that not all airlines, flights or fares are posted online; you might want to check with some airlines directly if you don't see something available that fits your needs.

EasySABRE also has a hotel reservation system. Again, you simply fill in your destination, the number of people staying, and any criteria, such as maximum rate or distance from the city center or airport. Details include rates, amenities offered, and even distance from popular tourist attractions (see Figure 11.15).

Most travel reservation systems online work similarly. They have straightforward, simple text interfaces, as opposed to a fancy graphic look. Some include several services, such as easySABRE's hotel, car rental, or airline features. Others are specialized by types of travel, such as cruises. Many hotel chains, like Hyatt and Hilton, have their own reservation Web pages, and several car rental agencies are online for direct booking as well.

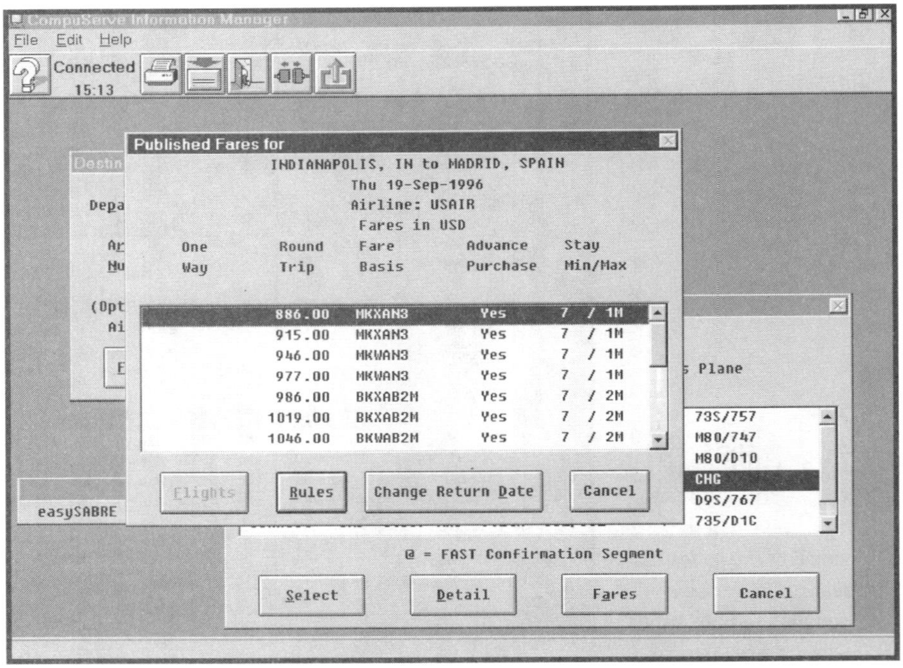

FIGURE 11.14

Minimum and maximum stay requirements are listed in the Published Fares For window.

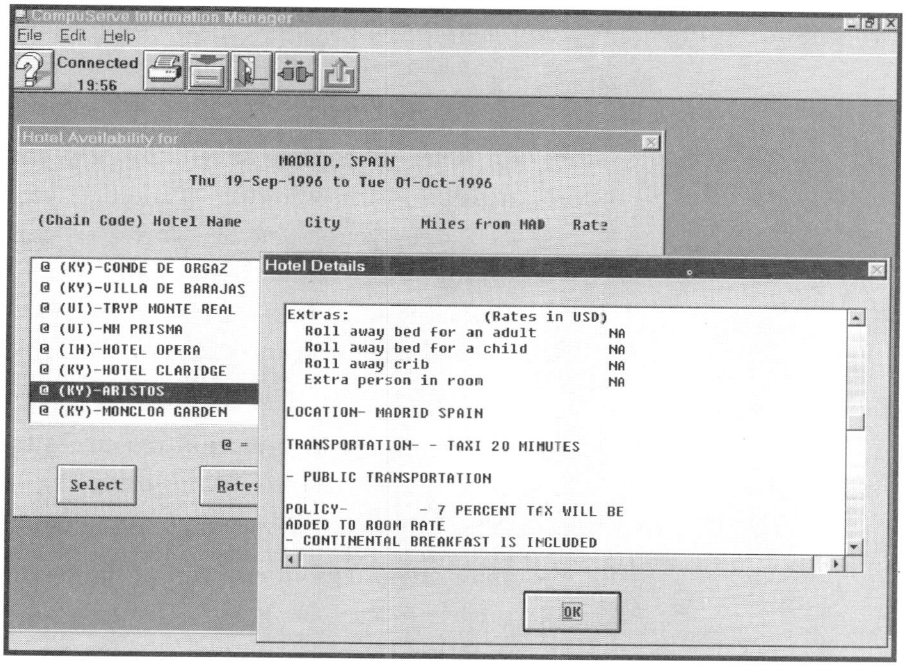

FIGURE 11.15

If you have a favorite hotel chain, you can search for hotels only in that chain.

Tips for the Online Traveler

Buying travel online is just another form of shopping online. For that reason, there are some tips and warnings you should know, as well:

- **Look for travel bargains.** There are several travel clubs and discount travel services online. Some give discounts to groups, such as senior citizens. Others offer discount tour packages. A few ask you to pay a fee to join and take advantage of their specials.
- **Remember comparison shopping for a $350 CD player?** That goes double for a $5,000 trip. A lot of the low-price airlines (such as Southwest Air) don't have an online presence because it doesn't pay for them. Check the fares you get online against other published fares in the travel section of your newspaper, for example. And don't forget to take advantage of those frequent flyer miles by making note of your award number when booking travel online or offline.
- **There are many ins and outs to the travel industry that travel agents are well-acquainted with.** They may know to look for restrictions or requirements you're not aware of. One great way to use online resources is to become an educated travel shopper. I looked up airfares to Austria a few years ago, then went to a travel agent to book the trip. The first price she

came up with was twice as expensive as the fare I'd seen online. When I presented her with that information, she suddenly found a fare to match the one I'd found.

- **Consider issues like cancellation fees and penalties when booking travel.** You may find a great rate, but if you find you can't make the trip, it could cost you big time. Read travel service policies before booking travel with them, and consider buying travel insurance to help protect you before and during travel. By using online resources to compare rates and policies, you may find that a lower fare—even with fees for changing your plans—might still be cheaper than a more expensive ticket.
- **Do use online information resources for travelers** to learn about essentials like climate, visa or passport requirements, and even State Department travel advisories for unstable destinations before you go.
- **Take advantage of the global nature of the Internet** and online services to learn about destinations, customs, and attractions. Chat with people in discussion groups or in forums to find out first hand what a location is really like (not what the brochures tell you it's like).
- **Remember you can buy luggage, travel books, maps, and even language courses online.** Because it's so easy to shop online, you might remember to pick up a few essentials you'd forget if you had to go to the mall.

Finding a Job Online

Perhaps not as pleasant as shopping or planning a trip to Spain, job hunting is nevertheless a necessary task you're likely to encounter at least once or twice in your life. Online resources can make it a little less painful and possibly more successful.

At this time, the odds of you getting a job by cruising the Internet for a few hours are slim. However, as more companies get online and as more people learn to do business online, you're likely to see a change. For now, the greatest strength online resources have is probably in the areas of learning about the types of opportunities that are out there, honing your resume preparation skills, and getting job hunting advice.

Online job resources fall into these categories:

- Employment services which post listings of jobs for employers for a fee.
- Classified ads where either you or a potential employer can place an ad.

- Career counseling services which give advice about topics, such as writing an effective resume and interview skills.

You can also use business information and directory services to look up information about prospective employers, such as number of employees and credit rating, before sending your resume. Posting your resume might get you some valuable feedback on how well it's been written, as well.

Employment Services

Employment services, such as Help Wanted USA on America Online and E-Span on CompuServe, allow you to search job listings by category (see Figure 11.16). E-Span also allows you to narrow your search by the area of the country you want to work in.

An interesting feature of America's Job Bank (**http:/www.ajb.dni.us/**) is a connection to state employment offices, such as the one for Idaho shown in Figure 11.17. (I'm not sure whether surfing for work qualifies with state agencies as time spent job hunting for the purpose of justifying your unemployment check, but it couldn't hurt.) If you're truly interested in finding a job, these state agency connections offer valuable information on available jobs, job training, and special work programs you can take advantage of as a resident of that state.

You can also find sites where companies have posted information about themselves to attract job applicants. A good place to find many of these is through *Career Magazine* on the Internet (**http:www.careermag.com/careermag/**). There's a section on this Web site where employers can post their own company information and job lists, like the MCI site shown in Figure 11.18.

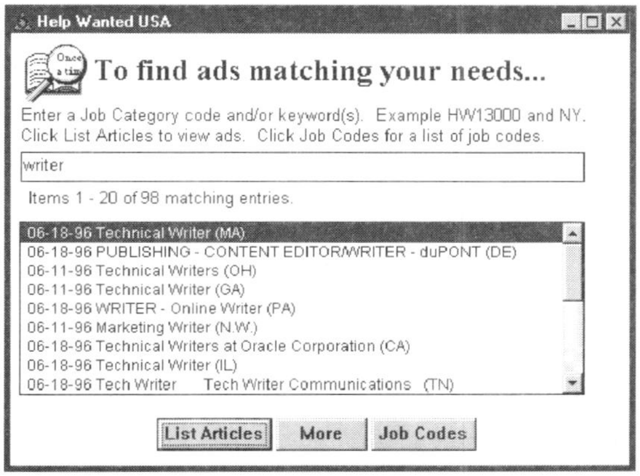

FIGURE 11.16

Searching by the word "writer," I found 98 job postings in Help Wanted USA.

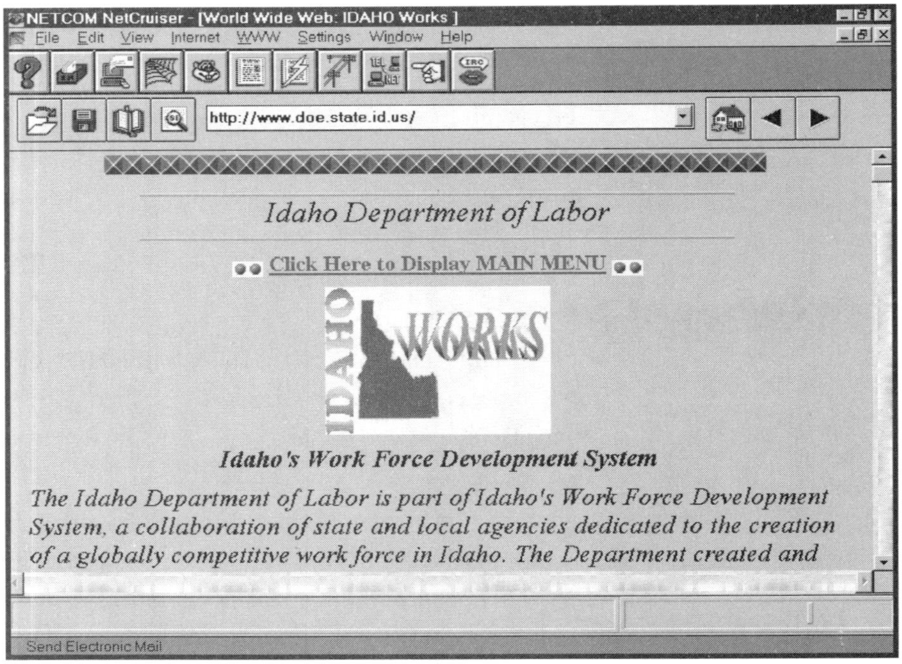

FIGURE 11.17

Your state may offer job listings right online.

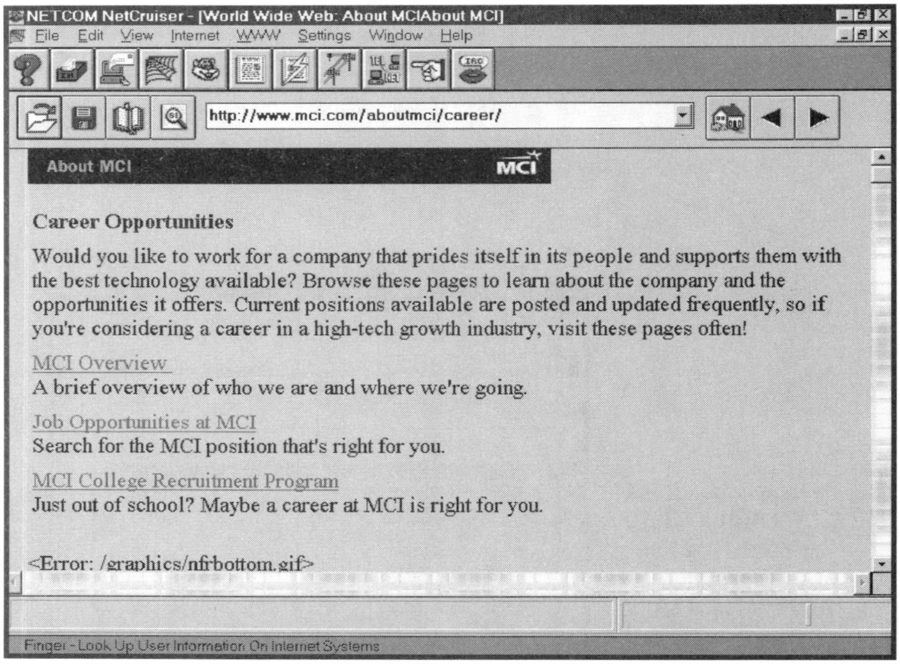

FIGURE 11.18

MCI wants to tell you why they're the best company to work for.

Finally, there are specialty categories (such as job hunting for college grads, women, or Hispanics) that you'll come across all around the Internet using a little creative browsing.

Classifieds

Classified ad services were described in the context of buying things online earlier in this chapter. They're basically areas where you can post or read ads. If you choose to advertise yourself to potential employers in the classifieds, your ad for work will be up there with offers for herbal remedies and astrology charts for a dollar. Classifieds are divided by topic, however, so your ad will be "placed" in a help wanted or employment section.

One such service, iMALL (at **http://www.imall.com**), charges a fee for ads (see Figure 11.19). Most online service classifieds don't charge fees.

WARNING

Use caution with classified listings. Ads have been known to appear that offer quick money working at home, only to charge you money for

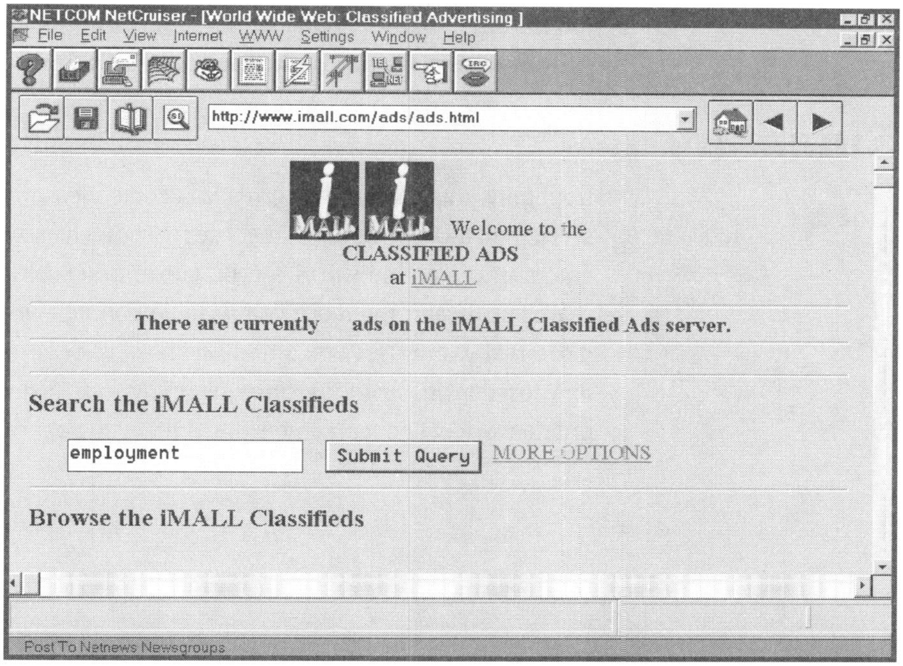

FIGURE 11.19

iMALL has ads in all kinds of categories, including help wanted.

supplies or equipment. If a business opportunity involves you sending cash or making an investment, investigate it thoroughly before sending any money.

Career Counseling

There's so much out there that might fit into this category, it's hard to get your arms around it all. Put your thinking cap on for this one and you can probably come up with all kinds of resources for career advice, including:

- Professional association forums where you can chat with others in your field about what they look for in prospective employees.
- Help wanted listings in online versions of publications like *The New York Times* or your local newspaper.
- Books on finding your perfect career, resume writing, or interviewing skills that you can buy in online bookstores.
- Articles on job hunting in places like *Career Magazine* online or publications related to your industry.

A good place to start might be by looking up a document titled "Guide to Internet Job Hunting," published by the University of Virginia. You can get to it at **http://minerva.acc.virginia.edu/career/GUIDE/guide.html**.

Summary

Hopefully, this chapter has given you some ideas for particular sites or types of services to look for while online. The real point here was to show you that all those places in the online world can be put to practical use. The more creative your search skills and the more comfortable you become getting around online, the more real world uses you'll find for those resources. Whether it's locating your long lost cousin, buying perfume, planning your next vacation, or getting a job, the online world will open up new possibilities to you in almost any area of interest.

12

ONLINE SECURITY AND ETHICS

Privacy and security are key issues in everyone's life. If you feel threatened in a situation, you try to get out of it. But what if you aren't sure if you're being threatened. In the online world, you may never know your privacy is at risk. What do you do then?

The online world provides a unique way for people to gather information about you, even without you knowing it. No longer is it necessary to make a trip to a public library or visit another city to obtain phone numbers and addresses of people living in other cities, states, or countries.

Just as there's no way to guarantee 100 percent safety when walking down the street, there's no way to ensure your online safety as well. However, you can take precautions by educating yourself on the potential online dangers threatening users as well as what rights you have while online. This chapter looks at ways you can protect yourself and others while online.

What Kind of Personal Information Is Available Online?

Have you ever looked up your last name in a phone book when you're on vacation or business trip? If you have an unusual or unique last name, you may find one or two matches every once in awhile. Now, with a computer, phone line, and modem, you can tap into various directory resources from all over the country from the comfort of your own home or office. Although your purpose may be for fun or to contact a relative or friend, others may use this information to send you junk mail, and direct marketing schemes. This information can even be used to harass you or to illegally obtain your credit information.

How to Find Online Personal Information

Even before you get an online account, your name and other personal information is probably available online someplace. For the most part, this information is readily available in telephone and business directories, and newspaper articles. If you've ever published an article, book, pamphlet, record album, or other copyrighted material, your name is likely to appear online someplace.

NOTE

Most of the information discussed in this chapter focuses on the Internet and World Wide Web because of their size and global availability. Other services, such as CompuServe, MSN, and America Online, have the same concerns about security and privacy, but these systems usually have more built-in controls than the Internet or WWW. Also, because these other services are commercial, they have more influence over the content and membership behavior found on their services. You should use the same caution as you do on the Internet or Web when using a commercial online service.

To get an idea of the type of personal information available online, run a search on your name. It's that simple. You can do this from any search engine (sometimes referred to as online *directories*, like your telephone directory) on the Web, such as the one shown in Figure 12.1. The following is a list of search engines and their URLs:

- Alta Vista **http://www.altavista.digital.com**
- Who Where **http://www.whowhere.com/**
- Lookup USA **http://www.lookupusa.com/**
- Yahoo! People Search **http://phone.yahoo.com**
- Excite **http://www.excite.com**
- Internet Address Finder **http://www.iaf.net**
- Four11 **http://www.four11.com**
- Bigfoot **http://www.Bigfoot.com**
- Switchboard **http://www2.switchboard.com**

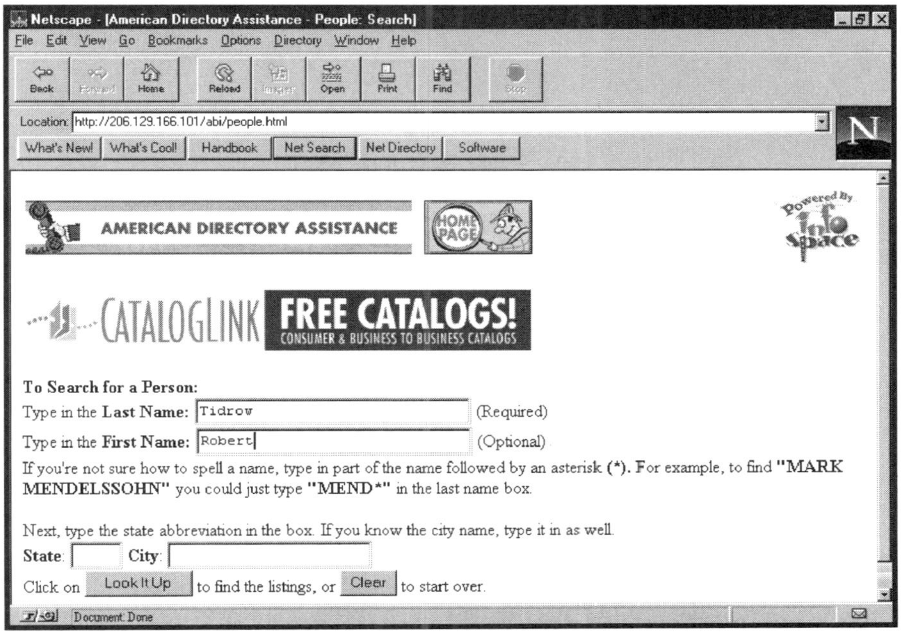

FIGURE 12.1

Many search engines, like Lookup USA, contain names, addresses, telephone numbers, and e-mail addresses.

The reason so many of these directories have your information is because the owners of the data sell it to the search engine companies. Any time personal data appears in a telephone book (white or yellow pages) or other public document, its available for others to reuse it. The data itself isn't copyrighted; the presentation of the data is. This means someone cannot photocopy the white pages and resell it. Someone can, however, create new documents, mailing lists, databases, and other publications based on that data. Web-based search engines tap into these repositories to populate query results.

One such company is Database America (see Figure 12.2). Database America (**http://www.databaseamerica.com**) compiles information from various sources and then makes it available for customers in the form of mailing lists, reunion or holiday lists, business directories, and mortgage information. Because demographic and marketing companies like Database America earn money by providing their customers with this data, they seldom—if ever—turn over a complete database to a search engine or Web site. Instead, they co-market their other services. So, Database America may include names and addresses for a search engine to use, but they don't include more specialized data, such as mortgage or business information. This data is sold to customers in more traditional ways and has more stringent privacy laws applied to it.

FIGURE 12.2

You might be able to find information about you or a friend by visiting demographic and marketing Web sites like this one.

NOTE

Several laws protect private information you've provided to institutions, such as banking and lending companies. These are usually governed by state legislation, not federal, which makes it difficult to enforce them once a transmission crosses state boundaries. Moreover, some legislation, like the Freedom of Information Act of 1972, allows courts to be petitioned for the public release of certain documents.

Online documents, messages, and electronic commerce are not yet protected by strong federal legislation, although a few laws are on the books. The 1986 Electronic Communications Privacy Act (ECPA) restricts law enforcement agencies to record wire and oral transmissions over electronic communications devices. ECPA, however, does not include restrictions for the provider of the service, such as employers, who can post or review your online documents.

Why Does Unlisted Information Appear?

Believe it or not, some search engines return unlisted or private information. Depending on how each search engine company obtains data for its searches, it may contain unlisted telephone numbers and addresses. Recently, Yahoo! removed over 32 million unlisted names and addresses from its database under pressure from users. Many users who found their own unlisted numbers displayed as search results complained to Yahoo!.

Although phone companies include unlisted numbers in databases they sell, the information is often obtained directly from the users. (See the guidelines in the section called "Tips on Protecting Your Family" on ways to keep personal information off the Internet.) When you fill out registration forms, magazine subscriptions, contest forms, warranty cards, and so on, the receiving company enters that information into marketing, demographic, and sales databases. As more companies are using the Internet and Web for business and customer service, the chances of that information being used in some capacity (such as searching for customers who use similar products) increases. Visit some of these directories and query on your name to see if any of your personal information appears. If so, you may want to contact that service and ask how to remove your name from their list.

Also, as direct marketing continues to grow as an economical and efficient way to pinpoint potentially new customers, *data* becomes a hot commodity. The size of a database and the way it can be filtered into demographic segments (such as age groups, family incomes, and purchasing patterns) often determines the success or failure of a product line or marketing campaign. Many consumers don't think about that when they receive product literature in the mail or watch television commercials. Advertisers pinpoint selected time slots during specific programming to run particular ads. This same paradigm is used on many search engine sites; specific ads display depending on the types of links a user clicks (see Figure 12.3).

Recently, the Lexis-Nexis research firm discontinued the dissemination of several million Social Security numbers in its product called P-TRAK Person Locator. By purchasing P-TRAK at a cost of $125 a month, customers could search over 300 million names, addresses, phone numbers, and Social Security numbers. After only 10 days of the service being available, Lexis-Nexis removed the Social Security searching mechanism on this product, but still allows the other information to be searched.

One of the problems with Social Security numbers being available in electronic format is the potential for fraud. Several law enforcement agencies complained about the Lexis-Nexis service and cited instances where Social Security numbers were being used for credit card fraud and illegal immigration. In some cases, people can "steal" your identity by knowing your Social Security number, name, and address.

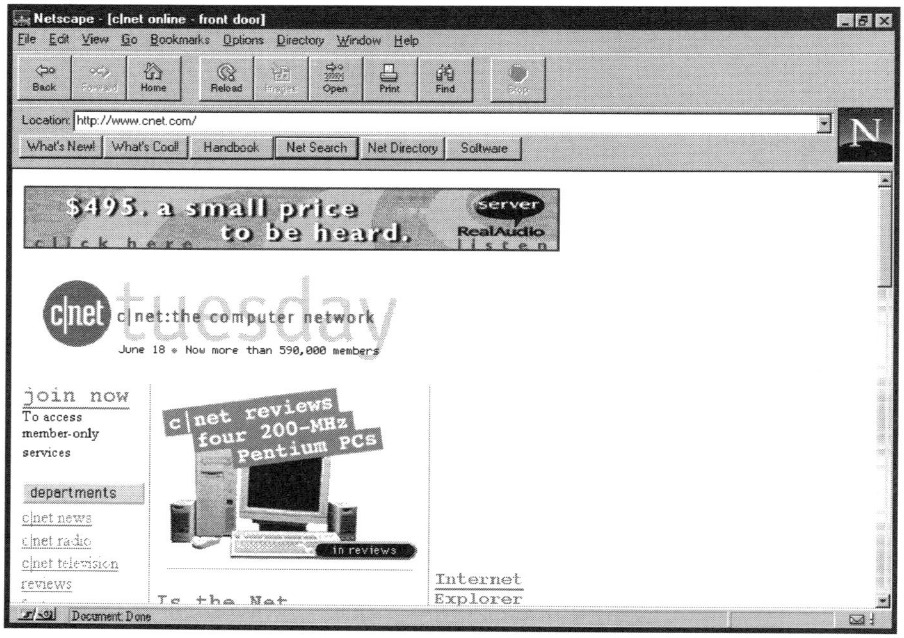

FIGURE 12.3

Many sites now display targeted advertisements depending on the links you click.

NOTE

For more information on Lexis-Nexis and the P-TRAK product, point your browser to ***http://www.lexisnexis.com****.*

You can learn how to take steps to protect yourself and unlisted numbers in the section "Tips On Protecting Yourself" later in this chapter.

Leaving a Trail

You may not know this, but you're like Hansel and Gretel when you enter a Web site. You leave a trail for others to follow. Web servers can track information about you when you enter a Web site, such as the type of browser you use, the time you visited the site, the amount of time you were there, and your IP address. This information can be stored in a text file (called a *log*) on the Web server and used by the site administrator to create a history of you and other users who pass through the site.

The server also can capture the links you click to track the information and ads that receive the most activity. Most sites don't distribute your personal information (such as IP address) to firms who do unsolicited e-mailings. Some sites, however, use the information they obtain when you visit their site to send you information about their products or services, or to welcome you to their site. These activities are mostly harmless, but they can be annoying if you receive a number of unsolicited e-mail messages from sites you just passed through. This is similar to receiving a product catalog from every store you pass as you drive down the street. Only with e-mail you pay for the postage (because you pay for the time to receive any e-mail messages sent to you).

NOTE

If a site has a user form or guestbook users can fill out, the type of information is even more personal. Unless you need to fill out a form to get access to additional resources, such as c|net, you should provide only required information and never give out credit card numbers, Social Security numbers, or phone numbers you want to keep confidential (see Figure 12.4).

So, regardless of how much direct information you actually supply, a site can make a record of all users who pass through. Further, data pertaining to users is an important commodity to commercial entities online. The more focused the

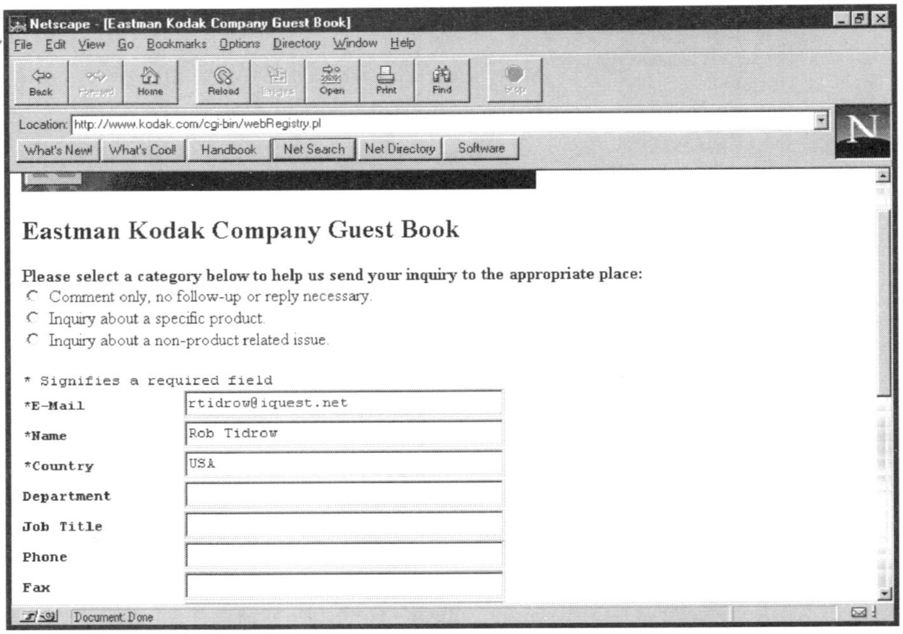

FIGURE 12.4

Guestbooks and user forms are one of the primary ways companies gather information about you.

information is, the better, which many times results in sensitive and private information about you being transmitted to other people.

Dealing with Viruses and Hackers

Not only is your personal information threatened when you're online, but so is your computer. When you're dealing with threats to your data, the main culprits are virus programs and hackers. Virus programs range from being relatively harmless to extremely dangerous to your computer system. Likewise, hackers can be the online equivalent of your pesky little nephew, or as sinister as Hannibal Lechter. The following sections discuss viruses and hackers in more detail.

Computer Viruses

A few years ago, you probably heard about the Michelangelo virus that was being spread. It activates on the artist's birthday and erases the infected hard drive's data. The story made network television news, magazine covers, and quickly spread through the computer industry. It was predicted that millions of users were infected. Unfortunately for many users, the virus wreaked havoc on their systems and caused untold loss of data. However, the majority of users were not infected and escaped harm. Since then, as Michelangelo's birthday approaches, managers, users, and administrators prepare themselves for the worst. And the worst is a computer or system-wide crash.

A *computer virus* is a program created to cause your computer, the software you're running, or the files stored on your computer to behave in a way they were not originally designed to. Some viruses are programmed to activate as soon as the virus installs on the user's computer. Other viruses, such as the Michelango virus, are set to go off at specified times or under certain conditions, such as opening or closing files. The following is a short list of virus names:

- Stoned
- Jerusalem B
- Data Crime
- Tequila
- Pakistani
- Maltese Amoeba
- Brain
- Joshi

Although you may encounter problems in your programs due to software bugs, viruses pose different problems. First, a virus is purposely created to infiltrate and damage your computer or files. Bugs are not created; they're problems in the program when the software developer writes the program. Second, viruses are seldom, if ever, loaded on a system knowingly. Except in cases when an infected file or program is being diagnosed or when a virus is known to be harmless, you don't install an infected program unless it's by accident. On the other hand, almost every program you install has at least one bug in it, which you come to realize after gaining some experience with computers. Finally, you can't remove a virus by uninstalling it; you must use an anti-virus program. Problems associated with buggy programs usually end after you uninstall the program or upgrade to a newer version.

NOTE

One virus that millions of users have knowingly installed on their system is the Microsoft Word Prank virus, a minor virus that is more of a nuisance than problem. This virus surfaced shortly after the release of Windows 95 and Word for Windows 95. It causes Word to save every file as a document template (DOT) file instead of a document (DOC) file. The virus is not part of the Word for Windows program, but infects the user's system from a document file shared from another infected user. Microsoft quickly responded with a set of macros *(short programs) to clean up the problem, but millions of users installed and used Word for Windows without too much worry. You can get the anti-virus program from the Microsoft Web site at* ***http://www.microsoft.com****.*

One way virus developers are successful at spreading viruses is via Internet and online service file downloading. America Online, CompuServe, Prodigy, The Microsoft Network, and other commercial online services ensure all programs and files are tested for viruses and are virus-free before they're posted for users to download (not to be confused with files sent via e-mail between you and someone else, which are not scanned by the online service). If you download any applications or files from the Internet, you open yourself to possible virus infection. This is because most sites don't guarantee that their programs are virus-free.

Fortunately, the majority of programs and files available online do not contain viruses. Millions of users download files without the threat of a virus. However, only one file can disrupt your work. If it spreads to other users or clients, it can result in loss of work and data for entire departments or businesses.

NOTE

Because the risk of contamination by a virus is so high, some companies have strict guidelines on downloading and running files from online resources. The guideline is often simple: It's against company policy for anyone other than information systems (IS) or technical support personnel to install any software on any system. Before you download files while at work, or bring in a file from home, check your company's guidelines.

Before you download any file or program from an Internet or Web site, understand that it may contain a virus. Although there's no guarantee that you won't encounter a virus while online, you can use some procedures to decrease the likelihood of infection. Anytime you go online, use the following guidelines:

- **Make backup copies of all files on your system.** You should do this daily for files you update frequently. You should also create a system disk so your computer can be rescued in case of a virus infection. You should perform system backups weekly or monthly depending on your system. If you're on a local area network (LAN) at work, your computer may get regular backups now. If not, copy files onto floppy disks or tape backup machines in case you encounter problems later.

TIP

The best way to approach routine backups is to consider the amount of time it would take to recreate any corrupt files. If you can't afford to start over, get in the habit of backing up. It's not necessary to backup full programs, such as Windows, Word for Windows, or WordPerfect (assuming you have the original system disks). You should, however, backup programs you've downloaded and don't want to re-download. Also, if you use financial software such as Quicken, Microsoft Money, or Peachtree Accounting, make daily backups of your data.

- **Install and run an anti-virus program.** If you use Windows 3.*x*, you have a built-in anti-virus program called Microsoft Anti-Virus. If you use Windows 95, you need to acquire a separate program, such as Norton AntiVirus for Windows 95, available at **http://www.symantec.com**, or McAffee VirusScan 95, available at **http://www.mcaffee.com** (see Figure 12.5).

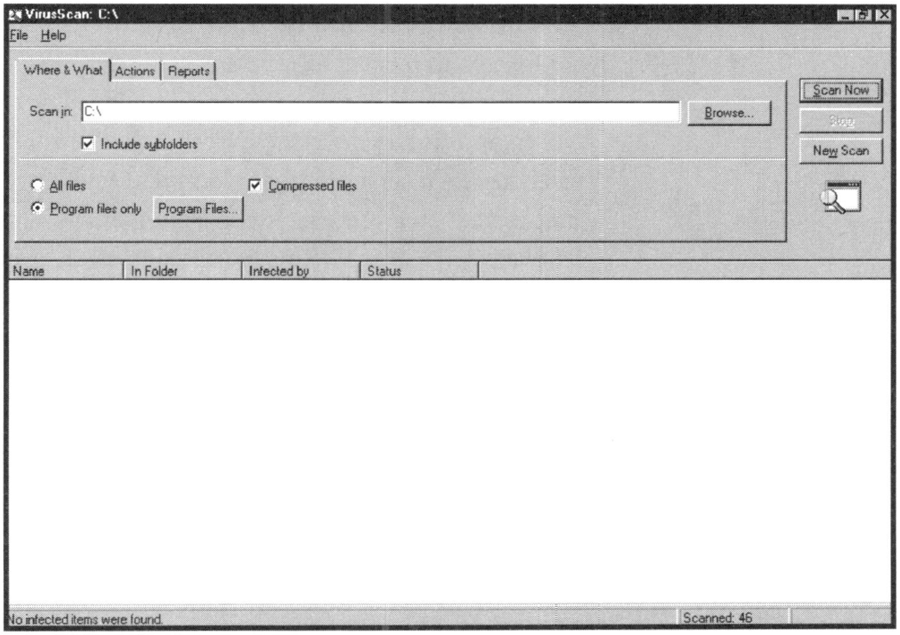

FIGURE 12.5

Install and use an anti-virus program regularly.

- **Update your anti-virus program.** According to James Daehn in an article from *Pitch Magazine*, each day two dozen new viruses are introduced. The best anti-virus program in the world cannot detect and remove viruses created since you purchased it. Many anti-virus programs include update offers you can download or purchase at computer stores.
- **Practice safe computing.** Don't install any software unless you know its source and know it has been scanned for viruses. Users on USENET newsgroups often post infected software for unsuspecting users to download and run on their machines. Unless absolutely necessary, stay away from these files. As the Web grows and more reputable software companies come online, such as Microsoft, Netscape, Sun Microsystems, and Adobe, more places to download safe software become available. Check any new program for viruses using the anti-virus software prior to installing the program.
- **Stay informed.** You can find a wealth of information on viruses at various sites, including the previously mentioned Norton and McAffee sites, as well as Microsoft and Pitch Magazine (**http://www.mediasoft.net/pitchmagazine/internet/jimsurf2.htm**).

If you encounter a virus on your computer and you're unfamiliar with your computer's systems files, the best bet is to stop what you're doing (keep your machined turned *on* though) and contact someone who can review the situation for you. If you're prepared to work out the situation on your own, you can do several things that might help. You may still—after working through all these steps—not be able to recover all your infected files. First, if you can reach a command prompt in DOS or can run Explorer or File Manager in Windows, back up your system or at least your critical files. This way you have your most current work saved in case you have to *repartition* your hard drive. When you repartition your hard drive, you erase everything from the hard drive, losing all data, files, and programs on it. You essentially have to start all over again. If you can't back up your files, you better hope you made backups prior to this incident.

Next, run an anti-virus program. If you don't have one installed, get one and run it. The anti-virus program may be able to detect the virus, clean your system, and remove the virus from it. If the anti-virus program works, your computer should be fine. Just make a habit of running the anti-virus program periodically.

If you can't install or run an anti-virus program, run the system disk to restore areas on your hard drive that may be infected. The process of restoring a hard drive is too lengthy for this book; consult your Windows or DOS documentation for more information.

Hackers

You may have heard of people who enjoy breaking into computer systems. These people generally are referred to as *hackers* or intruders. Hackers usually can access a computer system by getting around password and username authentication. Once on the system, hackers may steal information, erase data, access confidential or sensitive documents, or just have fun. One hacker who recently gained a lot of attention was Kevin Mitnick (see Figure 12.6), who stole mobile telephone numbers and hacked into computers at Digital Equipment Corporation. He was charged with 23 counts of computer fraud and is currently awaiting sentencing.

NOTE

A recent report by the Senate Permanent Investigations Subcommittee estimates that in 1995 over $800 million worldwide was lost to hackers. The businesses affected by break-ins included banks, large businesses, hospitals, and research firms. Many of these break-ins are not publicized because of potential negative press on the business. Also, almost half of the break-ins were done by employees or internal users of the network, which makes it easier for employers to punish the culprits without bringing criminal charges against them.

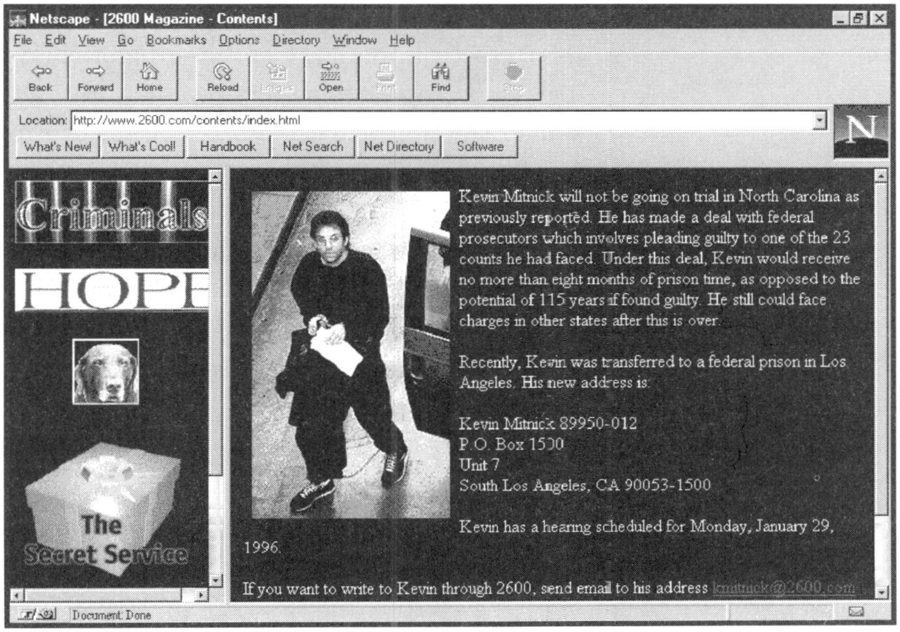

FIGURE 12.6

Some hackers break into computers for monetary gain, espionage purposes, or just for fun.

One misconception about hackers is that they can infiltrate your personal computer and steal or corrupt your data. Although it is possible, it is not likely your computer will be a target for hacking unless you have connections to sensitive data or secret software. If you're running a computer at home, hackers cannot break into your system if your modem is connected to the Internet, Web, or other online service. It becomes dangerous when someone can dial into your computer, or into a local area network like one you might have at work (see following note on information about remote access software). Further, unless you're running a supercomputer in your basement for the government or have access to sensitive company data, hackers wouldn't want to break into your computer anyway. It would be a waste of time. Usually, hackers can steal the type of data and software you have on your computer from other systems that have faster connections.

NOTE

If you use a remote control application or Remote Access Services (RAS) in Windows 95 or Windows 3.x, your computer is vulnerable to attacks from other users. Hackers or other users can dial up your computer (they would have to now your phone number, of course) and log into your system via the remote control or RAS software. If you use these types of systems, especially if the computer you're dialing into is connected to a LAN at work, make sure the password and usernames are unique and difficult to guess.

Although you may not directly encounter a hacker, you should be aware of them. This is especially true if you work in environments where sensitive data is stored. Some hackers access computers by getting to know the employees of the site they want to hack and eventually using that person's or a coworkers login information. Because many people create passwords that are easy to remember (favorite music group, family names, and so on) hackers can guess the passwords of many people they meet. They then dial into the company computer using stolen phone card numbers or modified phones that cannot be traced to the hacker. Once in, they appear as the employee because they're using that person's login information.

The following are some guidelines to protect you and others from potentially harmful encounters with hackers:

- Never post passwords, usernames, or phone numbers to newsgroups, chats, or other sources.
- Keep sensitive and confidential information protected. Don't let others know if you have access to this type of information.

- If you use remote control software, protect your username and password. Also, change your password periodically.
- Report any mysterious or questionable activities you see while online. The best person to report this to is your system administrator if you suspect someone is threatening your system at work.

For more information about hackers and unauthorized use of computer systems, check out these sites:

- Computer Security Institute (CSI) **http://www.fedcenter.com/fedcenter/foscis.htim**
- Federal Bureau of Investigations (FBI) **http://www.fbi.gov**
- Computer Emergency Response Team **http://www.cert.org**
- Center for Democracy and Technology **http://www.cdt.org/**

Online Scams

Another way online users are being threatened is through the use of online scams. Con artists are as prevalent on the Web as they are in everyday life. Many of the same scams that work offline now work online as well. One such scam is equivalent to the familiar pyramid scheme in which members pay to join and then, as new members join and send in money, each member ascends the pyramid and receives money from all those below him.

The Web offers a unique way to advertise and purchase products and services. It also allows scam artists to advertise bogus products and services to prey on other users. Some things you may see promoted online include the following:

- Weight-loss programs and products that don't work
- Entrepreneurial opportunities that require large quantities of up-front money with nothing in return
- Useless health products that also may be dangerous to some people
- Bogus gemstone and gold-mining opportunities
- Stock offerings that are not worth the paper they're printed on
- Credit repair scams

There are a variety of scams. Some scam products and services are sold as legitimate products through advertisements. You might see these ads in classified ad sections on the Web promising ways for you to make "$4,000 per month" with a spare computer. You might also see advertisements for setting up 900 numbers to make a few dollars per minute for each call.

Another way you may encounter scams is through subtle advertisements. These types of advertisements appear in chat sessions and newsgroups as normal posts, but are thinly disguised sales pitches for a product. Be wary when you see numerous "set up" questions for products or services out of context, such as "What's the best weight-loss diet?" during a serious weight loss or support thread. The question will probably be followed by a series of messages promoting a diet service and how to reach that company. The poster may in fact be one who sent the original question, only using a different user account or username.

NOTE

Another type of online scam is chain letters that appear in your e-mail inbox. These chain letters usually are nothing more than a nuisance to you. You are not obligated in any way to answer these messages or to send them along to others. In fact, the best action you can take is to delete them from your system. Also, if they contain file attachments delete them as well. You never know when one of these may contain a virus that can damage your system.

The bottom line in dealing with these types of potential scams is to ignore them or to ask for additional information. Don't rely on an e-mail message from the poster to settle your skepticism. Scam artists know how to say the right things to make you feel like sending money to them. Just like you wouldn't send money to someone calling you on the telephone promising you a great investment opportunity (or at least you shouldn't), don't do it over the Internet either. If you're interested in a product or service, ask the company to send you product brochures, business telephone numbers, and a business abstract that includes full product warranties, a history of the product, and references.

WARNING

Think carefully before you send your credit card number to someone online. If you want to purchase something with credit card from a vendor online, see if the vendor has a 1-800 number you can call to place your order. If you don't see a 1-800 number, send e-mail to the company asking for a sales representative to call you or to send you information on how you can contact them. Also, never write a check or money order to someone until you first gather ample information about

the business and product. Many scam artists set up businesses and fake "storefronts" on the Web to bilk users out of their money. If you get ripped off by one of these people, there's usually little you can do to get the money back except notify local authorities in that person's area, which could be a city or municipality thousands of miles away from where you live. And then you still probably won't see your money again.

The Federal Trade Commission (FTC) has released the following signs that may tip you off to online scam artists:

- Claims that seem too real to be true. Product descriptions or investment opportunities that include the phrase "hot" may indicate a scam.
- Outlandish earnings or profits. If it's too good to be true, then it's probably false.
- Descriptions of having an "inside" edge or confidential information.
- Stock opportunities that promise high returns on low investments. The FTC describes these as "Pump and Dump" promotions.
- Opportunities in outrageous areas, such as gold mining, ostrich farming, and wireless cable television (hint, cables are not wireless).

NOTE

For more information about online scams, advertisements, or promotions, contact the FTC, a consumer protection agency, or your state Attorney General. You can reach the FTC at the following address:

Correspondence Branch
Federal Trade Commission
Washington, DC 20580

For information on whether an investment person is licensed or a security is registered, contact the following group:

Office of Consumer Affairs
Securities and Exchange Commission (SEC)
(202) 942-7040

You also can check out the National Fraud Information Center (NFIC) on the Web at **http://www.fraud.org** *(see Figure 12.7). The NFIC can provide information about online scams, as well as phone and mail solicitations.*

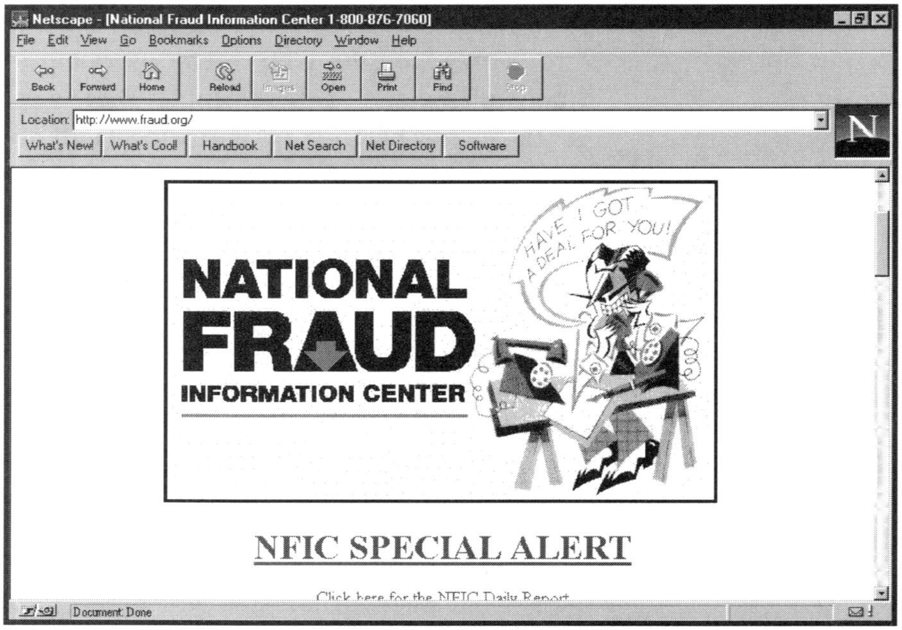

FIGURE 12.7

Beware of numerous online scams; use services like the National Fraud Information Center to help you avoid scams and frauds.

Understanding Privacy Issues and Rights

Throughout this chapter you've read about some potential online threats and pitfalls. Fortunately, the majority of the time you're online will be pleasant, and you won't have to deal with these problems. Unfortunately, there are times when understanding your online rights will payoff.

One of these areas concerns the issue of privacy. You read earlier that there's no real legislation that protects your desire for full privacy online. Personal information about you can appear online and there's not much you can do about it but confront the company or person who posted the information and ask for it be removed. Even personal medical records can be posted online.

NOTE

Privacy issues don't include defamation of character or slander. You are covered against someone using online resources to damage your reputation or character.

Is Your Mail Being Read?

Believe it or not, your e-mail is probably being read by someone. Of course, if your messages are boring and don't contain personal or confidential information, the person reading the messages isn't getting much. On the other hand, messages you want only select people to read may contain sensitive information about you, a product your company is offering, or research you're undertaking.

One way e-mail is read is by using search utilities to scan e-mail text to locate certain phrases or words, such as sex, product names, or management names. When these programs find these words or phrases, the messages are pulled out and saved for someone to read later. They can also be printed to make hard copy documentation to be placed in personnel files.

For the most part, the person reading your e-mail may not be a hacker or stranger out on the Internet someplace. It's probably a manager or company official inside your company who's doing it. If you use e-mail only from home, you don't have much to worry about unless you're conducting business. Then you might want to make sure your e-mail is secure before sending sensitive information over the Internet (see the list of tips at the end of this section for information on securing e-mail).

TIP

Even if you pay for a separate private account and you use it at work, your employer still has the right to read your mail. This is because you're using company equipment to send, retrieve, store, and read your mail.

Employers often read e-mail to see patterns of Internet use. Employers monitor online activities of employees to ensure company online and Internet usage policies are being followed. If they're not, companies can reissue policies, conduct training sessions on how to use the Internet effectively, discuss the matter with individual employees, or invoke disciplinary measures. In extreme cases, online privileges may be revoked if the employee cannot use his or her time online in appropriate ways.

Another reason for reviewing e-mail is to catch company security violations. Most companies have confidentiality clauses relating to products or services. Employers feel that one way to check up on the way their employees follow these clauses is to read e-mail messages sent by them.

Your rights against your employer reading company e-mail (even Internet e-mail routed through your network) are very slim. In fact, court cases have supported the employer's right to maintain a copy of all e-mail sent by employees. Even if you delete a message, it stays on the network server until it's been purged. By that time, a backup copy of the message has probably been made and has been retained someplace for safe keeping.

The following are some ways to avoid being put on the spot by your employer for e-mail infractions:

- **Know your company policy.** Ask your manager or human resource manager for a written policy on what is appropriate or inappropriate e-mail activity.
- **Use discretion: Don't defame or curse your employer in a message.** Calling someone derogatory names is not appropriate in a workplace environment; don't use them in your e-mail either. This type of information may be used against you later.
- **Send secure e-mail messages by encrypting them.** When you encrypt a message, you encode it so it is unreadable by everyone except the recipient, who then decodes it for viewing. One software you can use to encrypt your messages is Pretty Good Privacy (PGP), which can be downloaded from **http://web.mit.edu/network/pgp.html**.
- **Copy e-mail messages you want to keep to text files, and then delete the original e-mail message.** Although this may not delete it from the network server, the chances of someone accessing the message

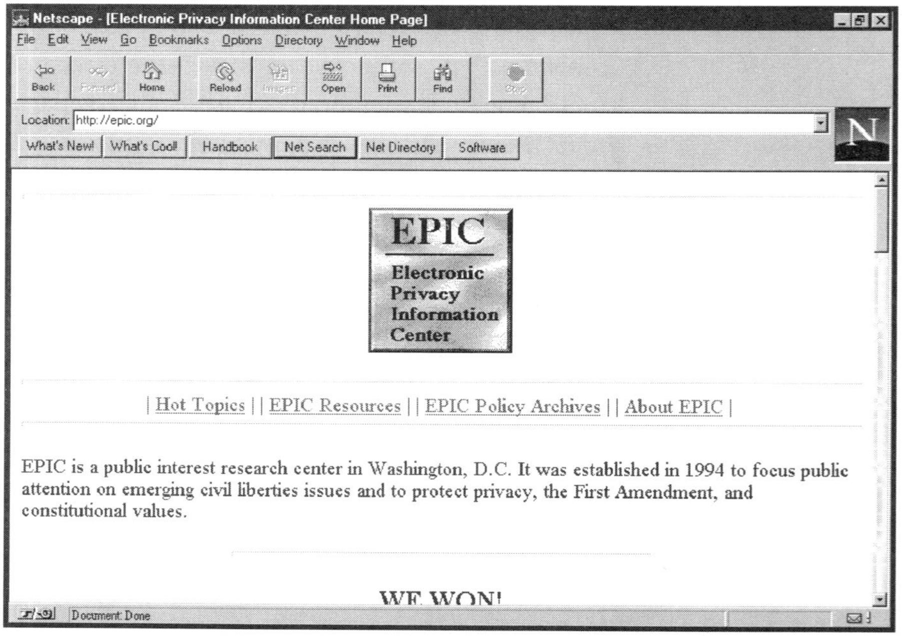

FIGURE 12.8

The Electronic Privacy Information Center includes numerous articles about online privacy and civil liberty issues.

is made a little more difficult. Be sure to empty any "trash" folders your e-mail program may use. Usually, trash folders are used to store deleted e-mail messages in case users want to undelete a message.

- **Don't send confidential or personal information over e-mail.** Even if you're using a private account from home, your messages may be forwarded to other users by the person who received the original message.

NOTE

You can find tons of information on privacy by visiting the following links:

The Electronic Frontier Foundation (EFF) ***http://www.eff.org***

Electronic Privacy Information Center (EPIC) ***http://epic.org/*** *(see Figure 12.8)*

Privacy Rights Clearinghouse (PRC) ***http://pwa.acusd.edu/prc/***

Computer Professionals for Social Responsibilities (CPSR) ***http://www.cpsr.org/dox/home.html***

The Communications Decency Act (CDA)

Recently, a U.S. District Court in Pennsylvania found the Communication Decency Act unconstitutional. The CDA (passed in February 1996) made it unlawful to distribute indecent and obscene material over the Internet. This made it was unlawful to distribute pornography, as well as information concerning AIDs, birth control, legal abortions, and other documents and pictures.

In a widely debated case (ACLU vs. Reno) the court found that the CDA was not enforceable and that it abridged rights protected in the First and Fifth Amendments. One justice stated that the Internet is essentially a "neverending worldwide conversation" which should not be interrupted by the government.

NOTE

For more information on the CDA and this case, see ***http://www.epic.org/cda/highlights.html****. There you can find excerpts of the summary and an analysis of the case.*

Although the CDA was overturned at this level, United States Attorney General Janet Reno may not appeal the case to a higher court. The government is, however, looking at ways to use technology to help parents monitor what children view on the Web. Some of these issues are covered in the next section.

Protecting You and Your Family While Online

Understanding how to protect yourself and your family while online is important. If you've spent some time online already, you know that there are many places not suitable for children. Similarly, there are many areas where you may not want to venture.

Not only do you need to keep an eye on the sites and information your family may be viewing, you need to make sure personal information is not being released to the public. Many marketing firms specialize on targeting children to exploit them and to solicit directly to them. This category of Internet users is typically referred to as the "cybertot" category.

Protecting Children

Among the primary reasons for placing restrictions on Internet usage is to protect children. Besides the CDA, other legislation is being introduced that makes it tougher for people to obtain information about children. One of these is called the Children's Privacy Protection and Parental Empowerment Act and is outlined as follows:

- Firms cannot sell personal information about children without the authorization of the parent(s).
- People cannot purchase personal information about children without the authorization of the parent(s).
- List brokers and solicitors must provide the source and content of personal information about a child upon request by the parents.
- List brokers and solicitors must provide the names of people who requested personal information about a child upon request by the parents.
- Would make it illegal for prisoners and sex criminals to obtain personal information about a child.

NOTE

How easy is it to obtain data about children? Very. One reporter of a Los Angeles television station sent $277 to a database company in Chicago and received hard copy of names, ages, and addresses of 5,500 children who live in Pasadena, California. That's how easy it is.

Until laws are created and followed, the responsibility of maintaining your child's safety is yours. When your children go online, don't just block out sites they shouldn't go to, but help them find ones they'll enjoy. Make sure you work with them and guide them to areas suitable to them. All children are different, but they all love games and interactive experiences.

One way to set up a list of sites for your child is to create a Web page you can load each time the child goes online. You can create this page using simple HTML commands and then load it onto your browser (see Figure 12.9). Your child can then follow the links you created for him or her. As you find more sites, you simply edit the HTML file and add the new sites. Easy to use HTML tools are available that help you create Web pages, including Netscape Navigator 2.0 Gold, Microsoft FrontPage 1.1, and HTML Assistant Pro 2.0. They are all available at local computer stores and retail outlets. When you use this method, remember that most of the pages on the Web contain hyperlinks to other sites. These other sites may be less suitable for your children, so always keep an eye on where they go.

The following are some sites you might want to include:

Trees of the World **http://www.hipark.austin.isd.tenet.edu/home/trees/main.html**

Blustery Beginnings **http://sln.fi.edu/tfi/units/energy/blustery.html**

Library of Cool Graphics Art **http://ra.nilenet.com/ifish**

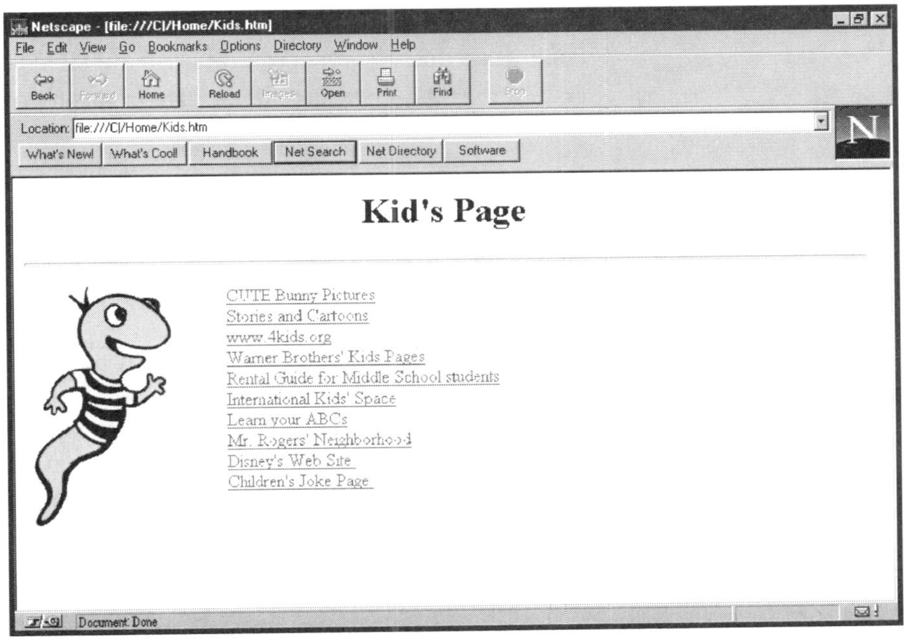

FIGURE 12.9

By learning a little HTML, you can create a simple Web page that lists your child's favorite Web sites.

UFO Sightings by Astronauts **http://www.cs.bgsu.edu/jzawodn/ufo/astro-sightings.html**

Boggle **http://www.cs.mu.oz.au/dnich/boggle_intro.html**

WebBattleship **http://info.gte.com/gtel/fun/battle/battle.html**

Nancy Drew **http://ils.unc.edu/nancy.drew/ktitle.html**

NOTE

For information on creating HTML documents, see Family PC *magazine's "Make Your Own Web Page" at* ***http://www.zdnet.com/familypc/content/960119/special/onln_mak.html****. Or see the "Comprehensive Guide to Publishing on the Web" at* ***http://www.webcom.com/html/****.*

One way to block access to certain sites is to use parental control software, such as Cyber Patrol or SurfWatch. These tools work by restricting access to a list of hundreds of Web sites, FTP servers, newsgroups, and IRC channels. Because the Internet changes every day, this list gets updated and you can routinely download updates to your system. Another way this type of software works is by listing thousands of family-oriented Web sites your children can access. You should, however, review these sites beforehand to ensure their content is not offensive to you and your family.

Software like Cyber Patrol enables you to restrict specific times when an Internet application doesn't work. You can regulate the hours your child can use a program to surf the Internet and navigate from site to site.

TIP

One rule of thumb about pornographic and other questionable material to keep in mind is that if you can find the material, so can your kids. Even with the best controls to keep children from accessing these types of sites, children will undoubtedly find ways to "beat" the software and locate these sites. One of the best deterents is to monitor your childrens online activities, much like monitoring the television shows and video tapes they watch.

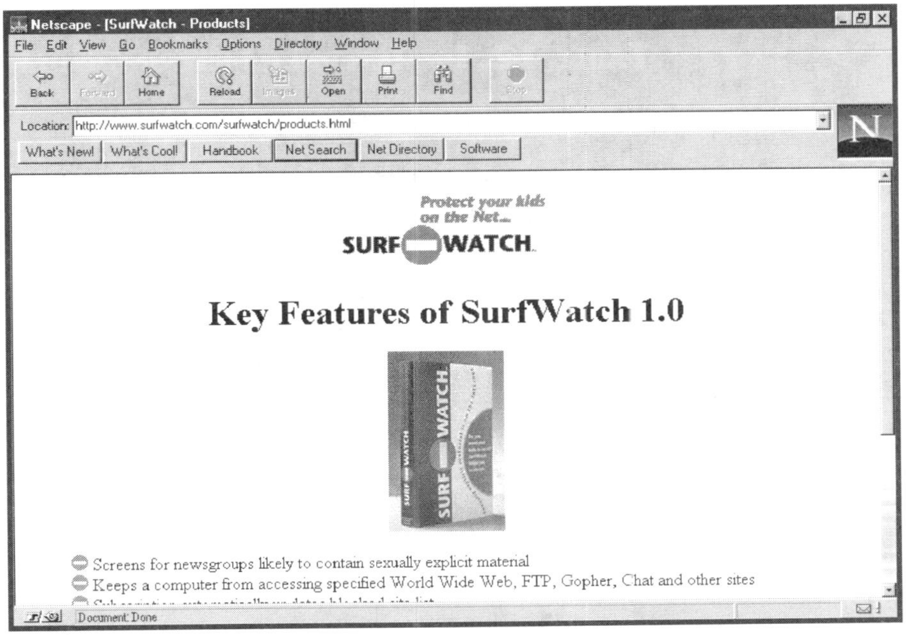

FIGURE 12.10

SurfWatch keeps children away from Web, FTP, Gopher, and chat sites that contain sexually explicit material.

Most of the filtering software available retails for about $49.95, such as SurfWatch (see Figure 12.10). To get updated lists, you need to purchase monthly subscriptions, which usually cost about $5.95 per month. If you belong to CompuServe or Prodigy, you can download the Cyber Patrol software for free, and then just pay for the monthly subscriptions.

Table 12.1 lists some of the common filtering software.

Tips on Protecting Your Family

What can you expect when you go online? Are you free to do as you want? Is there an established government to mediate problems? How can you protect the information you send across the Internet from falling into the wrong hands? Are credit card transactions secure online? Can you keep your children (and yourself) away from sites displaying obscene or pornographic material?

These are questions most users of the Internet and commercial online services ask before getting an online account. Not only should you concern yourself with your name and address being available for the whole world to see, you should be wary any time you send a confidential message or fill out financial data.

The following are some tips on how to protect yourself and your family when you go online.

TABLE 12.1 INTERNET FILTERING SOFTWARE		
Product Name	**URL**	**Phone Number**
SurfWatch	**http://www.surfwatch.com**	800-458-6600
Cyber Patrol	**http://www.cyberpatrol.com**	800-489-2001
NewView	**http://www.newview.com**	415-299-9016
NetNanny	**http://www.netnanny.com/netnanny/**	800-340-7177

- Think carefully before you give out credit card information over the Internet. Even if a form is available online, your best bet is to look for a telephone number to call and perform the transaction with a live person.
- Inform your children to never give out personal information, such as their real name, age, address, and sex while online.
- Never agree to meet someone in person you've recently met while online. Spend some time getting to know the person before rushing out to meet him or her. You might also want to exchange photographs, send "regular" mail to each other, and talk on the telephone to get to know the person better. If you do agree to meet the person, meet in a public place or take a friend with you in case the meeting doesn't go as well as you expect. However, advise your children and teenagers to never meet someone without first talking to you and getting your approval.
- Don't include personal information in forms or search engines. If you find confidential information in a search site (such as Yahoo!), read the policy statements at the site to learn how to remove your information from the site. The policy statement for Switchboard is located at **http://www.switchboard.com/policy.htm**.

NOTE

There is no one solution to erasing your name from all of the search engines on the Web. If you want to remove your information from these sites, you need to do it one at a time. To see a comprehensive list of search engines, go to ***http://home.netscape.com/home/internet-search.html****.*

- Respond "No" to any requests to be placed on mass mailings. If you answer "Yes," your name is included in different databases and mailing lists, which may eventually be sold to other companies. Also, if you get unsolicited e-mail from a company or user, send e-mail back to them asking to be removed from their database.
- Use an alias as much as possible. When you're in a newsgroup or chat room, don't use your real name. Choose an alias you like and use it.
- Stay informed of online privacy issues by visiting sites like c|net and the Electronic Privacy Information Center (EPIC).

Summary

Some good news: The Internet and online world have opened a wealth of information for almost every kind of user. Even with the risks involved, the time you spend online should be enjoyable and educational. And, as you may already realize, highly addictive.

As you've seen in this chapter, being online requires more than just getting your modem configured and installing the right software. You need to think about privacy issues important to you, as well as how to protect your family while they're online.

The key to online security and privacy is to take it into your own hands. No one else will protect you as well as you can yourself. The same holds true for protecting your children. Although Congress is reviewing some important legislation designed to protect children, Congress does not have full responsibility for your children—you do. So don't sit your child in front of the computer screen and walk away hoping for the best.

Above all else, have fun.

INDEX

A

Q

R

S

Available Now!

1-2-3 for Windows: The Visual Learning Guide	$19.95
Access 2 for Windows By Example (with 3½-inch disk)	$29.95
Windows Magazine Presents: Access from the Ground Up	$19.95
Access from the Ground Up, 2nd Edition	$19.95
Access for Windows 95: The Visual Learning Guide	$19.95
ACT! 2.0: The Visual Learning Guide	$19.95
Build a Web Site: The Programmer's Guide to Creating, Building, and Maintaining a Web Presence	$34.95
The CD-ROM Revolution	$24.95
CompuServe Complete Handbook & Membership Kit, Second Edition (with CD-ROM)	$24.95
CompuServe Information Manager for Windows: The Complete Membership Kit & Handbook (with two 3½-inch disks)	$29.95
Computers Don't Byte	$ 7.95
Computer Gamer's Survival Guide	$19.95
CorelDRAW! 4 for Windows By Example (with 3½-inch disk)	$34.95
CorelDRAW! 5 Revealed!	$24.95
Create Wealth with Quicken, Second Edition	$19.95
Create Wealth with Quicken, Third Edition	$21.95
Cruising America Online 2.5	$21.95
Cruising CompuServe	$21.99
Cruising The Microsoft Network	$21.95
DOS 6.2: Everything You Need to Know	$24.95
Data Security	$34.95
Essential Book for Microsoft Office	$27.99
Excel for Windows 95: The Visual Learning Guide	$19.95
Excel 5 for Windows By Example (with 3½-inch disk)	$29.95
Excel 5 for Windows: The Visual Learning Guide	$19.95
Excel for the Mac: The Visual Learning Guide	$19.95
Free Electronic Networks	$24.95
WINDOWS Magazine Presents: Freelance Graphics for Windows: The Art of Presentation	$27.95
Harvard Graphics for Windows: The Art of Presentation	$27.95
IBM Smalltalk Programming for Windows & OS/2 (with 3½-inch disk)	$49.95
Interactive Internet: The Insider's Guide to MUDs, MOOs, and IRC	$19.95
Internet After Hours	$19.95
Internet After Hours, 2nd Edition	$21.99
Internet for Windows: America Online Edition	$19.95
Internet for Windows: America Online 2.5 Edition	$19.95
Internet for Windows: The Microsoft Network Edition	$19.95
Internet Information Server	$40.00
The Internet Warp Book: Your Complete Guide to Getting Online with OS/2	$21.95
Introduction to Internet Security	$34.95
KidWare: The Parent's Guide to Software for Children	$14.95
Lotus Notes 3 Revealed!	$24.95
LotusWorks 3: Everything You Need to Know	$24.95
Mac Tips and Tricks	$14.95
Macintosh Design to Production: The Definitive Guide	$34.95
Making Movies with Your PC	$24.95
Making Music with Your PC	$19.95
Managing with Microsoft Project	$30.00
Microsoft Office in Concert	$24.95
Microsoft Office in Concert, Professional Edition	$27.95
Microsoft Works for Windows By Example	$24.95
Microsoft Works for Windows 95: The Visual Learning Guide	$19.95
Migrating to Windows 95	$39.95
Moving Worlds (with CD-ROM)	$35.00
OS/2 WARP: Easy Installation Guide	$12.95
PageMaker 5.0 for the Mac: Everything You Need to Know	$24.95
PageMaker 5.0 for Windows: Everything You Need to Know	$19.95
Paradox 4.5 for DOS Revealed! (with 3½-inch disk)	$29.95
Paradox for Windows Essential Power Programming (with 3½-inch disk)	$39.95
A Parent's Guide to Video Games	$12.95
PC DOS 6.2: Everything You Need to Know	$24.95
PowerPoint: The Visual Learning Guide	$19.95
PowerPoint for Windows 95: The Visual Learning Guide	$19.95
WINDOWS Magazine Presents: The Power of Windows and DOS Together, Second Edition	$24.95
PROCOMM PLUS for Windows: The Visual Learning Guide	$19.95
Quicken for Windows: The Visual Learning Guide	$19.95
Quicken 3 for Windows: The Visual Learning Guide	$19.95
Quicken 5 for Windows: The Visual Learning Guide	$19.95
QuickTime: Making Movies with Your Macintosh, Second Edition	$27.95
Researching on the Internet: The Complete Guide to Finding, Evaluating, and Organizing Information Effectively	$29.95
The Slightly Skewed Computer Dictionary	$ 8.95
Smalltalk Programming for Windows (with 3½-inch disk)	$39.95
The Software Developer's Complete Legal Companion (with 3½-inch disk)	$32.95
Software: What's Hot! What's Not!	$16.95
Sound Blaster: Making WAVes with Multimedia	$19.95
Stacker Multimedia	$19.95
Superbase Revealed!	$29.95
SuperPaint 3: Everything You Need to Know	$24.95
Symantec C++: Object-Oriented Programming Fundamentals for the Macintosh (with 3½-inch disk)	$39.95
Think THINK C! (with two 3½-inch disks)	$39.95
Thom Duncan's Guide to NetWare Shareware (with 3½-inch disk)	$29.95
UnInstaller 3: Uncluttering Your PC	$19.95
Visio 4: Drawing Has Never Been Easier!	$19.95
Visual Basic for Applications Revealed!	$27.95
The Warp Book: Your Definitive Guide to Installing and Using OS/2 v3	$24.95
Web After Hours	$22.95
Web Browsing with America Online	$22.95
Web Browsing with Netscape Navigator 1.1	$24.95
Web Browsing with NETCOM NetCruiser	$24.95
Web Browsing with Prodigy	$22.95
Web Browsing with The Microsoft Network	$22.95
WinComm Pro: The Visual Learning Guide	$19.95
Windows 3.1: The Visual Learning Guide	$19.95
Windows 95: The Visual Learning Guide	$19.95
Windows 95: A to Z	$34.95
Windows 95: Easy Installation Guide	$12.95
The Windows 95 Book: Your Definitive guide to Installing and Using Windows 95	$24.95
WinFax PRO 4: The Visual Learning Guide	$19.95
WinFax PRO 7 for Windows: The Visual Learning Guide	$19.95
Word 6 for the Mac: The Visual Learning Guide	$19.95
Word for Windows 2: The Visual Learning Guide	$19.95
Word for Windows 6: The Visual Learning Guide	$19.95
Word for Windows 95: The Visual Learning Guide	$19.95
WordPerfect 6 for DOS: How Do I...?	$24.95
WordPerfect 6 for DOS: The Visual Learning Guide	$19.95
WordPerfect 6 for Windows: How Do I...?	$24.95
WordPerfect 6 for Windows: The Visual Learning Guide	$19.95
WordPerfect 6.1 for Windows: The Visual Learning Guide	$19.95